THE MAJOR COMEDIES OF
ALEXANDER FREDRO

Columbia Slavic Studies
A Series of the Department of Slavic Languages
Columbia University

The Major Comedies of
Alexander Fredro

Translated, with an Introduction
& Commentaries, by

HAROLD B. SEGEL

PRINCETON, NEW JERSEY

PRINCETON UNIVERSITY PRESS

1969

Printed in the United States of America
by Princeton University Press

This book has been composed in Linotype Baskerville

*Publication of this book has been aided
by the Whitney Darrow Publication Reserve Fund
of Princeton University Press and by the
Department of Slavic Languages
of Columbia University*

FOR MY MOTHER

PREFACE

It is a fact, which I do not doubt in the least, that Fredro is one of the world's greatest writers of comedy, one of the small number of born comic geniuses. On the other hand, it is also a fact that he is these things only for us, that his contribution to world drama has been virtually nil. This in no way depreciates his value. In this respect he just shares the fate of our best writers.[1]

IT WAS in this way that in 1934 the brilliant Polish critic and scholar Dr. Tadeusz Boy-Żeleński summed up the paradox of Poland's major comic dramatist, Alexander Fredro (1793-1876). Although Poland's undisputed master of comedy, Fredro is little known beyond the borders of his own country. The reasons are not difficult to discover. Since the partitions of the late eighteenth century, Poland has been dispossessed of any great political significance in Europe, and it would be unrealistic to deny the importance of a nation's prestige in attracting foreign interest to its cultural achievements. Fredro, moreover, is not an easy author to translate. His best plays were written in verse, which at once erects a formidable barrier to foreign transmission. Fredro was also a master of language. His comedies abound in verbal humor, and the color and texture of his idiom which together with a superb gift of characterization have made his works immensely popular in Poland, suffer greatly in translation. Ironically, the very features that make Fredro a delight to Polish audiences now as in the past—despite the sweeping changes in Poland's political and social structure—are precisely the reasons why communicating the values of his comic art to foreign readers is such a difficult task.

The neglect of Fredro is reflected in the very small number of his plays available in translation. Within the past decade or so, however, there have been signs that this neglect is being overcome. In July 1954, during a festival of dramatic art in Paris, the Warsaw Kameralny Theater performed Fred-

[1] Tadeusz Boy-Żeleński, "Obrachunki fredrowskie," *Pisma*, Vol. v, Warsaw, 1956, p. 191.

ro's *Husband and Wife* before enthusiastic French audiences. The following year, in response to the interest in Fredro evoked by these performances, the Słowacki Theater in Cracow arranged for the publication of a French rhymed verse translation of Fredro's best comedy, *The Vengeance.* In 1956, the first book-length collection of Fredro's plays in a foreign language appeared in a Soviet edition of six comedies in Russian translations.

Since the end of World War II, there has been a marked increase in serious Western interest in the Slavs and their cultures. It began for obvious reasons and appropriately with Russia. But time has brought a widening of the horizon and with it a curiosity about the other Slavic nations which, though not politically important like the Soviet Union, have cultural heritages no less rich or impressive in their own way. This is especially true of Poland, and over the past two decades Western interest in and regard for Polish culture have risen greatly. It is in this spirit of expanding knowledge and understanding that the present contribution—the first collection of Fredro's most popular comedies in a Western language —is offered.

Because Fredro—and Polish literature generally—are still more remote than they deserve to be, I have felt it necessary to present more information on the author and his plays than is usual perhaps for a book of this sort. In addition to as complete a biographical sketch of the dramatist as space permits, the introduction also includes a brief survey of the development of Polish comedy to the time of Fredro and an attempt at an assessment of Fredro's place in the history of Polish and European drama. Furthermore, each individual play is preceded by its own introduction. The appendix at the end of the book contains bibliographical information on Polish editions of Fredro, a survey of Fredro scholarship in and outside of Poland, and a note on other translations of his plays. It is my hope that the background material and commentaries will provide sufficient initiation into the world of Fredro and Polish comedy to enable the reader to find interest in the plays despite the loss that translation inevitably involves.

PREFACE

At this time I should like to acknowledge my gratitude to Columbia University's Council for Research in the Humanities for the generous assistance that enabled me to spend the summer of 1960 familiarizing myself for the first time with the vast Fredro material in Polish libraries.

H. B. S.

CONTENTS

A Guide to Polish Pronunciation[1]

WITH the exception of Fredro's Christian name, which has been Anglicized (it would be Aleksander in Polish), all other Polish names in the expository parts of this book are given in their original form. In the translations of the comedies, names of characters have been Anglicized or translated where it was convenient to do so without too much distortion. With telling names it seemed impossible to pursue a consistent policy. Again, where appropriate English equivalents could be found, they have been used. Elsewhere, the Polish forms appear with explanatory footnotes. To facilitate the pronunciation of Polish names retained in their original spelling, the following guide may prove helpful.

1. *Accent*: All Polish words are stressed on the next-to-last syllable.

2. *Vowels*: *a, e, i, o, u* are pronounced as in most European languages (*a* as in *father*; *e* as in *met*; *i* as in *machine*; *o* as in *more*; *u* like the double *o* in *proof*; *ó* is pronounced the same as *u*). There are also two nasal vowels in Polish: *ą* (o^n) *ę* (e^n).

3. *Consonants*: Those different from English are:
   c = *ts*
   ć (or *ci*) = like *ch* in *chime* (soft *ch*)
   cz = like *tch* in *patch* (hard *ch*)
   ch = *kh* (like German *ch*)
   h = never silent in Polish
   j = *y*
   l = like *l* in *lure* (soft *l*)
   ł = like English *w* (hard *l*)
   ń (or *ni*) = *ny*, as in *canyon* (soft *n*)
   ź (or *zi*) = *zh*, as in *leisure* (soft *zh*)
   rz, ż = *zh*, as in *rouge*, or *sh* after *p, t, k* (hard *zh*)
   ś (or *si*) = *sh*, as in *sure* (soft *sh*)

---

[1] This guide is intended solely as an aid to the reader knowing no Polish; it makes no claim to any scientific exactness. The English equivalents are fair approximations at best.

sz = *sh*, as in *harsh* (hard *sh*)

w = *v*

A few examples:

Tadeusz = Tadéush
Żeleński = Zhelénski
Słowacki = Swovátski
Sejm = Seym
Józef = Yoo'zef
Józia = Yoo'zha
Dobrójska = Dobroo'yska
Twardosz = Tvárdosh

THE MAJOR COMEDIES OF
ALEXANDER FREDRO

INTRODUCTION

Polish Comedy to the Time of Fredro[1]

THE beginnings of Polish comedy date back to the second half of the sixteenth century when writers, mostly of burgher origin, began to publish plays in the old capital of Cracow in the southern part of the country. The plays were not very sophisticated in form or content. Most dealt with the adventures of former Cracow Academy students and teachers who were driven by the harsh economic conditions of sixteenth-century Polish burgher life to search for work as parish school teachers in the extensive parochial school system organized in Poland after the Council of Trent.

Political and economic power in Poland in the sixteenth century rested in the hands of the gentry (szlachta), a numerous class representing about 10 percent of the population of the country. This power was achieved at the expense of the Crown, which by the end of the century the gentry succeeded in making an elective office with candidates to be drawn from among the gentry or subject to the approval of representatives of the gentry convened in the national parliament known as the Sejm, and at the expense of the town bourgeoisie, the fledgling Polish middle class. When gentry pressure against the burghers increased in the second half of the century mostly in the form of repressive legislation, the burghers turned to literature to express their indignation and to demand a redress of the wrongs to which they had been subjected. One of the most productive forms of this "literature of protest" was comedy. In its early stages of development it was reminiscent of the old German Fastnachtsspiele or Shrovetide plays and reflected also the influence of the *intermedia* inserted in the school plays of the contemporary religious

---

[1] On Polish drama and theater to 1765, see Stanisław Windakiewicz, *Teatr polski przed powstaniem sceny narodowej* (Cracow, 1921). For a brief survey of Polish comedy, see Marian Szykowski, *Dzieje komedii polskiej w zarysie* (Cracow, 1921). See also Julian Lewański's introduction to *Dramaty polskie*, Vol. 1 (Warsaw, 1959), 7-92.

theater for comic diversion.[2] Some of the burgher comedies were just expanded versions of such *intermedia*.

The first burgher comedies for which we have texts are two simple dialogues dating from the last decade of the sixteenth century: *The Parish Priest's Expedition* (Wyprawa plebańska, 1590) and *Albertus Returns from War* (Albertus z wojny, 1596). The hero of these comedies is a village sexton named Albertus who is sent off to the wars Poland was waging at the time against the Swedes in Livonia. As a comic character Albertus belongs to the family of "soldier braggarts" whose genealogy can be traced as far back as Plautus' *Miles Gloriosus* (The Soldier Braggart), a type popularized in sixteenth-century Poland not only by the revival of interest in the theater of Plautus, but also by wandering troupes of Italian *commedia dell'arte* players.[3] The success of the "Albertus" comedies gave rise to a new series of plays dealing with the military adventures of simple recruits: *The Minister's Expedition to the War in Livonia* (Wyprawa ministra na wojnę do Inflant, 1605), *The Major Expedition of Ministers to the War in Wallachia* (Walna wyprawa do Wołoch ministrów na wojnę, 1617), and *Matiasz's Return from Podolia* (Zwrócenie Matiasza z Podola, 1619). Modeled directly on the "Albertus" series, this group of works has as its central character a brawling, drink-loving minister's son named Matiasz, conceived as the Protestant counterpart of Albertus. Of particular interest in the "Matiasz comedies," as they are known, is their reflection of a growing religious intolerance in the reign of Sigismund III (1586-1632) of the Swedish House of Vasa.

The majority of the old burgher comedies dealt with the contemporary parochial school life. Those that have been preserved include, in chronological order: *Janas' Meeting with the Sexton Gregorias* (Spotkanie Janasa z Gregoriasem klechą, 1598), *The Synod of Sub-Carpathian Sextons* (Synod klechów podgórskich, 1607), *The Old Itinerant Schoolman*

---

[2] On the old Polish burgher comedy, see my article "The Beginnings of Polish Comedy," *The Polish Review*, Vol. III, No. 3 (1958), 69-81.

[3] On the soldier braggart in Polish literature, see my article "From Albertus to Zagłoba: The Soldier Braggart in Polish Literature," *Indiana Slavic Studies*, Vol. III (1963), 76-112.

(Rybałt stary wędrowny, 1632), *School Misery* (Szkolna mizeria, 1633), and *Janas Knutl's Colloquy* (Colloquium Janasa Knutla, 1633). The plots of these primitive comedies are quite artless: a number of teachers, sextons and cantors (the next most important personages in the village parochial school system), unable to bear further the abuse of parish priests and the annoying interference of the priests' cooks, assemble, usually in pairs, to discuss possible courses of action open to them. Some choose to abandon the parishes and search for work elsewhere, mostly in agriculture and the trades. Others prefer to try their luck as soldiers and serve in the Polish campaigns in Livonia and Wallachia. Still others feel it would be best to take holy orders themselves and become priests. Separating, they abandon their parishes and set out in search of their fortunes. Much to their dismay, however, they discover that conditions are no better, if not worse, elsewhere in Poland. Sadly, many return to the parishes they so eagerly left behind them a short time before, finding some consolation in the knowledge that they really could do no better.

Two interesting phenomena with which the itinerant burgher comedy writers came into contact on their travels in south and southeast Poland were the contemporary practice of the "stacja," i.e., the enforced quartering of soldiers in villages during wartime, and the "Confederates," Polish veterans of the Muscovite campaign of 1609-1613 who, unpaid and hungry, roamed the Polish countryside marauding and plundering. The fragmentary *The Extraordinary Levy* (Niepospolite ruszenie, 1621) and *The New Schoolman Comedy* (Komedia rybałtowska nowa, 1615) contain vivid descriptions of these less familiar aspects of old Polish life. The *dziady*, who were beggars, magicians and medicine men as well as vital sources of information for remote villages in outlying districts, wandered the length and breadth of Poland in this period and represent the subject of one of the most interesting of the burgher comedies, *The Beggars' Peregrination* (Peregrynacja dziadowska, 1612).[4]

---

[4] On the *dziad* in Polish literature, see my article "Two Old Polish Wayfarers: The Dziad and the Pilgrim," *The Polish Review*, Vol. VI, No. 1-2 (1961), 107-117.

From the *intermedia* of the popular religious and, to a lesser extent, Jesuit theaters, the burgher comedy writers learned something of the fundamentals of the dramatic art. Their characters, drawn generally from everyday life, were allowed to speak their natural idiom, a crude but often colorful colloquial language. The presentation of pairs of opposites, the "duality" method of characterization known from classical Roman comedy, introduced dramatic conflict. Riotous farcical scenes, at times entrusted to the improvisation of the actors somewhat in the tradition of the commedia dell'arte, hastened the pace of the action and tended to overcome the deficiencies of episodic construction. The many forms of verbal play so common to the *intermedia* were also used abundantly: dialectisms, malapropisms, coined names and macaronisms (mixed Polish and Latin verse).

Jesuit school drama, which flourished in Poland from 1571, when the Order was introduced, to 1774, when it was expelled, proved to be an influential agent in the transmission to the developing burgher comedy of at least the externals of Humanist play construction. The burgher writers now began to introduce the previously unknown unities of time and place, act and scene division, prologues and epilogues, and inter-act diversions, usually in the form of choruses, monologues and *intermedia*. They began to show greater care for plot design and attempted to develop their characters beyond mere stock types.

Within twenty years after *The New Schoolman Comedy* (1615), the highest achievements of Polish sixteenth- and early seventeenth-century burgher comedy were reached. These were the *mięsopust* or Shrovetide comedies. Such works as *The Courtly Wooer* (Dziewosłąb dworski, 1620), *Marancya* (1620-1622), *Shrovetide* (Mięsopust, 1622) and *The Peasant Become King* (Z chłopa król, circa 1634) heralded the transformation of the primitive burgher playlets into full-fledged comedies. Until the reemergence of Polish dramatic art in the second half of the eighteenth century, these plays remained the limit to which Polish comedy had developed.

Although we still know little about actual performances or contemporary theater conditions generally, it is safe to assume that the old burgher comedy enjoyed considerable popularity in its day. The masses of the Polish bourgeoisie of the sixteenth and seventeenth centuries had little opportunity to enjoy the "official" drama, Humanist and classical, of the royal court. The lavish Jesuit school productions were also beyond their reach for the most part. The troupes of popular mystery players who traveled throughout Poland from the later Middle Ages offered a fare of religious plays enlivened only by the comico-realistic *intermedia*. These *intermedia* are not to be overlooked, however, for they served an important function—they whetted the audiences' appetite for living drama, an appetite that came to be satisfied in time by the burgher comedies.

Primitive in structure, weak in the essentials of dramatic art, crude in language and humor, the old Polish burgher comedy nonetheless occupies a position of some importance in the history of Polish comedy. As we have seen, the sixteenth and seventeenth centuries were not productive periods for drama in Poland. The popular mystery theater represented simply a continuation of the medieval dramatic tradition. The Jesuit school plays, despite their occasional brilliance, were seldom very original creations and have value only within the narrow framework of the history of Jesuit drama itself. As elsewhere in Europe, they exerted no great influence on native dramatic developments. While it is true that contemporary translations and adaptations from Roman comedy, such as Piotr Ciekliński's adaptation of Plautus' *Trinummus* (Potrójny in Polish, published in 1597), were often good and made some contribution to the theater of the period, they were still not original works. The poet Jan Kochanowski's *Dismissal of the Greek Envoys* (Odprawa posłów greckich, 1578) stands as the only highlight of old Polish drama. Essentially a typical Humanist tragedy on a classical subject, there is little natively Polish in the play save veiled allusions to political dangers facing the Polish Commonwealth at the time.

This older period in the history of Polish drama appears, therefore, somewhat desolate, but the picture is made brighter by the isolated phenomenon of the burgher comedy, a vibrant

7

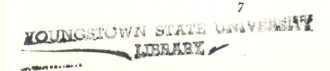

and original native comic art for all its crudities and primitiveness.

To attempt to find exact parallels of this comedy in the history of European comedy presents certain problems. The peculiar gentry-burgher relations of sixteenth-century Poland, and the special conditions of the contemporary parochial school life from which the old comedy ultimately sprang, created a milieu which did not exist in precisely the same way elsewhere in Europe. Only when the burgher comedies are viewed as part of the general outgrowth of European secular comedy from the comico-realistic scenes of medieval drama can this unique Polish literary phenomenon be related to the late medieval and Renaissance dramatic scene in western Europe. It must be remembered, however, that a secular drama had established itself much earlier in the West than in Poland, or for that matter, in the other Slavic lands.

The special socio-economic and cultural conditions out of which the old Polish burgher comedy emerged also contained the seeds of its destruction. When the bases of the burgher culture disappeared after the middle of the seventeenth century, so did its literature. Had the development of this native comic drama not been cut off by the decline of the Polish bourgeoisie, the collapse of the parochial school life and the devastation Poland suffered as a result of the wars and internal upheaval of the seventeenth century, it is possible to speculate that its cultivation in time would have produced a native Polish comedy comparable to that of the West European countries in the Baroque age. Such a development came, however, only in the first half of the nineteenth century in the works of Fredro.

The old Polish burgher comedy reached the peak of its development in the third decade of the seventeenth century, in the Jesuit-influenced Shrovetide comedies. It disappeared sometime around the middle of the seventeenth century; 1655 is the date of the work generally regarded as the last extant burgher comedy, *The Best and Most Useful Pleasures* (Uciechy lepsze i pożyteczniejsze).

The Chmielnicki revolt in southern Poland (1648-1654) and the wars with the Swedes, Muscovites and Turks depopulated and crippled Polish town life sweeping away the supports of the burgher culture. Polish political and intellectual life began a downward trend that continued virtually unchecked through the rule of the Saxon kings Augustus II (1697-1733) and Augustus III (1734-1764) whose reigns are viewed traditionally as landmarks in the decline of Poland. In 1764, however, a native Pole, Stanisław August Poniatowski, was again on the Polish throne and with his support a devoted group of political, social, and cultural reformers launched a vast program of national regeneration. Spearheaded by the National Commission of Education (founded in 1763 and the first of its type in Europe) and inspired by France of the Enlightenment, the attempt was made to unite the Stanislavian age (as the reign of Poniatowski is known) with preceding periods of Polish political and cultural dynamism. This meant above all a return to the ideals of the Polish "Golden Age," the sixteenth century, the time of a true florescence of Polish Renaissance culture. Hereditary ways of thinking and speaking were laid open to revision by the reformers and the way began to be paved for a new era of resurgent national growth. For literary culture, the period was one of rebirth to which the whole subsequent culture of Poland is indebted. Consonant with the ideology of the Stanislavian reform movement there was a marked reawakening of interest at this time in drama and especially in comedy, which in the spirit of the age was to be cultivated because of the possibilities if offered for a corrective influence on contemporary society.

In response to this lively interest in drama, a National Theater was founded in Warsaw in 1765. This was the first public stage in the history of Poland.[5] From its very inception however, the Theater was plagued by financial and administrative difficulties. During the first two years of its existence, from November 1765 to early in 1767, some Polish plays were presented but there was very little in the way of a Polish repertoire. The old burgher comedy by now had been entirely forgotten and consigned to oblivion (interest in it reawakened only toward the middle of the nineteenth century) and there

[5] For a brief survey of the Polish theater in English, see the album *Theatre in Modern Poland*, Warsaw, 1963, pp. 5-16.

9

appeared to be no native drama, no native comedy capable of sustaining the fledgling National Theater. In 1767 the directorship of the Theater passed to an Italian named Carol Tomatis who exhibited little interest in the struggling Polish stage and concentrated more on the revenue brought in by foreign troupes (particularly French and Italian). The performance of Polish plays virtually ceased at this time. The situation changed little during the next seven years until in 1774 the Polish stage was reopened in the Radziwiłł Palace. It was to remain in this location until a permanent theater building was erected in 1779.

The problem of a repertoire now became especially acute. In response to the challenge Polish dramatists gradually began to build a repertoire by the practice of so ingeniously adapting foreign works (mostly French comedies from Molière down to their own time) that they could offer them to domestic audiences as products of the native genius.[6] Often highly original in their own way, these adaptations, or "Polonizations," played a vital role in keeping the Polish stage alive in the trying period of its infancy. In the absence of a native dramatic tradition they supplied the much-needed repertoire and provided a firm base on which an original Polish drama could be—and was—constructed. The most successful practitioners of this art of adaptation were the Jesuit priest Franciszek Bohomolec (1720-1784), a number of whose comedies are skillful adaptations of Molière, and Franciszek Zabłocki (1754-1821), like Bohomolec a prolific provider of plays for the National Theater. Zabłocki was the most talented writer of comedies of the Stanislavian period. Adhering to the theoretical proposals on adaptation expounded by Count Adam Kazimierz Czartoryski (1734-1823) in the introduction to his comedy *A Marriageable Miss* (Panna na wydaniu, 1770, itself an adaptation of David Garrick's *A Miss in Her Teens or The Medley of Lovers*, 1747), Zabłocki produced two admirable comedies, *The Dandy A-Wooing* (Fircyk w zalotach, 1781) and *Sarmatianism* (Sarmatyzm, 1785), based on the

---

[6] On these adaptations, see my article "Foreign Drama in Eighteenth Century Polish Dress," *Slavic and East European Journal*, Vol. xvii (New Series Vol. iii) (1959), 35-42.

works of such minor seventeenth-century French dramatists as Romagnesi and Hauteroche. Before the second and third partitions (1793, 1795) completed the dismemberment of Poland begun in 1772, the Stanislavian age succeeded in producing two original comedies that brought to fruition the preparatory work of the translators and adaptors. They were the musical comedy based on folklore motifs, *The Imagined Miracle, or Cracovians and Mountaineers* (Cud mniemany, czyli Krakowiacy i górale, 1774) by Poland's first professional man of the theater, Wojciech Bogusławski (1757-1829), and *The Deputy's Return* (Powrót posła, 1790), a political comedy dealing with the reforms embodied in the liberal Polish constitution of May 3, 1791, by Julian Ursyn Niemcewicz (1757-1841), one of the most outstanding Polish literary personalities of the late eighteenth and early nineteenth centuries.

This ferment of dramatic activity of Stanislavian Poland briefly surveyed above culminated in the work of Poland's foremost comedy writer, Alexander Fredro (1793-1876), whose plays may be regarded as the fulfillment of the long unrealized promise of the primitive burgher comedy of the sixteenth and seventeenth centuries and the reunion of this tradition with the new dramatic and theatrical culture of the second half of the eighteenth century.

Alexander Fredro: A Biographical Sketch[7]

ALEXANDER FREDRO was born on June 20, 1793, one year after the second partition of Poland by Prussia and Russia, to a family of landowning Polish gentry in Surochów near Jarosław in southeastern Poland, then a part of Austria as a result of the first partition of 1772. The Fredro home, which the dramatist was later to characterize in his memoirs as "a true Polish gentry home, well-to-do but not to excess, tranquil and hos-

[7] Biographical sketches of Fredro appear in Aleksander Fredro *Komedie*, ed. by Eugeniusz Kucharski, Vol. 1 (Lwów, 1926), 3-59; Aleksander Fredro, *Komedie*, ed. by Henryk Mościcki, Vol. 1 (Lwów-Warsaw, 1930), 111-xliv; *Aleksander Fredro*, ed. by Tadeusz Sivert (Warsaw, 1962), pp. 7-57. See also Ignacy Chrzanowski, *O komediach Aleksandra Fredry* (Cracow, 1917), pp. 1-50.

pitable,"[8] embraced in addition to Alexander and his parents Jacek and Maria, two older brothers (Maksymilian and Seweryn), three younger brothers (Julian, Henryk, Edward), and three sisters (Ludwika, Konstancja, Cecylia).

Fredro's early years were spent on the family estate of Beńkowa Wisznia not far from Lwów, the capital of the province of Galicia and a lively commercial and cultural center of some 40,000 inhabitants. After building up a sizeable estate through clever investments and sheer hard work, Fredro's father Jacek had been granted the Austrian title of count (*hrabia* in Polish) —which thereafter became hereditary in the Fredro family—and was serving at the time as royal vice-marshal of the regional diet (sejm) that convened regularly in Lwów. The education of young Alexander followed the traditional Polish gentry pattern: little formal training in favor of home tutors (whom Fredro describes vividly in his memoirs) with the main emphasis on the gentlemanly arts of fencing, horseback-riding and dancing, and punctuated, in Alexander's case, by vacation-time trips with his father to the smaller family estate in Cisna, in the mountain country around Sanok.

When Fredro was thirteen years old, in January 1806, his mother died and the family moved into the city of Lwów with the exception of his brothers Maksymilian and Seweryn who were sent to further their education at the court of Prince Adam Czartoryski in Puławy. With the eruption of the Franco-Austrian war in the spring of 1809, Fredro, still in his teens, followed the example of his older brothers who had donned Polish uniforms and enlisted in the army of Prince Józef Poniatowski which was forming in Sandomierz, eventually to become a part of the *Grande Armée* of Napoleon. By June of the same year, he reached the rank of lieutenant and was made a member of the eleventh regiment of uhlans then commanded by Adam Potocki.

In the short period of calm between 1809 and 1812 achieved by the Peace of Schönbrunn, the life of a young Polish officer not too near the front was hardly one of deprivation and

[8] Aleksander Fredro, *Trzy po trzy*, Introduction by Adam Grzymała-Siedlecki, Notes by Henryk Mościcki (Warsaw, 1957), p. 177.

discomfort. Fredro was stationed in the district of Lublin in eastern Poland where his frequent visits to the home of General Ludwik Kamieniecki brought him into contact with his first romantic love, Aniela Trembicka, whom he was later to immortalize in the character of Aniela in his comedy *Maidens' Vows or the Magnetism of the Heart* (Śluby panieńskie, cyzli Magnetyzm serca, 1828, 1834). In the memoirs he began to write in the late 1840's and to which he gave the title *Topsy Turvy Talk* (Trzy po trzy), Fredro gives this description of the pleasant dalliances the young Polish officers enjoyed in Lublin just a few years before Napoleon's great campaign against Russia:

> Whoever had seen me as I jumped from stone to stone, a sword under my left arm, my hat set at a jaunty angle, would have been able to guess that I was off for Lublin for an evening at the home of General Kamieniecki, where there awaited me the friendly smile of Miss Aniela [Trembicka] and slippers. . . . Not Turkish slippers, and still less Jewish slippers or slippers in the figurative sense of the marital yoke, but slippers—the card game, not very clever, but of inestimable value for people in love, better than all the other social games people played in those days. With us in the Sambork area, between Grodek and Rudki, the game used to be called Gap or Castellan which was definitely most embarrassing for castellans and certainly for that reason the Senate decided to rename it innocently *slippers*. Those were good times in that Lublin. General Kamieniecki commanded the division—he had a worthy wife and nice, pleasant step-daughters, Miss Pelagia and Miss Aniela Trembicka.[9]

By April 1812, Fredro had advanced to the rank of captain-adjutant-major in the fifth cavalry regiment which saw action in almost all of Napoleon's battles in the eastern campaign. Fredro himself tasted the bitter pill of war at Romanów, Smolensk, Moscow, and Borodino—on the retreat of the *Grande Armée*. When he succumbed to an attack of typhus during the disastrous exodus from Russia, he was forced to

[9] *Ibid.*, p. 147.

lag behind and fell captive to the Russians who imprisoned him in a military hospital in Wilno (now Vilnius, the capital of Soviet Lithuania). This seemed the end of the young officer's military career, but with the return of his strength Fredro succeeded in escaping from prison and eventually crossed the Russian border at Tarnogród on July 8, 1813. In the disguise of a simple peasant, he slowly made his way back to Lwów and home. The entire trip took about four weeks. After spending a short time in Lwów, where he completely regained his health, he proceeded to Dresden in Saxony and in August 1813 rejoined the army of Prince Poniatowski. He was soon made a member of the imperial staff with the rank of captain and participated in the campaigns of 1813 and 1814 alongside his brother Seweryn who at this time commanded a battalion of the Imperial Guard. Fredro saw action at Dresden, Leipzig, and Hanau, and for his courage and heroism in the campaigns was awarded the Order of the Virtuti Militari, the highest Polish military decoration, and was made a Chevalier of the Legion of Honor.

With the final defeat of the *Grande Armée* Fredro, like so many thousands of other Poles who were serving in the Emperor's forces, dutifully followed Napoleon back to France. Although old acquaintances (such as the family tutor Trawiński) and frequent visits to the theaters of Paris made life in the French capital tolerable despite the humiliation and frustration of defeat, Fredro soon succumbed to the mood of despair and mute anger that gripped the Polish troops who had returned to France with Napoleon. The Emperor's promises of a liberated Poland had proven empty and in the sober reassessment of their destiny that came in the wake of the collapse of the *Grande Armée* the Poles now fully understood perhaps for the first time the cynical use Napoleon had made of them and the reward of misery their devotion and blood had won. Years later, in *Topsy Turvy Talk*, Fredro was to recall the bitterness that overwhelmed the Polish troops after the Battle of Leipzig:

On the nineteenth of October [1813], on the last day of the four of what was and perhaps will be the bloodiest battle

14

of Leipzig, between the hour of nine in the morning and noon, we were standing, the officers of the staff of Prince Neufchâtel, under the trees which surround the city [of Montereau] like a street. We were waiting for orders—we heard no shots because it was already hard to distinguish these, but rather some thundering more or less which flowed all around us. At that time we already had an idea of how things stood. With the fall of French power, Polish hopes also fell. But we thought that it was just at Leipzig that we were losing the Fatherland for the second time. We did not know that Napoleon as easily as possible always accepted the condition of returning it to a third yoke of captivity. Devilish illusion! Satanic politics! So much devotion, so much blood to accept for hopes which at the bottom of his heart he had no hopes of fulfilling. He bound us with this Duchy of Warsaw, with this Saxon king, and when he deprived us of all independence, he was always ready to dispose of us like some dead possesssion of his. Woe to the man whose fate depended on someone else, but woe twice over to the nation that depended on the interests of another nation. Nations have no consciences.[10]

The final scene of the Polish Napoleonic drama was played in St. Denis, when the Polish forces passed under the domination of the victorious Russians. The moment stands out vividly in Fredro's memory, which time could not erase:

> After the denouement of one of the biggest, if not the biggest historical dramas ever staged in Fontainebleau, the Polish staff officers betook themselves with a regiment of Polish uhlans of the Guard to St. Denis where the rest of our army gathered under the command of General Wincenty Krasiński. There, with inexpressible repulsion, we passed under Russian command. Grand Prince Constantine accepted the command of the Polish army. When the Emperor Alexander I arrived in St. Denis from Paris in order to take review of or rather to come into actual possession of the army representing Poland still garbed in the name of the Duchy of Warsaw, we stood in the ranks silent and

---

[10] *Ibid.*, p. 58.

melancholic. On the right wing were the Chevaux légers
lanciers de la Garde Impériale, about whom it was possible
to say that their tears had not yet dried—yes, that's right,
tears. For leaving Fontainebleau a few days ago, they were
crying, and here and there even out loud in the ranks of
these veterans who from the battle of Somo-Sierra right
up to the last battle of Paris, sans peur et sans reproche,
held up before the whole world the glory of the Polish soldier. Further, there was a brigade of uhlans under the command of General Kurnatowski, and the infantry, artillery,
and light cavalry of General Dwernicki. The Grand Prince,
at the head, set forward at a manège gallop for the meeting
with Tsar Alexander, and describing a circle with his
horse with great precision, delivered the report to him.
Throughout the whole line a dumb silence reigned, and
when afterward General Krukowiecki shouted: "Long live
the Tsar!—only a faint echo resounded. A person in whom
an honest heart beat, whether he wore a Russian or Polish
uniform, had to admit a feeling of pain at hearing that
shout in which, thank God, there could be no sincerity. If
it had been sincere, it would at the same time have been
base."[11]

It was in such a frame of mind that in June 1814 Alexander and his brother Seweryn took the discharges that brought
their military careers to an end. Their brother Maksymilian
chose to remain in the service, however, and from the rank of
colonel eventually rose to that of general-flügel-adjutant of the
tsar. On the way back to Poland Fredro stopped briefly in
Vienna, a visit that was to have far-reaching consequences for
the future dramatist for it was here in the Austrian capital
that he met the woman who was to become his wife only years
later and after much hardship and bitterness: Zofia Jabłonow-
ska, the very young wife in a loveless family-arranged marriage of the powerful and wealthy Count Stanisław Skarbek.

In his native Galicia again after the years at war, Fredro
visited the old family estate at Beńkowa Wisznia, then settled
at nearby Jatwięgy, which also belonged to the Fredros and

which his father Jacek had entrusted to his management. His brother Seweryn remained at Beńkowa Wisznia until his marriage to Countess Domicella Konarska, when he moved to the neighboring village of Nowosiółki. The quiet life of a country-gentleman, which Fredro was never to completely abandon from this time on, doubtless suited his mood upon his return from France and he threw himself into it with unconcealed pleasure. The tranquility of the provincial routine was interrupted from time to time by occasional trips to Lwów where the still young and decorated former officer in the *Grande Armée* enjoyed not only the city's cultural attractions, particularly the Lwów Polish theater directed at the time by the prominent Galician intellectual Jan Niepomucen Kamiński, but also its bustling social life.[12]

It was in this immediate post-military period—between the years 1816 and 1819—that Fredro began his literary career, at first modestly with the publication of a few poems in the leading Galician journal, the *Lwów Review* (Pamiętnik Lwowski). On the tenth of March, 1817, his first play, the one-act comedy in verse *Intrigue in a Hurry or There Is No Bad Without Good* (Intryga na prędce, czyli Niema złego bez dobrego), written two years earlier in 1815, was presented publicly in the Lwów Theater. In a poem, "Pro Memoria," composed in 1872 and appendixed to his memoirs, Fredro gave a succinct account of how he became a writer:

I longed for the camp . . . and soon became bored,
And to do something, I became a poet.
A poet! . . . Deuce take it! . . . That, Sir, is no joke!

Were you at least supported by good schooling?
What do you mean! . . . Why, there I was 'midst
two tutors

A complete sixteen-year-old dunce;
I never wrinkled my brow over any book—
The hunter's horn in the forest was my school.[13]

---

[12] On the Lwów Theater in Fredro's time, see Stanisław Pepłowski, *Teatr polski we Lwowie* (*1780-1881*) (Lwów, 1889).
[13] *Trzy po trzy*, p. 224.

Fredro, we know, began to become interested in poetry and drama around 1810, despite his lack of serious formal education. An early crude attempt at play-writing in the form of the comedy *The Terrified Demon* (Strach ustraszony) —which has since been lost—was long forgotten; another comedy about General Jakub Jasiński, one of the legendary heroes of Kościuszko's uprising in 1794, never got beyond the planning stage. But in camp, after his enlistment in the Polish army of Prince Poniatowski, Fredro thought seriously about writing. He later recalled:

> Some event, I don't remember whether happy or sad, gave me an opportunity for writing verses which passed from hand to hand and enjoyed unheard-of fame in my regiment. One of my more enlightened colleagues, however, noticed and brought to my attention that in many of my verses a caesura was lacking. A caesura?—I asked surprised —I never heard of it. My colleague undertook to explain to me the meaning of the caesura and that was my first lesson in the rules of Polish versification.[14]

It was in Paris, however, that Fredro enjoyed his first meaningful contact with the world of the theater, and it made an indelible impression. He has left an account of this contact in his memoirs:

> Thanks to my stay in this capital [Paris] I became familiar with the French theater which made an indescribable impression on me, corresponding to my internal disposition, and yet entirely new; for Lwów at the time had no permanent Polish stage, and if I happened to be at theatrical presentations then they were performed most frequently by amateurs and so I could have no clear idea of the power of this art.[15]

These French theatrical experiences, followed by his subsequent immersion in Molière and the French comedy writers of the eighteenth century, all of whom he doubtless had a

---

[14] In Lucjan Siemieński, "O Aleksandrze Fredrze i jego twórczości," *Kronika rodzinna*, Series II, No. 21 (Warsaw, Oct. 22–Nov. 1, 1876) , 321-322.
[15] *Ibid.*

chance to see on stage in Paris, bore fruit when in the postwar tranquility of Jatwięgy Fredro turned again to the literary art, this time far more seriously than he ever had previously. When *Intrigue in a Hurry* was finished it was brought to the attention of Kamiński, who praised it and accepted it for staging in the Lwów Theater. Although the play attracted little attention, Fredro was not disheartened and in a short space of time turned out two more dramatic works: *We're Even* (Kwita) and *Theater in a Theater* (Teatr w teatrze). When Kamiński suggested that the first be shortened and the second provided with musical accompaniment, Fredro lost interest and abandoned further work on these plays, which no longer survive. In 1818, however, his first full-length play was written, the Molièresque three-act comedy in verse *Mister Moneybags* (Pan Geldhab) about a bourgeois social climber of the species of Jourdain of *Le Bourgeois Gentilhomme*. Because of the lukewarm reception of *Intrigue in a Hurry*, Kamiński was somewhat reluctant to take a chance on a new Fredro play, so the dramatist made an effort instead to bring the work to the attention of the Warsaw theatrical world. In 1819, he made a trip to Warsaw where he counted on the assistance of an old army friend, Franciszek Morawski, who exhibited no great interest in the work and entertained Fredro instead by reciting some fables he had written. The director of the National Theater in Warsaw, Ludwik Osiński, was approached next. Osiński liked parts of the comedy but suggested that it be staged in Lwów since, as he put it, "there are no such people as Mister Moneybags in Warsaw." After further negotiations, however, Osiński agreed to stage the play and it was mounted in Warsaw two years later, on October 7, 1821.[16] The first serious review of the new play appeared in the influential *Warsaw Gazette* (Gazeta Warszawska) on January 1, 1822. Generally favorable, it was sent to Fredro by a Warsaw friend, Franciszek Kisieliński.

Other plays followed now in rapid succession: the one-act comedy in verse *Nagging and Contradiction* (Zrzędność i przekora), the three-act comedy in verse *Husband and Wife*

---

[16] For a detailed history of the stagings of Fredro's plays, see Stanisław Dąbrowski and Ryszard Górski, *Fredro na scenie* (Warsaw, 1963).

(Mąż i żona), written between 1820 and 1821; the *New Don Quixote or One Hundred Madnesses* (Nowy Don Kiszot czyli Sto szaleństw), a three-act "sketch" in verse; and the three-act comedy in verse *The Foreign Way* (Cudzoziemczyzna). *Husband and Wife*, the best play of Fredro's earliest period as a dramatist, was performed for the first time in the Lwów Theater on March 29, 1822, and in Warsaw on June 22, 1823. Kisieliński, who had intervened with Osiński in the matter of *Mister Moneybags* and was keeping the dramatist informed of the progress of his plays in Warsaw, could report that the work was received warmly and that the author's reputation was well on the way to being firmly established. Later, however, the play was attacked on moral grounds by the critic Alexander Dunin-Borkowski. The *New Don Quixote* appeared for the first time in Lwów in 1824. Although it is not one of Fredro's best plays and later served as the basis for a vicious attack on Fredro by the revolutionary poet and critic Seweryn Goszczyński, it was set to music by the composer Stanisław Moniuszko in 1839 and has survived in this form to the present day. *The Foreign Way*, a satire on the aping of foreign customs written as early as 1822, was staged in Lwów on February 29, 1824, and in Warsaw on March 11 of the same year. In 1823 Fredro wrote still another one-act comedy in verse, *The First Is Best or The Saving Art* (Pierwsza lepsza czyli Nauka zbawienna). It was performed for the first time in Warsaw on May 15, 1824. This brought to an end the vigorous first period of Fredro's career.

Writing plays was one way—certainly a very productive one —for Fredro to find some outlet for the frustration he was experiencing in his relationship with the Countess Skarbek with whom, it will be remembered, he became acquainted during a brief stopover in Vienna on his way back to Poland from Paris. After an unsuccessful romance with Karolina Potocka (whom he had met in the home of the widow of Adam Potocki, his old commander of the eleventh regiment of hussars), Fredro had a fresh opportunity to renew his acquaintance with the Countess. From the time he had settled in Jatwięgy upon his return to Poland, the dramatist had maintained close contact with the Jabłonowski family through his sister Cecylia, who married Leon Jabłonowski, and through his brother Henryk, who married the daughter of Kazimierz Jabłonowski. When Countess Skarbek separated from her husband, she came on a prolonged visit to the home of her parents which was situated not far from the Fredro estate at Jatwięgy. Fredro lost little time now in strengthening his friendship with the young beauty whom he could not get out of his mind since their first brief meeting in the Austrian capital. Whenever possible, the dramatist sought the company of Zofia Skarbek and sometime in 1819 the two exchanged vows of mutual love. Fate decreed, however, that another nine years would pass before they would become man and wife. In addition to the anticipated difficulties in obtaining a divorce from the ecclesiastical authorities (Fredro and Countess Skarbek were Roman Catholics), there was a great deal of opposition from both families, particularly from Fredro's future mother-in-law who, apart from other considerations was disappointed to see the break-up of her daughter's marriage to one of the wealthiest landowners in Galicia.

In his memoirs, Ludwik Jabłonowski, the Countess Skarbek's brother, conveys something of the hostility his parents felt toward Fredro when the young dramatist began to call frequently on his sister:

> Although mother guessed nothing, she looked with a jaundiced eye at these visits, since she had no love for the whole Fredro family, especially from the time that one of its daughters [Cecylia] crawled into our nest by marrying Leon Jabłonowski.[17]

When matters reached an impasse and there seemed no way out of his troubles, Fredro accepted an invitation to visit his brother Maksymilian and his family who were then staying in Florence, Italy. On February 13, 1824, he left Galicia. With Alexander's best interests at heart, Maksymilian and his wife made every effort to interest him in a cousin of Maksymilian's wife, the wealthy Russian countess Eugenia Buturlin. Their earnest efforts were to no avail, however. Fredro could

---

[17] Ludwik Jabłonowski, *Pamiętniki*, ed. by Karol Lewicki (Cracow, 1963), p. 110.

not forget Zofia Skarbek and terminated his Italian sojourn within six months. He left Florence for Naples, but broke his trip in Rome and then headed directly back to Galicia. In July or August, 1824, he was again in the city of Lwów. If there were any positive gains from the Italian trip they could only have been the confirmation of his love for Countess Skarbek and the opportunity while in Italy to become familiar with the comedies of Goldoni and the still living traditions of the Italian commedia dell'arte, echoes of which can be discerned in his own playwrighting.[18]

The years 1823 and 1824 saw only the production of plays Fredro had written earlier, but no new work flowed from his pen during this two-year period. Apart from the turmoil of his romantic life, another contributing factor to this temporary lull doubtless must have been the long delay the dramatist experienced in the staging of *Mister Moneybags*. In 1825, however, Fredro returned to active playwrighting and in the course of a single year wrote the one-act comedy in verse *Outcasts and the Poet* (Odludki i poeta), the three-act comedy in prose *Ladies and Hussars* (Damy i huzary), the one-act comedy in verse *The Letter* (List), the one-act operetta *A Night's Stay in the Apennines* (Nocleg w Apeninach), the one-act comedy in verse *Nobody Knows Me* (Nikt mnie nie zna) and the longer four-act comedy in verse *Friends* (Przyjaciele).

Outcasts and the Poet was presented for the first time in the Lwów Theater on November 10, 1825; *Ladies and Hussars* premiered also in Lwów on November 18, 1825; *The Letter* was staged first in Lwów on October 28, 1825; *A Night's Stay in the Apennines* was first presented with the music of Franciszek Mirecki in Lwów on June 16, 1841; *Nobody Knows Me* had its premiere in Lwów on July 7, 1826; and *Friends* made its debut in the National Theater (Teatr Narodowy) in Warsaw on September 27, 1828.

Following upon the initial successes of the stage productions of his plays, Fredro made an effort to have them published. Despite the good offices of his friends Kamiński and Kisieliński, a publisher could not be found. The dramatist

---

[18] On Fredro and Italian comedy, see Eugeniusz Kucharski, *Fredro a komedia obca* (Cracow, 1921).

nonetheless was adamant and with the considerable assistance of his brother Maksymilian, who was spending the year 1825-1826 in Galicia and was on hand to help him in the matter of his suit of Zofia Skarbek's hand, he went ahead with the publication at his own expense. Two volumes of his collected plays appeared in Vienna in 1826. Volume One contained *Mister Moneybags, The Foreign Way, Ladies and Hussars,* and *Nagging and Contradiction;* Volume Two, *Husband and Wife, The New Don Quixote, The First Is Best, The Letter,* and *Outcasts and the Poet.*

In the next two years—1826 and 1827—Fredro turned out two more plays: the three-act prose comedy *Heavens, What's Happening?* (Gwałtu, co się dzieje), which premiered in Cracow on May 6, 1832, and the first version of *Maidens' Vows* (Śluby panieńskie), which bore the title *The Hatred of Men* (Nienawiść mężczyzn) after the title originally planned for the work—*Magnetism* (Magnetyzm)—was abandoned. In its original version the comedy had four acts and was written in unrhymed thirteen-syllable lines. A new draft of the play was ready only five years later. Also in 1827, Fredro wrote another five-act comedy, *The Post Coach* (Dyliżans), which had its premiere in Lwów on March 22, 1833. The play *The Defense of Olsztyn* (Obrona Olsztyna) was probably also written at this time. Although it was published in 1830 in the Lwów *Galician* (Haliczanin), one of the leading Galician journals of the period, it was never performed during Fredro's lifetime. Its stage career began late in the nineteenth century, on December 31, 1889.

After the great productivity of 1825, 1826 and 1827, Fredro's literary activity again slowed down noticeably for the next few years. Because of the illness of his father, the dramatist left Jatwięgy and settled down on the old family estate of Beńkowa Wisznia where he and his brother Seweryn, who had been living nearby at Nowosiółki, busied themselves with the management of the property. Jacek Fredro's death not long after Alexander left Jatwięgy, on February 7, 1828, came as a profound shock to the dramatist who was deeply devoted to his father. In his memoirs he recorded the pain he felt at his loss:

I loved and respected my father, but to the extent that time presents me with points of comparison, esteem for him seems to increase in my heart. Now I often repeat more than one of the things he used to say, his advice, which I never thought I would remember when I heard them for the first time. My father's life became a model for his children. His righteous character, his intelligence—not sparkling with any fine learning, but profound, logical—an extreme goodness, kindness, helpfulness, earned him universal respect. As a person and as a Pole—he was in the full sense of the term: *Without blame.* About him one could say scrupulously: Le Ciel n'est pas plus pur, que le fond de son âme. . . . I like to recall my father as often as possible, to make him a participant in my happy and good moments—it seems to me that at such times he is smiling at me. Rest! Rest in God, you good, righteous, dear, beloved father![19]

Fredro knew not only tears and sadness in 1828. On November 8 of that year, after what seemed an eternity of waiting and struggle, he received word that the Vatican finally agreed to approve Zofia Skarbek's petition to divorce her husband. She and Fredro were at last free to marry. The wedding, a simple, quiet affair, took place in the parish church in Korczyn near Krosno, an estate belonging to the bride's family. The bitter hostility of the Jabłonowski family toward Fredro was still so great, however, that no member of the family attended with the sole exception of Ludwik Jabłonowski, who describes the occasion in his memoirs as "a painful ceremony for us" where the service itself was "more like that of a funeral than a wedding." In the celebration that followed the wedding the bridegroom standing next to his sister reminded Jabłonowski of "Mephisto whispering in Margareta's ear."[20] This, no doubt, remained the Jabłonowski family image of the dramatist.

After their wedding, Fredro and his wife settled in Beńkowa Wisznia, going into Lwów only for the winter months. In the fall of the following year, 1829, their first child was born, a son, named Jan Alexander, who later followed in the

[19] *Trzy po trzy*, pp. 195-196.   [20] Jabłonowski, *op.cit.*, p. 111.

footsteps of his father by becoming a comedy writer, though he never attained the stature nor did he command the talent of his more famous father.[21]

The domestic tranquility of the Fredros was shattered in 1830 by news of the ill-fated November Insurrection in Warsaw. Although he was sympathetically disposed toward the insurrection against the Russians in the part of Poland that had fallen to them in the Partitions, Fredro's conservative, realistic nature somewhat tinged with pessimism held out little hope for the success of the venture and he was not overly enthusiastic. When toward the end of 1831 plague swept through Galicia and there was tumult over the possibility of the insurrection spreading into the Austrian-ruled province, Fredro moved himself and his small family to the safety of Vienna. Here he continued his literary activity, writing poems of a generally patriotic nature such as "Poland Has Not Yet Perished" (Jeszcze Polska nie zginęła), "An Old Uhlan" (Stary ulan), and "Leave-taking" (Pożegnanie), and a poem in prose "An Exile's Diary" (Dziennik wygnańca) full of personal reminiscences and reflecting the author's attitudes toward the frustrated hopes of the November Insurrection.[22]

By the beginning of 1832, when the danger of plague in Galicia had subsided and the insurrection in Warsaw had been crushed, Fredro and his family were back in Lwów. In the next three years, no longer threatened by internal or external crises, he was to enjoy his most productive period as a dramatist and produce his best-known and best-loved works. In April 1832 his comedy *Mister Joviality* (Pan Jowialski), the first version of which was a three-act play, was enlarged to four acts. It premiered in Lwów on June 22, 1832, with premieres in Cracow on March 28 of the same year and on May 10, 1835, in Warsaw. One of Fredro's better comedies and virtually impossible to translate because of the great amount of verbal humor, *Mister Joviality* provoked considerable controversy over the titular character, an old Polish Galician

---

[21] Jan Alexander Fredro (1829-1891). In 1880-1881 a four-volume edition of his works, containing thirteen comedies, appeared in Warsaw.

[22] Fredro's poetry appears in Vols. XI and XII of the most recent edition of his collected works, *Pisma wszystkie*, ed. by Stanisław Pigoń (1955-1962).

squire, and over Fredro's attitude toward the contemporary social and political role of the Polish gentry in Galicia.[23] This controversy over *Mister Joviality* reached the boiling point in the twentieth century when Tadeusz Boy-Żeleński set about methodically "revising" traditional views on Fredro, particularly those advanced by the respected "Fredrologist," Professor Eugeniusz Kucharski.

Eight months after the premiere of *Mister Joviality*, the final revised version of *Maidens' Vows*, now a five-act comedy in rhymed verse, had its first stage mounting in Lwów on February 15, 1833. It was an immediate success and at once established the author as the foremost Polish writer of comedy. The Warsaw premiere of the play took place on the evening of November 16, 1834. After 1863 the role of Aniela in the comedy became something of the private preserve of the distinguished Polish actress Helena Modrzejewska, best known in the United States as Helena Modjeska. The year that witnessed the overwhelming success of *Maidens' Vows* also produced the comedy recognized as Fredro's best, *The Vengeance* (Zemsta). Based on the account of an actual feud between two old Polish squires of the seventeenth century, *The Vengeance* doubtless was conceived by Fredro during the brief period when he and his wife were residents on the estate of Korczyn. Part of the ruined castle of Odrzykoń was located here and its archives, which he read avidly, acquainted the dramatist with the story of the land feud between Jan Skotnicki and Piotr Firlej who appear in the comedy as the Cup-Bearer and the Notary, respectively. The play was performed for the first time in the Lwów Theater on February 17, 1834.

In late 1833 or early 1834 Fredro wrote the comedy *Auntie* (Ciotunia), based on the pursuit of remnants of the hapless Zaliwski "expedition." In March 1833, Colonel Józef Zaliwski crossed into the Kingdom of Poland at the head of partisan units formed in Great Poland and Galicia with the purpose of inciting a revolt in the Russian provinces. The adventure proved a complete fiasco. After its collapse its participants

---

[23] On *Mister Joviality*, see my article "The 'Awakened Sleeper' in Polish Literature," *Comparative Literature*, Vol. XVI, No. 2 (Spring 1964), 138-157.

were hunted down by the Austrian authorities from one end of Galicia to the other. *Auntie* was presented by the Lwów Theater on June 16, 1834; on May 9, 1858, it was permitted to be staged in Warsaw for the first time and in Cracow only in 1866. The last full-length comedy Fredro wrote before his retreat from literary activity in 1835 was *The Life Annuity* (Doyżwocie), a comedy of intrigue about a usurer and an annuity contract that faintly echoes Molière's *L'Avare* and ranks certainly as one of Fredro's better plays. Work on the comedy was finished by the beginning of 1835 and the text was published in Volume Five of Fredro's collected works, which also contained *Auntie* and *The Vengeance*. Its premiere was celebrated in the Lwów Theater on June 12, 1835. Performances in Cracow (and Poznań) came only four years later, with the Warsaw and Wilno premieres delayed until 1845.

With *The Life Annuity*, Fredro's most brilliant period as a creative writer came to an end. Until the early 1850's the only really significant new work the dramatist undertook was his book of memoirs, *Topsy Turvy Talk*. But we are not dealing here with a simple case of the drying up of the wellsprings of a creative artist's inspiration. Fredro not only produced little of enduring merit in the period from 1835 to 1852 or 1854, but almost completely cut himself off from literature during this time. Polish literary historians and "Fredrologists" usually characterize this bleak period in Fredro's career as the *milczenie*, the time of silence. The reasons behind the apparently sudden cessation of literary activity have been the subject of investigation and controversy for some time now. This is not the place to consider the different theories that have been put forth in the attempt to explain and document chronologically the author's withdrawal from the literary community of contemporary Galicia, but simply to present, in brief, the main developments in the episode.

The immediate cause of Fredro's "silence" was the devastating attack on his work leveled by the Romantic poet, critic and revolutionary Seweryn Goszczyński. The attack came in a lengthy article on contemporary Polish literature published by Goszczyński under the title "The New Epoch in Polish Poetry" (Nowa epoka w poezji polskiej). It appeared in 1835 in Volume II of the *Universal Journal of Science and Learning* (Powszechny Pamiętnik Nauk i Umiejętności), which was published by Goszczyński and the publicist and political activist Leon Zienkowicz.[24] In the section of the article dealing with French literary influences in contemporary Polish literature (against which, incidentally, Goszczyński takes a decidedly hostile stance), Fredro's work is condemned as slavishly imitative of foreign models, especially French, and devoid of any originality save in the matter of names and settings. Technically, the plays are dismissed as lacking individual color or shades of character. The success of Fredro's comedies in the theater Goszczyński ascribes to two factors, principally: first, Fredro's *superficial* polish and wit, his verse as "smooth as water, but also having the taste of water" and, second, a public hungry for dramatic poetry and who "like a starved beggar accepts whatever is thrown into his empty bags even if it is a piece of stale bread, regardless of whether the gift is made out of pure love on the part of the benefactor or from the desire to glory before the world, or if it is accompanied by consideration of whether it was even proper nourishment."[25]

The play that served as the principal example of Fredro's deficiencies as a playwright was *The New Don Quixote*, admittedly not one of Fredro's best. Goszczyński seized on one line in the play—"One has to be insane to wish to transform the world, to struggle with the entire world"—and deliberately misread it as proof of Fredro's ultra-conservatism that rejected the active struggle against oppression and social and political injustice. Moreover, the critic leveled the quite unjust accusation that when Polish artists were addressing themselves above all to the grave questions of national independence and cultural survival after the political disasters of the late eighteenth and early nineteenth centuries, Fredro gave no evidence in his comedies of sharing these concerns. Indeed, claimed Goszczyński, one could even detect in Fredro's writings a certain *disinterest*. At a time when Polish literature, and particularly the poetry of the great émigré poet Adam Mickiewicz, was com-

[24] The complete text appears also in Seweryn Goszczyński, *Dzieła zbiorowe*, ed. by Zygmunt Wasilewski, Vol. III (Lwów, 1910), pp. 177-237, particularly the section "Francuszczyzna," pp. 224-230.

[25] *Ibid.*, pp. 228-230.

mitted spiritually to the cause of the Polish nation, Goszczyński's attack was especially damaging.

To discover the true reasons behind this bitter condemna-
tion of Fredro by Goszczyński we have to leave the field of literature and enter the maze of contemporary Polish politics.
Goszczyński was an active member of an émigré revolutionary
group committed to fomenting an uprising in Galicia against
the Austrian government.[26] The organization took the name
of the *Association of the Polish People* (Stowarzyszenie Ludu
Polskiego, SLP). In late 1832, at a meeting of a citizens' committee in Lwów attended by Fredro, a plan was put forth to establish a literary journal that would be published jointly with
Polish writers living abroad (most were located at the time in
Paris where the majority of the Polish émigrés fled after the
defeat of the November Insurrection). Fredro was entrusted
with the direction of the journal's editorial policies. Conservative as he was by nature, the dramatist wanted to make certain that the journal would carry nothing that would threaten
its existence or bring harm to any of its contributors. He insisted, furthermore, that he would support the project only if
the articles submitted to the journal were reviewed by a censorship committee prior to publication. In his own memoirs
Goszczyński maintained that Fredro held up his [Goszczyński's]
vitriolic poem "The Banquet of Vengeance" (Uczta zemsty)
as an example of the type of offensive work that had to be
excluded from the pages of the proposed journal.[27] Although
Goszczyński insisted that his "Banquet of Vengeance" was
singled out by Fredro, Polish literary historians generally
agree that Fredro probably mentioned another poem by
Goszczyński, the "Prayer of a Free Man" (Modlitwa wolnego),
and not the "Banquet of Vengeance." In any case, that
Fredro did illustrate his point about prior censorship with
some work of Goszczyński which resulted in antagonism be-

[26] On Goszczyński's activities in Galicia in the 1830's and 1840's, see
Zygmunt Wasilewski, *Z życia poety romantycznego: Seweryn Goszczyński
w Galicji, Nieznane pamiętniki, utwory i listy z lat 1832-1843* (Lwów,
1910).

[27] On the Goszczyński–Fredro confrontation over the matter of the journal, see Józef Tretiak, *Bohdan Zaleski na tułactwie 1831-1838*, Vol. I (Cracow, 1913), 57.

tween the two writers cannot be doubted. In consequence of Fredro's stand, Goszczyński wrote: "I lost all respect for Fredro and showed that to him a few years later in my article 'The New Epoch in Polish Poetry.' "[28] This is more than sufficient evidence of the fact that the basis of Goszczyński's attack was personal, political and *essentially non-literary*. In this light it is easy to understand why Goszczyński used one of Fredro's weakest plays, *The New Don Quixote*, to demonstrate Fredro's "deficiencies" without any consideration or *even mention* of such far better works as *Mister Moneybags* or *Husband and Wife*, both of which appeared *before The New Don Quixote*.

The confrontation between Fredro and Goszczyński over the matter of the literary journal in Lwów in 1832 not only set the stage for the denigration of Fredro's literary talent by Goszczyński some three years later, but also tended to estrange Fredro from the younger generation of Galician writers who inclined to the political left and were strongly under Goszczyński's influence. When political intrigue increased in Galicia in the mid-1830's, the relations between Fredro and the younger writers worsened. Fredro's lukewarm response to the revolutionary schemes of Goszczyński and the Association of the Polish People and his reluctance to assist them with monetary contributions raised under his leadership from among the more well-to-do Polish Galician landowners resulted in a further deterioration of the situation. When Goszczyński's "The New Epoch in Polish Poetry" made its appearance in 1835, it was as though the clarion call to battle had been sounded. In the same year as the Goszczyński attack, the first volume of the *Scientific Quarterly* (Kwartalnik Naukowy) —the Lwów-Cracow journal published in 1835-1836 by the prominent political writer and radical Antoni Zygmunt Helcel (1808-1870) —carried the article "The Theater and Alexander Fredro" (Teatr i Aleksander Fredro) by the Galician author Wincenty Pol (1807-1872).[29] Here Fredro was attacked again, this time for the "salon atmosphere" of his plays,

28 Wasilewski, *op.cit.*, p. 24.
29 *Kwartalnik Naukowy*, Vol. I (Cracow, 1835), pp. 347-363, esp. pp. 355-357.

though in fairness to Pol it must be said that his attack lacked the bitterness of Goszczyński's and that he did express his recognition of Fredro's qualities as a dramatic artist.[30]

Few voices were raised in Fredro's defense. One of these belonged to the old Warsaw critic, Franciszek Salezy Dmochowski, who countered Pol's attack in the twenty-ninth number of the journal *The Domestic Museum* (Muzeum Domowe) of 1835.[31] In number forty-two of the same publication, Dmochowski made a brave effort to expose the weaknesses in Goszczyński's arguments. Despite occasional sallies against his detractors such as Dmochowski's, Fredro was stunned by the attacks against him. Unlike Molière in his *Critique de L'École des femmes* or the *Improvisation en Versailles*, he made no attempt to defend himself against his critics. Instead, like Grillparzer after the disastrous reception of his comedy *Weh dem, der lügt* in Vienna in 1834, Fredro chose the path of quiet retreat and simply withdrew from further participation in the contemporary literary life of Galicia.

For some time it was assumed that Fredro's break with literature followed immediately in 1835 upon the appearance of the Goszczyński article. This is the view expounded by, among others, Ludwik Jabłonowski, Fredro's brother-in-law, in his own memoirs. Research into the period of Fredro's "silence" in this century has produced convincing evidence to show that Fredro's withdrawal was only gradual, however, and that there was no sudden rupture.[32] Toward the end of 1835 Franciszek Mirecki urged Fredro to write a national opera. Mirecki had written to Fredro earlier from Geneva about the matter of such an opera. In 1836 the dramatist sent him *Rajmund the Monk* (Rajmund mnich), later titled simply *Rymond*. In 1838 Fredro prepared for publication the fifth volume of his

30 For the general background of this period, see Pol's memoirs *Pamiętniki*, ed. by Karol Lewicki (Cracow, 1960).

31 Dmochowski's memoirs contain much interesting material on the literary climate in Poland in the first three decades of the nineteenth century. See Franciszek Salezy Dmochowski, *Wspomnienia od 1806 do 1830 roku* (Warsaw, 1959).

32 On Fredro's withdrawal from literature and his activities during and after the "period of silence," see Kazimierz Wyka's introduction to Fredro, *Pisma wszystkie*, Vol. VII (Warsaw, 1958), 7-63.

comedies and the following year he worked on a new edition of the first and second volumes. In 1841 he twice published his novel *The Misfortunes of the Happiest Husband* (Nieszczęścia najszczęśliwego męża). Then, in 1842 a fresh wave of attacks was launched against him. It appeared that his opponents were to be satisfied only with Fredro's complete cessation of all literary activity. The most vehement attacker this time was probably the Galician liberal and staunch supporter of Goszczyński, Alexander (Leszek) Dunin-Borkowski, a representative of the younger generation of Galician writers who had been angered by Fredro's conservatism and lack of support for the revolutionary cause. The scathing denunciation of Fredro attributed to Dunin-Borkowski came in the article "General Remarks About Literature in Galicia" (Uwagi ogólne nad literaturą w Galicji) published in numbers fifty and fifty-one of the Poznań *Literary Weekly* (Tygodnik Literacki) for 1842. Since the article bore no signature it is of course difficult to positively identify its author as Dunin-Borkowski, but very strong evidence points to him, or at least to a coalition of Dunin-Borkowski and other Galician radicals such as the publicist Jan Dobrzański (1820-1886) and the historian and journalist Karol Szajnocha (1818-1868).[33] The nature of this new attack is manifest in the following brief excerpt:

> Educated superficially, since any other way was not possible in the country, disposed to glittering in salons rather than to the laborious pursuit of study, given over to military service under Napoleon and later to amusements and love affairs with the other youth of his class, amidst an idle life and landowners' pursuits, with a taste spoiled by French models, having experienced no misfortune or pain, which particularly excite the poetic mind, Alexander Fredro could not become an author except accidentally. For the companions of his youth, for the participants in his expeditions, his licentious and low pranks, he

[33] A very convincing argument for the exclusive authorship of Dunin-Borkowski is put forth by Kazimierz Pecold in "O autorstwie 'Uwag ogólnych nad literaturą w Galicji'" *Pamiętnik Literacki*, Vol. LII, zeszyt 4 (Warsaw-Wrocław, 1961), pp. 577-587.

first composed an obscene drama . . . full of coarse humor and unbridled gaiety. Soon the work circulated widely in numerous transcriptions, seized with eagerness by the young people who learned the bawdiest places by heart and repeated them with great pleasure, and called the author's attention to his previously hidden talent that could have been used for something better.

His first thought then was to write comedies. But since such things cannot be shaken out of a sleeve because apart from talent some preparatory disposition was necessary, he threw himself into the reading of as many French and German comedies and happy tales of all kinds as possible. The traces of such study we can discern in all his works, for obviously swallowing too many models at one time he could not digest them and just threw them up whole.[34]

As in 1835 Fredro was not entirely without defenders. This time the cudgel was taken up by the eminent Polish historical novelist Józef Ignacy Kraszewski (1812-1887) in his *Literary Studies* (Studia literackie), published in Wilno in 1842. The article in which Fredro's work was discussed bore the title "Truth and Life in the Comedies of Fredro" (Prawda i życie w komediach Fredry). Although he pointed out that Fredro's plays were by no means without their faults, they were the work, nonetheless, of a great talent and had a permanent place in Polish literature. Kraszewski wrote:

> There are so many of our own people in them, so much truth, so much true comicality, so strongly do they move each viewer with the remembrance of a live, personal world that, apart from the countless weaknesses that everybody sees in them and certainly the author himself, nobody will deny them the first place in our dramatic literature, which is decidedly poor.[35]

Despite such recognition and support from so important a literary figure as Kraszewski was in his day, Fredro had been

[34] *Tygodnik Literacki*, No. 50, Poznań, Dec. 12, 1842, p. 398, No. 51, Dec. 19, 1842, pp. 405, 408. See also Sivert, *op.cit.*, p. 98.
[35] Józef Ignacy Kraszewski, *Studia literackie*, ed. by Adam Zawadzki (Wilno, 1842), pp. 209-212. Also Sivert, *op.cit.*, pp. 100-101.

subjected to too much abuse on the part of his critics and detractors. Fatigued by this abuse and by what he considered the indignity of personally defending himself against unwarranted attack and unjustified criticism, he broke off completely now from the literary community. Some years later, however, in *Topsy Turvy Talk* he revealed the depth of the wound Goszczyński and his other critics had opened:

How many times I dissected myself morally, compared myself with other men, tried to fathom why I was almost always badly understood by others. Each simplest, clearest word of mine in the most indifferent conversation took on a different meaning in another person's understanding than it actually had, a meaning always harsh, always disparaging. My letters, usually written carelessly, became for me the cause of more than one deep pain for they fell subject to analysis just like some highly enigmatic utterances; they were interpreted, but always for the bad, never for the good. But my great single weakness was and is that I think out loud, that I express my opinion openly but always more to subject it to discussion than to pass judgment with it. The world does not understand frankness except in the case of someone stupid; on the part of an intelligent person, however, it is always taken for a well-calculated ghost. It's possible to renounce gratitude; every intelligent person should even avoid it. But always, continually, the purest intentions, the most eager favors, the most innocent words one sees twisted, changed into poison, and not being in a position to discover the reason in oneself this must ultimately rouse faith in some sort of unbreakable fatalism. This can repel me from this world that does not want me. Few are the walls between me and people so that I could enjoy the tranquility which is my only aim, that happiness which God has granted me in my domestic life. I broke my author's pen not, as it is supposed, on account of the bad as well as stupid article published anonymously, because the author of that article sold himself to an alien hostility, and to a hostility that was the reward for friendship and even for an important favor. I gave up my career where my self-love could have succumbed to the desire to pursue popularity. I tried, in a word, to remain stupid before the world. I hid myself in the shadow of stupidity before the slash, and before the still more unbearable clatter of human gnats, drones and gadflies—but in this thick shadow, however, I cannot avoid contact with a world that always remains the touch of electric current—annoying and often even painful. To blame the whole world—madness; to blame myself—unfair. It's best, then, to keep silent and not to think, just to keep on traveling farther the rough road, an exiled pilgrim![36]

In 1872, in his lengthy autobiographical poem "Pro Memoria," Fredro again took up the matter of the attacks against him:

Some Minos rose up and barked madly,
He'd have liked my five volumes in five hells.
I wrote badly. Agreed. But to write badly's no crime;
It used to happen before and it still happens now.
I was more surprised by the anger than the contents,
And when nobody undertook my defense,
I couldn't understand, I couldn't guess,
Whether it was by counsel or treachery,
And understood only that I had to be silent.[37]

The years of silence, extending from 1842 to the early 1850's when Fredro reappeared on the stage of Polish literature, were devoted mainly to non-literary interests and activities. In addition to the satisfaction he found in his family life (a second child, his daughter Zofia, was born in 1837) and the management of his estates, he began to take a more active part in Galician political life.[38] As early as 1832 the dramatist had become a member of the Provincial Diet that convened in Lwów. Because of his title of count, which he inherited from his father, he was one of the representatives of the so-called "magnates' estate." On October 26, 1833, he was pre-

---

[36] *Trzy po trzy*, pp. 165-166.   [37] *Ibid.*, p. 225.
[38] Fredro's political activities in the "period of silence" are treated in some detail in Stanisław Pigoń, *W pracowni Aleksandra Fredry* (Warsaw, 1956), pp. 217-283.

sented as a "deputy" or member to the Provincial Department (Wydział Stanowy), a permanent representative body connected with the Galician gubernatorial administration. This appointment, which was renewable every six years, gave Fredro an opportunity to work actively for the betterment of social and economic life in the Galician province. In recognition of this work he was made an honorary citizen of Lwów on September 17, 1839. This same year he was reappointed for a third term as deputy extending to 1845, but in 1842 he resigned the commission on the grounds of ill health. Although he was beginning to suffer greatly at this time from the discomfort of rheumatic attacks, it is difficult not to believe that his decision to give up his deputyship was partly a reaction to the new attack leveled at him in 1842 in the article Dunin-Borkowski is presumed to have written. Fredro remained a member of the Diet itself, however, until 1845.

In his role as a member of the Lwów Diet Fredro aligned himself with the prominent Galician nobleman and philanthropist Leon Sapieha (1802-1878) and campaigned enthusiastically for the alleviation of the economic misery of the Galician province. Toward this end he promoted plans for the extension of the Galician railroad system, the foundation of an Economic Society (Towarzystwo Akcyjne), a Land Credit Union (Towarzystwo Kredytowe Ziemskie) and a Fire Insurance Union (Towarzystwo Ubezpieczeń od Ognia). Encouraged by the work of such men as Sapieha and Fredro, Prince Adam Czartoryski, who directed the conservative wing of the Polish emigration from his quarters in the Hôtel Lambert in Paris, suggested to Fredro in 1842 that he found a journal in Lwów that would rally the Galician Polish gentry to support of the various programs for social and economic reform. On account of political reasons it was impossible for Fredro to carry out the proposal. On July 7, 1842, Czartoryski nonetheless pleaded with the dramatist at least to resume his literary work. "When Polish literature," he wrote, "in all parts of the country appears alive and fertile as never before, despite all obstacles, must it be abandoned by you? You are not permitted to be indifferent and inactive."[39]

[39] Quoted by Sivert, op.cit., p. 46.

When the famous Ossoliński National Institute, one of the leading Galician Polish cultural organizations, was deprived by the Austrian authorities of its right to publish, and its director, Konstanty Słotwiński, was arrested for the publication of patriotic songs and leaflets, Fredro intervened and was able to achieve some positive results. On September 18, 1845, he joined Kazimierz Badeni in the Provincial Commission for the Sambork region which was then engaged in the struggle for the autonomy of Galicia and a reform of the laws governing serfdom in the province.

The activity of this commission and in fact of the entire Provincial Diet was halted by the political events of 1846. The revolt that erupted in Cracow in February of that year—and of which far wider ramifications were anticipated—resulted in Galicia in a misconceived peasant uprising that took a bloody toll of the landowning gentry of the province. By April the Austrian army succeeded in quelling the insurrection but with no little brutality and at the cost of many lives. Polish attempts to gain independence by armed revolt had failed once again. In consideration of the social injustices that had precipitated the Galician revolts Fredro was moved to write in July or August 1846 a study (a memorial, "memoriał" in Polish) entitled "Observations on Galician Social Conditions" (Uwagi nad stanem socialnym w Galicji). It was translated into German and sent to the appropriate Austrian authorities in Vienna. Count Rudolf Stadion, in 1847 and 1848 the Austrian governor of the province of Galicia, welcomed such petitions from the more influential representatives of the Polish nobility and agreed to consider Fredro's proposals. Dealing with the genesis of the peasant movement in Galicia and drawing particular attention to contemporary Galician social conditions and problems, Fredro's memorial treated the Galician outbreaks as an attempt on the part of the peasantry to overthrow serfdom by destroying the "hated order." Although without immediate effect, it is generally accepted now that Fredro's work proved influential in the 1870's in the formation of a new Hapsburg policy for the province of Galicia.

Fredro's pen again served the national cause in 1848, during the "Spring of Nations," when the European revolutions of that year excited Polish hopes for the liberation of the fatherland. The dramatist joined the National Council (Rada Narodowa) founded in Lwów to press for a liberalization of Austrian Galician policy and accepted the rank of captain with command of the third company of a battalion in the recently formed Galician National Guard. When the Lwów National Council drafted a petition calling for increased autonomy for Galicia, Fredro submitted a new memorial distinguished by a sharp formulation of Polish demands for reform in the Austrian-held province. Along with the petition of the National Council this was taken to Vienna by a deputation of Galician Polish gentry for presentation to the emperor.

During the uprisings in 1848, Fredro's son Jan Alexander took an active part in the Hungarian revolution, over his father's objections. He went to Budapest where he joined the Polish forces under the command of the Polish General Józef Bem and fought in the battles of Tarcsal and Tura. He was decorated for his heroism in action. After the campaign of Temesvar he went to Turkey along with the Polish troops serving at the time under the command of General Dembiński. He remained in Turkey until 1850, then emigrated to Paris. Permission to return to his home in Galicia was to be denied him until 1857 because of his activities during the Hungarian rising.

Between 1850 and 1855 Fredro and his wife spent considerable time in Paris visiting their son, returning to Poland only for relatively short visits. One of these return trips to Galicia was necessitated in late 1852 by a charge placed against the dramatist of having insulted and committed treason against the Austrian imperial family.[40] The evidence against Fredro rested almost entirely on a speech he had made in 1848 during a meeting of members of the National Council in Rudki (near Lwów) during which he outspokenly attacked the Austrian

---

[40] For an extensive discussion of the whole case, see Bronisław Łoziński, "Sprawa kryminalna Alexandra hr. Fredry o zdradę stanu," *Przegląd historyczny*, Vol. I, zeszyt 1 (Warsaw, July-Aug. 1905), 89-106; Vol. I, zeszyt 2 (Sept.-Oct. 1905), 264-278.

bureaucracy and is reported to have said, among other things, that the time had come to throw out the "devil in the three-cornered hat." The Austrian authorities at once assumed that the remark referred to the emperor. The vehemence of Fredro's memorials, his stubborn resistance to the attempts of Count Stadion to badger Polish representatives during the Council meeting called by the Galician governor in 1848 to deal with the then deteriorating political situation, and his son's participation in the Hungarian revolution had already caused them to regard the dramatist with a certain suspicion.

Fredro arrived in Galicia to answer the charges brought against him in June 1853. The matter dragged on for more than half a year and in December the dramatist was even threatened with arrest. But on March 8, 1854, the court decided that there was not sufficient evidence to support the contention that Fredro was guilty of anything more serious than a lack of judgment in his choice of language during the meeting in Rudki. In his poem "Pro Memoria," written in 1872, Fredro was to describe the incident with wry humor.

After his trial Fredro received a passport to travel to the West again. He returned to Paris and remained there until the end of 1855, when he left to take up what was to become more or less permanent residence on the Lwów estate of Chorążczyzna, which the Fredros had acquired in 1848. In 1860, during a visit to Cracow on his way back from the "cures" at Karlsbad, the dramatist was tended an enthusiastic reception by a group of friends and admirers who pleaded with him to permit a public viewing of any new works he might have written during the period of his "silence." The novelist Józef Ignacy Kraszewski also voiced similar sentiments the same year in the *Daily Gazette* (Gazeta Codzienna) of which he was chief editor at the time.

During his long period of withdrawal from the literary life of Galicia Fredro never completely stopped writing although most of his energies as we have seen were devoted to social, economic, and political problems. Some time before 1848 he began his book of memoirs, *Topsy Turvy Talk*, very much in the casual, loose manner of Laurence Sterne's *Senti-*

mental Journey.[41] The work is interesting not only for the vivid, detailed picture of Fredro's childhood and adolescence, but also for the colorful and often amusing depiction of his adventures during the Napoleonic campaigns. When Fredro actually resumed the writing of comedies is difficult to determine with any real accuracy, but the two earliest dates accepted by Polish scholars are 1852 and 1854; that is the time when the dramatist's important political activity was behind him and his love of the theater was again excited by frequent visits to the theaters of Paris during his stay in that city on and off between 1850 and 1855. From 1852 or 1854 to 1867-1868, some nine years before his death, Fredro wrote altogether sixteen new dramatic works. These constitute what we may consider the second major period of his literary career.[42] These works of the post-"silence" period include:

1852 or 1854   *A Great Man for Small Matters* (Wielki człowiek do małych interesów), a five-act comedy in prose.

1854 or 1855   *Two Scars* (Dwie blizny), a one-act comedy in prose.

1855 or 1856   *The Ward* (Wychowanka), a five-act play (sztuka) in verse.

1857   *Lita et Compagnie,* a one-act comedy in prose.

1858   *What's the Trouble Here?* (Co tu kłopotu), a four-act comedy in verse.

1859   *I Can't Get Married* (Ożenić się nie mogę), a three-act comedy in prose.

1859   *Mister Benet* (Pan Benet), a one-act comedy in verse.

41 On Fredro's memoirs, see Wacław Borowy's afterword (pp. 183-216) to the edition published in Cracow, 1949, in the series *Biblioteka arcydzieł poezji i prozy.* Also Adam Grzymała-Siedlecki's introduction to the edition published by Książka i Wiedza (Warsaw, 1957), pp. 5-43.

42 On Fredro's "post-silence" comedies, see Kazimierz Wyka's introduction to Fredro, *Pisma wszystkie,* Vol. VII, 7-63.

1860	*Whom You Associate With You Become* (Z jakim się wdajesz, takim się stajesz), a one-act prose "proverb."
1860	*The Candle Blew Out* (Świeczka zgasła), a two-character one-act prose comedy.
1861	*The Revolver* (Rewolwer), a five-act comedy in verse.
1862	*Worthy of Pity* (Godzien litości), a three-act "serious comedy" (komedja serio) in prose.
1862	*Now* (Teraz), a one-act prose sketch.
1862–1867	*From Przemysl to Przeszów* (Z Przemyśla do Przeszowa), a two-act prose comedy.
1864	*I Am a Killer* (Jestem zabójca), a one-act prose comedy.
1867–1868	*The Last Wish* (Ostatnia wola), a three-act comedy in prose.
1867–1868	*Brytan-Bryś*, a political satire in the form of a four-part "dramatic fable."
	The Concert (Koncert), a one-scene prose "intermezzo."

In "Pro Memoria" Fredro was to offer this humorous explanation of his return to literature:

I was silent fifteen years, and grew thin not at all;
How did I suddenly find myself in my old madness?
I wrote a comedy . . . but this time in prose,
And having written one, after a happy confinement,
I returned, alas, to my former habit.
But now I write just for my drawer,
For I don't believe praise . . . and for advice it's too late.[43]

The dramatic works Fredro wrote during his later period were never produced during his lifetime, despite the mount-

43 *Trzy po trzy*, p. 226.

41

ing chorus of demands for their public exhibition. Some were
staged posthumously, but because only a few of them can bear
comparison with the best of his works from the 1820's or 1830's
they have never won permanent places in the classical Polish
repertoire as have *Husband and Wife, Ladies and Hussars,
Maidens' Vows, The Vengeance, Mister Joviality,* and *The
Life Annuity.* Of the later plays the best are *A Great Man for
Small Affairs, I Can't Get Married, The Ward, Worthy of
Pity,* and *Revolver.* The other works are generally weaker, less
vivacious, and often sharply satirical (a quality found only
rarely in the works written before 1835) ; significantly, the majority are in prose. The most satirical plays of the later period
are *The Revolver* and *Now* in which Fredro excoriates the
state of political life in Galicia and the conduct of the im-
potent Galician Provincial Diet.

The last years of Fredro's life were characterized generally
by a mood of frustration and keen disappointment over Galician social and political conditions, and the snail's pace at
which reforms were instituted by the Austrian government. In
1861, when Austrian Galician policy began to show signs of
improvement and the first elections to a General Diet (Sejm
Powszechny) were called, Fredro was asked to accept the man-
date of an envoy. He agreed, but only to withdraw in a few
months' time on the grounds of poor health. In a poem printed in the paper *Time* (Czas) on December 23, 1865, he expressed his true feelings on the conduct of the Diet. The atmosphere of Diet elections was further roundly criticized in
his "dramatized" fable, *Brytan-Bryś.* When the ill-fated January Insurrection of 1863 erupted, the second major attempt by
the Poles in the nineteenth century to regain their independence by force of arms, Fredro greeted it with little enthusiasm
and dissuaded his son Jan from taking part in it. Illness also
continued to aggravate the dramatist's disposition. He fell
subject to a particularly severe case of arthritis which often
made writing physically difficult and lingered until his death.
If there was any real comfort in Fredro's last years, apart from
his close family ties, it was in the public recognition that
again came his way after so many years. In the anti-Romantic
reaction that swept through Poland in the wake of the dis-

aster of the January Insurrection and in the calm rationalism fostered by the positivist Weltanschauung that dominated Polish thinking almost to the end of the century, Fredro's work was reappraised and his true contribution to the development of Polish drama hailed. The public now began to clamor for more of his comedies to fill the Polish stage with warmth and good humor as they had in the second and third decades of the century. On March 26, 1865, in a public ceremony in Lwów, Fredro was honored with a medal presented by Count Józef Załuski in recognition of his literary and civic work, and the occasion provided another opportunity for a demand that Fredro share with his public the fruits of his newest efforts. But the dramatist's answer was not very different now from many he had already given:

> I could have, I should have done more in the field of literature. I confess it; I regret it. Now it's too late. Whatever my works were, they were always nourished, however, by a pure source, to the very depths of my conscience. Posterity never, never confesses this: envy, the desire for retaliation, malice or calumny did not break my pen. My only desire was to earn the respect of my fellow men, of all my fellow men of equal love for and dedication to the good of our dear fatherland. . . .[44]

In August 1868, the journal *Ears of Corn* (Kłosy) dedicated a special number to Fredro. Its editor-in-chief, Kazimierz Władysław Wojcicki, hoped to convince the dramatist that he should produce his unpublished work. Fredro refused and sent the following response to Wojcicki and the editorial board of the journal:

> It is true that after a long interruption I gave in to my old habit and wrote a few plays, but erroneous is the opinion, which seems to be general, that my silence was caused by any offended author's self-love. No!—I remain silent because I know that society demands continually newer forms, that stone monuments may be pretty, but fresh flowers are always nicer, even though scattered in disarray. I am silent

---

[44] Quoted in Sivert, *op.cit.*, p. 56.

because I am already very old, because I don't want to enter new contests in rusted armor. Its remains, however, I am leaving in my legacy. . . .[45]

The many demands for the public exhibition of his new works thus had little impact on Fredro and he could not be swayed from the course of silence he had determined for himself. In a token gesture, however, he agreed in 1869 to the publication of a new edition of the previously published six volumes of his collected works. This appeared in 1871, a publication of the distinguished old Polish publishing house of Gebethner and Wolff.

The remaining five years of Fredro's life were spent mostly at his home in Lwów with the family to which he was always deeply devoted. His last literary work was *An Oldtimer's Notes* (Zapiski starucha), a collection of aphorisms and maxims on a great variety of subjects. His own physical condition by now had deteriorated rapidly and as he himself wrote in a short poem at the end of his life:

> I've grown deaf, my eyes are weaker,
> It's already hard to read or write
> And frequently there is a lack of words.
> In this time of woe, sometimes half-dreaming,
> I'm forced to converse with myself
> In order to still live a little.[46]

In 1875, one year before his death, Fredro was elected a member of the Academy of Sciences (Akademia Umiejętności) in Cracow—the last public recognition accorded him in his long life. By an ironic twist of fate worthy of his own comedy Fredro and his family were living now in Lwów directly opposite another prominent Polish literary personality, none other than Seweryn Goszczyński. On July 15, 1876, Fredro died, outliving his old adversary by four months. He was buried in Lwów where he had spent the last years of his life, where he had been presented honorary citizenship, and with which his career as a dramatist was intimately bound. In mem-

---

[45] *Kłosy*, Vol. VII, No. 167 (Warsaw, Aug. 29-Sept. 10, 1868), 130.
[46] *Pisma wszystkie*, Vol. XII, 143.

ory of the great playwright the city erected a monument in his honor. When Lwów was ceded to the Soviet Union after World War II, thence to begin its career as the Ukrainian city of Lviv, the monument was transferred to Wrocław, in Poland's regained western territories, where it now stands in the city square. The posthumous publication of Fredro's later works was entrusted to his son, Jan Alexander, with assistance in the project requested also of the old family friend, Franciszek Paszkowski, and the Cracow literary historian, Professor Stanisław Tarnowski.[47] Within a year after his passing, Fredro's post-"silence" plays began appearing on Polish stages. From that time to the present day he has become the subject of many studies and appreciations that have fixed his place in the history of Polish literature as Poland's greatest comic dramatist. No other writer of comedy in Polish has yet appeared to challenge that position.

Fredro in Polish and European Drama

FREDRO's position in the history of Polish drama is in some ways paradoxical. He is viewed, justifiably, as the culmination of the spirited dramatic and theatrical activity of Stanislavian Poland. Without the groundwork laid by Bohomolec, Czartoryski, Zabłocki, Niemcewicz, and Bogusławski it is very doubtful that an outstanding Polish comic dramatist could have appeared in Fredro's time. But in the emergence of an original Polish comedy, represented by Fredro, in the first half of the nineteenth century we encounter our first paradox: Polish comedy through Fredro reached the fullest, most impressive level of its development precisely at a time when comedy was suffering a decline elsewhere in Europe.

Fredro's most appealing and enduring comedies were written at the height of the Romantic period, an age hardly devoid of humor but less inclined by its very nature to foster a vibrant comic art—unlike the Baroque which, after all, had spawned Molière. Romanticism in fact did little to further the cause of drama generally. Successful in shattering the rigid conventions

---

[47] The first real appraisal of Fredro's work was Tarnowski's *Komedie Aleks. hr. Fredry*, which appeared in Warsaw in 1876.

of classicist forms under the banners of Calderonian or Shakespearean dramaturgy, the Romantics so poeticized and rhetoricized the drama that the theater ceased to be its true home. Compounded of ponderous historical plays such as Victor Hugo's *Cromwell* (1827) and *Hernani* (1830), Alexandre Dumas père's *Henri III et sa cour* (1829) and *Charles VII chez ses grands vassaux* (1831), of "cosmic" dramas such as Byron's *Manfred* (1817), of neo-Elizabethan revenge drama such as Shelley's *The Cenci* (1819), of the all but forgotten mythical-knightly tragedies of Tieck, Arnim and Brentano, of the *Schicksalstragödien* or "fate tragedies" of Zacharias Werner and Grillparzer, and of neo-Shakespearean histories such as Pushkin's *Boris Godunov* (1825)—this literary or bookish drama of the Romantics has survived only as academic reading or found its proper resting place, like *Boris Godunov*, in opera. Its life in the theater was destined to be short.

For the Poles during the Romantic period the same situation prevailed. Apart from the fact that Polish romanticism blossomed on the foreign soil of western Europe where the leading writers sought refuge—as did thousands of other Polish émigrés—after the defeat of the November Insurrection of 1830-31, Polish Romantic drama developed along more or less the same lines as the English, French or German. One qualification, however, should be made. The West European Romantics had *theaters* where they could see their works on the stage. The fact that their dramas have been unsuccessful theatrically was due to their having been written by poets fundamentally disinterested in the theater and for whom the drama existed as a genre of poetry. The Poles living in emigration had no theater, and the plays written by the émigré Romantic writers were of necessity "literary," that is, designed primarily for a reading and not a theatergoing public. The eventual staging of these plays, beginning in the late nineteenth century in the Cracow Theater directed by Tadeusz Pawlikowski, remains one of the most outstanding achievements of the modern Polish theater and the collective test of the mettle of Polish directors and actors to the present day.

The major Polish Romantics—Adam Mickiewicz (1798-1855), Juliusz Słowacki (1809-1849), and Zygmunt Krasiński

(1812-1859) —drew inspiration for their dramatic works from the same medieval, Shakespearean and Calderonian sources as their English, French and German counterparts and created a Polish Romantic drama which, though much less known, compares favorably with the best of the contemporary West European. But in the literary hegemony of Polish émigré romanticism which came to assume the spiritual and even political direction not only of the emigration but of the Poles in occupied Poland who turned to the work of the great émigré poets for guidance and hope, what room could there be for the survival of a comic art such as Fredro's? Free of any marked tendency, undidactic, uncommitted in the sense of the Polish Romantics' dedication to the Polish national cause with which the bulk of their work was concerned, Fredro's playwriting at its best sought its justification only in its fidelity to the spirit of the purely comic. And here we have the second great paradox in studying Fredro. Not only did Polish comedy attain the apex of its development at a time when comedy elsewhere in Europe was declining as an art, but also when the triumph of romanticism in the 1830's and 1840's engendered the eventual rejection and lack of appreciation that Fredro in fact was made to endure in 1835 and again in 1842. Unless we consider the background role of Polish émigré romanticism itself, the attacks leveled against Fredro by Goszczyński and Dunin-Borkowski are less easy to appreciate and less meaningful. In the post-Romantic period, particularly after the collapse of the Polish January Insurrection of 1863 when a sharp anti-Romantic reaction began to pervade Polish thinking and the emphasis shifted away from the émigrés to internal Polish developments, Fredro's position in the eyes of his fellow Poles changed drastically. He was beseeched with requests to return to literature, to make public any works he might have written privately in the long period of "silence" and he was finally—and belatedly—hailed as Poland's greatest comic dramatist.

In the history of Polish drama Fredro's position is no more paradoxical than it is unique. His best work was done in the time of the romanticism that must bear responsibility, however indirectly, for his self-exile from literature. Although his major plays were written when the Polish literary scene was dominated by Mickiewicz, Słowacki and Krasiński, his own work had little in common with that of the Romantics. Recognized as Poland's master of the art of comedy in an era when romanticism gave way to the sobriety of positivism, Fredro returned to literature in a climate favorable to his talent, yet the works he produced in the last period of his life only marginally and not at all consistently relate to the main currents of Polish literary positivism and are as a group of less consequence than those written before 1835.

For all his greatness, Fredro nonetheless left no heirs. Imitations of his comedy appeared in the second half of the nineteenth century—those by Józef Bliziński (1827-1893) and Michał Bałucki (1837-1901) have long been regarded as the best of them—but there emerged no new comic dramatist with anything approaching Fredro's talent. In the period of Polish literary history known as Young Poland (Młoda Polska) and extending approximately from the 1880's to World War I, neo-Romantic literary tastes sounded the death knell of positivism as a literary style and, to a lesser extent, as an ideology. For the contemporary dramatists, chief among whom was Stanisław Wyspiański (1869-1907), the fount of inspiration was the drama of the émigré Romantic poets Mickiewicz and, most especially, Słowacki whose lyric and dramatic poetry began to be considered the finest achievement of Polish romanticism. Comedy all but disappeared in the neo-Romantic ethereality; when it was cultivated anew in the time of independent Poland (1919-1939) it never reached the level on which Fredro's work had once placed it, and theatrical triumphs were scored by the stagings of the old Romantic plays and—comedies of Fredro. Since the end of World War II the satires of Sławomir Mrożek and Tadeusz Różewicz have marked positive gains in contemporary Polish dramaturgy and have even attracted attention outside Poland, but it is still too early to determine whether their works possess those qualities that will enable them to endure beyond their own time. The interest in and success of these contemporary Polish dramatists notwithstanding, Fredro continues to be handsomely represented in the repertoires of Polish theaters and continues to attract large audiences—of all ages.

Assessing Fredro's place in the history of European drama is much more difficult than determining the role he played in the development of the drama of his own country. For the sake of neat categorization Fredro at times had been presented to the non-Polish world as the Polish Molière, or the Polish Goldoni, or even the Polish Musset. None of these appellations is particularly accurate, convenient though they may sometimes be.

However fluent he may have been in Molière's comedy, however much he may have admired Molière, Fredro was not greatly in the French master's debt.[48] This is quite evident in *The Life Annuity*, which some consider his most Molièresque comedy after *Mister Moneybags*. Traces of Molière certainly can be found in *The Life Annuity*, as well as in *Mister Moneybags* and *Mister Joviality*, but comparison of these comedies with Molière's work will show that the similarities are considerably less significant than the differences. Like *Husband and Wife*, *Ladies and Hussars* and *The Vengeance* these plays are original works which owe no more to Molière than to other sources of Fredro's genius: the old Polish burgher comedy of the sixteenth and seventeenth centuries, the comedy of Stanislavian Poland, the commedia dell'arte and Goldoni, Marivaux and Kotzebue.

During his stay in Italy Fredro, as we have seen, had a chance to become familiar with the traditions of Italian comedy and especially Goldoni, to whose plays he took an immediate liking. Polish scholarship (I have in mind above all the work of Eugeniusz Kucharski) [49] has explored with painstaking thoroughness the connections between Fredro and Italian comedy and demonstrated, quite convincingly, that while some motifs in Fredro may be traced to Goldoni, the two dramatists share only an ability to develop fine character studies within the context of the comedy of intrigue. In any less general way they have little in common.

[48] On Fredro and Molière, see Boy-Żeleński, "Obrachunki fredrowskie," pp. 168-198.
[49] *Fredro a komedia obca* (Cracow, 1921) .

Characterizing Fredro as a Polish Musset is even less sound than trying to make of him a Slavic Molière or a Slavic Goldoni.[50] *Maidens' Vows* is the only play of Fredro having anything of the aura of a Musset comedy about it, but here it would be more productive to look back to the inspiration of Marivaux—who was a source common to both Fredro and Musset—than to the kind of romantic comedy Musset's name has become identified with and from which Fredro was quite alien.

What then is the proper historical frame in which Fredro's comedy must be set? Despite the neglect of comedy by the Romantics, the art did not die out completely in the time of their eminence; comedy continued to exist, but on two very distinct levels. There appeared from time to time—as isolated phenomena—such comedies of lasting appeal and merit as Grillparzer's *Woe to Him Who Lies* (Weh dem, der lügt), Kleist's *The Broken Jug* (Der zerbrochene Krug), Gogol's *Inspector General* (Revizor), and Griboedov's *Woe From Wit* (Gore ot uma). But these works were the products of writers whose importance for the history of comedy rests only on one or two plays and whose most serious literary efforts came either in other areas of drama (the "fate tragedies" of Grillparzer) or in other literary genres (Gogol's novels and short stories). Something of an exception to this was Musset in France. Although he earned a reputation as well through his lyric poetry and the novel *Confession d'un enfant du siècle* (1836), Musset wrote some of the best French comedy of the period in such works as *Les Caprices de Marianne* (1833), *Fantasio* (1833), *Le Chandelier* (1835) and the dramatized proverb (a genre he became identified with) *Il ne faut jurer de rien* (1836), and never abandoned dramatic writing for the lyric or the novel. Musset's most notable achievements in the field of drama, however, developed strongly within the context of romanticism. By emphasizing romantic love to the extent that it dominates the action of his plays and in the prominence given the role of the tragic, Musset was consciously drawing away from the traditions of classical comedy, away

[50] The possible connections between Fredro and Musset are taken up in the discussion of *Maidens' Vows*.

from the traditions of Molière and his eighteenth-century successors and in the direction of the neo-Shakespeareanism of the Romantics. It is for these reasons that Musset, unlike Fredro, must be placed in the center of romanticism rather than considered a development tangential to it.

The other level on which comedy continued its precarious existence during the Romantic period is represented by the mass of sentimental melodramas, fantasies and formulaic "well-made" plays of intrigue churned out by such amazingly fecund minor dramatists as Pixerécourt and Scribe in France, and Nestroy and Raimund in Austria, for a public whose taste for the theater could not be satisfied by the literary drama of the Romantics. The pattern for this "popular theater," which came to take the place of classical comedy in the age of romanticism, had already been established in the late eighteenth and early nineteenth centuries by August von Kotzebue (1761-1819). Most of the works of these dramatists were of slight value, but they were enormously popular and even influential in their own day. Since then they have all but vanished from memory as well as from the boards of European theaters; the many volumes of their plays sit in libraries and gather dust, opened once in a while by the professional scholar or the curious student of drama.

Fredro was by no means aloof from the work of these artisans of comedy. This is reflected above all in his attention to plot and the reluctance to assume any discernible moral posture. But with these popular practitioners of the comic art Fredro ultimately shares little more than an admirable productive capacity and an almost total commitment to the genre of comedy at a time when in the history of European drama comedy had fallen from grace. What Fredro possessed that these writers did not was a genius that made him far more than a manufacturer of mediocre comedies and indeed placed him as a comic dramatist among the major talents of his time. In common with Grillparzer, Kleist, Gogol and Griboedov, Fredro sought to reaffirm the values of classical comedy in an age that for the most part spurned it. But his contribution in this respect must be measured not in terms of a single work or two but a substantial body of plays of considerable variety representing collectively a career of devotion to the art of comedy. This is where Fredro departs from these other dramatists and wherein his uniqueness for European drama is no less important than his uniqueness for Polish.

Comparing Fredro's work to that of his Polish and European predecessors and contemporaries, what can we isolate as the distinguishing characteristics of his comic genius? Fredro was, to begin with, a master of complex but skilfully executed plot design; this is evident in each play in the present collection where intrigue is as important as character. In his deft handling of plot, however, there is seldom the reliance on contrivance and straining of credulity that we have come to expect as somehow indispensable in comedy. The resolution of the plot flows plausibly from the course of the action and the relationships of the characters. Improbability enters rarely; some older Polish critics insisted on singling out *The Life Annuity* as the weakest of Fredro's better comedies from this point of view, but close examination of it discloses on the contrary a carefully and logically elaborated plot structure that shows up the author's sure hand as well as any other of his major plays. Writing about *The Life Annuity* in his introduction to the most recent edition of Fredro's collected works, the late Polish literary historian and critic Kazimierz Wyka was quite right when he said: "If Fredro thought in terms of action [myślał akcją], then *The Life Annuity* represents one of the very best examples of this kind of thinking, and not just in the history of Polish comedy."[51]

Another area in which Fredro reveals a fine talent and in which he has few superiors in European comedy is characterization. Through all the intricacies of plot character is never neglected, with the result that the easily recognized comic types—the young lovers, cheating husbands and wives, husband-hunting widows and spinsters, servants, cantankerous old country squires, petty usurers, professional soldiers, bachelors and braggarts—are transformed into well-rounded, highly individualized creations who are rarely mere abstractions and rarely implausible.

[51] *Pisma wszystkie*, Vol. I, 131.

In creating his own gallery of comic portraits Fredro was greatly aided by a feeling for language no less remarkable than let us say Gogol's. His characters, primary and secondary, have their own distinct idioms and it is through these idioms as much as through appearance and manner that the characters are recognized. The succulence, color, and variety of his language make Fredro a continuous source of delight to Polish audiences, but it is precisely this feature of his style that has denied him the recognition he deserves beyond the borders of his own country.

Like Kleist and Musset among his contemporaries Fredro also wrote comedies in verse. But here, no less than with his language, he again proved his considerable talent and originality. Whereas verse is most of the time a convention in European comedy, in Fredro's most impressive verse plays (*Maidens' Vows, The Vengeance, The Life Annuity*) it was a convention to which—like other comic conventions—he brought a new life. Breaking with the traditional verse pattern for comedy in *Husband and Wife*, Fredro went on to exploit verse as a technique of style in *Maidens' Vows* and as an instrument for effecting the light, vivacious tempo that remains one of the major sources of appeal of *The Vengeance* and *The Life Annuity* and without which it is difficult even to imagine these plays.

From the foregoing, we can see that the most outstanding characteristics of Fredro's technique—the sources of his appeal and impact as a comic dramatist—are the absence of moral tendentiousness and his welding of plot, character, and idiom into a single dramatic entity in which no one element carries greater weight than others. For this reason Fredro's best plays do not lend themselves to ready classification. The characters are usually so well drawn and so much individualized beyond mere types and the intrigue usually so ably structured that the traditional lines of comedy are blurred. Is *Husband and Wife* a comedy of intrigue, or a salon comedy of manners? Can we say that character is more important than situation in *Maidens' Vows*? Are *The Vengeance* and *The Life Annuity* primarily comedies of intrigue, or comedies of character? The questions are not easily answered because the plays are so composed that they cannot adequately be defined by one classification or the other. Even in the farce *Ladies and Hussars* the characters come off so well—with their own distinct personalities—that we feel we have gone beyond the traditional limits of the genre.

Fredro's importance in the total picture of European comedy rests then not only on the fact that he was a productive, talented writer of comedies who like Kleist, Gogol or Griboedov—though in a more substantial way—sought to preserve a classical comic art during the time of romanticism. In his dedication to classical comedy Fredro was not bound by its traditions. It had taught him the fundamentals of his craft, but he approached its traditions and conventions with a freshness and originality that enabled him to reshape it into something uniquely his own. In so doing he gave Polish drama a comic tradition it can take pride in and European drama a page in its history it has yet to appreciate.

A NOTE ON THE TRANSLATIONS

THE preface to this book opened with a quotation from Tadeusz Boy-Żeleński's *Settling Accounts About Fredro*. I should like to introduce my remarks on the translations with the rest of the paragraph from which the quotation was extracted. Taking up the matter of the Fredro-Molière parallel so often made in Poland, Boy-Żeleński writes:

> In contrast to Fredro, I am struck by the phenomenon of the universality and transmittability of Molière. Molière conquered the world in poor adaptations. *The Miser* can be played in any kind of translation, but what would remain of *The Life Annuity* without its wonderful intoxication with the word? In Fredro's play there is some delicate fragrance that evaporates. One can play *Tartuffe* even in prose without grief, but just let someone try to translate *The Vengeance*! It is possible to find equivalents for all the famous sayings of Molière, but who can transfer to a foreign language the music, which is wonderful in its almost coarse finesse, of some line of Fredro's such as: *Co skłoniło Podstolinę—wdówkę tantną, wdówkę gładką* . . . [What inclined our Podstolina/ a well-off and comely widow]. This is a positive gauge that the very essence of Fredro's comedies lies entirely in something other than that of Molière's and that all attempts at measuring these two writers with the same ell of aesthetic parallels are basically wrong.[52]

Boy-Żeleński has isolated the chief problem facing the translator of Fredro: his language. The highly individual and idiomatic language of the comedies at times seems to defy translation. Equivalents in other languages may be found, but the special flavor of Fredro's language does not filter through the language barrier, particularly in the case of a language so different from Polish as English. Boy-Żeleński quoted one line from *The Vengeance* to illustrate his point. It is worth examining more closely for it can tell us much about this "flavor" of Fredro's language. The line in Polish reads:

[52] *Ibid.*, p. 191.

Co skłoniło Podstolinę/ Wdówkę tantną, wdówkę gładką. . . .
The literal translation is: What inclined Podstolina/ Well-off widow, comely widow . . . To begin with, the highly inflected nature of Polish (the most inflected of the Slavic languages) which has no definite or indefinite article and permits of a much freer word order than English makes possible the parallel structure *wdówkę tantną, wdówkę gladką* (widow well-off, widow comely). This cannot be preserved in English—in the framework of the original metric pattern and context—without distortion and shift of meaning. Furthermore, *wdówka* is a diminutive from *wdowa* (widow). To be perfectly accurate the translation would have to suggest this diminutive quality ("nice little widow"). The final result in English would be a line twice as long as the original Polish and without the rhythm of the original Polish. We notice in the Polish line also the feature of ellipsis within the parallelism of *wdówkę tantną, wdówkę gladką*. The connective "and" has been omitted. It is one of the most characteristic features of Fredro's language and a frequent source of trouble for the translator. Sometimes it can be transferred smoothly into English, like this line of Patch from the beginning of *The Life Annuity*: *Tu dudziarze, tu opoje/ Fiddlers here, drunkards there.* More often it cannot be, as in the following examples, also drawn from *The Life Annuity*. At the end of Act I, Scene 1, Philip says, as he is about to take his leave:

> Ale czas też i mnie w drogę,
> Bo się diable wiatr odmienia:
> U mnie kieska, u mnie sprzęty . . .

This means literally: But it's also time for me (to be) on the road,/ For the wind is changing devilishly:/ By me little purse, by me belongings. For the last parallel-elliptic line no real equivalent can be found in English and a free translation is necessary. This may be rendered in the same meter and line length: I've my bag and my belongings. The sense of the original is retained but the "fragrance" Boy-Żeleński has spoken of is lost.

In Act III, Scene 2, of *The Life Annuity* when Patch pleads with Raphael and Michael to spare Leon's life, he says in one place:

> No, no—prawda, często gęsto
> Figi-migi w jego głowie:
> Lecz serce—blank! blank, panowie!
> Jego słówka jak gotówka . . .

An unrhymed translation in the trochaic line of the Polish might read:

> Well, well—it's true, all too often
> His head's filled with silly nonsense.
> But his heart—is pure I tell you!
> And his word as good as money!

The translation is accurate and reads smoothly, but see what flavor has been lost from the original. In the first line *często* (meaning: often, frequently) and *gęsto* (thickly) make a rhyming pair within the line and represent together a colloquialism meaning "pretty often." In the following line *figi-migi*, representing another rhyming pair structurally similar to *często gęsto* and meaning "pranks," "jokes," etc., has no adequate English equivalent. The next line is elliptical: *Lecz serce—blank! blank, panowie!* and is literally "But heart— pure! pure, gentlemen!" To make sense in English "his" modifying heart must be introduced and also "is"—the ellipsis does not carry over into English effectively. Furthermore, there is no English equivalent for Patch's colloquial *blank*. "Pure" is as near as I was able to come. The last line has the diminutive *słówka* (from *słowo*, word) meaning "little words," and the untranslatable internal rhyme of *słówka* and *gotówka* (a colloquialism meaning "ready cash") .

The Slavic diminutive suffixes pose another serious problem for the translator. Most simply cannot be rendered into English without the introduction of the auxiliary "little" and an accompanying loss of flavor. One of the best examples of extensive diminutive usage I have come across in Polish occurs in Fredro's *The Life Annuity*, Act II, Scene 3, where Patch offers Rose an engagement ring. He first tells her how happy he is that the time has come when he can put on her *luba rączka* (dear little hand; *rączka* is diminutive of *ręka*, hand) a real gold *obrączka* (band; diminutive of *obręcz* although no longer felt as a diminutive). When Rose is reluctant to accept the gift, Patch tries to coax her with a string of diminutive terms of endearment that border on the absurd:

> Weźże, moja turkaweczko,
> Gołąbeczko, kukułeczko,
> Wiewióreczko, kochaneczko.

In English a fair translation might be:

> Take it, little turtledove mine,
> Little pigeon, little cuckoo
> Little squirrel, little darling.

The diminutives are: *turkaweczka* (from *turkawka*, turtledove), *gołąbeczka* (from *gołąbka*, pigeon; dove), *kukułeczka* (from *kukułka*, cuckoo), *wiewióreczka* (from *wiewiórka*, squirrel), and *kochaneczka* (from *kochanka*, darling).

Patch's coaxing reaches the height of absurdity when he pleads further:

> Weź, weź na ten cieniuteńki
> Na ten, ten, ten maciupeńki
> Palususio.

> Put it on this little thin one,
> This one, this one teeny weeny
> Little finger.

Cieniuteńki, the first diminutive, is really a double diminutive. That is, it is a diminutive of *cieniutki*, itself a diminutive of *cieńki*, thin. The rhyming diminutive is a similar form *maciupeńki*, from *maciupki*, tiny. The last diminutive, *palususio*, is delightful and loses greatly in translation. It is based ultimately on the word for finger, *palec*, but is a diminutive of the diminutive *paluszek*, little finger. The absurdly comic effect it produces in the original Polish cannot be duplicated—unfortunately—in English.

There are many forms of verbal humor in Fredro's comedies. These are also difficult to capture in another language. Let us take one typical example, again from *The Life Annuity*, Act II, Scene 2. Leon orders Philip to throw one of his creditors out of his house. The line in Polish reads: *To ze schodow strąć zuchwalca!* / Then toss the upstart down the stairs! One of the musicians who has been asleep is awakened by Leon's shout. Hearing just the last part of the word *zuchwalca* (genitive singular of *zuchwalec*, upstart) —*walca*, he thinks he has been ordered to strike up a waltz and answers:

> Walca!—zaraz . . .
> (do muzykantów)
> Walca! Walca!

> A waltz!—In a second . . . (To the
> musicians.) A waltz! A waltz!

I have made an attempt to preserve the original play on words by using the verb "waltz" in the colloquial sense of "toss out," "boot out." My translation of this line is: Then waltz the upstart down the stairs. It is possible to imagine the musician aroused by a word in the middle of the line as well as at the end, but the tempo of the original is lost in the translation and what remains is just a fair approximation of the Polish.

In connection with the language of Fredro's comedies, there are a few other points I would like to mention briefly. (1) The profuse Galician Polish expressions of politeness, in which *The Vengeance* and *The Life Annuity* especially abound, do not make much sense in English and have been treated freely. Here are few examples from the original, literally translated: *Ściskam nóżki pańskie* (I embrace your little legs), *Trzykroć twoje ściskam nóżki* (I thrice embrace your little legs), *Sługa, służka uniżony* (Humble servant, little servant), etc. (2) Old Polish gentry terms of address such as *waćpan, mospan, waszmość, mocium panie, jaśnie panie*, etc., generally meaning "your lordship" have been translated as "sir" when appropriate to the situation or just "you" or omitted altogether. (3) Diminutives of personal names do not translate well into English; the regular, non-diminutive forms have been used in most cases. (4) The frequent terms of endearment among men such as *moje serce* (my heart), *bratek* (little brother), *mój kochany* (my dear), *moja duszka* (my little soul), *droga dusza* (dear soul), etc., sound odd in English and have been rendered generally as "dear sir," "good fellow," "good man," "brother."

Let us consider now the matter of verse. Of the five comedies in the present collection, only one was written originally in prose: *Ladies and Hussars.* The remaining four were written in verse: *Husband and Wife* and *Maidens' Vows* in mixed syllabic meters ranging from the six-syllable to the thirteen-syllable line (but concentrating primarily on the interplay of the eight-, eleven-, and thirteen-syllable lines); *The Vengeance* and *The Life Annuity* were both written entirely in the eight-syllable (four-foot) trochaic line with which Fredro scored his greatest triumph. There is no doubt that from the point of view of metric structure these latter two plays are his best. In *Husband and Wife* and *Maidens' Vows* Fredro broke with the conventional pattern for comedy by mixing lines of different length. This was the main reason for the alternation of shorter and longer lines in *Husband and Wife,* chronologically the earliest play in this group. With *Maidens' Vows* Fredro used verse more effectively than in *Husband and Wife* by assigning it a stylistic function it had not enjoyed previously. In spite of this notable advance in verse technique, the appeal of *Maidens' Vows* does not depend on its metric structure. This is one of the reasons I chose to translate the comedy, like *Husband and Wife,* into prose. Also, the Polish eleven- and thirteen-syllable lines really have no exact equivalents in English and would have to be rendered by the iambic pentameter used so much for English poetry and poetic drama or the alexandrine. The result would be a dissipation of the effects achieved in the original Polish by the alternation of these lines—with their traditional associations—with the shorter eight-syllable line. With *The Vengeance* and *The Life Annuity,* however, the matter is quite different. Here the verse is so much a source of appeal in these plays, so vital an element in the structure giving the plays their own unique rhythm, that for one who knows the original Polish it is almost impossible to imagine them in prose.

My original purpose was to translate *The Vengeance* and *The Life Annuity* into rhymed verse, using the four-foot trochaic meter of the Polish. It was not long before I found myself forced to operate much more freely with the original texts than I wanted to because of the search for rhymes. I then abandoned rhyme and concentrated solely on preserving the meter and line length of the original. The four-foot trochaic line in which the two comedies were written is an accepted English meter, although it has not been used often. This is readily understandable in view of the English stress pattern. In its use of the trochee English poetry has frequently substituted in place of the perfect four-foot line the so-called cataleptic or imperfect (seven instead of eight syllables) four-foot trochaic line. This proves much easier to maintain than the perfect trochaic tetrameter. Since the trochee is more natural in Polish than the iamb (unlike English) there is no need for cataleptic lines and the regular tetrameter—with the exception only of a few lines—is employed throughout *The Vengeance* and *The Life Annuity*. I had in mind preserving the same pattern in my translations.

Although many lines presented problems, the first English versions of these two comedies were in verse, in the original meter, but unrhymed. This permitted considerably greater fidelity to the originals than the rhymed versions. Upon completion of these translations I felt that the effort was, on the whole, successful. But readers of the typescript found the regular four-foot trochaic line unfamiliar, particularly in the absence of rhyme. The reading, instead of being enhanced by the verse, as I had hoped, seemed to be awkward and at times difficult. It was suggested that I think of redoing the plays in prose. I reread my translations a few more times in the light of these comments and came, with some regret, to the conclusion that while more work could possibly strengthen the rythmically weaker lines, the verse translations did not consistently capture the tempo and vivacity of the Polish and that the rhyme could not effectively be ignored. This meant that the most that could be expected was that the English reader would occasionally experience some feeling for the form of the originals but that he could not conceivably react to the plays as a Polish audience. The translator who hoped to be able to evoke the same kind of response was, I accepted finally, doomed to disappointment. In such a spirit I redid the two comedies in prose. If there is any solace I can extract from this compromise it is that it has been possible to achieve still greater accuracy in the translations, that the reading in English is now smoother, and that the plays seem less alien. And perhaps—hopefully—the readers may yet experience some feeling for the gaiety of the originals.

HUSBAND AND WIFE

A Comedy in Three Acts

*Acquiring someone else's, we often
lose our own. Who goes after another
person's stake, has to risk his own
and sometimes even loses.*

ANDRZEJ MAKSYMILIAN FREDRO*

* The epigraphs of Fredro's plays are
drawn from the collection of proverbs
Przysłowia mów potocznych, published in
Cracow in 1658 by a distant kinsman Andrzej
Maksymilian Fredro (1620-1679), a writer in
Latin and Polish.

INTRODUCTION

ONE of Fredro's best comedies of intrigue, *Husband and Wife*, was presented for the first time in 1822. The play was written in 1820 or 1821—the exact date is uncertain—but in either case not long after Fredro returned from military service and threw himself into the social whirl of Lwów where he was received with near adulation. He was, after all, a decorated soldier who had fought valiantly in the cause of Polish freedom under the banners of Napoleon and, moreover, an eligible bachelor less than thirty years old, of good family, for whom the matrons of Lvovian society competed with each other to arrange a suitable marriage.

Although he doubtless enjoyed the fuss that was made over him and all the social lionizing, Fredro was able to maintain a certain distance, perhaps an emotional aloofness bordering even on coldness from the milieu that rushed to embrace him and in which he had begun to move quite freely. The relations between the sexes in Lwów in the immediate post-Napoleonic period reflected a certain libertinism and cynicism; the young ex-officer observed this dispassionately and captured the atmosphere with rich irony in his comedy *Husband and Wife*. Boy-Żeleński, in his *Settling Accounts About Fredro* (Obrachunki fredrowskie, 1932), sums the matter up in these terms:

> It was the atmosphere of the famous Lwów carnivals, of the crapulous, amour-ridden, somewhat cynical Lwów world of which the ex-Captain Fredro was at the time more of a happy observer than a stern judge.[1]

This last remark of Boy's is noteworthy. Despite the attempts by Polish literary historians and critics to reduce *Husband and Wife* to the level of a didactic French comedy of marital infidelity, sober analysis of the play reveals a negligible didactic element. Perhaps it was for this reason—the absence of any obvious moral stance on the part of the author —that the play was for a long time unjustly neglected in Po-

[1] Boy Żeleński, "Obrachunki fredrowskie," p. 63.

land and, consequently, seldom performed. This also explains why the play has two different endings. After Fredro's death, the second, much weaker moralistic ending was added (possibly by Fredro's son Jan). There were four editions of *Husband and Wife* in Fredro's lifetime: 1826, 1839, 1853, 1871. The original ending appears in all four. Only in the fifth edition of the play, the posthumous edition published by Gebethner and Wolff in Warsaw in 1880, do we find the second, revised ending used for the first time. This second ending was printed in later editions of the play and in acting versions, with the original completely ignored. In the twentieth century, however, the tendency has been to restore the original ending. For the sake of comparison, both are given in the present collection.

Fredro's achievement in *Husband and Wife* lies not in the power of satire with which he castigates the moral laxity of a jaded contemporary Lvovian society, but in his adroit handling of a complex plot that maintains audience interest at a high level in spite of the fact that there are only four speaking parts in the comedy. Through the complicated but logically elaborated intrigue, which he manipulates with all the talent of a virtuoso puppeteer, Fredro explores with his audience the superb irony in the relationships of his characters: a wife unfaithful to her husband, the wife's lover a close friend of the husband whose vanity makes it impossible for him to see the infidelity of his wife under his very nose and even casts him in the Ovidian role of tutor in the art of love to his wife's lover; and, to bring the irony to the peak of its development, the husband unfaithful to his wife with her servant—with whom the wife's lover is also carrying on an affair at the same time!

The subject of *Husband and Wife* brings to mind the antimarital comedies of Molière, but as Boy-Żeleński demonstrated so convincingly in *Settling Accounts About Fredro*, Fredro's originality as a comic dramatist enabled him to revitalize the Molièresque theme in entirely new ways.[2] Let us now consider what these were: (1) In Molière (and in later French comedy—Beaumarchais and Musset, for example) the de-

2 *Ibid.*, pp. 68-69.

ceived husband or guardian is usually old or unattractive, for which reason the deception of the wife or the expected wife is plausible. In *Husband and Wife*, on the other hand, the husband is both young and attractive. The wife's deception is motivated not by repulsion but by frustration, for the husband's weak point is his inability to appreciate what he has in his own home. Boy-Żeleński poses the question, a quite valid one; if Elvira were someone else's wife, what then would Vatslav's attitude to her be? It is easy to imagine. (2) Unlike Molière, or the French comedy writers of the eighteenth century, Fredro devaluates and deemphasizes the extra-marital romance itself. After the initial sweetness, in part the natural result of the clandestine nature of their affair, the illicit relationship of Alfred and Elvira takes on all the semblance of a second marriage with its own routine pattern of conduct, its bickering and boredom, its problems without its pleasures. In Molière's comedies the "forbidden love" was never demasked in this way. Maintained conventionally, for the most part, as off-stage action, rarely was it ever treated with the contempt characteristic of its treatment in *Husband and Wife*. (3) In *Husband and Wife* we find that Fredro has drastically revamped the traditional character of the soubrette. Traditionally she had been a confidante of her mistress whom she ably assisted in her romantic intrigues. Often she was the lever of much of the action. Sometimes, as in Beaumarchais, she could become the rival of her mistress, but when this happened it was not of the soubrette's volition and more a chance occurrence. The guilty party was always the male. In *Husband and Wife* the soubrette Justysia, one of Fredro's most successful characters, is at the very center of the intrigue. Not only is she the mistress's rival with her own husband, but in a quite original twist, her rival also with her mistress's lover, Alfred! Both husband and lover, tired of the mistress of the house, seek a new adventure and find it in their romantic intrigue with the same woman, who happens to be the mistress's servant. The attractions of Justysia for both the husband and the lover are not difficult to discover: unlike Elvira, Justysia, as a servant, offers both men the chance to be themselves because of the difference in class. For Vatslav there is no necessity to maintain the formality of conventional relationship with his wife dictated by the mores of time and place. For Alfred, there is relief in his affair with Justysia from the necessity of maintaining the stylized sentimentalism of his relationship with Elvira (conveyed so effectively by the language of the characters from the very first scene of the play) which her own nature no less than her "sentimental" upbringing and training demand. As in the case of the romantic relationship between Valère and Lisette in Destouches *Le Glorieux* (before the discovery of Lisette's noble origin), *Husband and Wife* rediscovers the truth that love is the great equalizer, that in love class differences vanish and that at a certain moment in time there is neither servant nor mistress, but just two women—Elvira and Justysia.

Like the other comedies in this collection, with the sole exception of *Ladies and Hussars*, *Husband and Wife* was written in verse. The verse structure of the play marks an important stage in Fredro's development as a dramatist. Until *Husband and Wife*, Fredro had followed the conventional Polish dramatic practice of using for all dialogue the thirteen-syllable line divided by the caesura into two groups of seven and six syllables (the so-called Polish "epic" line, because it has been the traditional meter for Polish heroic poetry). This is the Polish equivalent of the French twelve-syllable alexandrine. It is the meter of such early comedies as *Mister Moneybags* and *Nagging and Contradiction*. With *Husband and Wife*, however, Fredro abandoned the thirteen-syllable line in favor of a mixed verse pattern of six, eight, eleven, and thirteen syllables. By this innovation, he was aiming at greater flexibility and naturalness in dialogue. Generally speaking, the eleven-syllable line was to be used for most of the dialogue, the longer thirteen-syllable line for greater solemnity, for "serious" moods, and the shorter six- and eight-syllable lines for lightness and vivacity. We notice, however, that these lines are not always used so consistently in *Husband and Wife*. Characters shift from longer to shorter lines (and vice versa) within a single monologue and for no apparent stylistic purpose. This means that in *Husband and Wife* Fredro sought above all to liberate dramatic dialogue from the fetters of the conventional thirteen-syllable line. He did this by alternating lines of different length but he had not yet worked out completely the specific stylistic functions of these lines. He was to do so in his next major play in verse, *Maidens' Vows*.

CHARACTERS

COUNT VATSLAV

ELVIRA, *his wife*

ALFRED

JUSTYSIA

The scene is set in the town residence
of Count Vatslav.

HUSBAND AND WIFE

ACT I

A room. On one side a sofa, on the other a round table with a lamp on it. In the rear of the room, a piano.

SCENE 1. Elvira, Alfred seated next to each other on the sofa.

ALFRED. [*Holding Elvira's hand.*] Dear Elvira, love of my soul, when will your eyes be dry of tears? Why do you let so many regrets throw a veil of mourning over the rare, dear moments we can spend with each other? Is the strength of love so weak already that my happiness, which you created, cannot obliterate some trifling memory, or change idle thoughts?

ELVIRA. I love you, Alfred, I love you more than life, but even those words are too weak. What pleasures can life have if we have to love each other secretly? The thought that, becoming the reward of love, I caused your happiness, is perhaps more like the sweetening of sorrow; it is what I fear even to say . . . But can I, without secret grief, completely forget about the responsibilities, the virtues with which I have been inculcated from my youth, and which I recalled in an unhappy moment? And then, the constant fear . . .

ALFRED. Fear?

ELVIRA. Alfred, our love isn't right; the world has penetrating eyes . . .

ALFRED. Our love not right—why that's nonsense! If nature placed in every being the seed of its flame, the flame whose captivating strength changes insensitive existence into life, likewise, it seems, has it arranged every love. Do I then become a criminal because my heart, confined in too small a space, loving beauty, intelligence, goodness, charm, had also to love Elvira? After all, it was the sacred hand of nature that bestowed her charm and my faithful love, and if the heavens had to single out someone for me, did it have to be Elvira?

ELVIRA. Ah, and that love, for which, alas, I threw over the virtues of an innocent soul, for which, always seeing only you, I forgot myself, I forgot the whole world—oh if sometime your heart consumes its ardors, if it becomes frozen, what kind of an opinion will you have of me? Perhaps the proof will come today . . .

ALFRED. What? What did you say? When I stop loving you? Oh no, Elvira. The union of our hearts, this equal beating of mine with yours, this affinity at once beloved and fiery which justifying itself with a secret word joined our sensitive souls, and this haze that covers the world when I take you in my embrace—oh, do I have to repeat it to you? It's more than the ardor of ordinary love! This divine feeling, which I never knew before, which once I sought in vain, has fused with life in me. The heavens will not undo the knots, they must endure and perish together.

ELVIRA. Oh, how I love to listen to your voice! Bewitched by its charm, I forget about my fate and I see only you before my eyes. I cannot find the words within me, I feel ecstasy, grief, and anxiety. A pleasant fire goes through me, I burn and am afraid to burn, and I hardly have enough strength to throw myself into your embraces. Why did not the powers of predestination which were able to unite us, which know our hearts, give you to Elvira as a husband? And perhaps Vatslav, living with another wife, would be happy, and today I would not be forced to be cunning and false with him. Only love for you conquers my natural repulsion at having to deceive my husband each hour of my life.

ALFRED. The reason for your grief is unfair. It's not your own fault that he was never able to please you, though at first he was loved, and that he blindly understood the love of his wife as a duty. Vatslav is attractive, rich, intelligent, in the first flower of youth. Renowned and proud because of so many love affairs everyone would have thought that his wife from any point of view would be one of the happiest women on earth. No sooner did he marry you, when he was envied everywhere. However, he grew cold to his wife and no longer liked his home. As much as he is the object of admiration with other people because of his rare affability, so much is he unbearable when he's taken by himself. He left his wife, if I may say so, in need of searching for a warmer soul, of searching for someone to share her feelings, and of submitting little by little to the power under which nature inclines us.

ELVIRA. If I was not always left alone, oh, I would be a very different wife!

ALFRED. Tell me, did you spend at least some pleasant moment with him?

ELVIRA. Oh no, never, alas, he was so little with me!

ALFRED. If he comes to you, he just sits and yawns.

ELVIRA. And then, because he's bored, he gets angry at his wife.

ALFRED. It gets worse as we go along.

ELVIRA. He always grumbles, nags, scolds . . . How much grief he causes me with the false embraces he usually presents me with when a third party is present. He talks about the ecstasy and happiness enjoyed by married people; he embraces me, fondles me, falls to his knees, calls his wife his own goddess—but no sooner does the door close after the visitor than love and sincerity die, and just as though he wanted to redeem the pleasantness of that moment, right away he strengthens himself for a thousand unpleasantnesses.

ALFRED. He's unbearable!

ELVIRA. Nasty.

ALFRED. Soulless.

ELVIRA. Nothing touches him . . .

ALFRED. Or moves him.

ELVIRA. A person doesn't know how to please him.

ALFRED. And yet you say it's painful to deceive such a man? No, no, he deserves it, let it be payment for his lack of feeling.

ELVIRA. [*Joking.*] I see you like to punish husbands.

ALFRED. One has to look after the good of all.

ELVIRA. And sometimes this concern excites still more ill will!

ALFRED. Oh, who on earth has not experienced the ingratitude of man!

ELVIRA. Still, no matter how many unpleasantnesses I suffer with him, I feel sorry for him.

ALFRED. [*With a long sigh.*] The poor thing!

ELVIRA. [*Laughing.*] Don't pity him, please!

ALFRED. But how can I help sincerely pitying him and sighing when Vatslav takes me under his wing in order to teach me how to go about winning the attention of someone I love: when and how long I must love in secret, when to declare my love, when to groan, sob, what streets to take, how to deceive sleepy husbands, in a word—he is teaching me the art of love.

ELVIRA. [*Laughing.*] You?

ALFRED. Me.

ELVIRA. And you?

ALFRED. I take notes.

ELVIRA. [*Laughing.*] Marvelous, superb! It's true, he is a poor thing; I don't understand him at all . . .

SCENE 2. Elvira, Alfred, Justysia.

JUSTYSIA. [*Running in.*] The master, the master, for God's sake! The Count is coming.

ELVIRA. [*Tearing herself away.*] He's returning so early, who would have expected it?

JUSTYSIA. [*Opening a window.*] Quickly, quickly, or we'll be in for trouble.

ALFRED. Unbearable individual . . . !

JUSTYSIA. Tomorrow you'll be upset . . .

ALFRED. [*Standing in the window.*] Doesn't even let a person spend a peaceful evening! He's coming back just to grumble.

JUSTYSIA. Go on, or I swear, I'll push you out!

ELVIRA. [*To Alfred.*] When . . . ?

ALFRED. I'll return in a little while. [*Elvira sits at the round table, takes her handwork and begins to sew; Justysia runs out.*]

SCENE 3. *Elvira, Vatslav. Vatslav enters, looks at Elvira and shrugs his shoulders; throws his hat down and walks around the room for a while.*

VATSLAV. [*Standing in front of Elvira.*] How is it that at least once a year you don't go out? Once in a while you should show yourself in the world. You're always at home; I always see you alone.

ELVIRA. I like to be alone.

VATSLAV. And I hate it. [*Paces. A short pause.*] Unusual taste, always sitting at home!

ELVIRA. A taste that harms no one.

VATSLAV. Oh certainly, certainly it harms no one, but it is boring, you have to admit that. [*Paces. A short pause.*] Do you also like this gloomy darkness? [*Rings loudly and calls to a servant.*] Candle! [*Two candles are brought. He sits down and yawns.*] Oh, put your work away! Always that needle and thread. Women have no idea of moderation. Either dances, parties, fun, or eyes lowered over embroidery they sew and putter days on end, just as though they had grown into their chairs. [*A long silence; Elvira sits at the piano, begins to play quietly, but gets increasingly louder.*]

VATSLAV. [*To himself.*] Ah—a six, four honors, ace, queen of diamonds, and let them finish the rubber! That's a brand new game! Unheard of! And he plays whist! And still growls and throws the cards. I play the ace because I'm afraid of my opponent . . . Oh, dear Elvira, my ears, my ears! Enough of that allegro, those trills; this harmonic racket is too much, you're striking the keys mercilessly. It's impossible to think, I can't even hear myself! [*Elvira gets up and sits by the table, opens a book. A short pause.*] I don't know what it means— everywhere you go it's full of people, yet we rarely have anyone in and everyone's bored. Ha! Everyone avoids melancholy, and seeks merriment. Oh, to make a home pleasant—that's a great art! [*A short pause.*] What kind of serious or amusing work is it that has caught your attention so?

ELVIRA. The Journal.

VATSLAV. Aha, the Journal—no joke. For two weeks it's lain there open, until at last it's lived to see a reading I don't know whether out of boredom or desire. [*Elvira pushes the book away; long silence.*]

ELVIRA. You came back early today.

VATSLAV. And where was I supposed to stay?

ELVIRA. [*After a short pause.*] No whist game?

VATSLAV. Of course there was.

ELVIRA. [*A short pause.*] You played?

VATSLAV. I played.

ELVIRA. [*A short pause.*] Lucky?

VATSLAV. No. [*Yawning.*] Was anyone here?

ELVIRA. No one. [*After a short pause, also yawning.*] Are you gambling much at cards?

VATSLAV. Not much.

ELVIRA. [*A short pause.*] A bad frost today for sure.

VATSLAV. Bad.

ELVIRA. [*Yawns.*] Very bad?

VATSLAV. [*Getting up.*] Enough of this frost—don't bore me anymore! What could I possibly care about a frost or a heat spell? [*Paces; a long silence.*] But today's the theater, don't we have a box?

ELVIRA. We have.

VATSLAV. Then we must go, for the custom has changed; now we judge the work from the fifth act. [*Elvira goes out.*]

SCENE 4.

VATSLAV. Ah, before a man gets married, alas, how little he values his freedom! Once he tastes this bitter fruit then he wants what he once had.

SCENE 5. Vatslav, Justysia. Justysia runs in to fetch Elvira's work.

VATSLAV. It's good you came, Justysia dear, from morning on I've been waiting just for a moment to spend with you. I want to see you and talk to you. There's so much I have to tell you.

JUSTYSIA. Oh, if you really wanted to, then you'd find not a moment, but surely a whole hour!

VATSLAV. How can you put all the blame on me? After all you know that no matter how much I ask, implore or rage, nothing moves my wife from the house. Her whole life she sits indoors, and if I want to love you, it has to be in secret. But, tomorrow, when she goes to church . . .

JUSTYSIA. I understand, I understand, let me go—she's calling!

VATSLAV. It just seems that way to you.

JUSTYSIA. She'll come in, for heaven's sake!

VATSLAV. Don't forget me, dearest; try to get away from everyone. At least we'll have an hour to amuse ourselves in. Remember me, because I always have you in mind. Look for how long I've been carrying around this ring for you. Please take it, I beg you; let your hand adorn it. [*Justysia bows.*] Is that how you thank me?

JUSTYSIA. [*Coquettishly.*] How am I to thank you?

VATSLAV. How, Justysia? Kiss me. [*He tries to kiss her.*]

JUSTYSIA. [*Holding him off.*] Please, what are you doing? [*Elvira enters, Justysia pushes away Vatslav who stays with his back to Elvira.*]

SCENE 6. Elvira, Vatslav, Justysia.

JUSTYSIA. [*Holding herself by the head.*] Oh, oh! My head! [*Cries.*] Honestly, I must say the Count always walks just as if he were alone in the house. Who ever heard of breaking a person's head this way! Oh, what pain! I can't even open my eyes.

ELVIRA. You'd best put some cold water on it right away. [*Rings and goes to the door; to the servant.*] Water! Water quickly! [*To Justysia.*] That's the only way. You'll be well again in half an hour.

JUSTYSIA. Well—but the bruise?

ELVIRA. It won't hurt so much. [*They bring in water.*]

JUSTYSIA. Faugh!

ELVIRA. Justysia's worried about her looks.

JUSTYSIA. Enough, I'd rather fast three days than wear any bruise on my brow. [*Elvira sits Justysia down and ties a kerchief round her head.*]

ELVIRA. Where do you feel it?

JUSTYSIA. Here, here—oh, how it hurts!

ELVIRA. Here?

JUSTYSIA. Here—Oh, slowly!

ELVIRA. There's no sign of anything—but let the kerchief stay on anyway.

JUSTYSIA. [*Threatening the Count from behind Elvira.*] I swear, I could have gotten a good bump.

ELVIRA. Send someone over there to tell them to hold up harnessing the horses a while! [*Justysia kisses Elvira's hand and goes with lowered head slowly toward the door. She glances from beneath her eyes; seeing that Elvira has her back turned, she smiles, makes a threatening gesture at the Count and then runs out.*]

SCENE 7. Elvira, Vatslav.

ELVIRA. There's still time for the theater, it's not six yet.

VATSLAV. [*Who has stood immobile from Elvira's entry, as though suddenly awakened.*] Not six, not six; so, seven already ... Or five ... five-thirty ... Let them undo the horses ... Or do them, as you wish. [*Aside.*] That girlish intellect! ...

ELVIRA. What's girlish?

VATSLAV. Nothing, I'm just sorry she suffers so much on my account.

ELVIRA. Not much; she just indulges herself a great deal.

VATSLAV. It's true, she does like to indulge herself.

ELVIRA. There's not much pain; she was more afraid than anything else.

VATSLAV. So it seems to me, too.

ELVIRA. Sometimes such an accident serves as a warning. She'll be more careful now.

VATSLAV. For my part, I'll also watch out for myself. But speaking frankly, she's quite a scatterbrain.

ELVIRA. Justysia? Sensible, to say the least.

VATSLAV. And interesting.

ELVIRA. What interesting things could go on here?

VATSLAV. She's always twisting about, singing.

78

ELVIRA. She's usually happy.

VATSLAV. She wants amusements.

ELVIRA. Nothing can tempt her from this house.

VATSLAV. And she's a flirt.

ELVIRA. Be that as it may, I always have my eye on her and without me, rest assured, she can't even take a step.

SERVANT. [*Announcing.*] Count Alfred.

VATSLAV. Show him in—he's rarely here.

ELVIRA. I'd say too often.

VATSLAV. I see he's not in your favor.

ELVIRA. That is true.

VATSLAV. A real chimera! What everyone praises, my wife deprecates. He's courteous, clever, honorable—what can you charge him with, even from appearances?

ELVIRA. He's shrewd and false, especially with women.

VATSLAV. Excuse me, he's sincere, sometimes too much so.

ELVIRA. Concerned only with himself.

VATSLAV. It just seems so, because he's not bold.

ELVIRA. Unfaithful . . .

VATSLAV. [*Laughing.*] Ah! From that point of view . . .

ELVIRA. That means he's really unfaithful? . . . Then you see that I am not wrong, and are those his only faults? He's a gambler.

VATSLAV. Him? He knows nothing about cards.

ELVIRA. He's bad . . .

VATSLAV. The best there is. Let him be as he wishes, but please accept my friend graciously.

ELVIRA. My opinion, I am sure, does not divide you. You'll find no opposition in me; let him amuse himself here if you find it pleasant.

VATSLAV. Truthfully, when friendship today is becoming something unknown, he gives me rare proof of kindness.

SCENE 8. Elvira, Alfred, Vatslav.

VATSLAV. You've forgotten us entirely, dear Alfred! But today some fair goddess leads you here; three days without seeing you is really an eternity.

ELVIRA. Surely, he's seldom in this part of the city, otherwise he'd never pass his friends by.

ALFRED. There couldn't be any more delicate reproaches, but nonetheless undeserved.

VATSLAV. Then let us hear the defense.

ALFRED. Is it our fault that the mistress is fond of solitude? Although I am here rarely, I am not forgotten. But in pleasant company, when one loses track of time, I'd soon be very much at home, and a nuisance to you.

VATSLAV. A bad, bad defense!

ALFRED. You will confess yourself, my friend, that you are rarely found at home.

VATSLAV. I should say very frequently, today almost the entire day. Since I have no desire to leave a weak woman alone, I am staying with Elvira.

ALFRED. [*To Elvira.*] Are you weak?

ELVIRA. [*Confused.*] Yes . . .

VATSLAV. [*Approaching.*] Poor weak thing. [*Fondles her.*] My darling, my dear woman . . .

ALFRED. Probably a headache, you can see it from her face.

VATSLAV. Yes . . . a cold . . . a cold changes the eyes.

ALFRED. There are a lot of colds around now. She shouldn't go out.

VATSLAV. [*In haste.*] Oh, not at all, not at all; she can't harm herself. Sitting at home—that's not healthy. [*To Elvira.*] Dearest, how is your head?

ELVIRA. I don't know if I'll be . . .

VATSLAV. [*Not hearing her answer; to Alfred.*] You know, I got a collie; what a treasure, magnificent! Something worth seeing. It'll kill Henry, because he doesn't have one like this. I'm sure no other can be compared to him. Oh, and your Falcon is nothing, you'll see now. So big! Black as a ball, and the crest—you'll see! But now tell me, what's been happening to you? One sees you around so seldom. Especially evenings, you seem to be avoiding merriment. What did you do today? I want an accurate accounting.

ELVIRA. Maybe he has a secret, something that should not be investigated.

VATSLAV. Certainly not from me.

ALFRED. Oh, I can tell everyone and give an accurate accounting of how I spent this day. I was at the Pantler's.* For what,
I myself don't know.

VATSLAV. What did you hear there? Share it with us.

ALFRED. A lot of coughing.

VATSLAV. That's not much.

ALFRED. And a few rumors.

ELVIRA. Ah, and that's too much!

ALFRED. Nonetheless, one can repeat them openly, because if
anything, they serve as a warning—old things that have
been long forgotten; the Pantler's wife spreads the stories
herself and even laughs herself.

ELVIRA. Yes, but she speaks well.

VATSLAV. Oh, very eloquent!

ELVIRA. A very worthy person.

VATSLAV. The best.

ALFRED. Respected.

VATSLAV. But dull! As soon as she begins to speak, you've got
to have tremendous strength to keep from dozing.

ALFRED. Soon Aniela came dressed in mourning clothes.

ELVIRA. For whom?

ALFRED. Her husband.

VATSLAV. He died?

ALFRED. No, he's alive, but he went to the country today and
is coming back tomorrow.

VATSLAV. What feeling! But why doesn't she stay home and
grieve?

ALFRED. Stay home? A good question. Who would know about
it then? No sooner had her brother told me all about it
when Julia appeared in our midst.

ELVIRA. In a bad mood?

VATSLAV. As usual.

ALFRED. Tucked in tight . . . beauty spots all over her face.

VATSLAV. Powdered.

ALFRED. The dread of my evening jacket.

ELVIRA. With someone like that around—it's hard to doze.

---

* The Pantler or Master of the Pantry (*stolnik* in Polish) was a dignitary
of the old Polish Commonwealth. By Fredro's time, such titles were
ceremonial and carried no functions.

VATSLAV. Because she smokes like a man.

ELVIRA. And she's sharp-tongued.

ALFRED. Especially when she's close.

VATSLAV. Why does she dress herself that way, gild herself, make herself so white from powder, tie herself in so? What's the use of fighting nature?

ALFRED. [*Finishing.*] Once upon a time she was a lizard; now she's a salamander.

VATSLAV. She's always reproving something, finding something laughable; she's always pouting, always making fun of something . . . But talk about someone else, I don't like that witch.

ALFRED. Well, Erasmus was there—ruddy-cheeked, though apparently weak, always sweet-talking, though with half a voice. He most tenderly congratulated the Pantler's wife on her birthday, me belatedly on my name's day, Master Jan because he's living in Warsaw, the Prince because two children were waiting for him when he returned from abroad. He was spinning around and wearing himself out at such a wild pace that he wound up congratulating the *starosta** on the burial of his wife!

VATSLAV. When he comes to me or stands near me, it seems at once that I'm a celebrity. To tell the truth, this person, always congratulating, laughing, loving, is a frightful bore.

ELVIRA. He has a good heart.

ALFRED. Just like a lamb.

VATSLAV. Sweet as licorice, good as camomile.

ALFRED. I would have had even more time there for observation if the *castellan** hadn't frightened me out of my wits. When I saw that he let out his sails in my direction I had no desire to hear about his law suits and I beat a hasty retreat.

VATSLAV. Where to?

ALFRED. To the Baron's.

VATSLAV. How is zee gut Baron?

* A district official of the old Polish Commonwealth.
* Kasztelan in Polish; originally the "Keeper of the Castle." In Fredro's time no more than a title.

ALFRED. Zee gut Baron is happy, he luffs his vife.

VATSLAV. Did you find the Colonel there?

ALFRED. What kind of a question is that? It's understood—who doesn't find him there?

ELVIRA. It's a lovely pass you've come to—you've been talking for a whole hour now.

ALFRED. Am I not allowed to say what everyone knows? Am I in any way to blame . . .

VATSLAV. That the Baroness favors the army. Anyway, is that today's discovery?

ELVIRA. Certainly, it's her own fault, no one else's. But who's without a "but," as they say.

VATSLAV. But the Baroness's "but" is too big, and I ask you not to defend her at all.

ELVIRA. You were praising her yourself.

ALFRED. You also have to consider the weaknesses of women, their so agreeable little faults.

VATSLAV. [*To Alfred.*] Jokes! [*To Elvira.*] I was praising her intelligence, but I said nothing about honor. If such a woman could desire respect who, after trampling on humility, duties and honor, has already given up being ashamed and revels in her disgrace which has passed from clandestine love affairs into open harlotry, a woman whom respectable people despise, whom her children will despise—if such a woman gets a favorable opinion what then remains for the one who brings happiness with her wherever she goes, is a model of virtue and the adornment of the fair sex?

ALFRED. What a discourse, thunderingly delivered!

VATSLAV. Let's return to something happier, let's return to the Baron. That his wife should . . . er-r-r . . . uh-h-h . . . we know what's going on . . . Well, what can be done about it? But what I'm laughing at is that she's so much in love with this Colonel who sometimes deliberately avoids her. The Baron, on the other hand, lodges him at his own place, invites him here and there, holds on to him; it's a wonder he doesn't fondle him. He has to be with him always, everywhere—in a word, should the fellow ever go away, the Baron wouldn't live. [*Laughs.*] Oh, it is funny!

ALFRED. True, it's amusing.

VATSLAV. To be so blind! And for such a long time! And they live together peacefully; they get along just the way you and I do. [*He laughs.*] And what makes the whole thing all the funnier is that the Baron closely follows other people's doings. He's able to observe, even scoff, and can see everything—except himself.

ALFRED. Simple soul!

VATSLAV. Ah, he's a real idiot!

ALFRED. Oh! That's too sharp! Why so impolite?

VATSLAV. Idiot, idiot—for such a husband that's the only word.

ALFRED. So be it, if that's the way you want it.

VATSLAV. That certainty of his that he rests on amuses me at times, but at times it also angers me, and once in a while I get the desire to tell him everything straight out. [*He laughs.*] He would be surprised!

ALFRED. And he'd have reason to be.

VATSLAV. Just imagine the kind of face he'd pull.

ALFRED. He'd refuse to believe it.

VATSLAV. I'd offer him proof.

ALFRED. Then he'd be angry.

VATSLAV. No—he'd stand as if nailed to the spot [*imitating the Baron's expression*], his eyes bulging and his mouth gaping.

ALFRED. [*Laughing, to Elvira.*] Just look—how superb—the Baron himself!

[*Until now, Elvira, her head lowered, looking over some book, has been laughing quietly to herself. Now she laughs out loud after taking a look at her husband. A short pause.*] I'm looking at the clock, for if you people are planning to go to the theater—it's already after seven.

VATSLAV. [*Rings, then to the butler.*] The carriage!

BUTLER. Already harnessed.

VATSLAV. You're invited to our box. Come tomorrow, too; I'll wait for you with the horses till ten in the morning, then you'll stay later for lunch. All right, Alfred?

ALFRED. [*Extending his hand to Elvira.*] I willingly accept all of your invitations, except the one to your box at the theater; I have something to take care of . . .

VATSLAV. Then, until tomorrow.

ALFRED. [*Going toward the door.*] Yes, tomorrow, Vatslav, I shall present myself for your kind orders.

SCENE 9. *Servants carry out the candelabra with candles, leaving just the lamp behind.*

JUSTYSIA. [*Alone. Looks around, then runs out, looks beyond the door through which they went out, locks it and returns.*] I know, I know who'll return; I'd almost swear to it—Soon I'll hear a knocking at the window. Ah, it was a wise man who thought up an apartment on the bottom floor! [*Touches her fingers together.*] To open, or not to open? To open, to open, to open!—Aha, so was it destined! But I must also humiliate the young gentleman a little, let him have a look in his own mirror just once. Justysia's no scatterbrain, she thinks about herself, she doesn't want to risk everything in one day. Tomorrow's time enough for me to change the whole shape of things. [*Loftily.*] That's how honor and conscience direct me! [*She sits by a table. A short pause.*] But what does it mean that he hasn't come until now? After all he did give me a sign with his eyes. If . . . Ha! . . . Quieter . . . something's stirring in the garden. Yes . . . it's he . . . unmistakably. I can tell by his walk. [*She turns with her back to the window and begins to read. A knocking is heard at the window. She jumps back into the middle of the room.*] Oh! Oh!

ALFRED. [*Behind the window.*] Justysia! It's me, open up.

JUSTYSIA. I'm afraid.

ALFRED. Open quickly, I'm standing here in the cold. Justysia! [*Knocks.*]

JUSTYSIA. [*Quietly.*] I'll shout! Franciszek, Stefan! I'll cry for help; Jan! Jan!

ALFRED. But Justysia, what are you doing, for heaven's sake? It's me, it's me! What's this noise all about, what are you afraid of?

JUSTYSIA. [*Opening the window.*] Oh, it's you!

SCENE *10. Justysia, Alfred.*

ALFRED. [*In the window.*] And who else could it be, so courageous and bold?

JUSTYSIA. I was so frightened, it's a wonder I'm alive. How my heart is beating!

ALFRED. [*Putting his hand on her.*] Is it really beating?

JUSTYSIA. I still can't come to. How can you cause someone so much anxiety?

ALFRED. I'm sorry, I'm sorry.

JUSTYSIA. Yes! It's unheard of. That window—it's a door for you.

ALFRED. True, it is convenient.

JUSTYSIA. Oh, I know it's not much trouble to crawl through a window, but to frighten people . . .

ALFRED. [*Bowing in jest.*] I beg your forgiveness, Queen!

JUSTYSIA. [*In the same tone.*] I forgive you.

ALFRED. Then I shall sit down.

JUSTYSIA. [*Standing before Alfred who has seated himself on the sofa.*] Why is it I never give you a piece of my mind? What do you come here for, to deceive me and my mistress?

ALFRED. [*Taking her by the hand.*] Bravo, Justysia, principles!

JUSTYSIA. They'd seem that way to you!

ALFRED. You think so?

JUSTYSIA. Certainly, because . . .

ALFRED. [*Seating her next to him.*] Just talk closer, I can't hear anything from a distance.

JUSTYSIA. Please don't squeeze me.

ALFRED. Can't be otherwise—since I want to grasp your principles, they have to be nearer my heart.

JUSTYSIA. You're a great tease!

ALFRED. A wonderful beginning!

JUSTYSIA. But how does it look for me to deceive my mistress so horribly?

ALFRED. And who is deceiving her?

JUSTYSIA. Fine question! After all, you do swear eternal love to her. And today, standing on the other side of the door I heard how you delude her with pretty words [*imitating Alfred*]: "I would like to forget you, but I cannot. Love has

86

become intertwined with life in me, even heaven can't undo the knots; they must endure and perish together."

ALFRED. [*Laughing.*] Well, and what else?

JUSTYSIA. Isn't that enough?

ALFRED. What seemed so strange to you about this? I tell her I love her, and she remains with this belief, because I also do love her sincerely.

JUSTYSIA. Hm, is that so? And me?

ALFRED. I'm mad about you!

JUSTYSIA. But my mistress has other hopes; loving you alone, she wants to be the only one loved by you.

ALFRED. The only one? There was nothing said about that. I never swore to that; it's something new. But listen, Justysia, soon it'll be a year, a year that I love Elvira and she is favorable to me. A year, Justysia, that's not a day! What's so strange then, about my liking that nice little face of yours, that clever look that now threatens destruction, now hurls flames, that smile that likes to merge with a scowl, the deceiving smile that destroys everyone, that little mouth created for kisses, that caresssing embrace, that divine friendliness, that whole divine figure of yours—in short, what's so strange about the fact that my heart has grown fond of Justysia?

JUSTYSIA. You've no lack of words, and even though I don't believe them, I don't know why I still sincerely love you, but if you love for no more than a year, then all I have left is just about six months.

ALFRED. No, I shall love you more than every other love, as long as I can love, as long as I am alive, I swear it!

JUSTYSIA. Hold on! Wait, Sir, don't swear, please! Where vows are necessary, pleasures vanish.

ALFRED. And what kind of mood is Justysia in today? You scold me constantly, and I listen in humility.

JUSTYSIA. I'll scold you just once more.

ALFRED. Once more—I accede. But then . . .

JUSTYSIA. Why write so many letters? They can give us away, cause some painful moments. Before the mistress carried them with her, but now she's got such a pile of them it's hard to carry them around, so she puts them everywhere.

The bed is full of them and every chest . . . By the way, I understand French.

ALFRED. I know—perfectly.

JUSTYSIA. So I took a few of them.

ALFRED. Quite unnecessary.

JUSTYSIA. I wanted to know about everything, so I read them. How dull! I would never want someone to write to me like that. Isn't it more fitting for someone to come in person and be amusing and present everything in a better way?

ALFRED. Justysia is sensible and wishes to explain how to amuse oneself with little letters. But your mistress has other wishes and it is with these that I must comply.

JUSTYSIA. But the letters can betray my mistress, me, and you, and bring all of us unhappiness.

ALFRED. Not me, because I'm not the one who writes them.

JUSTYSIA. Who then? Not you? What do you mean?

ALFRED. Where would I be in a position to write such things? But since I have to send her one letter a day, I keep some old Frenchman by my side who chats a lot and writes endlessly. Sometimes I dictate to him, sometimes he copies without me, sometimes he adds something, I correct him afterward and so each day present her with one letter.

JUSTYSIA. But even such letters can give us away.

ALFRED. I mention no one in them and the writing isn't mine, therefore I'm afraid of nothing.

JUSTYSIA. Does the mistress know it?

ALFRED. God forbid!

JUSTYSIA. And is that good? Aren't you deceiving her then?

ALFRED. Ah, today you're prattling to excess! So kiss me then as punishment. [*Justysia draws away.*] What, you don't want to? Then I shall kiss you four times for all your insults.

JUSTYSIA. Nothing doing. [*Runs away.*]

ALFRED. Come closer!

JUSTYSIA. Go away!

ALFRED. I'll force you.

JUSTYSIA. I'll stop you. [*She runs away and barricades herself behind some chairs.*]

ALFRED. Please!

JUSTYSIA. No!

ALFRED. No?

JUSTYSIA. No.

ALFRED. But if I catch you! . . . [*Alfred chases after Justysia among the chairs; the curtain falls.*]

ACT II

SCENE 1

JUSTYSIA. Always being afraid, always being on guard, while another love thrives without danger . . . There's nothing to think about, the choice has already been made: Vatslav stays, Alfred goes. Yes—but how to get him away from the mistress? So that I don't get myself in trouble?—There has to be proof . . . Must I be the one to get it and reveal our past behavior? No—letters . . . jealousy . . . I'll make up a little story, the mistress will believe it . . . he'll get entangled. Yes, good idea . . . Besides, if he doesn't know who deceived him and I can keep him from finding out through tears, oaths, despair and sobbing, what was will remain a secret forever.

SCENE 2. Justysia, Vatslav.

VATSLAV. [*Looking around.*] The mistress is still at home?

JUSTYSIA. No she's not, she's already in church.

VATSLAV. Oh, how I've come to love Sundays! It's only then that I can stay with you a while. Yet I have to continue to think of a way for the two of us to bestow on each other the proofs of mutual feeling without constant interruption. But, tell me, when I rush to you with the passion of tender love, when I am happy beforehand with my good fortune, why do I see you sad, cold, timid? And tears . . . What is it . . . what's happened?

JUSTYSIA. Please, Sir, don't look for the reason, don't be anxious about the fate of an unhappy girl.

VATSLAV. You think your sadness doesn't concern me? Is this the kind of love you see in me?

JUSTYSIA. Nothing can sweeten my grief. Why disclose it for nothing?

VATSLAV. Your only relief is to reveal the cause of your sadness. Tell me then, why are you crying? If you love me!

JUSTYSIA. Ah, what a wish!

VATSLAV. [*Pleading.*] Dear Justysia!

JUSTYSIA. Dear, dear Sir! Please allow me to keep silent.

VATSLAV. No, that can't be.

JUSTYSIA. You'll find out later.

VATSLAV. No, I want to know now.

JUSTYSIA. You won't remove the sadness.

VATSLAV. I'll put an end to it.

JUSTYSIA. I can't tell you.

VATSLAV. Fine, you can't tell me. I know, those tears of yours, I know what could have caused them. You're crying because you can't bring yourself to tell me to my face that you've stopped loving me the way you used to. That's your whole secret.

JUSTYSIA. What did you say! Oh, such an opinion calls from my lips the painful confession that I must part with you forever. That's the secret that's tormenting my soul.

VATSLAV. Part with me?

JUSTYSIA. Yes, and this very day.

VATSLAV. Justysia is just making jokes!

JUSTYSIA. No Sir, I am not joking. I would prefer to lose my place here than repay kindness with ingratitude. No, I shall never cause my mistress suffering, the mistress with whom I grew up almost from the cradle, who continuously favors me with her kindnesses and regards me not as a servant, but as a friend.

VATSLAV. Then be her friend, but be mine too!

JUSTYSIA. No, such ties are not at all fitting for us. I've already made too many mistakes, but I know what they are—And since every person can repent sincerely I shall enter a convent today. There, in bitter penance, I shall redeem all my past sins and put out this wrong feeling that I have. Oh, this is something I should have done long ago! But I didn't know what it is to be happy with you; I didn't know what would happen if I loved you, for, alas, I didn't know cruel love.

VATSLAV. But why "cruel," Justysia dear? The cruelty exists only for those who don't know love. Old matrons are just frightening you about love. Let them say what they want— love is our pleasure! What's so frightful in the innocent sweetness of embraces? Certainly nothing, since everyone wants to be embraced. And as far as the convent is concerned, I must say that I'm somewhat of an unbeliever. Such plans are frequently changed. They're the usual girlish dreams and the one who rushes off to a convent I'm sure dies of longing for a wedding ring.

JUSTYSIA. You think I'm making it all up?

VATSLAV. I don't say that you're making it all up, but I do say that you're wrong. Anyway, why go—whether your calling is sincere or not, it's enough that it will never be fulfilled. I love you, you love me, let it suffice at that, for I shall make you at peace with the world in every way.

JUSTYSIA. But even if I didn't go into a convent, I'd have to leave here for the sake of my honor. What kind of a future is waiting for me, what hopes can I have? Poor, abandoned . . . Oh, I'm trembling all over! . . .

VATSLAV. Oh, have a better opinion of my honor! It's entirely possible that sometime we'll part, but Justysia will never be abandoned. I'll have her fate in view above anything else. A dowry used to augment a girl's charms; if Justysia adds one to hers, certainly more than one admirer will desire her hand. So everything doesn't end in a convent. And if perhaps you don't believe my words, then I shall put it in writing this very day. After all, it would be a shame to veil that pretty little face with bars. Well, what about it? Just one little word! You're thinking . . . you'll be persuaded? . . .

JUSTYSIA. Ah, you carry off an easy victory over me, for I can't refuse when you ask something!

VATSLAV. Then you'll remain?

JUSTYSIA. I'll remain.

VATSLAV. That makes me very happy. But who conceals the

truth, sins the more. Confess honestly, I won't be insulted: did you really intend to go off to a convent? Or did you just want, in a less painful way, to take a comrade with you into your penance?

JUSTYSIA. That's a fine question! [*Weeps.*] There's the reward for my loving!

VATSLAV. Right away you start crying!

JUSTYSIA. I should cry that I must love you even if it brings me unhappiness. I could have gotten married, been a wealthy woman, but on account of you I didn't consider it. [*Weeps.*] But when . . . when you think the way you do, when you no longer have any faith in my virtue, I shall find a husband, I shall have my own home and I shall love others kinder than you!

VATSLAV. But, Justysia, what kind of a silly thought is that? When a woman gets married, she doesn't love others.

JUSTYSIA. And when a man gets married?

VATSLAV. When a man gets married, you say? A man who is already married . . . that is, who has a wife? That's something else, for although his state changes . . . a man is permitted everything.

JUSTYSIA. [*Running to the window.*] Someone's riding in . . . the mistress! . . . [*She runs out of the room.*]

VATSLAV. [*Alone.*] She's here, she's coming back! Well, I ask you, what annoyance I suffer with that wife of mine. This is something unbearable, even perverse, that in my own home I can't do as I please!

SCENE 3. Vatslav, Elvira.

VATSLAV. Believe me, Elvira, you're choosing a bad road! I can't look on calmly and say nothing. Whether it's the style now or someone's advice, you should give up both of them. Gaiety, amusements, fashion—they all have their place. But responsibilities, especially as regards heaven— those must always be placed before everything else. It will never do to get them mixed up! And the person who fears censure, plans his deeds accordingly.

ELVIRA. But I don't know what you're talking about.

VATSLAV. Then I shall tell you that it isn't at all nice when someone falls into church like a windstorm, moves herself around a dozen times, gets up, sits down, amuses herself this way a quarter of an hour, then flies out in a rush, throws herself into a carriage with the same hustle and bustle and enjoys the admiration of the lazy gaping crowd that usually stands on exhibition in its Sunday finery in all the public places.

ELVIRA. Are you speaking about me?

VATSLAV. You weren't in the church three minutes! I won't argue the point too much, but I'll just say that it's very amusing when women scorn appearances. It's not enough to be pious, virtuous in one's soul; it's not enough to be attentive and tender-hearted, for lest your honor suffer even in the slightest, you also have to have some regard for external appearances.

ELVIRA. This very fair warning I have heeded for a long time, so I cannot therefore accept it now. Because I see happiness in quiet virtue, I don't think about the tumult of the world. But since I am pious by nature, I also pay close attention to appearances.

VATSLAV. Why did you return so quickly?

ELVIRA. For the best possible reason. I couldn't be comfortable and drive from my memory the fact that the coachman has to stand outdoors in such a frost, that he has to suffer just on my account.

VATSLAV. Frost? Today frost? It's hot! There are few such pleasant days.

ELVIRA. It really isn't cold? It seemed so to me. I am sincerely pious and I go to church often and I very much heed the fact as well as the appearance, but I feel that the holiest of all our obligations is to bear the relief of suffering mankind.

VATSLAV. Although you speak very nicely and you argue warmly, where does humanity, especially suffering humanity, figure here just because a coachman waits an hour in a warm fur coat? How quickly your mind gets off the point! Pity mixed with judgment—fine; I like and value it. But exaggerated—it changes itself into amusing day-dreaming.

ELVIRA. Into amusing day-dreaming, I confess; but even though the intention is not realized, a good desire remains of true advantage for us. Oh, how sweet and pleasant when I can think that someone found help in me, that I can bring relief to someone's sufferings. Ah, my husband, say what you want, count it among the vices, but there can never be enough of pity and gooddoing! Ah, humanity is my God! Its appeal, its strength . . . [*Before she finishes, Vatslav shrugs his shoulders and leaves without Elvira noticing his absence.*]

SCENE 4. *Elvira, Justysia.*

JUSTYSIA. You came back so soon, my lady?

ELVIRA. Oh, I had to come back soon since I forgot to give Alfred a letter! Take it and deliver it to him as soon as he comes, and then I will get an answer by dinner-time.

JUSTYSIA. [*Taking the letter and shaking her head.*] A letter to Mr. Alfred?

ELVIRA. Why do you make such faces?

JUSTYSIA. I'm afraid to say.

ELVIRA. Just tell me straight out.

JUSTYSIA. It would be better not to deliver it.

ELVIRA. Not deliver it? For what reason? . . .

JUSTYSIA. Will you believe me, my lady?

ELVIRA. Don't beat around the bush; tell me what you have to tell me without hints! I'll believe anything, so long as you can prove it.

JUSTYSIA. But you must promise to keep this secret for someone could try to get even with me. And if something happens, promise you won't tell where you heard what I'm going to tell you now. Very often the good reputation of an innocent girl can be destroyed in half an hour because of these fine gentlemen.

ELVIRA. I promise you everything, I give you my word, I swear it, but don't keep me waiting any longer.

JUSTYSIA. I'll tell you in all honesty . . . But someone is coming now . . . Let's go to my room, no one will disturb us there.

ELVIRA. Good heavens! What's going on! What am I going to hear? I'm trembling all over! [*They leave.*]

SCENE 5.

ALFRED. [*To the butler.*] Please tell your master that I am waiting for him. [*A short pause.*] For a long time I've been postponing the break with Elvira, but this Justysia is some girl! She's beginning to have some strange power over me. Her gaiety and her charms make up for Elvira's constant nagging. And this innocent child loves me so much that she sees no one but me in the world. I am so surprised at my feelings for her! Then finally the thought, indeed pleasant, that I was her master in the science of love—everything turns me to her whether I want to or not.

SCENE 6. Alfred, Vatslav.

ALFRED. Oh, why such a face? What's the matter, Vatslav?

VATSLAV. A headache.

ALFRED. I don't think so; rather an obstruction in some delicate matter is standing in your way.

VATSLAV. What? You speak to me now as you used to two years ago? Have you forgotten that I'm married?

ALFRED. By no means, how can I forget. But though you've chosen this difficult road, I know you faithfully preserve your principles: you pluck just the flowers and pass over the thorns. I know you don't want to be the model of an idyllic husband, though you've followed a well-worn path, and placing no limits on the marital rights—you know, distaff in hand, at your spouse's feet—you wouldn't want to enjoy a freedom as heavy as lead. Besides, you've lived in the world and you're still young. How would it be for that Vatslav, the object of so much envy, the child spoiled by happiness and love, a third person in every marriage, never satisfied with anything but victory, who's gained a reputation as the woe of husbands, the deceiver of wives, who's caused so much pleasure and then so many tears, to put an end to his old ways and be content to rest on his laurels?

VATSLAV. Yes, Alfred, I am resting on my laurels. While we're free we have it much better. The title of husband adds gravity, and that we need the least of all. Furthermore, once the right to confidence is already acquired, it's hardly anything flattering for us. I always prefer to be feared, then no one is deceived by my friendship. My words are taken at their face value and the usual way is cut in two.

ALFRED. You've really surprised me with this new approach! Oh, my worthy master, why do your ideas seem so settled to me?

VATSLAV. Oh, dearest pupil, you will find out in due time that it cannot be otherwise! Let a married man succeed somewhere—how many obstacles he has! His own wife, the lady's husband, domestic peace, family councils, and the worst of all things, the hundred-tongued matrons who've already lived through their sins and descend like crows over a dead hawk! But if I do get by their owl's eyes and am cautious at every step I take and, unknown, outsmart and fool them all, all the guardians and rivals, and even if I do become fortunate in every respect, what will I get out of it if no one is to know about it?

ALFRED. May all husbands be calm then?

VATSLAV. As calm as possible, and not just because of me. No one will bother them now. And even if someone tries—it will be for nothing. Today's youth, in love with itself, concerned only with its own adornment for which it has adopted all the vanities of women and lacks just fainting-spells and beauty-spots to complete the picture, thinks it just has to exhibit itself, just show itself off in order to inflame all hearts with love. Who knows how to really love today, how to forget himself and make sacrifices, almost renounce his own personality and be happy or sad, hopeful or frightened all for the one for whom he sighs . . . [*in a lower voice*] until he gets what he wants?

ALFRED. And when he gets it? What then Vatslav?

VATSLAV. One has to suddenly change his shape and from a snake—become a lion.

ALFRED. Oh, I could embrace you for such lessons! I beg you, publish all your ideas and your grateful great-grandchildren will hail your name!

VATSLAV. Don't make fun of it; these ideas of mine could serve as certain principles.

ALFRED. That you should publish them, that was just a joke. But I really believe that since you happily carried the art of attraction in love so far, you're worth emulating. That way, no one will achieve distinction in this regard unless he's like you. One should follow in your steps and you, on the other hand, should freely give your advice to others.

VATSLAV. Give advice? To whom? For what? Why? Youth has gone to sleep—husbands won't lose a thing. Since I'm a husband myself now, I'm happy about it and I'm in no rush to enlighten others. However, to a good friend like you, I will gladly help with advice. And if with the help of my advice you succeed, then my efforts will be rewarded. Did you think I'd become sad when I turned to matrimonial comforts? Oh, no, I am only stating what should be stated, that there is no ingenious youth today.

ALFRED. Don't despise them so much; avengers might rise from the ashes.

VATSLAV. They say who cheats will also be cheated, that husbands and wives are always the same and no one is spared: *hodie mihi, cras tibi.* But I don't believe it. I have my own way of taking care of things, and all the proverbs on this score I fear no more than the avengers.

ALFRED. You don't fear them! Ha, that does amuse me! For who'd ever put himself up beside you. Whoever'd try to contend with you for superiority would be committing suicide!

VATSLAV. I'd recognize a suitor like that from the first glance.

ALFRED. With your experience, it's easy.

VATSLAV. No one can escape my piercing eye.

ALFRED. You see right through people, that's what everyone says.

VATSLAV. If I wanted to, I could almost guess their thoughts.

ALFRED. And their shrewd little schemes.

VATSLAV. I won't fall into any traps because I'm very careful.

ALFRED. You surprise me very often.

VATSLAV. But I'm never jealous!

ALFRED. Very fair. There's nothing worse than jealousy and a jealous husband—always deserves his punishment.

VATSLAV. And on the other hand, I am reassured by my wife's virtues. Her sincere love, her fine upbringing . . .

ALFRED. These qualities take the place of a hundred Arguses!

VATSLAV. She loves solitude.

ALFRED. You doubtless put her mind at ease.

VATSLAV. She's bashful, modest.

ALFRED. Oh, I know her well!

VATSLAV. But above all, she is very pious.

ALFRED. And could one ask for more assurance?

VATSLAV. I am secure, then, in every way: I trust the times, Elvira, and above all myself. After all, I know all the ways and byways—I walked them myself—which the cunning enemies of husbands may follow: I have all the stratagems perfectly in memory. No one can get ahead of me, no one can outsmart me! Believe me, an old and experienced soldier will always upset a youngster's plans in the first battle. The art of love is like a game of chess: one covers up his moves until he wins. But if some champion coldly observes two passionate players opposing each other, he'll easily guess their plans and find their weaknesses. And if he wants to give one of them advice, and be with him constantly like a guard when he takes the bishops and stops them in their tracks, and beats the knight at just the right moment, and especially when he keeps the queen from check, then the second player hasn't a chance: he must give in or be check-mated.

ALFRED. You deserve a university chair, I always say. I consider your teaching really important, and if I ever directed a school somewhere I'd do away with such unbearable stuff as law, for example. Why should we bother studying now how the Romans governed themselves years ago? Or is it worth so much study just to learn how to reach heaven in the robes of a cardinal? In the place of the eminent judges then you'd sit upon a soft throne surrounded by your numerous students, male and female. You'd teach them the most essential thing in life. Yes, the most essential, for who'd dispute that the way of getting the greatest pleasure is what each of us spends his whole life seeking.

BUTLER. [*Coming in.*] It's already eleven and the horses are ready.

VATSLAV. Talking to you, I almost forgot about our ride. I am at your service, I'll go wherever you want.

ALFRED. It's all the same to me.

VATSLAV. You don't have to tell me, and I'm not asking, but in any necessity you can always count on my being blind and deaf. [*They are about to leave when the butler enters and gives Vatslav a note.*]

VATSLAV. [*After reading the note.*] I have no luck today . . . ! Do me a favor, my dear Alfred; wait for me a while, it won't take long. I'll just find out about a matter I can't put off any longer, or if you want, we'll meet somewhere.

ALFRED. No, no, I prefer to wait here; we still have plenty of time. [*Vatslav goes out.*]

SCENE 7.

ALFRED. It's not people who rule us but our own weaknesses. That's the moral of what's been said. Who finds out a person's weaknesses has a key to his home. Everything is opened to him and he can go in the easy way . . . Yet my conscience, my conscience—to deceive a friend! Ha! But a husband and wife ought to get along. If I like the husband less, because I like the wife more, then my heart is always divided between them. Have fun, Alfred, the world will pay you back, no deed ever loses its value. Oh, can't anything be done to change the customs when I get married?

SCENE 8. *Alfred and Elvira.*

ELVIRA. Oh! [*Aside.*] God, he's still here!

ALFRED. [*With sympathy.*] My dear Elvira, what is the matter, why have you been crying? If you still value my life, tell me the truth, don't hide it from me. Tell me, darling, what's wrong?

ELVIRA. Traitor! You dare to ask me why I'm crying? And even look me straight in the eye? Do you have any conscience at all? You return my tender love with deceit, you make vows, then deceive me, twice in the same day. There's ice in your soul, while I am burning—and you still ask me, why am I crying? Yes, I was crying, because I despise myself; and now I am still crying because I see you! Don't think, however, that love will dry my tears. Your cunningness has separated us forever. As much as I loved you before, now I hate you! I'm even happy, I feel an ecstasy in my soul, because you have freed me from the bondage of love and because you have shown me how worthy of trust creatures like you really are!

ALFRED. Calm yourself, Elvira . . .

ELVIRA. My downfall was an easy success for you. Without experience, without the advice of parents to guide me, I was thrown into this corrupted world with a soul yearning for affection. It didn't take you long to win my trust. My husband was cold, and your qualities, of which, alas, I always heard so much, inclined my heart to you, and conquered the little resistance I still had. You won. But while I was sincerely miserable because I felt guilty that I gave myself to you out of love, you were secretly enjoying your teachery! But your treachery would have been nothing, your whole art of deceit nothing if only I had loved you less!

ALFRED. Could you think . . . If my life is still dear to you, allay your uncertainty, which is worse than any discovery.

ELVIRA. I am guilty, I admit it, I don't want to conceal my mistakes. My shame remains open and isn't worth any consideration. I trampled on the sanctity of modesty and faith and I deserve a heavy punishment, but why should you be the one to punish me, to bloody the heart that took you as its god? And if you never loved, if you never knew the fire of the soul that extinguishes the source of life with a passionate flame, that presses the heart and together with sweet pleasure puts in it the most awful pains—what could unhappy Elvira have done to you that would cause you to try so hard to make her guilty?

ALFRED. What did I do . . . ?

ELVIRA. Oh, Alfred, it can't be, a wicked thought must be deceiving me! You can't have so base a soul that you could step on people out of vain pride and build your glory on my tears. You had to give me up, your honor ordered you to—isn't that true? Tell me, you had to deceive me, and with such a heavy blow strike my heart. Tell me, I beg you, make your guilt smaller, conceal it! Give me good reasons, invent them, I'll believe anything you say—I want to! I'll cling to anything sincerely, not so I can remain in my old day-dreams, but so I can see you more honorable than you are.

ALFRED. Now I've guessed the reason for your worries: you are jealous, and of whom? Poor Alina! How could you even compare yourself to her, you who are the adornment of the fair sex, you before whom half the world bows? How could you lower yourself to such an extent, and take as love—just some diversion on my part? In order to convince you how I treasure every token of Alina's affection—look, here's a letter of hers, unique in its taste, strong in morals and premature defense, along with promises which were not requested—[tearing the letter] I'm tearing it into pieces, and believe me, I do it sincerely, and I place it at your feet as a sacrifice. [Comes closer.] Let's have peace again, Elvira. For the sake of it, I even forgive your unjust opinion of me.

ELVIRA. Get away from me, you monster! Oh, good heavens! How much meanness I must discover! Alina? You and Alina? . . . Do I hear correctly? The same day, the same moment when you swear to . . . ? No, no, great God! Oh, I can't even express my anger! [To herself.] Here's the man I worshipped! [To Alfred.] So Alina has also awakened desire in you? Now you are even more guilty, and a new guilt is added. But it's not Alina that we've been talking about.

ALFRED. About whom, then?

ELVIRA. About Justysia, you traitor!

ALFRED. [Aside.] Now I've had it . . . !

ELVIRA. Don't look for a scheme, don't bother to think of some way of putting everything in another light. I know everything, you won't be able to deny it or explain it. Therefore, I don't want to waste even another minute with you. I'll shorten this upsetting episode and put an end to our relationship. I'll go and repent my sins, and you I'll leave to your misery. But no; I, unhappy woman, must still ask a favor of him who blemished my soul. My accomplice in sin! My first step in shame! I implore you then on the holiest rights of pity, if not honor, to preserve Vatslav's friendship!

ALFRED. Now listen to me . . . !

ELVIRA. Too sudden a break might be a source of gossip. If I have to suffer so much, let me suffer secretly . . . Or—go, go ahead, brag about it, poison a miserable life, tell the whole world, amuse it with the picture of my mistakes, make it happy; but also tell it, as much as I suffer for losing my honor, I am just as much ashamed to have made you my choice! [*She goes out.*]

SCENE 9.

ALFRED. [*After a short pause.*] Ah, how beautiful she is when she gets angry! I have never seen her so beautiful! I'll beg her forgiveness, she isn't counting on that . . . But wait! Hey! Didn't I want to break off with her? It's a good chance, but this way—thrown out, scolded and scorned? . . . No, no, I'll go and beg her forgiveness, and then . . . What then? I'll leave her . . . Hm! What would I gain that way? Perhaps I should let her think what they all want, that it was she who left me. [*A short pause.*] I've torn the letter, the devil knows why; I didn't act as smoothly as I should have. [*Collects the torn pieces of the letter.*] But these pieces don't lose their value. Actually, they gain double their value. I'll say I saved them from a jealous hand; anyway, Alina's charms . . . Well, I must admit, she hardly has any: tall, plain, pale, and one could say quite stupid . . . The only consolation is her husband, her jealous husband! And if Alina deprives me of pleasure, her husband repays it twofold by his jealousy. But poor Justysia, who could have betrayed us . . . ? Never mind that now . . . she might lose her job . . . One has to help her, and I have just the way! I'll settle her with Alina! Bravo, bravo, excellent!

Enjoy yourself, Alfred, life is short! I would still like to make up with Elvira, at least on the surface. But how can I soothe her?

BUTLER. [*Comes in.*] The Count is waiting and asks you to come.

ALFRED. [*Taking his hat.*] Ha! We'll see, a plan will come at the right time. [*He goes out.*]

ACT III

SCENE *1.* Elvira, Justysia. *Elvira sits down, leaning on a table, holding a handkerchief to her eyes.*

JUSTYSIA. [*Carrying several packages.*] Here are Mr. Alfred's sweet little notes. From all over, wherever I could find them, I gathered up the packets: from the middle of the sofa comes the biggest bundle here, this one from under the embroidering frames, and this one from the small table. Another one from the chest of drawers, tied 'round with a little string, this package was behind the bureau, and these two behind the bed. I really looked everywhere, and it seems to me this is all there is.

ELVIRA. It's still not all.

JUSTYSIA. Still not all? Then tell me please where these abundant treasures are hidden.

ELVIRA. There are still some behind the portrait.

JUSTYSIA. Which portrait?

ELVIRA. [*With a sigh.*] My husband's. [*Justysia starts to leave the room.*] Oh, and underneath the little altar where I say my prayers! [*Justysia goes out.*]

SCENE *2.*

ELVIRA. Oh, how worthy of pity is a person whom love oppresses! In vain does he call on reason and incite hatred in himself. Turbulent feelings tear down everything; his whole world is centered about the person he loves. I repeat in vain that I hate him, that I loathe such a person. Ah, in vain do I arm myself against him with courage, disgust, and loathing. My heart searches for his. Wanting to grasp the reason for my unhappiness, I apologize for him at my own expense; wanting to lament my guilt, I cry only for the loss of him.

SCENE 3. *Elvira, Justysia.*

JUSTYSIA. This time I'm certain I have them all. There isn't a corner where I didn't search them out with my own eyes. And now I'll light a fire as fast as I can. Let one after the other burn like an evil-doer.

ELVIRA. How was it, Justysia—was he just waiting for your permission? Did he want to steal you away from her and did he swear faithfulness?

JUSTYSIA. I already told you: he wanted to abduct me, he swore that he loved me, but I, not wishing to deceive . . .

ELVIRA. He doesn't love you either and only deceives you.

JUSTYSIA. That I don't know.

ELVIRA. Oh, of course; how can you doubt it? How would Alfred fall in love with you?

JUSTYSIA. [*Insulted.*] Why not? Do you see anything in me that would make me repulsive to men?

ELVIRA. Oh well now, enough of this; let it be as it was. But you have to send back all his gifts; you can't keep them.

JUSTYSIA. Well, for better or for worse I took them and still have them with me. But whatever you order me to do with them today, I'll do.

ELVIRA. You mean, Justysia, it wasn't Alfred who wrote the letters?

JUSTYSIA. But I gave you clear proof of it, and he himself confessed that he was unfaithful. Isn't that enough? But why think about what's already happened?

ELVIRA. You're right, Justysia, there's no need to think about it any longer. To pay back my trust with such deceit, oh heavens! I believed him so, I loved him so, my whole soul went out to him!

JUSTYSIA. What kind of love is it when there's always anxiety, when because of it tears never dry? From the beginning, no matter at what kind of entertainment, I almost never saw you happy. The Parisian clothes that are so hard for other women to acquire are lying in the closet: the little hats, ribbons, cambrics and moires, and the pelerines, the marvelous pelerines, the heavenly flounces, especially the ones with rick-rack—they're all lying untouched, just like old hems. [*With feeling.*] You look at everything indifferently; the cashmere looks no different to you than chintz. [*More tenderly.*] You don't want to wear garlands, you turn away from the mirror, in short—something horrible has come into this household! And it's all the unfortunate result of this love. But now I say that when this gloom passes peace will return and the anxieties will diminish.

ELVIRA. You're right, Justysia, I will be calmer. Moments of joy! Nothing detains you, and there isn't even any hope! The dream of happiness has faded, my whole world has faded, only grief has remained to me!

JUSTYSIA. Even the grief passes, just as those other moments. But why recall so much, why keep bringing it all up in conversation?

ELVIRA. You're right, Justysia, one shouldn't talk about it. But tell me—what kind of a look did he have when he gave assurance of his feelings: that charming smile and that expression on his face which God grants only to those in love?

JUSTYSIA. True—he's pleasant, handsome, and not skimpy in his vows; but the Count doesn't take second place to him in anything. He is also friendly, handsome, and young. He wants a peaceful, domestic freedom and though he's cold now, I give you my word you'll be loving each other very soon. As soon as Mister Alfred leaves here.

ELVIRA. You're right, Justysia, we will be loving each other. But are you also certain that he wasn't just joking? Perhaps he was just testing my faith?

JUSTYSIA. Is that so? Well, I know what it all means. Just receive him here now. You could then explain yourself to him and even ask him to forgive you for the rebuke!

ELVIRA. Who? I? I should look at that traitor? Must I still make explanations to him? I can't stand him! I hate him! I loathe the very memory of him! Give me the letters!

JUSTYSIA. Why are you taking them?

ELVIRA. I'll go to my sister's.

JUSTYSIA. Then you can leave them.

ELVIRA. No, I'll avoid any guesses this way by just sending everything to him from there. You stay here. When Vatslav comes, tell him I won't be home for dinner for I'll be spending the whole day with my sister who's gotten weaker. [*Elvira gathers the packets of letters in her shawl and goes out.*]

SCENE 4.

JUSTYSIA. Be happy, Justysia, be happy, Vatslav! Here's no ordinary head for you, by God! Everything's working out just as I wanted it! Now I won't be afraid every moment. I'll be the mistress here, I'll love and live happily. Everything calmly, everything without slander. Bravo, Justysia, bravo! [*Sings and dances.*] Bravo, bravo, bravo! [*Vatslav enters and remains in the rear.*] Bravo, Justysia, bravo!

VATSLAV. [*Finishes on the same note.*] Bravo, bravo, bravo! [*Extends his hands. Justysia falls into his embrace.*]

SCENE 5. *Justysia, Vatslav.*

JUSTYSIA. Oh, hold me! My head is spinning . . . Oh, oh, I'm going to faint!

VATSLAV. No lack of desire on my part; I'll hold you even till night and even if I get weak, I'll get my strength back quickly.

JUSTYSIA. No, I want to sit down. [*She goes to the couch, leaning on Vatslav.*]

VATSLAV. Certainly, we'll both sit down. [*They sit down.*]

JUSTYSIA. It's all a trifle, but I do wrong to look for you when I should shun you; because of it, I'll shed many tears . . . I ask you, please sit a little farther away.

VATSLAV. What was and will be is all a trifle, just so long as I can embrace you . . . But listen, where is my wife?

JUSTYSIA. She went to her sister who's very sick. She sent for her, so she'll remain with her until evening, if not longer. She asked me to tell you about it.

VATSLAV. [*Singing the same tune Justysia sang earlier.*] Bravo, Justysia, bravo, bravo, bravo! There's no need now to torment yourself with fear. From morning to evening there'll just be the two of us. Oh, let me embrace you for the happy news you brought! [*Kisses her.*]

SCENE 6. Vatslav, Justysia, Elvira.

ELVIRA. [*Running in.*] I forgot . . . [*Starting.*] What is this? What is this? Vatslav!

VATSLAV. What is this? Uh . . . that is, these . . . that is, just some innocent joking . . . she was afraid of being tickled . . . [*Laughs with effort.*] Tickling . . . that's it . . . that's how it happened.

ELVIRA. [*To Justysia.*] Away! Out of my sight, treacherous lizard, whom I've fondled at my breast too long! Does affectionate friendship take such a reward? . . . Away from my home, right now, servant. You're not worthy of hearing even a word from me! Lead your life as miserably as you deceive! [*Justysia withdraws to the rear of the stage and remains there with her eyes lowered. To Vatslav, after a short pause.*] Oh, my husband, how could you forget in a single day what you owe to your wife, and what you owe to yourself! Does Vatslav honor himself with such a liaison? Does he give me, alas, such a rival? [*Looks at Justysia.*] But where's the beauty that captivates you? What attributes of hers, what qualities, so madly took possession of you? [*With irony.*] Let me know them, let me be the judge of them, since already I don't dare to compare myself with this divinity [*bowing to Justysia*]. Today let me erase with honor the old blame. Only now do I see the reason why you were always so cold to me. I kept you from the goal of your desires. I was unpleasant for you only at home. That was why you wanted always to get rid of me, so that you would have more time to spend with her. There you are—all men are the same! Tender, faithful, but only in word, not deed. [*Speaks more rapidly.*] You yourselves set the bad example, but you want to have good wives. You want your poor wife, though deceived and insulted, to love you just the same, to believe you, to listen to you and then to say thank you for all your tortures. You want her to respect just your will, conceal her own grief, and be only a servant . . . [*At this moment one of the packets of letters drops out of her scarf.*] Oh! Oh! [*She wants to pick it up, but a second packet drops, and then all of them.*] Oh, heavens! What have I done! [*She covers her eyes with her handkerchief and throws herself into a chair. Justysia approaches her.*]

VATSLAV. [*Lifting up one packet.*] What does this mean, Elvira? Eh . . . Elvira? Wife! What is it? These . . . these letters, no doubt written to you. Ah, that is lovely! It's comical! [*Turns the letters over.*] From whom? To whom? Tell me, whose letters can these be? [*Grasps a letter in his hand; with growing restlessness.*] Tell me, darling, I ask you very much, I'm not making anything bad out of it all, I'm not blaming you for anything, but it's not pleasant to wait until your husband discovers the secret by himself. Whose letters are they? My dear wife, darling! Just one word, one word—You've had so much to say up to now! Answer me, give me a sign, shake your head!

ELVIRA. I just can't!

VATSLAV. Strange! But I must know whose letters they are.

ELVIRA. I would willingly open my whole soul to you, but I swear to you, it's nothing that concerns me.

ALFRED. [*Coming in, then wanting to withdraw.*] Oh! Excuse me!

VATSLAV. No harm done.

ALFRED. Perhaps I've come at a bad time . . .

VATSLAV. On the contrary; I have to talk to you.

ELVIRA. [*Getting up.*] Oh, I can't bear any more of this. [*Goes out.*]

JUSTYSIA. [*Approaching Vatslav.*] In front of another person.

VATSLAV. He's gone away. [*Rings and calls to the butler.*] No one can come in here now; tell everyone that I'm not at home. [*Justysia goes out.*]

SCENE 7. *Vatslav, Alfred. Alfred, coming in and catching sight of his letters, reveals an inner confusion. He rubs his hands and hums from time to time looking now at the letters, now at Vatslav. Vatslav shuts the door through which Elvira went out.*

ALFRED. [*With a forced smile.*] What? You're shutting the door?

VATSLAV. I'm shutting it. [*A long silence. Alfred always uncomfortable. Then Vatslav shuts the second door.*] No one will bother us here. Alfred, an unfortunate event has come to my attention, and it's unfortunate to have to bring it up now. But knowing your heart, and knowing your sincere friendship, I'm not afraid to mention it. While dampening in myself my own love, I shall make a confession to you of my domestic tribulations. Just before you came in, a few minutes before, my wife, I don't know why, upset over something, dropped thousands of these letters. Her shriek, her confusion, her whole body trembling seemed to suggest that there was some secret she was afraid of. I picked up the letters, read them and just stood dumbfounded. Can you believe it? Look—confessions of love, some sort of secret arrangements, some advice, opinions, vows by the hundreds—in short, I found the kind of letters that are frequently written to a woman who no longer conceals her feelings about us, and with whom . . . at least, life is as good as it can be. I asked her about them, I begged her to tell me, I tried to guess, I beseeched her and expressed my amazement, but Elvira is silent . . .

ALFRED. She's silent?

VATSLAV. She's stubbornly silent, and through her whimpering the only thing I could find out was that she was keeping quiet for someone else's benefit. What am I to deduce from this, what has to be done, tell me, and let your advice enlighten me in this affair.

ALFRED. I judge that Elvira is entirely innocent, except for the fact that she is concealing from you what some other woman has done! But it is difficult to demand from a sensitive person that she confide to you the confidences of a friendship.

VATSLAV. But whose confidences can they be? Her associations are known to me, and besides—when are girlfriends so effusive that they'd confide such things to each other?

ALFRED. Right, a good observation! But who'd ever imagine, if those letters were written for at least a year, that this relationship could escape your eye?

VATSLAV. You know me, what can I say to you—I wouldn't have noticed! That's why I postponed this conversation with Elvira; I didn't want her to guess what was going on with me and for her to think that I have little faith either in her or myself. Then, taking everything carefully into consideration, I credit Elvira with more intelligence. A lover of hers would have written better.

ALFRED. Why?

VATSLAV. Some student knocked out the nonsense.

ALFRED. [*Insulted.*] Why a student?

VATSLAV. Because they're a little stupid.

ALFRED. But please, tell me, why a little stupid?

VATSLAV. Here you are, take a few of them, read them over, and then ask yourself why they're stupid. These letters weren't written to my wife, certainly. Still, I'm not satisfied until I learn the entire secret.

ALFRED. You've an unnecessary curiosity to investigate other people's affairs.

VATSLAV. Excuse me, but they're not other people's affairs if they concern my wife!

ALFRED. Come! For shame, now! Your envy is deceiving you, Vatslav.

VATSLAV. Envy?

ALFRED. Envy.

VATSLAV. You're wrong.

ALFRED. Then forget about any investigation, return the letters, ask your wife to forgive you, and that'll be the end of it.

VATSLAV. No, no. Envy, no envy, let it be as it may, but I must find out about this matter today. [*A short pause.*] Just let some idea come into my head . . . Who's Elvira living with? I know all her acquaintances perfectly.

ALFRED. Wait, what an idea! Perhaps . . . That's it, couldn't be otherwise: Justysia, her servant, rather friend, who often likes to boast about how well she understands French, could easily inflame someone into loving her and imitating the fashion and the customs of the age—though a Polish girl —she does not embark on love in the Polish style—but everything happens à la française, with little letters and conversation. So act our ladies, and so acts half the world. Why, then, shouldn't our Justysia act the same way and, though she could do differently, write her lovers in the Polish language? Remember when I entered unexpectedly—she was even coming and going and . . . Right, perfect! She wanted to interrupt you as you were speaking and keep you from making the discovery. Believe me, my guesses are not unfounded.

VATSLAV. Justysia? That can be, you know. I'm afraid of that.

ALFRED. What harm does it do *you*?

VATSLAV. It's not so much that it harms me, but here in my house . . . somehow it just won't do, right under my roof . . . offending morality.

ALFRED. [*Repeating with irony.*] Aha, morality!

VATSLAV. Besides, it's no small matter . . . But why should I hide before you. Since I began to confide in you, I'll confide everything to you. You see, Justysia . . . don't think she's just a servant in the ordinary sense; she grew up with Elvira, received an education good enough for someone of higher status, benefited much from her instructors, and knowing her well, I can confess openly . . .

ALFRED. [*Impatiently.*] Well—and what about Justysia?

VATSLAV. This girl . . . I just wish you could have a talk with her, she's a real treasure! It's really hard to believe what a good head she's got on her shoulders, how sensible she is, agreeable, gay in conversation . . .

ALFRED. Well, well—what about Justysia?

VATSLAV. I must confess everything. Well . . . and what honors her soul even more is that angelic goodness with that tender expression of hers . . .

ALFRED. [*Impatiently.*] But what has this . . .

VATSLAV. And especially she has . . . something . . . something . . . at the same time . . .

ALFRED. She has something, she has something, yes, yes; I know, I know, but finish, damn it all! What about Justysia, this adornment of the world . . . ?

VATSLAV. [*Interrupting him.*] I like her very much.

ALFRED. Yes?

VATSLAV. [*Rapidly.*] We are in love with each other and can live together happily. That's the whole thing.

ALFRED. You can live together happily?—A rare skill! But how long has this game been going on?

VATSLAV. For the past two weeks I'm sure she loves me now.

ALFRED. [*Aside.*] For two weeks she's been deceiving me!

VATSLAV. [*Hearing the last words.*] Deceives? There you are —and that does concern me! But I repeat, she isn't flighty and these letters in such a collection . . . No, that can't be! But, hm, true, I recall, someone young and rich was in love with her; once she mentioned him in a very strange way, and even laughed on account of her lover's loss. But if possessing those two attributes, that is, youth and wealth, the young gentleman didn't know how to devise a trap to keep a young girl like that for himself, he must be, speaking just between the two of us, an idiot, but an idiot of idiots.

ALFRED. [*Discontent.*] Well, how smart you are today!

VATSLAV. I'm not afraid of that. But our guesses are futile; I want to send Justysia here to you, and I want you to try, please, to make her confident that you want to help smooth this affair over. Offer yourself to her as a friend in need. Tell her you'll even take responsibility for the letters, and . . . but you'll manage yourself to come to some agreement with her, and I, in the meantime, even if I have to get down on my knees, will beg my wife for peace for all of us. [*He goes out.*]

SCENE 8. Alfred [hurling the letters to the ground.]

May you . . . ! Believe women, be sincere, be faithful, every one of them'll make a fool out of you! [*Takes big steps around the room.*] A child . . . innocent . . . tender little words . . . Well, I ask you, except her—everyone of us was deceived: the wife by the husband, the husband again by the wife, I deceived both the husband and the wife and, best of all, the darling little thing deceived me, the mistress, and the master!

SCENE 9. Alfred, Justysia.

ALFRED. Lovely, Miss Justysia, beautiful, excellent! Why are your little eyes lowered? Why so humble? Those feigned gestures of yours no longer deceive me—I know your heart now, I know it only too well. I want to hear nothing, nothing can calm me! [*A short pause.*] What, you're not saying anything? You don't dare raise your head? You deceived me for someone else, and someone else will supplant him, faugh! For shame, my dear woman! Nothing blemishes a person more than flightiness, shrewdness, changeability and lack of feeling, and the image of all of these things is—you! [*Justysia, who until now has remained standing with lowered eyes and heard everything humbly, bursts out in a laugh looking at Alfred straight in the eye. Surprised, Alfred is a little confused.*] What is it?

JUSTYSIA. [*Laughing.*] Oh, how you amuse me when you're angry! But why are you giving me this sermon, why are you insulting me so?

ALFRED. Why are you deceiving me and Vatslav, false one? In one and the same day, almost in the space of an hour, aren't you telling both of us that you love us and us alone?

JUSTYSIA. Neither you nor him have I been deceiving. I tell him I love him, because I do love him sincerely.

ALFRED. And me, you ungrateful one?

JUSTYSIA. [*Laughing.*] As for you—I go mad!

ALFRED. You're laughing!

JUSTYSIA. Because you're not laughing. But this is not the time to waste time getting into arguments—we have to save the mistress from misfortune. How can we get rid of the obvious proof, those letters of yours, those unfortunate letters?

ALFRED. [*Takes his hat and wants to leave.*] What has that to do with me? You know how to deceive us, you should know how to cook something up, how to smooth the whole thing over! [*Turns around and speaks the first line in reflection, then afterward in growing anger.*] Say that the letters were written to you, that—the whole town is in love with you, the council, senate, the entire army, all the students, professors, philanthropists and doctors . . . that you received letters from all of them, that . . . tell them whatever you want, and if Vatslav doesn't believe what you say, let him ask me, and he'll find out everything! [*He wants to leave; Vatslav, who came in just in time to hear the last few lines holding Elvira by the hand, stops him.*]

SCENE *10. Elvira, Vatslav, Alfred, Justysia.*

VATSLAV. He has already found out. [*To Justysia.*] You, my dear miss, you found an equal who also deceived you. Your little love-intrigues, deceits, generous services—we know everything now, everything is out in the open now; and since you have a sincere calling for the monastery, your desire today shall be gratified.

JUSTYSIA. [*Weeping.*] I go to a monastery! I'd rather die twice instead! [*Goes out sobbing.*]

VATSLAV. Alfred, I don't wish to recall the insult I received from you in exchange for my faith; I know your answer in advance. But knowing you well, and since you know me well too, I want to end everything in as honorable a way as possible. Moreover, since I am certain you know how much I value honor, you won't interpret this as base timidity on my part. Elvira herself has confessed her error to me. Her reputation is dearer to me than my vengeance. I believe her grief, I excuse youth, and so I respect her. I shall not bring damage to myself.

ALFRED. Since I have acted so criminally against both of you,

I won't dare ask forgiveness. But although necessity separates us at this moment, you always have a friend in me forever. [*Goes out.*]

ELVIRA. [*Wanting to get down on her knees.*] Forgive me, Vatslav!

VATSLAV. [*Not allowing her to get on her knees before him.*] And you me! With your faith in me you'll find mine in you, and our mistakes, being a warning to both of us, may in time bring us peace.

END

Revised version of the tenth scene according to the edition of 1880:

SCENE *10 and Last. Vatslav, Alfred.*

VATSLAV. Elvira has confessed everything. She's guilty, but all the guilt cannot fall on her alone. I place the greatest part of it in our consciences. Alfred, insults of this kind usually end one way. I know what you're going to say, but I know at the same time—and you'll admit it—that some crazy urge was boiling in us today. But we have to forget about ourselves. We are obliged by our honor to protect from insult, from the insult of gossip, her who too trusting, living only by the faith of her heart, today became the sacrifice of our degradation.

ALFRED. I understand, and swear by all that's holy that as regards this matter your wish, whatever it be, will be law for me. [*They bow to each other coldly and leave in opposite directions.*]

END

LADIES AND HUSSARS

A Comedy in Three Acts

*Flattery has its own special flavor,
for even though someone pretends to
reject it, it still tastes good.*

ANDRZEJ MAKSYMILIAN FREDRO

INTRODUCTION

THE farce *Ladies and Hussars* is the best of Fredro's light works. It was written in 1825, not long after Fredro returned to Galicia from Italy where his brother Maksymilian's plan to interest him in the Russian Countess Eugenia Buturlin met with no success. Upon his return to Poland, Fredro hurled himself into literary activity, perhaps in this way to console himself for the frustration he continued to experience in his seemingly hopeless love affair with the Countess Skarbek. In a single year's time, he succeeded in producing six plays: *Outcasts and the Poet, Ladies and Hussars, The Letter, A Night's Stay in the Apennines, Nobody Knows Me,* and *Friends.*

Ladies and Hussars is set against the background of the war between the Duchy of Warsaw and Austria in 1809 that ended in the seizure of the Galician province by the army under the command of Prince Poniatowski. The soldiers who appear in the comedy were probably modeled on the hussars of the thirteenth cavalry regiment of the Duchy of Warsaw which was formed in the Lublin region in the second half of the year 1809. Its commander was Colonel Józef Toliński, who died in 1813, the chain of command then passing to Józef Sokolnicki. There are clear autobiographical reminiscences in *Ladies and Hussars.* We know, for example, that Fredro himself, a lieutenant at the time, was transferred on January 23, 1810, from the eleventh regiment of cavalry to this thirteenth regiment of "silver" hussars, as they were known. He remained with them a few months. The year 1809, the time of the action of *Ladies and Hussars,* also had a particular significance for Fredro. This was the year when at the young age of seventeen he donned a Polish military uniform and for the first time went off to war in what was to be one of the truly splendid adventures of European history— the Napoleonic campaigns. In the light of this, *Ladies and Hussars* may be considered, as the Polish scholar Stanisław Pigoń has stated, "an act of sentiment on the part of the au-

thor, a sincere though humorous payment of a debt of gratitude to his old regimental superiors and comrades-in-arms."[1]

One of the rare prose comedies of Fredro's early period as a
dramatist, *Ladies and Hussars* is a briskly paced situation
comedy in which the solidly masculine world of a group of
hussars on leave is temporarily disrupted by the sudden in-
vasion of the Major's three sisters and their sprightly maids
Fruzia, Zuzia, and Józia. The women have one purpose in
mind: to marry the old bachelor Major to his pretty young
niece, Zofia, Mrs. Orgon's daughter. The farce reaches its most
hyperbolic expression when Mrs. Orgon's plans for her brother
are echoed on the more ludicrous level of the Major's spinster
sister Aniela's attempt to lead the Captain to the altar and
the old soldier Gregory's wish that he were a Turk so that he
could marry Fruzia, Zuzia and Józia at the same time. The
aggressiveness and scheming of the ladies almost produce the
desired result—the total submission of the hussars—until the
Major discovers his own folly and sets the pattern for the Captain and Gregory who one after the other extricate themselves from the ladies' gossamer marriage net, finally leaving
the way clear for the conventional young lovers, Zofia and
the Lieutenant, to unite in wedded bliss.

The dialogue of the comedy is effectively lively and sharp
(as good farce demands) and the characterizations plausible
and well done, especially that of the Major. Much of the success of *Ladies and Hussars* derives from Fredro's technique—
used in other works as well—of heightening the humor of a
central character or situation by means of secondary characters
or situations in which the major patterns of development
are repeated on a lower level of comedy.

Until the twentieth-century editions of *Ladies and Hussars*,
there had been a minor discordant note in the comedy which
should be mentioned in passing. In the *dramatis personae* the
Hussars' chaplain is described as a Lutheran minister. Since
the great majority of Poles are Roman Catholics this may
come as something of a surprise. However, we must remember
that in Fredro's time the Austrian censorship frowned on the
presentation of Catholic clerics on stage. For this reason the

[1] Stanisław Pigoń, *W pracowni Aleksandra Fredry*, p. 101.

character was first transformed into a regimental physician. But there were still incongruities in the part. Only later (after 1860), the character's real function in the comedy was restored, though Fredro still could not present a Catholic chaplain and was forced into the expediency of making the chaplain a Lutheran.

In a review of the comedy in 1932, the critic Boy-Żeleński described *Ladies and Hussars* as "a masterpiece of scenic dialogue."[2] Since the play was written in prose, this quality fortunately does not suffer much in translation. The farce, therefore, may prove as appealing to English readers as it has been to Polish.

[2] Boy-Żeleński, *op.cit.*, p. 313.

CHARACTERS

MAJOR
CAPTAIN
EDMUND, *a lieutenant*
} *of a regiment of Hussars, on leave*

MRS. ORGON
MRS. DYNDALSKA
MISS ANIELA (Anielka)
} *the Major's sisters, each one older and stouter than the next*

ZOFIA (Zosia)   *daughter of Mrs. Orgon*

JÓZIA
ZUZIA
FRUZIA
} *the ladies' maids*

GREGORY
REMBO
} *old Hussars*

The scene is set in the country estate of the Major.

LADIES AND HUSSARS

ACT I

A large room. Four side doors, two in the rear. In the center a table covered with maps. On the right, a small table set up for chess. Near it and a little to the rear, chairs. In the rear, different firearms: spears, a target, and Turks' heads which are used for a carrousel.

SCENE 1. Major, Captain, Chaplain, Lieutenant, Rembo. In the center the Major is examining a gun; on the left the Lieutenant is loading another; on the right, the Captain, leaning on a gun, is looking at the figures on the chess board; near him sits the Chaplain, busy with a gun; Rembo is in the rear. All are in spencers, dressed for hunting, with military caps on.

MAJOR. Are you really sure? Sometimes you like to . . .

REMBO. I'd never dare deceive the Major. I'd sooner die first if I didn't see with my own eyes a buck and two does. All three came out at once to Shady Valley, where the cattle were, near the corner, where the stream is . . . you know, near the willow tree where the Chaplain missed the hare . . . then the dogs went right after them, first one, then the other: woof, woof! . . . Eh, Sir, how those does cleared off! Terrible! The earth nearly trembled . . .! Across Knob, Big Gourd, up along Bartek Stream . . .

MAJOR. Ho, ho, ho! . . . By now the does are on the other side of the world.

REMBO. They got scared of the wagons going along the highway, so off they went along the meadows way back into the glen.

MAJOR. Now we've got to head them off from the hills.

REMBO. I'll quietly let the dogs out from the oak grove, and each deer will fall on a gun like a spit.

MAJOR. Let's go, gentlemen! Even on leave I won't let you idle.

CHAPLAIN. Coming, coming.

LIEUTENANT. I'll catch up.

MAJOR. [*Taking a pipe from the center table and shaking his head, to Rembo.*] Call Gregory. [*Goes out.*]

CAPTAIN. [*To the Chaplain, looking at the chess board.*] I'll win if I withdraw the castle.

CHAPLAIN. I doubt it.

CAPTAIN. Bet.

CHAPLAIN. All right.

CAPTAIN. No one will bother us here. After we get back I'll convince you and pocket my dollar.

SCENE 2. The same, and Gregory, an old hussar with huge moustaches.

MAJOR. How many times, Gregory, have I told you to put everything back in its place. Why do you leave my pipe here on the maps? There's a special place for it over there in the closet. I hate disorder. [*Puts away his pipe and blows off the maps.*] See here, see here, didn't I tell you? A spot . . . and this bastion . . . à propos, where's the housekeeper?

GREGORY. They took her off at a trot. [*Goes out.*]

MAJOR. Thank God.

CAPTAIN. Well, the last woman has been cleared out of our house. For once it'll be quiet and peaceful.

MAJOR. She was a terrible talker.

LIEUTENANT. Because she was old, old.

MAJOR. Oho, Lieutenant, I know what you have in mind, but nothing will come of it. I prefer the roar of mortars to the babbling of women. Nothing will come of it, and I'll show you that even a soldier can keep house without a woman.

LIEUTENANT. Some order!

CHAPLAIN. Good, good.

CAPTAIN. First rate.

MAJOR. First rate.

LIEUTENANT. Did you always find it first rate, gentlemen? Was this woman's babbling always distasteful? [*Long silence.*]

MAJOR. Let's go hunting.

REMBO. [*Running in.*] Guests are coming up!

MAJOR. Some of our comrades.

REMBO. Not on your life! A few carriages—it's a regular parade. [*He goes out. One after the other the officers slowly approach the window.*]

MAJOR. For heavens' sake, a landau!

LIEUTENANT. And a coach.

CAPTAIN. And a wagon.

LIEUTENANT. [*With displeasure.*] Oh! Ladies!

MAJOR, CAPTAIN. [*Jumping back to the middle of the room.*] Ladies!

LIEUTENANT. [*Counting.*] One, two three . . .

MAJOR, CAPTAIN. [*Looking at each other woefully.*] Three!

LIEUTENANT. Four, five . . .

MAJOR. [*As above.*] Five!

CAPTAIN. [*As before.*] Five!

LIEUTENANT. Still one more . . .

MAJOR, CAPTAIN. [*Together.*] Six!

LIEUTENANT. Another one.

MAJOR, CAPTAIN. [*Together.*] Seven! Seven!

CHAPLAIN. [*Getting up.*] Seven!

[*Blocking his ears he sits down again and remains this way, leaning on the table, until the end of the scene.*]

LIEUTENANT. What do I see! [*Runs out.*]

CAPTAIN. [*Approaching the window timidly.*] What women! What hulks! What bags!

MAJOR. [*Approaching the window.*] Oh, those are my sisters.

CAPTAIN. I'm sorry.

MAJOR. Forget it, I know them quite well! [*Walks around the room all the faster.*] Sisters, sisters, women, but still I have to receive them . . . Gregory, my uniform . . . my uniform! Greg . . . ! The devil cooked this up . . . Greg, the uniform! [*Gregory goes after him with the uniform.*] I have to be glad to see them . . . My uniform, Greg . . . my uniform . . . ! I have to be happy, devil take them!

GREGORY. Put your uniform on, Sir.

SCENE 3. *Major, Captain, Chaplain, then Mrs. Dyndalska, Józia, Miss Aniela, Zuzia, Mrs. Orgon, Zofia, Fruzia, Lieutenant, Rembo.*
On the left side of the stage the Major absentmindedly puts his uniform on over his other clothes. Noticing it, he wants to remove it and at the same time pulls off the sleeve of the spencer. He is unable to get his arm free when Mrs. Dyndalska enters with two little dogs in her hands. After her comes Józia, with a basket of puppies and a few boxes in her arms. Near the Major, farther to the rear, stands the Captain, behind him the Chaplain. Gregory goes out with the uniform.

DYNDALSKA. How are you, brother? [*To Józia.*] Careful, dumb-bunny! Don't drop the puppies!
MAJOR. [*Confused.*] Greetings, greetings.
DYNDALSKA. [*To Józia.*] What are you holding them for? Put them down! [*To The Major.*] How have you been? [*To Józia.*] Why not on the table? What a stupid girl! [*Józia puts everything on the chess board and goes out. Dyndalska sits down. Aniela enters, and after her Zuzia with two cages— a magpie in one, a squirrel in the other—and with various other paraphernalia.*]
ANIELA. It's been ages, brother dear, since we've seen each other. [*To Zuzia.*] Put the cages down, what are you standing for?
MAJOR. Greetings, greetings.
ANIELA. [*To Zuzia.*] Where, where, where? Are you blind? What's the matter, isn't there a table here? [*Zuzia puts the cages on the maps and leaves. The Major stirs. The Captain holds him back by his coat.*]
MAJOR. [*Quietly to the Captain.*] The maps.
CAPTAIN. [*To the Major.*] Sh! [*The Major tries to conceal his displeasure, and looks from time to time at the maps. From off stage an uproar is heard and the shouting of women.*]
REMBO. [*Off stage.*] Don't move! A whip! Faugh! Get away!
ORGON. [*Entering backward and shaking her hands.*] Get away! Away! I'm fainting. [*Rembo comes in after her holding above his head a cat which Mrs. Orgon takes from him at*

the door.] Poor little Filun! My little darling! How he's trembling! Poor Filun! . . . Brother, how can you keep such ugly old dogs? They tangled my feet with some sort of chains and almost tore dear Filun to pieces.

REMBO. Howler and Yelper were both on the leash when they sniffed the cat, but then off they went after the thing! Straight into your ladyship! And Thumper and Thrasher . . . [*Leaves at a sign from the Major.*]

ORGON. Faugh, what names! The ugliest curs . . . I can hardly breathe—I'm all in a sweat. [*Sits down beside Dyndalska and Aniela. Behind Orgon, Zofia enters with the Lieutenant carrying a cage with a canary, which they hang in the rear, conversing in low tones. In the course of this scene, the girls take out the cat and dogs.*]

SCENE 4. *Orgon, Dyndalska, and Aniela sit in a row on the right side of the stage. On the left side opposite them stand the Major, the Captain and the Chaplain. In the rear are Zofia and the Lieutenant. The first door on the right leads to Mrs. Orgon's room; the first on the left to Mrs. Dyndalska's. The second door on the right to the Major's; the second on the left to the room of the Captain and the Chaplain. In the rear one door leads to Aniela's room, and through the other, people come on stage.*

MAJOR. Welcome, welcome in my home, sisters, and I beg the cat's pardon for the inhospitality of Yelper and the rudeness of Howler.

ORGON. See, brother, this is my daughter. [*Zofia approaches and bows.*] This is little Zofia . . . You surely didn't recognize her . . . She's grown up, become pretty, isn't it true? And I need not be ashamed for her upbringing either. In the greatest capital of the world she could converse without trouble, and not in one language . . .

CHAPLAIN. [*Aside.*] Not in one! Terrible!

ORGON. And she had a governess, a well-known person, and she spent half a year in the city acquiring the higher studies.

ANIELA. When she develops her talents . . .

DYNDALSKA. Oh, Aniela dear, what on earth are you saying!

She has already developed her talents: doesn't she sing the whole of Rossini so that everyone just has to listen to her? Doesn't she dance so that she never loses a beat? Doesn't she paint so that her flower fooled everyone and the Judge when he tried to sniff it got paint all over his nose?

ANIELA. That was the Referendary, not the Judge.

DYNDALSKA. But it was the Judge, my angel!

ORGON. Quiet, quiet. You don't have to praise her to her face! She'll show you herself what she knows.

ANIELA. [*To the Major.*] How do you like her? . . .

DYNDALSKA. [*Nudging her with her elbow.*] What a question!

ANIELA. You don't let me talk, sister dear.

DYNDALSKA. Because you talk nonsense, my dear.

ORGON. Quiet, quiet, sister. [*To the Major.*] Who are these gentlemen?

MAJOR. Captain Slavomir. Friendship united us already in our schooldays; we put on the uniform together, wore it together, and perhaps together we'll put it aside in one grave. Our honorable Chaplain, also an old comrade, a true friend of men; he does much, says little. One should follow his example. This is my Edmund, you already know him somewhat from my letter. In one unfortunate skirmish, when everyone was thinking just about himself, and I was lying wounded under a fallen horse, he looked for me, saw me, gathered a few stout fellows, fell on the enemy, and protected me with his own chest. He retreated, charged, again retreated, and again charged, until the increasing number of our men returned the victory to us. It was there, defending me, me, that he got this slash across the temple which is worth more than ten laurel wreaths. [*Embraces him affectionately.*]

ZOFIA. [*Involuntarily.*] Oh, it's beautiful to be courageous! [*She lowers her eyes at a quick glance from her mother and aunts.*]

ORGON. Good, now enough of that! Let's get down to business. I want to have a little talk with you, brother, if the gentlemen will permit . . . [*The officers leave and Zofia returns to her room at a sign from Orgon.*]

SCENE 5. *Orgon, Dyndalska, Aniela, Major.*

ORGON. In one brief word I'll tell you everything; I don't like an unnecessary introduction. A person with sense can easily grasp and understand something when it's put before him clearly. Therefore, without any introduction: it's best to say briefly what the matter is about, and later give reasons and arguments. Besides, I am so well read, I have lived so much in society, I have so much discretion and acuteness that I never make a mistake in judgment and perhaps only an insane person would contradict me. Proceeding then to the matter at hand, I shall say that having received the news that you were on leave and that you went to your country place, I guessed at once that you must be bored with military service and want to throw it up and settle in the country. A laudable idea, but for this you need . . .

DYNDALSKA. [*Rapidly.*] Permit me, dear sister, to interrupt you! If one wishes to convince a person, the shortest speech is not always the best. First you have to give the reasons which incline us to something, then hear the matter out from beginning to end, and finally give arguments in support of your stand. But before I enter into the real purpose, one has to glance at preceding events and the present situation. And since this is an affair of some weight, I shall divide it into chapters by means of which I shall convince your brother that [*counts on her fingers*]: until now he's had only the wrong things on his mind, that he's suffering great losses, that the military career is worth nothing, that the best thing is to settle down in the country, that I wisely advise . . .

ANIELA. Better, my dear, write a book about it, and now let me approach the matter by the simplest road . . .

ORGON. Talk, go on talk, if you like talking so much. Talk, I beg you. I shall say nothing. I know nothing. I understand nothing. Talk, you'll do me a favor.

DYNDALSKA. Oh, on the contrary, I shall remain silent. Let our dear sister expatiate, if a moment of silence is so painful to her. Or perhaps the eloquent Anielka will substitute for her.

ANIELA. Ah, if I dared but compare myself in eloquence to my beloved little sisters! I shall listen to the chapters or the second preface without a preface.

ORGON. Please speak, I beg you.

DYNDALSKA. Without ceremony, I beg you.

ANIELA. Speak, speak, I beg you.

ORGON, DYNDALSKA, ANIELA. I beg you.

ORGON. [*Going toward the doors.*] I won't hinder you.

DYNDALSKA. [*Likewise.*] I am leaving you.

ANIELA. [*Also.*] I am leaving.

ORGON, DYNDALSKA, ANIELA. [*Bowing several times from the doors.*] Speak, speak, please. I beg you. [*They leave.*]

SCENE 6. Major, Captain, Chaplain, Lieutenant. They enter one after another deep in thought and stand beside the Major, who from the beginning of the last scene has been standing motionless in the middle of the room. The Captain and Lieutenant are in uniform; the Chaplain in a long coat.

CAPTAIN. [*After a short pause.*] What's going on there?

CHAPLAIN. Aren't they ordering their carriages?

LIEUTENANT. With what command have the ladies honored us now?

MAJOR. Ra, ra, ra, ra, ra, ra—understand?

CAPTAIN. Who'd understand that?

MAJOR. I didn't understand it; my ears are just ringing.

CAPTAIN. However . . .

MAJOR. I know nothing.

LIEUTENANT. But . . .

MAJOR. Nothing, nothing, damn it! When one of them speaks, the other envies her—each one thinks herself wiser than the other. Even though it's always "just a word" there's no end to their jabbering, and what the whole thing is about it would take a wise man to figure out. Nevertheless, whether we understand it or not—we are obliged to receive them in a dignified way. Let's unite our endeavors. It's just unfortunate that we have no one here in the house who knows how to receive ladies.

LIEUTENANT. Aha, you see it's bad—there are no women around.

CHAPLAIN. No one to nag you.

CAPTAIN. A shame, nonetheless, that we got rid of the last one.

MAJOR. Hey! Gregory! Rembo! Everything will be all right soon. [*Rembo and Gregory come in. To Rembo.*] Have Kutasiński mount Baldie and ride after the housekeeper. And when he catches up with her, don't let the old woman babble or discuss anything, just have her ride back with him as soon as possible.

CHAPLAIN. It won't do, it won't do.

LIEUTENANT. [*Laughing, to Rembo.*] And have them return at a fast trot.

CHAPLAIN. But it won't do.

MAJOR. Why not? Don't our camp followers trot? [*To Rembo.*] Well, do as you want, just so long as [*looking at his watch*] you bring the housekeeper here by eleven. March! One thing taken care of. [*Rembo goes out.*]

CAPTAIN. This is all a trifle, but dinner, dinner, there's the rub! For let's not deceive ourselves with Kordesz's talent. It's true he's considered the best cook in the camp, but what does he know how to do well? Just between ourselves: hussar's roast and roast for a hussar.

CHAPLAIN. It won't do, it just won't do.

CAPTAIN. For the ladies we need different delicacies. We have to have some decoration for the table; something pretty, something light.

MAJOR. I know, I know what we have to have. Greg will take care of everything. He's been in different cities, on different estates, he's seen different kinds of cooking. Greg, Greg will make the cakes.

GREGORY. But . . .

MAJOR. And you, Edmund dear, will busy yourself, if you will, with the order of the dishes. That is, I hear, a matter of great weight now, whether the fish comes after the meat, or the meat after the fish. And Gregory—nobody's fool—will do it, although he doesn't know how.

GREGORY. But . . .

MAJOR. But you'll make the cakes.

GREGORY. But, Sir, for heaven's sake, I don't know how.

MAJOR. You'll do it. I order you, and *basta*. Now a second problem solved. We're getting along well.

CAPTAIN. We still have to have some kind of entertainment for the ladies at the table.

MAJOR. A little music—What do you say?

CAPTAIN. Certainly, we need something—but where can we get it?

MAJOR. Where? Gregory and Rembo play the bugle perfectly.

CHAPLAIN. It won't do, it won't do.

MAJOR. Oh, give us some peace, Chaplain. You and your "it won't do, it won't do."

CAPTAIN. But have mercy, Major, you'll frighten every last one of them out of your own home.

MAJOR. With what, with what, damn it? Don't they bugle waltzes perfectly? Just let the Chaplain beat time for them with his head, and you'll see how smoothly they'll play. But what an idea just came to me! . . . Excellent, superb! . . . You, you, Captain, must take care of this: under the window of the dining room . . . have them put . . . you know what? Guess! . . . a loaded mortar . . . As soon as I shout: Long live the ladies! Boom! From the mortar.

CHAPLAIN. Oh, on my honor, it won't do. [*Gets up.*]

LIEUTENANT. [*Getting up.*] That can't happen under any circumstances! This isn't an affair with soldiers.

MAJOR. [*Getting up.*] But I implore you . . .

LIEUTENANT. But consider, they're women.

MAJOR. He's a preacher, too! Bravo, bravo—women; I didn't know. Damn it, why is it these young gentlemen think that the old timers were never young themselves. As you live now, so we used to live before—and perhaps even better, and more vigorously for that matter. I ask you! Hm! Only they know how to get along with women. But I haven't spent my whole life slashing, and I did amuse myself with the ladies and always seemed to be able to please them. So, talk or no talk, I'm going to fire the mortar.

CAPTAIN. Perhaps it's safe. Although they'll be frightened a little bit, there certainly won't be any ill effects from their fright.

MAJOR. So it is, there won't be any ill effects.

CAPTAIN. And we have to have some amusement.

MAJOR. We have to have some amusement. [*To Gregory.*] Put the mortar under the window. March! But, but—I ask you, my dear Gregory, when you play your bugle, don't blow so loud, especially in the second part; on that broken note there's always such a shrieking in your bugle, it's awful to listen to it. Lightly—and look at the Chaplain. [*Gregory goes out.*]

SCENE 7. Major, Captain, Lieutenant, Fruzia.
Fruzia enters, curtsying on both sides. Only the Lieutenant returns the bow; the Chaplain turns around and goes out.

FRUZIA. My mistress sends her respects [*curtsying*] and begs you to come to her.

MAJOR. Who? The Lieutenant?

FRUZIA. No, the Major. [*Curtsies.*]

MAJOR. Why do you look at him when you speak to me? [*A short pause.*] Go, tell your mistress that this evening I shall be at her service. Only I beg you to leave us alone; I have no time now. [*Fruzia curtsies and goes out.*]

SCENE 8. Major, Captain, Lieutenant.

CAPTAIN. Why postpone it? Earlier, a little later, it's always waiting for you.

MAJOR. Ah, my dear fellow, it's good to have a whole day.

CAPTAIN. But this will then delay their departure.

MAJOR. That's true! I must get this unpleasant talk out of the way. Oh, you have no idea what a frightful thing it is.

SCENE 9. The same, Fruzia.

FRUZIA. [*Curtsying.*] My mistress wishes to speak with you now, not this evening, and she will be here in a little while.

MAJOR. Your mistress, I see, does not like to repeat her orders.

FRUZIA. Oh, she doesn't like to at all!

CAPTAIN. [*To the Lieutenant.*] There's no place for us here to-day, I see. Let's take a walk for a while or go riding . . .

MAJOR. Don't leave me alone! Go to the garden but be on call. [*They leave. A short dumb scene. The Major does not want to notice Fruzia who makes eyes at him flirtatiously. He turns around, twists his moustaches, hums. However, when he looks at her involuntarily, he turns around the moment their eyes meet. Finally Fruzia leaves at a sign from Mrs. Orgon who enters the room.*]

SCENE 10. Major, Mrs. Orgon.

ORGON. We are alone.

MAJOR. Yes, we are alone.

ORGON. I shall finish the matter in just a few words.

MAJOR. That's just what I need.

ORGON. I shall do the talking.

MAJOR. Yes, just you.

ORGON. Let us sit down. [*They sit down.*] Beginning from the beginning . . .

MAJOR. It wouldn't be possible to begin from the end?

ORGON. What a wild idea.

MAJOR. Very prudent, for I remember what I learned from our last conversation, and if now the same way . . .

ORGON. What a gabbler you've become with age, brother!

MAJOR. I'll keep quiet.

ORGON. I cannot get a word in edgewise.

MAJOR. I'm listening.

ORGON. Since you want to give up the service . . .

MAJOR. But I don't want to leave the service . . .!

ORGON. Why hide it?

MAJOR. I'm speaking sincerely.

ORGON. You want to settle in the country . . .

MAJOR. I don't have the slightest thought of it.

ORGON. Just stop disagreeing with me, or I'll never finish what I'm trying to say.

MAJOR. Then I'll just listen.

ORGON. You're acting very wisely, but you have to . . . you have to, well, in a word, you have to get married.

MAJOR. [*Starting.*] Are you out of your mind?

ORGON. My, how polite we are.

MAJOR. I meant to say: I'd have to be insane!

ORGON. Why?

MAJOR. Look at me, and you have your answer. Me, at this age, to take a young wife? What an idea, what an idea! I was never a friend of marriage, and especially now. In camp my hair went grey, a sword and horse were my sweethearts, and if I did fall in love from time to time, then it was in the hussar style: as long as everything went along well, it was love. And now I have to give myself over to amours? I'd have to be crazy, but the woman who'd have me would be still crazier.

ORGON. Then I shall say nothing more today.

MAJOR. Talk to the four winds if you want, talk on to Judgment Day, for all I care, but not about my getting married.

ORGON. Be patient for just a moment. All marriages aren't the same.

MAJOR. [*Aside.*] None of them are worth a damn.

ORGON. You don't know whom I intend as a wife for you.

MAJOR. I'm not interested.

ORGON. My Zosia.

MAJOR. That child?

ORGON. She is eighteen years old.

MAJOR. And I'm fifty-six. Four years older than you are.

ORGON. Without the accounting, if you please.

MAJOR. It's even possible that you're fifty-three.

ORGON. I see, I get back only insults for my good wishes.

MAJOR. For your good wishes I thank you, but I do not accept your project.

ORGON. Just think about it, you stubborn Major! A maiden, piously brought up in the country, her whole life will be devoted to you. She will love you, she will respect you more as a father than as a husband. And you yourself, surrounded by children . . .

MAJOR. Not at all, not at all.

ORGON. You will bless the moment you yielded to my plans. I beg you, don't despise the happiness being offered you.

MAJOR. I don't despise happiness, but I don't see happiness

in poisoning someone's youth with the infirmities of old age and making myself the laughing stock of a whole regiment of hussars.

ORGON. What a care! Just let any one of the whole regiment of hussars come across a nice pretty girl, and you'll see that it is one thing to advise someone else and another thing to act yourself. And that's why I ask you, brother, to end all consultations with this Captain of yours, with your Chaplain and with that slim little Lieutenant. Each one will dissuade you, and would himself marry three times over if he had the chance. Think it over then, but by yourself, I beg you! [*Goes out.*]

SCENE *11.*

MAJOR. A short reflection, very short. I have a head, thank God. [*Calls through the window.*] Come in, fellows!—I'll tell them. Why shouldn't I tell them? They'll laugh along with me. Me marry? Me! I'm trembling all over. A young wife! Ha, ha, ha! I'd be beginning a fine campaign! . . .

SCENE *12. Major, Captain, Chaplain, Lieutenant.*

MAJOR. Sit down. [*They seat themselves around the table.*] I've at last found out what it's all about. A trifle! What do you say—they want to marry me off.

ALL. Marry?

MAJOR. [*Laughing.*] That's all.

LIEUTENANT. To whom?

MAJOR. To Zosia, my niece.

CHAPLAIN. It won't do, it won't do.

LIEUTENANT. [*Aside.*] What do I hear? [*To the Major.*] And the Major?

MAJOR. Do you have to ask?

CAPTAIN. He doesn't want to, obviously.

MAJOR. I'd have to be insane.

CHAPLAIN. Bravo.

MAJOR. But I suspect that my dear sisters won't give up the idea so easily.

LIEUTENANT. They can't force you into it.

MAJOR. Of course. But I'd like to hear as little about it as possible.

CAPTAIN. Let them chatter, but we don't have to listen.

MAJOR. It's impossible not to listen.

CAPTAIN. They'll get tired of it in the end.

MAJOR. What—talking? You're joking, dear fellow.

LIEUTENANT. We have to think it over.

MAJOR. Just so long as I don't marry.

CHAPLAIN. It won't do.

CAPTAIN. I think so too.

LIEUTENANT. And so do I. But what does Zosia have to say about it?

MAJOR. I still don't know.

CAPTAIN. Then my advice is . . .

SCENE 13. The same, Mrs. Orgon, Zofia.

ORGON. What's this? A council of war? [*They all rise. Silence.*]

MAJOR. [*Quietly to the Captain who is standing next to him.*] Captain, tell her, please, that it simply is impossible.

CAPTAIN. [*The same to the Chaplain.*] Chaplain, tell her what you think.

CHAPLAIN. [*To the Captain.*] It won't do. Let the Major speak.

CAPTAIN. [*To the Major.*] Tell her that you don't want to.

MAJOR. We have decided . . .

ORGON. Certainly nothing good. [*Silence. Taking the Major aside.*] Let us remain by ourselves.

MAJOR. Thank you, but it's not necessary.

ORGON. If you gentlemen permit . . . [*They bow—the officers leave the room.*] Well, Major, now you and Zosia can . . .

MAJOR. But sister dear . . .

ORGON. I leave the two of you alone.

MAJOR. But . . . wait a moment . . . later . . .

ORGON. The matter must be finished. Zofia, listen . . .

MAJOR. [*Going in the direction of the doors.*] Please . . . in a moment . . . my nose is bleeding . . .

ORGON. But you'll return?

MAJOR. I'll return, I'll return. [*Goes out.*]

SCENE *14. Orgon, Zofia.*

ORGON. Please knock out of your head all the romances you
ever heard anywhere or may have read yourself by chance.
One marries for fortune, not for love. Your uncle is an honest man, and he has good property which certainly will fall
into other hands if he doesn't marry you.

ZOFIA. But mother dear, I have too good an opinion of him
to believe that he would want me against my will.

ORGON. What did you say—against your will? Does your
ladyship have a will other than that of your mother?

ZOFIA. I can fulfill yours, but it would be difficult to order
my heart to have the same wish.

ORGON. Not a word about hearts now!

ZOFIA. Anyway maybe he himself won't want it.

ORGON. He'll want it, just as you will. I know him well. He's
often given in to me just so as to avoid a quarrel.

ZOFIA. But mamma, why do you absolutely want this marriage?

ORGON. For your happiness.

ZOFIA. And if it will be my unhappiness?

ORGON. You're still too young to be able to see far ahead. A
mother should decide for her daughter.

ZOFIA. I am, however, in a position to know that his age is
not at all suited to mine.

ORGON. My how you do fret! Who would have thought it . . .
His age unsuitable . . . Some youngster, a scatterbrain,
would be more fitting for your ladyship?

ZOFIA. The person I liked would be the most suitable of all.

ORGON. Enough of this . . . not another word more . . . If you
don't marry the Major, then you know what's waiting for
you.

ZOFIA. Oh, mamma dear, what did I do to deserve this?
[*Weeps.*]

ORGON. Listen, Zosia, I love you, I sincerely want your happiness. Don't be a child and throw away the fortune that's
being offered you. My brother is of a gentle yielding character. A wife will do with him as she wishes. Only there's
no need to lose courage just because there are some difficulties at first. In the beginning every husband thinks only

about not being henpecked. He rages, puffs himself up, issues orders, everything has to be done as he wishes. For the first few weeks he has to be a dictator. But just have a little patience, a little patience. The constant battle and the constant guard over himself exhaust him, become distasteful to him. But a sensible wife, who knows what she's about, should never succumb and, always staying on the same road, taking a step at a time, slowly, slowly, but infallibly she'll reach her goal, and that is—to be mistress in her home and [*humbly*] to acknowledge her husband as master. I am leaving you now. Be sensible, be obedient to your mother, and you'll come out well. The Major will be here soon, try to make him like you [*patting her under the chin*] and remember that on your marriage depends your mother's happiness. [*Goes out.*]

SCENE 15. Zofia, later the Lieutenant.

ZOFIA. [*After a short pause.*] I think and think, and I just can't think up anything good. It's hard to oppose mother; I have to renounce happiness. Oh, Edmund! Edmund! Nothing will come of our love!

LIEUTENANT. [*Who has been waiting in the rear.*] Why such a sad prediction?

ZOFIA. It's good you've come. Advise me as quickly as you can . . . I beg you . . . advise me what to do, or we'll both perish.

LIEUTENANT. Perish, but why?

ZOFIA. Don't you know it's my mother's wish that I marry the Major?

LIEUTENANT. And if it is?

ZOFIA. Edmund, what kind of a question is that? Wasn't your declaration just a while ago sincere? Was it just to deceive my heart?

LIEUTENANT. Not one or the other. Your mother wants to give you to the Major, but I am just coming from him with the assurance that he loves you very much and because he loves you he is not thinking of marrying you and doesn't want to marry you.

ZOFIA. But that's still not the end of it.

LIEUTENANT. Zofia dear! Let's have hope; let's want to have it. From the moment I saw you here, some inexpressible feeling of happiness filled my soul. I meet you here, you, for whom I've been searching so long in vain.

ZOFIA. All the efforts of my father were in vain, too. He couldn't even find out which regiment the soldiers were from whom you were leading when you saved him from death and me from a most terrible disaster. In the last hour of life he remembered you with gratitude and he left it to me in a single bequest.

LIEUTENANT. More than gratitude, I won your love.

ZOFIA. The most sincere, and the most sacred, because it was blessed by my father's last wish.

LIEUTENANT. I don't claim any other rights.

ZOFIA. And can I forget . . .

LIEUTENANT. Zofia dear! Believe me . . . my actions seemed like the work of an angel to one who was just coming out of danger. But as a matter of fact it's hardly worthwhile recalling them. I regretted only that the oncoming enemy didn't allow me to guard the rest of your journey and that in all the confusion I wasn't even able to find out your name.

ZOFIA. On the journey my father was forced by sudden weakness to stay for several days in a forester's cottage. Three days after the passage of our army several hundred soldiers of all kinds were stationed in the village. Plundering began soon and reached such a degree of fury that houses were burnt for no reason at all. Dragged away from my father, I could see the roof catching fire when your voice struck my ear. It seemed to me just then that I was hearing the voice of a friend, and later, how many times I remembered you, always like some old friend. My heart was yours even before you approached it.

LIEUTENANT. Every officer, just as I did, would have returned to your father and ordered the fire put out. It's just my luck that it happened to me. Look, Zofia, here's the ribbon you dropped. From that time on it never left my heart. Without knowing where or who you were, I was faithful to it.

ZOFIA. God has accepted our vows separately, I see. But, Edmund, my mother knows nothing about this. Unfortunately my parents did not live together for the last ten years and it would be enough to tell her that it was her husband's wish to make her unyielding forever.

LIEUTENANT. Then let's not tell her anything about it just yet.

ZOFIA. Confide in the Major, let's ask his help.

LIEUTENANT. I could rely on his help if it were not for this. He's a sworn enemy of marriage, and even if he didn't oppose me, I would certainly lose his friendship and perhaps even his respect.

ZOFIA. What an unfortunate prejudice!

LIEUTENANT. On the other hand, I am certain that he will not be my rival, first because he fears an entire enemy squadron less than a wife, and second, because he has too noble a mind to want to be the cause of someone's unhappiness.

ZOFIA. But you know if I don't marry him, then Smętosz, an ugly man, a stupid, dirty old moneylender, is to receive my hand.

LIEUTENANT. Is it possible? That your mother . . .

ZOFIA. According to her a fortune is happiness, and besides, just between the two of us, she is a bit stubborn.

LIEUTENANT. That's bad, very bad. [*Thinks.*]

ZOFIA. However, they say God doesn't forsake lovers. Perhaps my mother will be softened by our prayers.

LIEUTENANT. [*After a short pause.*] No, let's not trust our fate to chance.

ZOFIA. What can we do?

LIEUTENANT. [*After a short pause.*] It's a hard thing to pretend, especially with friends, but when they have prejudices that are often unfounded like the Major's against marriage, sometimes an innocent deception is necessary. You have to announce to the Major that you wish to marry him.

ZOFIA. For God's sake! Then I will have to marry him.

LIEUTENANT. There's nothing to be afraid of, I promise. If your mother sees that you're not opposed to her plan, she won't lose hope of carrying it into effect and she'll drop Smętosz. But the Major, urged on more and more, will easily accept the carefully insinuated idea of extricating himself through me.

ZOFIA. Oh, that would be good!

LIEUTENANT. You try, however, to make him like you, for he won't fall in love but it will be good if he understands why I love.

ZOFIA. Then I have to . . .

LIEUTENANT. Be agreeable to your mother and friendly to the Major.

ZOFIA. You're certain he doesn't want to? . . .

LIEUTENANT. Ah, I'm as sure as you of my love and I of yours.

ZOFIA. Whatever the outcome, Edmund, Zofia's heart is yours forever.

LIEUTENANT. [*Kissing her hand.*] That assurance is already my happiness. But come, we have to tell your mother of the Major's answer. And you act according to our agreement. Let love and hope be our watchword!

ZOFIA. Until death!

ACT II

The same room. In place of weapons, opened boxes with pieces of clothing; ladies' head-dress; in place of a chess board, a mirror. On a Turk's head, a cap; on the target, a dress. Maps and cages have been removed. Off stage, the sound of bugling followed by a powerful explosion.

SCENE 1. Fruzia, followed by Józia, Zuzia.

FRUZIA. [*Rushing out.*] Józia, Józia! Zuzia! Józia, Zuzia!

JÓZIA. [*Running in.*] What?

ZUZIA. [*Running in.*] What's going on there?

FRUZIA. [*Running around the room.*] The ladies were terrified; they're going to faint.

ZUZIA. [*Running in the direction of the door.*] For heaven's sake!

JÓZIA. [*Toward the door.*] Maybe they've already fainted?

FRUZIA. [*Running out.*] There's no one here! There's no one here!

SCENE 2. *The Major leads Mrs. Orgon slowly into her room.
She is leaning on him. Zuzia is by her side, and Fruzia behind her. After waiting, the Captain similarly leads in Mrs.
Dyndalska with Józia; they go across to her room. A few moments later, the Lieutenant accompanied by Gregory, bugle
in hand, leads in Aniela and stands at the door. The Chaplain enters at the end with a napkin tied around his neck;
he stands in the middle of the room at the front of the
stage and remains there motionless for the rest of the scene.
Voices are heard from the rooms: "Water! Water! Water!"
Gregory rushes in and soon returns, a bugle in one hand
and a garden watering pot in the other.*

FRUZIA. [*At the door.*] Water! [*Gregory runs to her.*]
JÓZIA. [*At the door.*] Water! [*Gregory runs to her.*]
ZUZIA. [*At the door.*] Water! Quickly! [*Gregory runs out after
her.*] *The girls and the Lieutenant run across the stage in
different directions with bottles, glasses, etc., etc.*

SCENE 3. *Major, Captain, Chaplain, Gregory. The Chaplain
always in the same place with his arms folded; Gregory out
of breath in the rear.*

MAJOR. [*Mopping his brow.*] Who would have expected it!
CAPTAIN. [*Similarly.*] Who could have foreseen it!
MAJOR. It shouldn't have been placed right under the
window.
CAPTAIN. The shot was too powerful.
MAJOR. That's just it, too powerful; who fired it?
CAPTAIN. Gregory.
MAJOR. You probably gave it more powder, eh?
GREGORY. A little, only a little, Sir.
MAJOR. [*Walking around.*] A little! To him it means nothing!
A little! Now you see what a little caused.
CAPTAIN. [*Walking around.*] They wouldn't have been so
frightened.
MAJOR. [*Walking around.*] Yes, perhaps then only one would
have fainted.
CAPTAIN. [*Walking around.*] Yes one, or perhaps two.

MAJOR. [*Walking around.*] Yes, two, maybe three!

CAPTAIN. All three at once!

MAJOR. Three, three at once!

CHAPLAIN. Send for the doctor . . . have them bled.

CAPTAIN. Before he comes . . .

MAJOR. Better have Gregory bleed them.

CHAPLAIN. It won't do, it won't do.

GREGORY. [*Standing directly in front of the Major.*] Sir, I shall undertake it.

CHAPLAIN. That's out of the question.

MAJOR. But as long as he knows how . . . I saw myself—he bled my bugler once when he was struck by a horse; it's true, not right away, but still . . .

SCENE 4. The same and the Lieutenant.

LIEUTENANT. Our ladies have finally come to. Mrs. Orgon now has only spasmodic hiccoughs . . . Mrs. Dyndalska a slight colic . . . and Miss Aniela is trembling somewhat.

GREGORY. The Major's orders?

MAJOR. Not necessary now. [*Gregory goes out.*]

LIEUTENANT. Everything will be all right after they rest a few moments.

MAJOR. Thank God.

CAPTAIN. Let's have lunch.

FRUZIA. [*Comes in and curtsies before the Major.*] My mistress asks you, Sir, that you order the horses in the stable not to make such noise. They are stamping and neighing terribly, and that gets on my mistress's nerves. [*She goes out. The officers look at each other in silence.*]

CAPTAIN. It gets on her nerves.

MAJOR. Order the horses not to make noise . . . Gregory! [*Gregory comes in. The Captain and Major walk around.*] Lead the horses out of the stable.

GREGORY. Where to?

MAJOR. Wherever you want—let them graze. [*Gregory goes out; Józia comes in.*]

JÓZIA. [*Curtsying before the Major.*] My mistress asks that you order all cannons, guns, and swords taken out of the house because she is afraid of a new accident and is unable to sleep. [*Józia goes out—A moment of silence.*]

CAPTAIN. Take out the cannons.

MAJOR. And the swords . . . Gregory! [*Gregory comes in.*] Gather the weapons and take them up to the attic. [*Gregory goes out; Zuzia comes in.*]

ZUZIA. [*Curtsying before the Major.*] My mistress asks that you have incense burnt under her window because the gun powder smells terrible and makes her chill worse. [*She goes out—A moment of silence.*]

MAJOR. Gregory!

CAPTAIN. What do you want? [*Gregory comes in.*]

MAJOR. Order incense burnt.

CAPTAIN. Outdoors?

CHAPLAIN. Goodbye!

MAJOR. Where are you going?

CHAPLAIN. I'm going away.

CAPTAIN. You're leaving us?

CHAPLAIN. I can't take it any longer.

CAPTAIN. Then I'm going too.

MAJOR. Then take me along with you too!

LIEUTENANT. But, my dear fellows, do you want to leave the ladies here alone?

MAJOR. They'll get along all right by themselves.

LIEUTENANT. But they won't let you go.

MAJOR. Shhh! [*Quieter.*] We have to get away secretly.

CAPTAIN. [*Softly.*] We have to escape secretly.

CHAPLAIN. Let's escape.

MAJOR. [*Quietly to Gregory.*] Saddle up the horses.

LIEUTENANT. Major, Captain! . . .

MAJOR. Pst . . . let's gather . . .

CAPTAIN. And off we go! [*They walk on tip-toes to their rooms.*]

LIEUTENANT. [*Alone.*] That's just lovely! I can't leave . . . I won't stay behind alone . . . what am I to do? I have to stop this flight of theirs. If I could just . . . [*He goes to Zofia's door and opens it slowly; at a sign from Zofia he enters.*]

SCENE 5. Lieutenant, Zofia.

LIEUTENANT. Zofia, there's trouble.

ZOFIA. What's the matter?

LIEUTENANT. The Major, Captain, and Chaplain, frightened by what's happened and still more afraid of what may be ahead, have decided to run away.

ZOFIA. What? They want to run away?

LIEUTENANT. Just that, secretly. Go, tell your mother. Only don't say that you know about it from me. I am also supposed to take off with the rest of them.

ZOFIA. How can my mother help?

LIEUTENANT. She'll think of something, only go and tell her. [*They go out on opposite sides. The Major, the Captain and the Chaplain leave very cautiously and move on their tiptoes; portmanteaus under their arms and their swords attached. They signal to each other to be silent, and having come together in the middle of the room they go out slowly looking around on all sides. Fruzia, followed by Józia and Zuzia, run across the stage from door to door as in the second scene.*]

SCENE 6. Mrs. Orgon, Mrs. Dyndalska, Aniela, Fruzia, Józia, Zuzia. The ladies run out of their own rooms; a maid behind each one, finishing their dressing. They stop breathless at the front of the stage close together in a circle. Not one of them is able to speak. A moment of silence.

DYNDALSKA. [*Gasping.*] They want to run away!

ANIELA. Run away!

ORGON. Run away! . . . away!

DYNDALSKA. Don't let them!

ORGON. Run, sister!

DYNDALSKA. Jump, Aniela!

ANIELA. [*To the girls.*] Run!

ORGON. Wait! Ask . . . Tell the Major to come here . . . Don't leave him alone for a moment—run!

SCENE 7. Mrs. Orgon, Mrs. Dyndalska, Aniela seated.

ORGON. An unheard-of thing!

ANIELA. Unbelievable.

DYNDALSKA. A trick of his advisers.

ORGON. Couldn't be otherwise! He himself wouldn't dare.

DYNDALSKA. I wouldn't trust the Captain.

ORGON. And the Chaplain.

ANIELA. Or the Lieutenant either.

ORGON. He doesn't count for anything.

ANIELA. Don't believe him, sister.

ORGON. I give you my word on that. He'll neither help nor hinder. Whether he's here or not, it's all the same. But those old ones, those old ones, as soon as they begin to move their moustaches, one would jump into the fire after the other.

DYNDALSKA. As long as they are with him, our efforts are in vain. We talk, and talk, but one of his fellows shakes his head and it's all over.

ORGON. The Captain is the most dreadful of all.

ANIELA. In that case . . . I'll sacrifice myself for the sake of all of you: I'll marry him.

DYNDALSKA. But he has a head, angel.

ANIELA. And wit . . .

ORGON. Let her try to make him like her . . . she'll either captivate him or frighten him; in any case, it will be a good thing.

ANIELA. I want to help you in spite of your sneers and you'll see what I can do.

ORGON. We have to soften up the Major.

DYNDALSKA. We won't let him breathe.

ORGON. Not for a moment! When we wear him down, then he'll agree to everything. I know him well.

DYNDALSKA. We'll set the Chaplain at odds with the two of them.

ORGON. We'll annoy him as much as possible.

DYNDALSKA. A word cleverly slipped in often divides the best of friends.

ORGON. I'll take that on myself; I am relying on your support.
ANIELA. Here's the Major.

SCENE 8. Mrs. Orgon, Mrs. Dyndalska, Aniela, Major, and the girls. Fruzia enters with a serious mien, the Major after her, followed by Józia and Zuzia; they remain at the door, giggling among themselves. A moment of silence. At a signal from Mrs. Orgon the girls go out.

ORGON. Welcome home from your trip. [*The Major bows.*]
DYNDALSKA. [*After a short pause.*] Where did you go, brother?
MAJOR. I wanted to go horseback riding.
ORGON. Horseback riding?
MAJOR. Horseback riding.
ORGON. So, just to take a little ride?
MAJOR. Just a little ride.
ORGON. And to return?
MAJOR. [*With a sigh.*] And to return.
ORGON. Quickly?
MAJOR. Yes . . . that is . . . I don't know . . . because . . .
ORGON. Why pretend? It's better to tell the truth.
MAJOR. You're right, I don't know how to pretend and I don't want to. [*They get up.*]
ORGON. Then you wanted to go away from us?
MAJOR. I wanted to.
ORGON. And leave us alone?
MAJOR. Leave you alone.
ORGON. Secretly?
MAJOR. Without saying goodbye.
ORGON. You've reached this degree of impoliteness.
MAJOR. You're wrong; it wasn't impoliteness.
ORGON. Only hospitality.
MAJOR. Nothing else.
ORGON. In an entirely new way; leave guests behind at home . . .
MAJOR. I thought that you'd be better off without me. I confess, I don't know how to receive ladies and with the best of intentions I could cause great harm on account of my ig-

norance. Already once because of me you fainted; who can swear that you won't die if I try to honor you still further? Could I guess that horses increase a person's spasms, that powder aggravates chills, and swords the colic? And how am I supposed to know what you need and what you don't need?

ORGON. You would know everything if you were happy about our being here. But, alas, your sisters who love you . . . who have not seen you for a long time . . .

DYNDALSKA. Pining to embrace their brother . . .

ORGON. In spite of all the trouble, they take themselves off to see you . . .

DYNDALSKA. Over a most uncomfortable road . . .

ANIELA. We got stuck twice.

MAJOR. [*With a sigh, aside.*] Oh, who pulled you out to my grief?

ORGON. We came because we are concerned about your happiness . . .

DYNDALSKA. Anxious about your welfare . . .

ORGON. And how do you receive us?

ANIELA. You want to throw us out.

ORGON. You run away from us.

DYNDALSKA. Without any regard for our weak health . . .

ORGON. Our shattered nerves . . .

DYNDALSKA. That's a brother's love!

ORGON. Such gratitude! Ah, it hurts! [*She begins to weep.*]

MAJOR. But, my dear sister . . .

DYNDALSKA. Ingratitude—and from a brother! [*She begins to weep.*]

MAJOR. [*To Dyndalska.*] But, sister dear . . .

ANIELA. He spurns our hearts! [*She begins to weep.*]

MAJOR. But sister . . .

ORGON. Be helpful here! Oh! Oh!

DYNDALSKA. Oh! Oh!

ANIELA. Oh! Oh!

DYNDALSKA. [*Throwing herself into a chair.*] Colic!

ANIELA. [*Likewise.*] I'm weak!

ORGON. [*Likewise.*] Spasms!

MAJOR. Just don't faint, for God's sake! [*Silence.*] They're fainting—what can I do? Hey! Is anyone there? . . . Water! Vodka! Vinegar! . . . Have they gone deaf . . . Gregory! Gregory! [*Returns to them.*] They're fainting! What to do? . . . Gregory, fire the mortar! [*They all start.*]

ORGON. Don't shoot, don't shoot!

DYNDALSKA. For God's sake, don't shoot!

ANIELA. I'm already a little better.

MAJOR. My dear sisters, speak, do what you want, only don't faint, or damn knows what . . .

ANIELA. Oh, shame! What nasty language!

MAJOR. You see, Ma'm, that I don't know how to receive ladies or how to talk to them. However, I'll do what you ask, except get married. That's one order I can't carry out. [*Dyndalska and Aniela, to whom Orgon was whispering, go off to their rooms.*]

SCENE 9. *Orgon, Major.*

ORGON. Who wants to force you into marriage? Who's dragging you to the altar? Everything depends on your will, after all, and we ask of you only a little politeness. Stay with us a few days, believe that we are advising you sincerely, don't listen to your colleagues and try to get to know Zofia.

MAJOR. What good will it all do?

ORGON. Say at least one word to her. Why do you despise the poor child so mercilessly! The poor thing's crying can't be stopped.

MAJOR. Crying again; but all of you . . .

ORGON. Here she is now . . . [*Zofia comes in.*] I am leaving the two of you alone. I expect that you'll like each other. [*To the Major, aside.*] Have regard for her youth! [*To Zofia, aside.*] Be wise, your future's at stake!

SCENE 10. *Major, Zofia.* [*A moment of silence.*]

MAJOR. Young lady . . .

ZOFIA. Uncle dear.

MAJOR. [*More gently.*] My little miss . . .

ZOFIA. What do you wish?

MAJOR. [*More gently.*] My dear little Zosia . . .

ZOFIA. I'm listening.

MAJOR. [*Aside.*] The devil cooked up such an affair! [*To Zofia.*] Certainly . . . doubtless . . . evidently . . . you know that . . . this . . . that is, as regards your mother's intention . . . as regards . . .

ZOFIA. I know.

MAJOR. What do you say about it?

ZOFIA. I, nothing.

MAJOR. Speak openly.

ZOFIA. I am speaking openly. [*Aside.*] The first lie.

MAJOR. Nothing then?

ZOFIA. Nothing.

MAJOR. [*Aside.*] Strange thing! [*To Zofia.*] Doesn't it disturb you a little, however?

ZOFIA. Not in the least.

MAJOR. I can see by your eyes.

ZOFIA. You are mistaken, uncle dear.

MAJOR. Mistaken? [*Aside.*] Strange thing! How can I tell the poor thing: I don't want you? A devilish state of affairs! [*To Zofia, after a short pause.*] My dear girl, I want us to understand each other.

ZOFIA. And that's the one thing I want too.

MAJOR. For the good of both of us.

ZOFIA. [*Aside.*] Ah, Edmund, Edmund, what a hard role you've given me to play.

MAJOR. I am sincerely interested in your fate.

ZOFIA. [*Aside.*] And I have to deceive him!

MAJOR. Tell me then—do you want to get married?

ZOFIA. Yes I do.

MAJOR. To me?

ZOFIA. [*After a moment's hesitation, softly.*] Yes.

MAJOR. That's bad.

ZOFIA. Why?

MAJOR. Why?

ZOFIA. Yes, why is it bad?

MAJOR. It seems to me that you can guess why easily.

ZOFIA. Not at all.

MAJOR. At least you see nothing good in it?

ZOFIA. On the contrary.

MAJOR. On the contrary? [*Aside.*] Strange thing! [*To Zofia.*] It seems to me that you would not be happy.

ZOFIA. That will depend on you.

MAJOR. Oh, that depends not only on my will, but on many, many circumstances.

ZOFIA. It's difficult to foresee them.

MAJOR. To some extent we can, my dear, to some extent. I've never fathomed what constitutes real happiness in marriage; I believe, however, that two people should match each other like a pair of horses—the same gait, the same turn, the same fire. Then one rides well and there's less fatigue. But when one is fast and the other lazy, one soft, and the other hard, one pulls, and the other jumps—then there's the devil to pay! Isn't it the truth, Miss? Tell me now, if we were to get married, which pair of horses would we resemble? The first pair or the second? Probably the second: you'd run, while I stumbled along; you'd be jumping, while I was already panting. Laugh, laugh: it's better to laugh than to act stupidly!

ZOFIA. It wasn't the idea, but the comparison that amused me a little.

MAJOR. Then without any comparison. You're young, you like to enjoy yourself, and it's good that you do, for this is the time for it. You need, then, a husband who would also like to have a good time, who would take you for walks, to parties, to dances, to the theater, who would play for you at night on the fife somewhere near a stream, somewhere by the light of the moon, as they describe it in those romances of yours. But I, my dear, am not for that; during the day I'm busy with my service duties, in the evening I smoke my pipe, and at night I snore until the windows rattle.

ZOFIA. Must one look only for pleasure and amusement in marriage? Is youth eternal, so that we should forget about older age? Do honesty, kindness, and steadiness of character count for nothing in the person with whom we have to pass the spring as well as the winter of our life? Men can win our hearts only by manly virtues. A husband's good repute is also his wife's, and steady peacefulness is the only real happiness as far as I am concerned.

MAJOR. Very sound, very very sound! But with all this, my age . . .

ZOFIA. The age of experience.

MAJOR. A few ailments . . .

ZOFIA. Who is without them?

MAJOR. My faults . . .

ZOFIA. Who has none?

MAJOR. I feel myself that I could be more polite, more friendly in society. It will be difficult for me to change; I can't beat around the bush.

ZOFIA. That proves your frankness.

MAJOR. Sometimes this soldier's frankness is painful.

ZOFIA. Not at all.

MAJOR. Not at all? [*Aside.*] Strange thing! A young, pretty and intelligent girl . . . strange thing! [*To Zofia.*] But, my dear, not speaking of you, very many girls marry in order to win their freedom . . . freedom . . . Do you understand it, as I do? If I'm not created to be a husband, the less was I created to be the sort of person who'd endure certain pranks.

ZOFIA. Excessive freedom, freedom without limits I do not desire, but I also do not expect to find bondage in marriage; there should be mutual obligations on both sides.

MAJOR. Very sound. [*Aside.*] And she wants to marry me . . . strange thing! [*To Zofia.*] With all of this . . . I think . . . that it would be necessary . . .

ZOFIA. [*Laughing.*] Don't hesitate, don't hesitate, uncle dear.

MAJOR. [*Aside.*] Sound! . . . She wants to marry me, it would hurt me to grieve her. [*To Zofia.*] But you see, my dear Zofia, that . . .

ZOFIA. Why look for reasons? You still don't know me well, uncle . . . that's enough . . . but you can get to know me better . . . Let's leave it to time, then, and I hope to gain by it.

MAJOR. That won't be difficult for you, Zofia dear.

ZOFIA. Really?

MAJOR. [*Approaching.*] With those eyes of yours.

ZOFIA. We're not talking about that.

MAJOR. [*Drawing close to her.*] With that little mouth.
ZOFIA. Oh, please . . .
MAJOR. [*Taking her by the hand.*] With this little hand.
ZOFIA. Oh, Major!
MAJOR. [*Embracing her.*] With this figure, with these . . .
ZOFIA. For God's sake! What are you doing?
MAJOR. I'm surprised myself.
ZOFIA. I should expect so . . .
MAJOR. Expect what you like.
ZOFIA. [*Tearing herself loose.*] Oh, enough of this! . . .
MAJOR. Still too little . . . [*Zofia runs off to her room.*]

SCENE 11.

MAJOR. [*Straightening himself.*] Oh! Oh! She's run away from
me! [*Walks around straightening himself.*] I've become
young again, I've become young again . . . 'pon my word,
I feel that I've become young again . . . and no wonder: a
charming girl, a pretty girl! And sensible! She's dying to
marry me! . . . And if I did marry? . . . Let it be as she wishes
. . . No, not that. Let it not be as she wishes . . . But I . . .
only that it . . . then again on the other hand . . . but however . . . after all, in case . . . Ah, devil take it, it's bad! What
am I to do?

SCENE 12. Major, Dyndalska.

DYNDALSKA. Well, brother dear, how are things coming along?
MAJOR. Fair, fair.
DYNDALSKA. Zosia confused, you sunk in thought; a good sign.
MAJOR. Not a bad sign, that's true.
DYNDALSKA. How did you like her?
MAJOR. A pretty girl, there's no denying it.
DYNDALSKA. There, you see.
MAJOR. She's pleasant.
DYNDALSKA. You see.
MAJOR. And good.
DYNDALSKA. You see.
MAJOR. Sensible.

DYNDALSKA. Didn't I tell you so?

MAJOR. Very sensible.

DYNDALSKA. Everybody knows that.

MAJOR. She's dying to marry me.

DYNDALSKA. Dying to.

MAJOR. That's not bad.

DYNDALSKA. Very good.

MAJOR. But on the other hand . . .

DYNDALSKA. There is no other hand . . . You liked her?

MAJOR. Liked her? I should say so.

DYNDALSKA. Well then, marry her.

MAJOR. Marry her, it's easy to say.

DYNDALSKA. What's preventing you?

MAJOR. What's preventing me?

DYNDALSKA. For example?

MAJOR. You guess.

DYNDALSKA. I don't want to guess.

MAJOR. Fifty-six years.

DYNDALSKA. A trifle.

MAJOR. Her eighteen years.

DYNDALSKA. A trifle.

MAJOR. Bad consequences.

DYNDALSKA. Trifles.

MAJOR. Oh, devil take your trifles!

DYNDALSKA. Women age quickly.

MAJOR. Well, that's true.

DYNDALSKA. Zosia is eighteen years old?

MAJOR. Eighteen.

DYNDALSKA. In ten years she'll be twenty-eight.

MAJOR. That's true.

DYNDALSKA. In fifteen years—thirty-three.

MAJOR. True.

DYNDALSKA. And no longer young.

MAJOR. That's true.

DYNDALSKA. What is the great difference between you then?

MAJOR. Well now.

DYNDALSKA. Well, now, none.

MAJOR. There's no denying it.

DYNDALSKA. Very small. And besides you're not fifty-six.

MAJOR. But I am, I am.

DYNDALSKA. But you're not.

MAJOR. I certainly must know.

DYNDALSKA. But I am telling you that you're not.

MAJOR. You're mistaken, mistaken.

DYNDALSKA. But I am not mistaken.

MAJOR. I have a certificate.

DYNDALSKA. It means nothing. Aniela is forty, I'm almost forty-three, Orgon is going on forty-six, and you're four years older than she is, which means that you are fifty; simple.

MAJOR. Perhaps a mistake in the certificate.

DYNDALSKA. Of course.

MAJOR. Well, fifty, that's something else.

DYNDALSKA. And besides, tell me, have you never come across a happy marriage where the people were of different ages?

MAJOR. Of course I have. Just recently Mr. Radoslav married a young woman.

DYNDALSKA. And he's satisfied?

MAJOR. Satisfied.

DYNDALSKA. Happy?

MAJOR. Happy . . . only they say that his own secretary . . .

DYNDALSKA. Secretary, secretary; but you don't have a secretary.

MAJOR. That's true. Ah! Mr. Fontaziński and his young little wife for the past three years . . .

DYNDALSKA. Are getting along all right?

MAJOR. All right, but the devil take it, I forgot—last year he had to get divorced and pay for the divorce himself.

DYNDALSKA. But you're hunting for examples . . .

MAJOR. Young Radost, who got married for an annuity . . .

DYNDALSKA. Is living happily.

MAJOR. He lived happily enough, but he soon went mad and they had to lock him up.

DYNDALSKA. Why look further? You know how old the late Dyndalski was when I married him. However, as God is my witness, he never had any reason to complain about me.

MAJOR. That's true. But your late husband was always like a late husband; you used to do just what you wanted.

DYNDALSKA. Honest soul! For that matter, he wanted it that way. But if you want it, your wife will also do what you want. Everything depends on the arrangement.

MAJOR. That's true, there's no denying it . . . everything depends on the arrangement.

DYNDALSKA. I'll go then . . .

MAJOR. But wait a moment . . .

DYNDALSKA. Rely on me.

MAJOR. But . . .

DYNDALSKA. Be calm.

MAJOR. At least . . .

DYNDALSKA. The matter is closed.

MAJOR. Let it remain between us for now, I have to first . . .

DYNDALSKA. Get the opinion of your colleagues.

MAJOR. Of course.

DYNDALSKA. Unnecessary.

MAJOR. Oh, please . . .

DYNDALSKA. So be it. [*Aside.*] Let's not lose time. [*She goes out.*]

SCENE 13. Major. [Alone.]

MAJOR. Well, when anyone says anything sensible to me, then I know how to give in, I'm not stubborn. I don't consider it bad just because I don't want to confess that up to now I've been wrong . . . Dear girl! . . . But what will they tell you? . . . Hm, hm, hm . . . Dear girl! . . . Here they are now: a little bothersome, to tell the truth.

SCENE 14. Major, Captain, Chaplain, Lieutenant.

MAJOR. [*With a forced smile.*] They're dying to marry me off; but I tell you, simply dying to.

CAPTAIN. They think that they've struck on someone with whom they can do as they wish, whom they'll be able to lead around by the nose [*the Major scowls*] wherever they want to.

LIEUTENANT. Don't let them crack their skulls for nothing. But they can stay here with us, if they want to.

MAJOR. I am fifty years old . . .

CAPTAIN. [*To the Lieutenant.*] Certainly they can, because it'd be hard to unseat them even with mines.

MAJOR. She's an entirely sensible girl . . .

LIEUTENANT. [*To the Captain.*] We don't even have to deprive them entirely of the hope of achieving their goal. Let them slowly figure it out for themselves.

MAJOR. [*With a forced smile.*] She's determined to marry me.

CAPTAIN. She doesn't show much sense.

MAJOR. I am fifty years old.

LIEUTENANT. [*To the Captain.*] Who knows what's forcing her; perhaps her mother's order . . . maybe a desire of becoming useful to her . . .

MAJOR. They are dying to marry me off.

CHAPLAIN. It won't do, it won't do.

CAPTAIN. But everyone knows that.

MAJOR. She's very sensible.

CAPTAIN. So she's sensible, sensible; as though the only thing that mattered was common sense.

MAJOR. Well, good sense is not such a small thing, to tell the truth.

CAPTAIN. Then you do want to get married?

MAJOR. I still haven't said so.

CAPTAIN. Still? But in time . . . ?

MAJOR. Everything must be weighed . . . everything depends on the arrangement . . . I am fifty years old.

LIEUTENANT. [*Aside.*] What kind of a change is this? I'm trembling, it can't be! [*To the Major.*] Don't joke with us, Major; we know you too well. The Captain is getting excited for nothing; I wager my neck that you'll never commit such madness.

MAJOR. Madness! Madness! I ask you to be more polite, Lieutenant! . . . Madness!

CHAPLAIN. The Lieutenant speaks well. My good Major, my good Major . . .

MAJOR. My good Chaplain, my good Chaplain, talk faster or don't talk at all.

CAPTAIN. Then you are getting married?

MAJOR. Marry or not marry, no one has the right to call my actions madness, and that's that.

CHAPLAIN. But it won't do . . .

MAJOR. Who's going to teach me what will do or won't.

CHAPLAIN. Do as you wish. [*Goes out.*]

LIEUTENANT. [*To the Chaplain.*] Wait a moment, we'll go together! I'd like just a word with you. [*To the Major.*] You're speaking sincerely, without jokes?

MAJOR. I don't have to give an account of myself to anyone. [*The Lieutenant goes out with the Chaplain.*] Hm, madness! madness! What a man for advice!

SCENE 15. Major, Captain.

CAPTAIN. You have no reason to get angry; you wanted advice, take it as it's given.

MAJOR. Advice is one thing, rebuke another. If up to now I've had a false image of marriage, I don't see the necessity of my holding it until death. The military profession is a fine thing, but it is possible for it to become distasteful in time. Freedom, freedom we always talk about, but we're always under orders and in the end there's no one to put a pillow under your head when you're old and sick. And what is so terrible about having a pleasant, fine, good, young person always around you, who thinks about you, who comforts you, strokes you, fondles you; what is really so terrible about it? And just because I'm not stubborn, I'm supposed to be mad! Mad? Mad is the person who thinks otherwise. Right?

CAPTAIN. Not right.

MAJOR. Not right?

CAPTAIN. Not right.

MAJOR. Goodbye.

CAPTAIN. Your servant. [*The Major goes out.*]

SCENE 16. Captain. [Alone.]

CAPTAIN. Three of them came at once, with cats, pug-dogs, magpies, monkeys, and as soon as they began their tyr-tyr-tyr, tur-tur-tur, tyr-tyr-tyr- they turned a wise man into a fool. He wants to get married, and married to a child! If he

absolutely decided to get married, let him at least find someone more mature . . . Only . . . hm, hm, hm . . . [*Sits down.*]

SCENE *17*. *Captain, Aniela.*

ANIELA. I am happy to find you here, Sir. How can you be so
calm, being a friend of the Major? How can you agree to
this marriage of his?
CAPTAIN. [*After a short pause, confused.*] I don't agree.
ANIELA. But you do not try to dissuade him from this mad
idea.
CAPTAIN. I can't forbid it.
ANIELA. Does he have to change his way of life? Let someone
tell me.
CAPTAIN. Of course not.
ANIELA. What could be more pleasant than the military life.
CAPTAIN. Of course.
ANIELA. He enjoys the present and doesn't worry about the
future.
CAPTAIN. Of course.
ANIELA. Subject only to his own sense of duty.
CAPTAIN. My own merits speak for themselves; I need no one's
favor.
ANIELA. Never alone, never forsaken.
CAPTAIN. Always in the company . . .
ANIELA. Of experienced friends. What better way to get to
know a person than in hardship, in grief, in danger?
CAPTAIN. That's true.
ANIELA. High-blown words count for nothing in the army.
CAPTAIN. Ho, ho!
ANIELA. There one has to *act*.
CAPTAIN. As befitting a man.
ANIELA. And a good soldier; bad or good—but always straight-
forward.
CAPTAIN. By the straight road, simply and boldly.
ANIELA. Never to be afraid.
CAPTAIN. Even of the devil himself!
ANIELA. Oh! [*Thinks better of herself.*] Oh, yes, yes! . . . Happy,

happy is the one who's chosen such a life! Ah, if I weren't a woman, I'd be a soldier my whole life.

CAPTAIN. I say! [*Aside.*] A woman of parts.

ANIELA. Even once the thought occurred to me, but that was some time ago, of concealing my sex, putting on a uniform and joining a regiment of hussars.

CAPTAIN. A regiment of hussars, and concealing . . . [*Aside.*] A rare woman.

ANIELA. But I would want to serve only in the cavalry.

CAPTAIN. In the cavalry?

ANIELA. I love horses so.

CAPTAIN. You like horses?

ANIELA. Madly.

CAPTAIN. A proof of good sense.

ANIELA. I even go riding myself.

CAPTAIN. You ride? [*Aside.*] What a woman!

ANIELA. What a pleasure it is to mount a good steed, one still young, a little wild . . .

CAPTAIN. [*With mounting excitement.*] To teach him how to walk correctly.

ANIELA. Slowly . . .

CAPTAIN. Patiently, as with a child.

ANIELA. Then, a little more lively . . .

CAPTAIN. But cautiously.

ANIELA. To trot . . .

CAPTAIN. Let him out.

ANIELA. To gallop.

CAPTAIN. In a circle, to the right, to the left.

ANIELA. To put the spurs into him.

CAPTAIN. But why that?

ANIELA. Sometimes, sometimes.

CAPTAIN. But why?

ANIELA. Yes . . . but . . .

CAPTAIN. Unless he's stubborn, and then . . .

ANIELA. Yes, yes, when he's stubborn, and then . . .

CAPTAIN. Carefully.

ANIELA. Oh, carefully!

CAPTAIN. Because it could make him restive.

ANIELA. Oh, it can make him restive! I'd spend the whole day in the stable. I'd order this one exercised, then that one, then this one again, or I'd exercise him myself. What a pleasure!

CAPTAIN. [*Aside.*] On my honor, a rare woman.

ANIELA. And then in the evening, to light up a little pipe.

CAPTAIN. It's hard for women to take to the taste.

ANIELA. How so? But there is one woman . . . I am the first to like tobacco.

CAPTAIN. You like it?

ANIELA. I smoke myself.

CAPTAIN. You smoke yourself! [*Aside.*] What a woman! What a woman!

ANIELA. I have such different tastes from the rest of my sex, that until now I haven't wanted to marry. Those city dandies want a woman just to dress herself up, be amusing, twist around, and act giddy; they can't understand a woman who'd prefer camp life.

CAPTAIN. Nitwits.

ANIELA. Marches, bivouacs, activity, work . . .

CAPTAIN. But why didn't you honor some military man with your hand?

ANIELA. I've just happened to meet flighty young men.

CAPTAIN. Flighty young men . . .

ANIELA. No one sensible . . .

CAPTAIN. No one sensible . . .

ANIELA. Who would value my kind of thinking.

CAPTAIN. Impossible.

ANIELA. [*Touching his hands.*] Soldiers' hearts are made of stone . . .

CAPTAIN. [*Kissing her hand.*] Not always.

ANIELA. Unmovable, hard.

CAPTAIN. Even solid ice melts from the sun. [*Kisses her hand.*]

ANIELA. [*As if pulling her hand away.*] Why, Captain!

CAPTAIN. No harm.

ANIELA. Oh, how warm I am!

CAPTAIN. [*To himself.*] What a woman!

ANIELA. Let's go to the garden, it's cooler there.

CAPTAIN. Perhaps to the stable?

ANIELA. Oh, later, later.

CAPTAIN. Perhaps a little pipeful?

ANIELA. Later, later . . .

CAPTAIN. I go where you command. [*To himself.*] What a woman! What a woman!

ACT III

The same room, decorated with flowers.

SCENE 1. Fruzia, Józia, Zuzia. Fruzia is ironing, Józia is sewing, Zuzia is straightening out the cap on a Turk's head.

FRUZIA. What do you think about it, Józia?

JÓZIA. What?

FRUZIA. These masters of ours. When we arrived, how they looked at us, how they glared!

JÓZIA. As though they wanted to devour us.

ZUZIA. Not one of them had a decent word to say.

FRUZIA. And now—they're like lambs.

JÓZIA. You could lead each one of them around on a silk string.

FRUZIA. My mother was right when she used to say that women were created to rule.

JÓZIA. But why don't they rule?

FRUZIA. Oh you child! Is that the only thing wrong with the world?

ZUZIA. I wouldn't want to rule here.

JÓZIA. Oh, neither would I; I'm afraid as soon as I meet any one of them, especially the Major.

FRUZIA. It seems to me that if I were the most courageous soldier, I'd run away as soon as I caught sight of him. What moustaches! God almighty!

JÓZIA. But the Captain is even more frightening with those brooms of his. [*Imitating.*] When one of them goes up, the other goes down; then this one goes up, and the other down, till you start trembling.

FRUZIA. It's true, that here, among all these moustaches—a person is just like in a forest.

ZUZIA. Horrible hussars!

FRUZIA. Oh, give us a rest, Zuzia—the Lieutenant . . .

ZUZIA. Ah, the Lieutenant . . .

JÓZIA. The Lieutenant—he's worthy of being a colonel!

FRUZIA. But what a wild one he is, my!

JÓZIA. Ask me about that . . . !

ZUZIA. How lucky you are; he hasn't talked to me at all.

JÓZIA. But then that Mr. Gregory . . .

ZUZIA. [*Laughing.*] That's my lover.

FRUZIA. [*Laughing.*] And mine, too.

JÓZIA. [*Laughing.*] I have to take him away from you.

FRUZIA. Pst!

SCENE 2. *Fruzia, Józia, Zuzia, Gregory.* [*A short pause.*]

FRUZIA. Why is Mr. Gregory so sad?

GREGORY. Ah!

FRUZIA. And sighing.

JÓZIA. He must be in love.

GREGORY. Ah!

ZUZIA. Happy is the girl who made him like her.

GREGORY. [*Aside.*] Which is the prettiest here?

FRUZIA. Are you really in love, Sir?

GREGORY. I am, by Lord, I am.

FRUZIA. Why don't you get married?

GREGORY. I'm thinking of it, by Lord, I am thinking of it.

JÓZIA. Is something still preventing you?

GREGORY. I don't know if she'll have me.

FRUZIA. Who wouldn't want you!

JÓZIA. Only you're probably a great flirt, Sir.

GREGORY. No, no; believe me, Miss, no.

FRUZIA. A giddy little butterfly, there's no doubt about it.

GREGORY. [*Aside.*] I don't understand . . .

FRUZIA. [*Shaking her head.*] What a fate it would be for a poor wife.

GREGORY. Why poor? My wife's fate would be the most pleasant.

FRUZIA, JÓZIA, ZUZIA. [*Surrounding him; ironic throughout the the entire scene.*] The most pleasant?

GREGORY. Right after the wedding, after I went back to the regiment, I'd buy her a pretty . . . little pony.

FRUZIA, JÓZIA, ZUZIA. [*Clapping their hands.*] A pony, oh, a pony.

GREGORY. Afterward a proper, strong—little barrel.

FRUZIA, JÓZIA, ZUZIA. [*As before.*] A little barrel, oh, a little barrel!

GREGORY. And then a pretty—little basket, with a cover, closed.

FRUZIA, JÓZIA, ZUZIA. A basket, a basket! Oh, how pretty! That's beautiful!

GREGORY. She'd have all kinds of things to eat and drink. And since I'm well known to the officers, my wife would serve only them.

JÓZIA, ZUZIA. Oh, how pretty! How beautiful!

FRUZIA. But Mr. Gregory, how will it be in time of war?

GREGORY. It'd be just the best then.

FRUZIA. But the dread of it!

GREGORY. Where's the dread? That could be the most beautiful part of it all. I beg you to look when a squadron of hussars rides off into a skirmish.

FRUZIA. To a skirmish, do you hear?

GREGORY. Pif paf, pif paf!

FRUZIA, JÓZIA, ZUZIA. Pif paf!

GREGORY. Later the infantry: brr . . . brr . . .

FRUZIA, JÓZIA, ZUZIA. Brr . . . brr . . .

GREGORY. Then the cannon: boom . . . boom . . .

FRUZIA, JÓZIA, ZUZIA. Boom . . . boom! . . . [*Running and jumping all around him.*] Pif paf . . . Brr . . . brr . . . boom . . . boom! . . .

GREGORY. [*Turning all around and looking after them.*] Dear, dear girls! Now I regret I'm not a Turk.

FRUZIA. Oh my! A Turk . . .

GREGORY. I know, I know. But this time it would be very good if I could marry all three of you at once.

JÓZIA. It certainly would.

DYNDALSKA. [*From offstage.*] Józia!

JÓZIA. I hear you; I'm coming right away.

GREGORY. [*Holding her back.*] Wait a moment.

JÓZIA. I can't.

GREGORY. A little . . .

JÓZIA. The mistress is calling. [*She goes out.*]

ANIELA [*From offstage.*] Zuzia!

ZUZIA. I'm coming.

GREGORY. [*Holding her back.*] Don't go.

ZUZIA. I must; bye. [*She goes out.*]

SCENE 3. Fruzia, Gregory.

GREGORY. Ah, Miss Fruzia, do you love me?

FRUZIA. How can I love you when you haven't yet chosen among us?

GREGORY. I choose you, my little magpie.

FRUZIA. For certain?

GREGORY. I'll marry you today if you want.

FRUZIA. Oh, there's enough time yet for that.

GREGORY. But my impatience . . .

FRUZIA. You love me so much?

GREGORY. More than my own horse. But I have to confess to you that I've described your future with me only from the prettiest side; there are certain . . .

ORGAN. [*From offstage.*] Fruzia!

FRUZIA. Right away, right away.

GREGORY. [*Holding her back.*] How will it be?

FRUZIA. Everything will be fine.

GREGORY. Oh, Fruzia!

FRUZIA. Oh, Gregory! [*She runs out.*]

GREGORY. [*Alone.*] I have whichever one I want. It's always best —strike while the iron's hot! What's there to think about! No one's done anything yet just by thought. And Józia is pretty . . . and Zuzia is pretty . . . and Fruzia is pretty . . . the prettiest . . . she'll be mine.

SCENE 4. Captain, Gregory. The Captain enters, dressed carefully, pouring perfume onto his handkerchief from a little bottle.

GREGORY. [Not seeing the Captain.] A dear girl!
CAPTAIN. [Not seeing Gregory.] A rare woman!
GREGORY. [Having heard him.] Did the Captain see her?
CAPTAIN. [With a smile.] I saw her.
GREGORY. It's true, Captain, she's just like a little fawn.
CAPTAIN. Like a little fawn? Hm . . . I don't find that.
GREGORY. She's always jumping about.
CAPTAIN. Jumping about? Hm . . . that I haven't seen.
GREGORY. Never at a walk, always at a trot.
CAPTAIN. Trot . . . hm? . . . You mean to tell me that she rides horseback at a trot?
GREGORY. Rides horseback?
CAPTAIN. Rides, rides.
GREGORY. The devil . . . With your permission, Sir, that's what gets me—everyone likes her, don't they, Captain?
CAPTAIN. [With a smile.] Greg has a head.
GREGORY. To marry such a woman . . .
CAPTAIN. What a flatterer.
GREGORY. I'll marry her this very day! [Starting, the Captain looks at him; silence.]
CAPTAIN. You?
GREGORY. I.
CAPTAIN. You, you?
GREGORY. You thinking about it yourself, Captain?
CAPTAIN. [In anger.] What are you talking about?
GREGORY. I . . . I . . . I . . .
CAPTAIN. Whom are you daring to marry?
GREGORY. Fruzia, by your leave, Sir.
CAPTAIN. Fruzia? . . . You old babbler! . . . Get out of here! [Gregory leaves. The Captain alone.] He's gone mad! . . . Him get married . . . at that age! What good can he promise himself? . . . But why is Miss Aniela taking so long? Perhaps she's already in the garden . . . [Looks through the window.] Can't see. [Listens at her door. Hearing someone coming, he jumps back into the middle of the room.]

SCENE 5. Captain, Lieutenant.

LIEUTENANT. Did you speak with the Major?
CAPTAIN. I spoke . . . but . . . [*Shrugs his shoulders.*]
LIEUTENANT. Stubborn?
CAPTAIN. Stubborn, if one can call it stubbornness.
LIEUTENANT. Who would have expected it?
CAPTAIN. A wise man, my dear fellow, expects everything. [*The Captain, becoming more and more absent-minded, looks frequently out the window, answering at random.*]
LIEUTENANT. No hope then that he'll give up the idea?
CAPTAIN. None, for sure none.
LIEUTENANT. I know it, I know it well and I'm still asking. It's true I can't advise him to, and I can't talk him out of it either.
CAPTAIN. It's for the best.
LIEUTENANT. He'll be happy with her.
CAPTAIN. He will be, he will be . . .
LIEUTENANT. I'm going away . . . but first I'm asking of your friendship just one favor. Listen to me: during the last war . . . [*Looking out the window, the Captain suddenly runs out.*] What does this mean? . . . I don't understand . . . Then I won't disclose my sad secret to him . . . and it's better . . . for how could I explain my sudden departure to the Major? Friendship will condemn me when I dedicate everything for it, and renounce everything because of it.

SCENE 6. Lieutenant, Zofia.

LIEUTENANT. Oh, Zofia!
ZOFIA. Edmund, what have we done! . . . Isn't there any hope now?
LIEUTENANT. None.
ZOFIA. Must we separate?
LIEUTENANT. Forever.
ZOFIA. Let's reveal our love to him.
LIEUTENANT. I can't. What's the purpose? The Major certainly would withdraw, but would you still be mine?
ZOFIA. My mother . . .

LIEUTENANT. Let's not deceive ourselves; she'll never allow it. I put all my hope in time and the help of a friend; but everything deceived me. Do I have to drag you with me into more unhappiness, and separate you from your family? In the end you'll become not the Major's wife, but Smętosz's.

ZOFIA. Terrible.

LIEUTENANT. I'm going away.

ZOFIA. When?

LIEUTENANT. This hour.

ZOFIA. Already, already so soon?

LIEUTENANT. Must I be a witness . . .

ZOFIA. Don't go on, don't go on. Leave me, leave me Edmund!

LIEUTENANT. Our secret must always remain such for the Major. Only the Chaplain knows and he is going away with me. This honest man supported my wavering purpose and has kept me steadfast on the road honor commands me to take.

ZOFIA. Then I shall remain alone; with no hope of relief, no hope of consolation!

LIEUTENANT. We have to endure a great deal, a great deal!

ZOFIA. Perhaps more than we can bear . . .

LIEUTENANT. No, Zofia. Our strength must suffice if the source of our unhappiness is pure.

ZOFIA. To love you and swear love to another!

LIEUTENANT. Loving me, you will love him like a father. You will find him the best, the noblest of men. My one and only relief, my one consolation is that I am giving up happiness for him, that he will surely find it with you. Ah, remember, Zofia, that I am entrusting to you his fate, happiness, and the peace of his days. Beautify every moment for him, and in that way my own life will be sweetened.

ZOFIA. [Drying her tears.] Oh, why must I love you more and more!

LIEUTENANT. Our hearts will remain together.

ZOFIA. For ever.

LIEUTENANT. Separated, far from each other—our thoughts will search for and find each other. Calm yourself; there are still . . . for us . . . pleasures . . . pure . . . sweet . . .

ZOFIA. Like the smile of the dying. [A short pause.]

LIEUTENANT. I see you surely for the last time now. After much time has passed, when you no longer hear any more of me, remind him of me from time to time; he also loved me. Tell him that it was for his sake that I renounced more than life, for I renounced you. [*Zofia sits down, covering her eyes.*] But no, no; don't disturb your peace and his! . . . [*Kneels and takes her by the hand.*] Zofia, with this farewell, with this embrace, I lose the right to your heart; forget me.

ZOFIA. Never!

LIEUTENANT. Be happy!

ZOFIA. Without you?

LIEUTENANT. For me.

ZOFIA. [*Crying.*] Oh, God!

LIEUTENANT. [*Kissing her hand.*] The last time then . . .

ZOFIA. Edmund! The last time . . . [*She throws herself into his embrace. At this point Aniela enters, discovers them, throws her hands up and runs to her room. After this the Lieutenant and Zofia leave on opposite sides.*]

SCENE 7. *The girls run across the stage in different directions, followed quickly by Orgon, Dyndalska, Aniela. The girls remain at the rear of the stage.*

ORGON. What is the matter?

DYNDALSKA. What is it about?

ANIELA. [*Between them.*] What is it about? What is the matter? . . . You'll soon find out.

ORGON. We're listening.

ANIELA. A terrible thing!

DYNDALSKA. Well, go on.

ANIELA. A terrible thing.

ORGON. Talk . . . !

ANIELA. Unexpected!

ORGON. What is it?

ANIELA. What?

DYNDALSKA. What? We're listening.

ANIELA. The Lieutenant . . .

ORGON. What about the Lieutenant?

ANIELA. The Lieutenant . . . is in love—with Zofia.

ORGON. Ha, ha, ha, ha . . .

DYNDALSKA. Too much perspicacity.

ANIELA. As long as it's perspicacity, as long as it's ha-ha-ha, then I won't say what I saw.

ORGON. What you saw?

ANIELA. With my own eyes.

DYNDALSKA. What did you see?

ANIELA. It's only perspicacity.

ORGON. Talk, angel. You're so good, you never get angry; faster, my angel.

ANIELA. Then listen.

DYNDALSKA. We're listening.

ANIELA. The Lieutenant . . .

ORGON. What?

ANIELA. The Lieutenant . . . kissed . . . Zofia's hand.

ORGON, DYNDALSKA. He kissed her hand?

ANIELA. Her hand . . .

ORGON. Is it possible?

ANIELA. That's not all.

ORGON. What is it?

DYNDALSKA. Talk faster.

ANIELA. The Lieutenant . . .

ORGON. What about the Lieutenant?

ANIELA. The Lieutenant . . . kneeled in front of her.

ORGON, DYNDALSKA. He kneeled in front of her?

ANIELA. He kneeled in front of her . . . here . . . on this spot.

DYNDALSKA. Horrors!

ANIELA. That's not all.

ORGON. For heaven's sake, what else?

ANIELA. The Lieutenant . . .

DYNDALSKA. Well, well . . .

ANIELA. The Lieutenant . . . was holding her . . . in his arms.

DYNDALSKA. Oh!

ORGON. And Zosia?

ANIELA. Zosia?

ORGON. Zosia, Zosia?

ANIELA. Zosia . . . was . . . in his arms.

ORGON. Terrible!

DYNDALSKA. Unheard of! [*The two of them walk around*

Aniela with long strides, halting at every question. Aniela stands with arms folded.]

ORGON. Is he in love?

ANIELA. He is.

DYNDALSKA. He kissed her hand?

ANIELA. He did.

ORGON. He kneeled in front of her?

ANIELA. He did.

DYNDALSKA. He held her in an embrace?

ANIELA. He did.

ORGON. Fruzia! Call Zosia! No! Wait . . . Józia! Run . . . wait . . . All of you, call quickly.

DYNDALSKA. Józia—Lieutenant, Lieutenant!

ORGON. No, no; wait, run, look for him; all of you, run, and quickly. Well, are you still here?

FRUZIA, JÓZIA, ZUZIA. [*Together.*] Where? What? Who?

ORGON. The Major, stupid things, the Major! [*The girls run out.*] Terrible thing! [*The two women throw themselves into chairs, exhausted.*]

ANIELA. And I told you, I told you that that Lieutenant was dangerous. I know what kind of a Lieutenant he is! But whatever I say is always bad . . . there's no reason to listen to me . . . I'm not even permitted to open my mouth! Now you see I have to talk. Now no one can convince me otherwise: I shall always, always talk.

SCENE 8. Orgon, Dyndalska, Aniela, Major.

ORGON. Brother dear, brother dear! For heaven's sake, come quickly. You have no idea what's going on; everything is falling in on our heads.

MAJOR. What's happened?

ORGON. He still asks!

MAJOR. But when I don't know, I have to ask.

ORGON. That slender little Lieutenant, that friend of yours, that comrade of yours, that, now I don't know what . . .

MAJOR. What did he do?

ORGON. He wanted Zosia . . . words fail me . . .

MAJOR. He wanted . . . ?

ORGON. He wanted to steal her, to steal her.

MAJOR. That can't be.

DYNDALSKA. Ask Anielka.

ORGON. She saw it with her own eyes.

MAJOR. What did she see?

DYNDALSKA. That he's in love with her, that he was kissing her hand, that he was kneeling in front of her, that . . .

MAJOR. That just cannot be. Aniela was seeing wrong.

ANIELA. If you'd see it yourself, maybe you also wouldn't believe it? There's a fine man for a husband!

MAJOR. But how, where, when?

ANIELA. How? The same as everyone else. Where? Here, on this spot. When? A quarter of an hour ago.

MAJOR. [*After a short pause.*] This I did not expect! And does Zosia also love him?

ORGON. Zosia? What a thought? If she did love him, she'd already be quite a few miles away from here with him.

MAJOR. Edmund! Edmund! My Edmund! To deceive me! If he had shot me, wounded me, it wouldn't have hurt me so much.

ORGON. There is the advice of your colleagues for you!

DYNDALSKA. No one's doing but the Chaplain's; he's trying frantically to block your plan.

ORGON. He tried to convince us of different things and he expressed himself regarding you in an altogether unpleasant manner.

MAJOR. The Chaplain? What did he say?

ORGON. To tell you the truth, I am ashamed to repeat it.

DYNDALSKA. He expressed himself quite unusually; let Aniela tell you.

ANIELA. I heard, but I did not understand; I still can't understand everything.

MAJOR. What, how can he know? What business is it of his? How can he be sure? But Edmund, Edmund!

ORGON. If you don't believe us, then ask the Captain. He's a worthy person.

DYNDALSKA. He will always be of the same opinion as we.

MAJOR. I doubt that very much.

DYNDALSKA. You have nothing to doubt—he is in love with
  Aniela.
MAJOR. That's not true.
DYNDALSKA. That's being polite.
MAJOR. I wanted to say that it cannot be.
ANIELA. Our wedding should convince you.
MAJOR. What? He wants to get married?
ANIELA. Exactly.
MAJOR. To you?
ANIELA. To me.
MAJOR. Has the old fellow gone mad!
ANIELA. The same as you.
DYNDALSKA. [*Aside, to Aniela.*] Be gentle—carefully.
MAJOR. But Edmund, Edmund! Leave me, please. Gregory!
ORGON. [*To her sisters, aside.*] I'm going to keep an eye on
  Zosia.
ANIELA. [*Similarly.*] And I—on the Captain.
DYNDALSKA. [*Similarly.*] And I'll keep an ear open . . .
ORGON. [*Similarly.*] But no, let's go put our heads together.
  We'll be alone there. [*They go into Dyndalska's room.*]
MAJOR. [*To Gregory.*] Ask the Lieutenant to come to me.
  [*Gregory goes out.*]

SCENE 9. Major. [Alone.]

MAJOR. If he had come to me and said: "Major, I like this girl,
  too. Let's oppose each other, but let's oppose each other
  openly." Openly, like men of honor; but not like snakes
  damn it, like snakes! Whom, whom am I to believe now? I
  loved him so! I wanted to share my fortune with him, I
  would have shared my life with him. Oh, it hurts, it hurts!
  But no more friendship, young man, no more! I have no
  need of an adjutant.

SCENE 10. Major, Chaplain.

MAJOR. It's good that you've come.
CHAPLAIN. I'm also looking for you.
MAJOR. What have you been babbling about me to the ladies?

I can imagine what . . . But this is slander . . . And what right have you to mix in? You said two thousand times: "it won't do, it won't do," and you were doing your duty; but I say "it will do," "it will do," and "it will do," and I'll do what seems best for me. But to hold discussions secretly with the ladies, to spread rumors about me—that I really did not expect!

CHAPLAIN. But Major, Major, what are you saying, what are you saying?

MAJOR. Ask yourself: What have I been saying, what have I been saying? Discussions with the Lieutenant, plots, elopement—does that befit your position? Phew! You ought to be ashamed. If an old comrade had said to me what I am now saying to you, I'd hang myself on the nearest tree. Do you understand? I would hang myself, damn it! [*He goes out.*]

CHAPLAIN. What is happening? What is happening?

SCENE 11. Chaplain, Orgon.

ORGON. Don't put your fingers in the door, and your fingers won't be jammed. Who repeats advice becomes a nuisance instead of an adviser. Evil eyes see everything crooked. The spider looks for poison, but the bee for honey; do you understand? Silence one regrets rarely, loquaciousness often. I beg you to remember that; your obedient servant.

CHAPLAIN. [*Bowing low and following her with his eyes.*] Must I regret speaking? What is happening, what is happening?

SCENE 12. Chaplain, Aniela.

ANIELA. Once upon a time I was at a friend's house; I gave her advice, advice which, to tell the truth, was more for my good than hers. She found out about it in the end; she told me that she needed no advice and that I had become boring to her. Do you know what I did, Sir, after such an announcement? I ordered my carriage and I went away . . . I went away. [*She leaves after Mrs. Orgon.*]

CHAPLAIN. [*As before.*] What advice? What did I do? What is going on?

SCENE *13*. Chaplain, Dyndalska.

DYNDALSKA. What is this, dear Sir? What kind of actions are these? Who asked you to mix into other people's affairs? How much longer are there going to be these rumors, these discussions, these intrigues? Is this the kind of a friend you proved to be? Is this the kind of adviser you are? Instead of encouraging harmony and trying to establish peace—you incite quarrels, set brother against sister, sister against sister, daughter against mother, friend against friend. You're creating discord here, you're hatching plots, you're dreaming up deceits, you're looking for quarrels, arguments, brawls, calamities, and murders! [*She goes out.*]

CHAPLAIN. [*Bowing low and looking after her as she leaves. Afterward mopping his brow.*] My good God—calamities and murders! What have I been guilty of? What have I been guilty of?

SCENE *14*. Chaplain, Captain.

CAPTAIN. [*Entering quickly.*] Where is the Major?

CHAPLAIN. I don't know.

CAPTAIN. To call me mad! Mad, because I want to get married!

CHAPLAIN. [*Lamenting.*] How is that—and you too?

CAPTAIN. I'm not talking about that. The Major has offended me, painfully insulted me . . . in front of Miss Aniela he called me an old madman.

CHAPLAIN. But from a friend . . .

CAPTAIN. Insult knows no friends. Where is the Major?

CHAPLAIN. I don't know.

CAPTAIN. I know that you know.

CHAPLAIN. But I don't know.

CAPTAIN. You don't want to tell.

CHAPLAIN. For God's sake, I do not know.

CAPTAIN. You'd hinder it . . . you'd oppose it . . . hm? Everything bothers you; our happiness is pepper in your eye.

CHAPLAIN. Some beautiful happiness!

CAPTAIN. I know, I know. Miss Aniela told me what you were prattling in her presence; but I'm not concerned about that! I don't need any advice . . . and for spite I'll get married, for spite . . . do you understand me, Sir?

CHAPLAIN. For heaven's sake, just listen . . .

CAPTAIN. I don't have to listen to anything.

CHAPLAIN. You want to get married?

CAPTAIN. I do, I do, I do—and you can't prevent it.

CHAPLAIN. But . . .

CAPTAIN. But!—You can't get married yourself, and you'd like it if no one ever married.

CHAPLAIN. Heaven forbid; but your age . . .

CAPTAIN. [In anger.] My dear Sir! Don't count my years for me. I know it's enough . . . Don't count! I am telling you, devil take it! [Goes out.]

CHAPLAIN. What is going on? For heaven's sake, what is going on? It seems to me they've all gone mad.

SCENE 15. Chaplain, Gregory.

GREGORY. I should like to ask you a favor.

CHAPLAIN. What is it, my honest Gregory?

GREGORY. That you intercede in my behalf.

CHAPLAIN. With whom?

GREGORY. With the Major.

CHAPLAIN. Of course; regarding what?

GREGORY. I want to get married. [The Chaplain jumps away from him. Pause.] To Fruzia, Mrs. Orgon's maid . . . [Pause.] A pretty girl . . . [Pause.] She's crazy about me . . . [Pause.] I'd like to ask you then . . .

CHAPLAIN. You want to get married?

GREGORY. This very day even!

CHAPLAIN. Oh, I just can't take any more! . . . [Walking away.] May God keep you in his care! [Going out.] What is happening? What is happening?

GREGORY. [Alone.] Hm, hm, hm; he's not himself! Well, delay is not loss! . . . They'll stay here for several days yet, I still have enough time. [Laughs.] My comrades will be surprised . . . they don't know what's awaiting them!

SCENE 16. Gregory, Rembo.

REMBO. I congratulate you, I congratulate you, Mr. Gregory!

GREGORY. On what?

REMBO. Oh! As if you don't know! What else would I congratulate you on, if not a pretty bride?

GREGORY. Ah, yes—thank you.

REMBO. When you get married, I shall congratulate you in the name of the whole regiment.

GREGORY. I don't understand. You speak very wisely; one can see you're the son of an organist.

REMBO. Everyone will be very happy.

GREGORY. That's good.

REMBO. How many friends Mr. Gregory will have!

GREGORY. As many as now.

REMBO. Everyone will love you.

GREGORY. Really?

REMBO. I vouch for it, but it won't be on account of Gregory—but Gregory's wife.

GREGORY. Oh, that I don't want at all!

REMBO. Want or don't want, that's the way it'll be.

GREGORY. Give me some peace, will you—I don't like such jokes.

REMBO. Get used to them a little.

GREGORY. You're crazy! As though it had to be that way.

REMBO. It will be, without fail.

GREGORY. I beg you, give me some peace.

REMBO. I won't, because it grieves me that you're doing such a stupid thing.

GREGORY. You're just jealous.

REMBO. But an old man, an old man!

GREGORY. [*Mocking.*] But a young man, a young man!

REMBO. Consider . . .

GREGORY. Go to the devil!

REMBO. Get married if you want; but afterward don't be angry when they point a finger at you.

GREGORY. No one will point any finger at me.

REMBO. I'll be the first.

GREGORY. Whoever points a finger at me, I'll slice his moustache off.

REMBO. When you go to cut off someone else's, you'll be risking your own.

GREGORY. Even if I do, it'll be safe—from you.

REMBO. Calm down! Or I'll show you that it isn't safe!

GREGORY. You'll show me? Come on, come on! Show me, show me!

REMBO. But . . .

GREGORY. Aha! you're afraid.

REMBO. What? I'm afraid? Come on, let's get our swords!

GREGORY. Come on! Come on! [*They leave in the direction of the Major's room.*]

SCENE 17. Major, Captain.

CAPTAIN. I repeat it once again: I'll take anything from you before our friends, who know how we get along, but not before Miss Aniela. That I cannot stand and you must apologize to me in her presence.

MAJOR. I apologize here, but before her it's not worth . . .

CAPTAIN. Major, with greater respect . . .

MAJOR. She's my sister—but I wish you better and I tell you that the old bag is worth nothing.

CAPTAIN. Major, damn it! . . . [*Gregory and Rembo come in with swords in hand.*]

SCENE 18.

GREGORY. Come on, come on, I'll show you right now!

REMBO. To the garden, to the garden!

MAJOR. What is this? What does this mean? Rembo, tell me at once, what does this mean?

REMBO. Since you order me, Major, I'll tell you what the whole thing is about. This Gregory here, just as we see him here, fell in love with Fruzia . . . at such an age. For that, I beg the Major's pardon, one has to be stupid.

MAJOR. Well, well—what more?

REMBO. And he wants to marry her. To get married in old age—for that, I beg the Major's pardon, you have to be mad!

MAJOR. Well, well—what else?

REMBO. I wanted to show him what trouble he's taking on; I wanted to tell him that he must remember that as often as an old husband takes a young wife, or an old wife a young husband, that's how often the marriage will be incompatible. For, I beg the Major's pardon, what is young is young, and what is old is old—fire burns, water extinguishes. I wanted to tell him that it will be the same for him as it was for anyone in the same position. For he, I beg the Major's pardon, thinks that a different kind of woman was born as a wife for him and that he is old in a different way than all the other people who have already been living a long time. So I began to talk to him about this, but he didn't want to listen to me, we exchanged words and from there it grew into a quarrel.

GREGORY. I couldn't stand it when he told me that my comrades would point their fingers at me, when my wife . . . when . . . that is . . . since . . .

MAJOR. I understand.

GREGORY. I know that I'm the same age as the Major, and since . . .

MAJOR. Quiet! Peace!

CAPTAIN. Why advise him so strongly when he doesn't want your advice?

REMBO. Because I'm sorry for him, Captain; on my honor, I am sorry for him. And I know he'll be sorry himself, he'll soon be sorry. Because a man who has had sense until this age can't lose it for long. Up to now he was a good soldier, a sensible person, everyone loved him, respected him; but now he wants to do such a stupid thing, to draw such ridicule on his grey head. It's painful to me; first because he's my friend, and then—because I have to stand in the ranks alongside a stag!

MAJOR. Quiet! Peace!

REMBO. Let the Major also tell him, if he will be so kind, that whoever has not married when young should not marry in old age, but if he does marry then he ought to have his head shaved . . .

MAJOR. Off with you! Enough of this! Peace! March!

SCENE *19. Major, Captain. They walk around for a long time whistling and humming. Afterward they get up, look at each other and, after breaking out in laughter, embrace each other.*

CAPTAIN. We both wanted to do the same stupid thing!

MAJOR. So it seems.

CAPTAIN. A very stupid thing!

MAJOR. There's no denying it, a very stupid thing!

CAPTAIN. May God love him for speaking out the truth to us so sharply!

MAJOR. Like a real hussar.

CAPTAIN. I haven't blushed so in a long time.

MAJOR. The sweat was running from me.

CAPTAIN. "Can't lose his sense for long."

MAJOR. And that's the truth!

CAPTAIN. [*Laughing.*] "A stag in the ranks."

MAJOR. [*Laughing.*] Right in the front lines!

CAPTAIN. What these women made of us!

MAJOR. In a single day.

CAPTAIN. They turned the whole house upside down.

MAJOR. And our heads as well.

CAPTAIN. We wanted to get married!

MAJOR. For what? Why?

CAPTAIN. We argued with each other.

MAJOR. But not for very long . . . [*Extends his hand to him.*]

CAPTAIN. They wouldn't have accomplished this for too long. [*They embrace.*] How you smell of sage.

MAJOR. And you of musk.

CAPTAIN. Miss Aniela gave this to me as a present. [*He produces a small bottle.*]

MAJOR. Dyndalska sprinkled me.

SCENE 20. *Major, Captain, Chaplain.*

CHAPLAIN. My dear Sirs, I do not know what is going on here . . . I do not want to know—I do not want to stay here any longer. Farewell . . . I wish you happiness—I wish you much happiness.

MAJOR. Joseph dear! Forgive us, forget what happened . . . Stay, stay—everything has returned again to order.

CAPTAIN. You're angry at me too, old fellow?

CHAPLAIN. At no one, at no one! . . . But what has happened here?

MAJOR. We've returned to our senses.

CHAPLAIN. Bravo. [*He removes his hat.*]

MAJOR. We fell in love, we wanted to get married.

CHAPLAIN. It won't do, it won't do.

MAJOR. Now we are no longer in love and we will not get married.

CHAPLAIN. Wise, wise.

MAJOR. But do you know, friends, I'm not upset because I went wrong for a while; after all, who doesn't stumble once in a while. But Edmund's action—that's on my heart —as heavy as a stone.

CHAPLAIN. What action?

MAJOR. Knowing that I liked Zosia he wanted to seduce her, he wanted to take her away.

CAPTAIN. That can't be!

CHAPLAIN. Major, Major, what are you saying?

MAJOR. That's the way it is, no doubt about it.

CAPTAIN. That can't be.

CHAPLAIN. Who told you about it?

MAJOR. My sisters.

CHAPLAIN. And you believed them—just as you believed that I spoke with them about you.

CAPTAIN. I believe nothing—that's all there is to it.

MAJOR. He was kneeling in front of her.

CHAPLAIN. True, when he said goodbye and entrusted your happiness to her.

MAJOR. I don't understand . . .

CHAPLAIN. Edmund and Zofia have been in love with each

other for a long time. Zofia, certain that you wouldn't accept her hand, pretended to submit to her mother's will in
order to win time and fend off some detestable suitor. But
when matters took a different course, Edmund decided to
go away, to renounce love, never to see Zofia again and, so
that you would never have his unhappiness on your conscience, to keep the whole thing from you forever; he sacrificed more than life for you . . .
MAJOR. Edmund thought that way, that way? [*Forcefully embraces the Chaplain.*] Edmund! Dear Edmund! [*Runs out.*]

SCENE 21. *Captain, Chaplain, then Orgon, Dyndalska,
Aniela.*

ORGON. Why all the celebration here?
CAPTAIN. We're celebrating the return of our reason.
DYNDALSKA. [*To the Chaplain.*] Are you still here, Sir?
CHAPLAIN. [*Bowing.*] Still here.
ANIELA. Flighty Captain, I was waiting for you.
CAPTAIN. To tell the truth, I am very sorry, but after weighing
everything, I see that . . . that however . . . that is . . . that
in spite of . . .
MAJOR. [*Offstage.*] Zosia! Zosia! [*Comes in leading the Lieu-
tenant.*] Zosia! [*Zosia comes in.*]

SCENE 22. *Orgon, Dyndalska, Aniela, Captain, Chaplain,
Major, Zofia, Lieutenant.*

MAJOR. [*To Zofia.*] My successor—your husband . . .
DYNDALSKA. What's this?
ANIELA. What does this mean?
ORGON. Brother? . . .
MAJOR. In addition to my estate, which I planned to leave
him for some time now, he will take my place at Zofia's side.
Chaplain, will it do?
CHAPLAIN. It will do, it will do—and I give my blessings.
LIEUTENANT. Didn't I tell you, Zofia, that you will love him
as a father?
ZOFIA. A pleasant obligation, so fitting to my feelings.

ORGON. I am happy to receive a son-in-law who has already earned my respect. Be happy, both of you.

DYNDALSKA. And remember your aunts.

ANIELA. [*To the Captain.*] What about us?

CAPTAIN. Out of the question, I'm afraid.

ANIELA. You gave your word!

CAPTAIN. I cannot be of service.

ANIELA. Traitor!

MAJOR. Gently! Gently! Let it be enough for you, my ladies, that you conquered hussars, that they were forced to capitulate and surrender one of their number to you in slavery, and—you will admit—the very best among them.

END

MAIDENS' VOWS
or
The Magnetism of the Heart

A Comedy in Five Acts

Man is ruled by reason, woman just by sentiment. One moment she loves, next moment she hates. Sentiment, not reason, is everything to her.

ANDRZEJ MAKSYMILIAN FREDRO

INTRODUCTION

Maidens' Vows remains after *The Vengeance* Fredro's most admired comedy. Its subject is a warm one: the birth and crystallization of love. In the original version of the play which bore the title *Magnetism* (but quickly dropped in favor of *The Hatred of Men*) Fredro at first planned a comedy about two girls who take vows never to marry but who are eventually won over by "the magnetism of the heart." The word "magnetism" is not without importance here. Elsewhere, I have written of the interest in Poland during the Romantic period in the theory of animal magnetism expounded by Franz Mesmer and his followers.[1] It is startling in searching through the great body of European Romantic literature (and American, for that matter, particularly Edgar Allan Poe and Walt Whitman) to find so many works dealing directly with various aspects of Mesmeric therapy or reflecting magnetic theories and the contemporary interest in and excitement evoked by these theories. Fredro's *Maidens' Vows*, in this one respect, is very much a product of his age but with this important distinction: the Romantics themselves were quite serious about magnetism; it was far from quackery or a joking matter with them. The magnetists' emphasis on nonrational modes of perception, their elevation of folk belief and folk superstition to the level of scientific fact, their profound belief in the great power of the human will, all harmonized with the beliefs of the Romantics for whom animal magnetism seemed to offer additional support for their anti-rationalism. Fredro, on the other hand, was less than enthusiastic about romanticism and his comedies abound in anti-Romantic elements.[2] This is true also of *Maidens' Vows*. The "magnetization" of Aniela by Gustav—a high point of the comedy—appears a parody of this aspect of the Romantic interest in the occult and

---

[1] "Animal Magnetism in Polish Romantic Literature," *The Polish Review*, Vol. VII, No. 3 (1962), 16-39.

[2] On the anti-romanticism of Fredro's comedies *Maidens' Vows* and *The Vengeance*, see Juliusz Kleiner, "Śluby panieńskie i Zemsta jako komedie antyromantyczne," *O Krasickim i o Fredrze. Dziesięć rozpraw* (Wrocław, 1956), pp. 189-194.

supernatural. The whole approach of Fredro to magnetism is in keeping with the overall tone of the play: it is light, amusing, free of any sharp edges.

The plot of *Maidens' Vows* revolves around the vows of two young girls, Aniela and Clara, never to get married. The idea of the "vows" probably derives from Kotzebue's *Mädchenfreundschaft oder Der türkische Gesandte* (1805). In this work three girls who are very fond of each other—Natalia, Lenora, and Wilhelmina—take vows never to separate. The influence of Kotzebue is reflected further in the crucial letter-writing scene between Gustav and Aniela in Act IV, Scene 5, when Gustav feigning an injured hand asks Aniela's help with a love letter to an imaginary Aniela. In Kotzebue's one-act *Der Mann von vierzig Jahren* (1795) the protagonist of the comedy, Herr von Wiesen, loves his ward Julie but feels that he is too old for her. Declaring that her sentiments are too delicate for her to utter and that she prefers to write them in the form of a letter to her chosen lover, Julie pretends that she has cut her finger and begs her elderly guardian to take her dictation. Through the device of the letter she discloses her true feelings for him, just as Gustav does for Aniela in *Maidens' Vows*. There are also echoes of Goldoni in Fredro's play. In her dislike and distrust for men and her desire to see them humiliated if necessary even by encouraging them to fall in love with her only to reject them after they declare themselves, Clara is reminiscent of Mirandolina in Goldoni's *La Locandiera* (1753), which Fredro could have seen during his stay in Italy. The relationship between Livia and Renaldo in another Goldoni comedy, *La donna stravagante* (1756), may also have suggested the Clara-Albin relationship in *Maidens' Vows*. Although certain motifs in Fredro's comedy can be traced to foreign sources, as we have seen, *Maidens' Vows* remains nonetheless a thoroughly original work which has never lost its power to captivate audiences.

The real instigator of the girls' plot in *Maidens' Vows* is the more aggressive Clara. Both girls have suitors: Clara—Albin, a parody of the sentimental lover always sighing, groaning and weeping from love, and Aniela—Gustav. At first Gustav is a most reluctant suitor. His visit to the home of Aniela's mother, Mrs. Dobrójska, has been arranged by his uncle Radost who would like to see him married to Aniela. But when he learns about the girls' vows, Gustav treats them as a challenge and devotes all his energy to the defeat of their scheme. In so doing, however, he gradually succumbs to the innocent sweetness of Aniela while she, on the other hand, slowly, perhaps even unwittingly, falls in love with him. By the clever ruse of the imaginary Aniela and the device of the letter described above, Gustav succeeds in winning Aniela and so humbling Clara that she is only too happy to marry Albin and forget all about the vows she and Aniela took never to be seduced into marriage.

The love Fredro depicts in *Maidens' Vows* is very different from that of the Romantics: it is carefree, happy, fulfilled. The tragic overtones of romantic love described, for example, in Musset's *Les caprices de Marianne, Le Chandelier* or *On ne badine pas avec l'amour* are totally absent. This anti-Romantic element in *Maidens' Vows* is set into bold relief by the figure of Gustav. The name Gustav itself was not common in Poland in Fredro's time. We may legitimately ask then, where did the dramatist get it? Did he have any special purpose in using it?

One of the outstanding monuments of Polish romanticism is the poet Adam Mickiewicz's drama *Forefathers' Eve, Part Three* (Dziady, część trzecia, 1832-33). The work deals with the harassment of students at the University of Wilno in 1824 on grounds of alleged anti-Russian political activity. Since Mickiewicz himself was involved in the incident and was subsequently deported to Russia for an exile that lasted four years, the drama is in part autobiographical. The central character of the *Forefathers' Eve* is a young poet of mystic inclinations named Gustav who under the impact of the events of 1824 undergoes a transformation from which he emerges as a *wieszcz*, the Polish for a "poet-seer," now the spiritual leader of his people who takes the name of Konrad.

Forefathers' Eve, Part Three, is the third though loosely connected part of a larger dramatic entity two other parts of which (II and IV) had appeared in 1823. In these parts, which preceded Part Three, the author traces the unhappy ro-

mantic life of his hero, a spiritual descendant of Goethe's
Werther, who is driven to madness and suicide by the despair
of unrequited love. The name Gustav became synonymous in
Poland with the romantic lover consumed and eventually destroyed by his love for a woman. By choosing this name for a
character so diametrically opposed to the romantic hero and
Mickiewicz's character of the same name, Fredro not only
sought to link in the reader's mind his own work with *Forefathers' Eve* but also, and more importantly, to establish de-
finitively the antithetical nature of *Maidens' Vows*. The comedy must be viewed in this light—as a rejection of the romantic concept of love, with strong parodic overtones.

Were the comedy only part of a running polemic with the
Romantics it could never have achieved the reputation it enjoys to the present day with Polish theatergoers. For all its
anti-romanticism, *Maidens' Vows* is a sparkling comedy of
clever intrigue and well-drawn characters. As we have seen
earlier, Fredro's talent as a comedy writer lay in three areas:
plot structure, characterization, and language. In the first
play in this collection, *Husband and Wife*, language and verse
are of less importance to the impact of the work than the in-
tricate web of character relationships. The verse of the
play is undistinguished and the language—save for the stylized
sentimental idiom of Elvira—little differentiated among the
characters who are drawn from the same milieu with the sole
exception of the servant Justysia, for whom this is of little
consequence since we are told that she grew up with her
mistress Elvira and was well educated as a lady. Thus, even
in the speech of a servant, there is little difference from that of
the masters.

In the farce *Ladies and Hussars* Fredro abandoned verse entirely in favor of prose, something he was to do rarely in the
most fruitful period of his career. With *Maidens' Vows*, however, Fredro proved his superb mastery of verse and idiom.
The basic meter of the play is the Polish hendecasyllable. This
is a line of verse eleven syllables in length divided into two
groups of five and six syllables, with a pause, or caesura,
after the fifth. It is a regular Polish meter and has been used
often by Polish poets. Unlike the shorter Polish eight-syllable

line which conveys the impression of greater vivacity, greater rapidity of movement, a certain "sauciness" and gaiety, and unlike the statelier thirteen-syllable line usually reserved for heroic poetry, for works of more exalted nature (Mickiewicz's classic *Master Thaddeus*, Pan Tadeusz, is written entirely in this meter), the Polish hendecasyllable is felt more appropriate for works that fall into the middle area between the two extremes of the eight- and thirteen-syllable lines: comedies, average dialogue in verse plays, love poetry (the Polish Romantic poet Juliusz Słowacki's long narrative poem *In Switzerland*, W Szwajcarji, is written in hendecasyllables). In *Maidens' Vows* most of the dialogue is in the eleven-syllable line. I quote just a few lines, in the original Polish, by way of illustration. Gustav and Aniela are the speakers:

> *Gustav*: Jeszcze, Anielo, w kwiat życia bogata,
> Znasz tylko rozkosz, a nie znasz cierpienia;
> Jeszcze szczęśliwa, a nie znasz oddalenia!
> Nie wiesz, że wtedy cały ogrom świata
> Jeden punkt tylko dla nas w sobie mieście,
> A tym jest chwila spodziewanej wieści.
> Jak każdy szelest dech zapiera w łonie,
> I jaka boleść, gdy mija godzina—
> Z nią wprzód spłacona pociecha jedyna!
>
> *Aniela*: Otóż to miłość! Kochajże tu, proszę!
> *Gustav*: Ach, kochaj, kochaj! Boskie to rozkosze!
> (Act IV, sc. 3)

Aniela, you're still rich in the flower of life, you know only pleasure and no suffering; still happy, you have no idea what separation means! You don't know how when you're separated the whole vastness of the universe concentrates only on a single point, and that point is the moment of expected news. You don't know what it is to strain the eye burningly as every rustle makes you catch your breath, and what pain it is, when an hour passes—and with it your only comfort paid for in advance!

Aniela: That's love! Go on fall in love then!
Gustav: Yes, love, fall in love! A divine pleasure!

Frequently, to break up the pattern and for greater rhythmic variation, Fredro divides a line between two (and sometimes three) speakers, as in the following example:

Aniela: Ach, nie!
Gustav: Dlaczego?/ = 5
Aniela: Nie wiem, lecz sie trwożę. +6 = 11
Gustav: Trwożysz?
Aniela: Lękam się . . ./ 5
Gustav: Jak dziecię lekarza . . . +6 = 11

Aniela: Oh, no!
Gustav: Why?
Aniela: I don't know, but I'm frightened.
Gustav: Frightened?
Aniela: I'm afraid . . .
Gustav: Like a child of the doctor . . .

The verse structure of the play is varied still further by the introduction of both shorter (eight-syllable) and longer (thirteen-syllable) lines. The eight-syllable line is used primarily in *Maidens' Vows* in a mocking or derisive way, as in Gustav's monologue spoken at the entrance of the parodic figure of Albin in Act II, Scene eight:

Otóż to!—To jest przyczyna,
To powód wszystkiego złego!
Chodzi, łazi cień Albina,
Płacze, diabli wiedz czego!
Pięćdziesiąt lat jęczy, szlocha;
Pięćdziesiąt lat wzdycha, kocha;
Teraz każda myśleć będzie,
Że to tak się miłość przędzie;
Niby wiekiem życie człeka,
Aby wzdychać mógł pół wieka!

Oh, there it is, there's the reason, the source of all the trouble here! Our Albin's shadow walks and crawls, weeping devil knows what about! Fifty years of groaning, sobbing; fifty years of sighing, loving. Now every girl is bound to think that that's the way that love is spun, as if we lived a hundred years with fifty set aside for sighing!

This is the same tone in which Clara had greeted the sighing Albin in the sixth scene of Act I:

Po raz pierwszy, drugi, trzeci!
Na wezwanie takie dzielne,
Powtórzone po trzy razy,
Nawet duchy nieśmiertelne,
Jak posłuszne ojcu dzieci,
Porzucając ciemne cele,
Stają władcy brać rozkazy.

Once, twice, thrice! At summons so valiant, repeated three times, even immortal souls, like children obeying their father, forsaking their dark cells, stand ready to receive their master's orders.

The eight-syllable line is continued for the first exchange of dialogue between Clara and Albin, since the tone is still mocking:

Albin: (całując w rękę) . Ach!
Clara: Nic więcej? / 4
Albin: To tak wiele! +4 = 8

Albin: (Kissing her hand) . Ah!
Clara: Nothing more?
Albin: That is so much.

But as the tone shifts with Albin's tortured pleas of love, the eight-syllable line gives way to the thirteen which, initially, is divided between the two speakers:

Albin: Ach, urągasz miłości! 7
Clara: (śmiejąc się) . Urągam?—Broń Boże! +6 = 13/
Albin: Twoje serce bez czucie! 7
Clara: Lwie, tygrysie może? +6 = 13

Albin: You insult love.
Clara: (Laughing) . Insult?—God forbid!
Albin: Your heart is without feeling.
Clara: Is it a lion's, a tiger's perhaps?

When Albin is given more opportunity to speak and tearfully describes the pain he suffers at the hands of Clara who rejects his love, the exaggerated solemnity of the monologue is heightened by Fredro's choice here of the thirteen-syllable line:

Albin: Zostań, okrutna! Uwolnię twe oczy
Od smutnego przedmiotu, co ich swietność mroczy.
Ciesz się moją meką?—Ciesz się więc do woli:
Żaden twój raz nie minął, każdy mocno boli;
Jedna tylko pociecha mej duszy zostaje,
Żem nie zasłużył wzgardy, który dziś doznaję . . .

Stay, cruel one, stay! I'll free your eyes from the sad object that darkens their brilliance. My torture delights you? —Then enjoy it to the full: not a single blow of yours passes me, each hurts frightfully. Only one comfort remains to my soul, that I did not earn the contempt which I receive today.

Again we notice that when representatives of the older generation (Mrs. Dobrójska, Radost) are admonishing the young people, the "weightier" thirteen-syllable line is also used. In the first example that follows, Radost is speaking to Gustav; in the second, Mrs. Dobrójska to Clara:

Mój Gustawie, dlaboga, porzuć myśli płoche
I raz tylko, raz pierwszy, zastanów się trochę?
Kilka dni jesteś pośród tak godnej rodziny,
I nie ma dnia jednego—gdzie tam dnia—godziny,
Żebyś czegoś nie zbroił, aż się serce kraje. (Act I, Sc. 4)

Gustav!—I beg you, give up these flighty thoughts, and just once, for the first time reflect a while. A few days now you're in among these worthy people and not a day goes by . . . what do I mean a day? . . . an hour, that you haven't done some mischief that'd break a person's heart.

Kiedy dwie głowy radzą, nie radzą daremnie.
Rozsądna za tym Klara rozsądnej Anieli
Zapewne tej uwagi rozsądnej udzieli,
Że grzeczność, a szczególnie w swojej matki domu,
Najmniejszej przynieść krzywdy nie może nikomu.

(Act I, Sc. 8)

When two heads advise, they do not advise in vain. So, wise Clara certainly shares with wise Aniela the wise conviction that politeness, especially in one's mother's home, cannot bring the slightest harm to anyone.

Although there are exceptions to be found, of course, the above formulas prevail generally throughout the comedy. The rhyme of *Maidens' Vows* is conservative: the basic pattern of the rhymed couplet is varied occasionally by cross rhymes (ababab and abba, etc.) and internal rhymes.

Polish writers have pointed out that the atmosphere of *Maidens' Vows*, the lyrical climate of awakening love, is very reminiscent of and indeed could have been inspired by Marivaux.[3] Like the birth of love in Araminte for Dorante in the French eighteenth-century dramatist's *Les fausses confidences* (1737; translated into Polish in 1784), so too in *Maidens' Vows*, in the relationship between Gustav and Aniela, is love treated not only *descriptively* but *genetically*. Fredro probably had some knowledge of Marivaux and may have seen his comedies performed during his stay in Paris after Napoleon's collapse. He succeeded in capturing the essence of "marivaudage" in *Maidens' Vows*, however, without being indebted to the French author in any more concrete way.

Of the five comedies of Fredro included in the present collection, *Maidens' Vows* is the only one that appears to have exerted influence outside of Poland, and particularly in France. Polish critics have discovered similarities of plot between *Maidens' Vows* and Alfred de Musset's comedy *Il ne*

[3] On Fredro, Marivaux, and Musset, see Boy-Żeleński, *op.cit.*, pp. 104-106, 109-118, and Bolesław-Kielski, "Śluby panieńskie jako ogniwo w rozwoju 'komedii miłości,'" *Pamiętnik Literacki*, Vol. XLVIII, zeszyt 3 (Warsaw-Wrocław, 1957), 47-60. Kielski considers in this article the question of Fredro's possible influence on Musset and expresses the opinion that such influence was doubtful. Rather, he finds a common source of the "love comedies" of both Fredro and Musset in Marivaux. Comparing all three dramatists in terms of their treatment of love, Kielski concludes that Fredro occupies a middle ground between Marivaux and Musset, that Musset's work represents a further development of Marivaux's techniques for which a comedy like *Maidens' Vows* would have presented a logical prior step. On Musset's *Il ne faut jurer de rien* and *Maidens' Vows*, see also Władysław Folkierski, *Fredro a Francja* (Cracow, 1925), p. 15. This work is a general study of French influences in Fredro.

faut jurer de rien, which was published in the *Revue des deux mondes* in 1836. In the Musset work, a bachelor, Valentin, takes a vow never to marry but eventually succumbs to the charms of Cecile. A somewhat more analogous work, however, would be Musset's *On ne badine pas avec l'amour,* also published in the *Revue des deux mondes* on July 1, 1834, almost a year and a half after the appearance of Fredro's *Maidens' Vows.* In this comedy, it is not a bachelor but a young girl, Camille, who takes a vow never to wed despite plans to marry her to her cousin, Perdican. Ultimately she succumbs to Perdican's love until his spiteful trifling with the affections of a simple girl, Rosette, results in tragedy. The similarities between *On ne badine pas avec l'amour* and *Maidens' Vows* are not difficult to isolate: Camille's vow, recalling that of Clara and Aniela, her mistrust of men, Perdican's use of strategy which, like Gustav's, feigns love for another woman (in Gustav's case imagined; in Perdican's real in the form of Rosette) .

Fredro's comedy was translated into French prose and published in a French "European Theater" collection in 1835.[4] This means that Musset could not have known the work directly before writing *On ne badine pas avec l'amour.* There were, however, many Poles in Paris in the 1830's, political refugees who fled Poland for the freedom of France after the defeat of the November Insurrection of 1830-1831. There was considerable sympathy for the Poles in France at the time. They were, to quote Boy-Żeleński, even "in fashion," and contacts between Poles and Frenchmen were lively. It is entirely possible that through Polish friends Musset became familiar with Fredro's work. If *Maidens' Vows* did not directly influence *On ne badine pas avec l'amour* it could have provided the stimulus—after he had the chance to read the play in French translation in 1835—for Musset to write a new comedy on the same theme of anti-marital vows, but this time without the happy ending of *Maidens' Vows.*

---

[4] Théâtre Européen, nouvelle collection des chefs d'oeuvres des théâtres, Un voeu de jeunes filles (Śluby panieńskie) . Comédie en cinq actes, par le Comte Alexandre Fredro, représentée, pour la première fois, sur le théâtre de Léopol, capitale de la Pologne autrichienne en 1833. Paris, 1835, ed. Guérin, Rue du Dragon 30.

Although the possible influence of Fredro's *Maidens' Vows* on Musset must remain, after all, problematical, there is stronger evidence pointing to the direct influence of the Polish comedy on the French vaudeville *Bocquet père et fils ou le chemin le plus long* by Laurencin, Marc-Michel, and Labiche, staged for the first time in the Théâtre de Gymnase Dramatique on August 17, 1840.[5] Here not only the main plot but even certain scenes appear to have been taken directly from the Polish original.

[5] Folkierski, *op.cit.*, p. 3; Stanisław Dąbrowski and Ryszard Górski, *Fredro na scenie*, p. 206. Foreign performances of Fredro's plays are discussed in the latter, pp. 205-212.

CHARACTERS

MRS. DOBRÓJSKA

ANIELA (Anielka), her daughter

CLARA, Aniela's cousin

RADOST

GUSTAV, his nephew

ALBIN, a young neighbor of Mrs. Dobrójska

JAN, a servant

The scene is set in the country,
in the home of Mrs. Dobrójska.

MAIDENS' VOWS

ACT I

A large room. Two doors in the rear. A third door on the right leading to the rooms of Mrs. Dobrójska. A fourth on the left leads to Gustav's room. A window.

SCENE *1. Jan alone, in a coat thrown over his shoulders, walks around, looks out the window, then speaks with a yawn.* "Wait for me, don't sleep, I'll be back at three." A fine three. The sun is bright as day, and my dear master's ruining himself at cards or with a bottle . . . or . . . Ah, well! I'd best say nothing.

SCENE *2. Jan, Radost.*

RADOST. [*Going to the door of Gustav's room.*] Gustav's asleep?
JAN. Asleep? . . . Like a corpse, Sir.
RADOST. The rascal loves to sleep.
JAN. [*Blocking the door.*] You had best not enter.
RADOST. And may I ask why?
JAN. Because he's sleeping.
RADOST. No harm.
JAN. [*Barring him.*] He'll be angry.
RADOST. Nothing will happen to me.
JAN. He's just dozed off—hardly half an hour ago.
RADOST. What did he do all night?
JAN. He didn't sleep!
RADOST. And for what reason?
JAN. For what reason? He got weak.
RADOST. [*Anxiously.*] He got weak?
JAN. [*With a sigh.*] Suddenly.
RADOST. What's the matter with him?
JAN. What's the matter? Some dizziness in the head . . .
RADOST. Hm!
JAN. A loathing for water . . .
RADOST. Hm!

JAN. A thirst for wine . . .

RADOST. Hm! Come, come, he was still well last evening!

JAN. [*Shrugging his shoulders.*] Ha! Illness, Sir, strikes like lightning!

RADOST. [*To himself.*] Hm! Loathing, thirst! Hm . . . Hm . . . dizziness in the head.

JAN. Let him sleep it off, he'll get up in the afternoon.

RADOST. I wanted to be home and back today. But with such goings on one can't think of it.

JAN. By all means, go Sir, go. I promise that in a little while . . .

RADOST. He's sound asleep?

JAN. [*Barring the way.*] The slightest thing will awaken him. Quiet, for God's sake.

RADOST. I'll just open the door a little.

JAN. But the door creaks.

RADOST. With my own eyes . . .

JAN. [*Giving up.*] Well, if that's it! Don't trouble yourself, Sir; you'll just waste your time—my master isn't in.

RADOST. Not in?

JAN. Not in.

RADOST. Where is he?

JAN. A mile away from here.

RADOST. How? What?

JAN. He went away.

RADOST. Where to?

JAN. To Lublin.

RADOST. To Lu . . . Lu . . .

JAN. [*With a bow, completing the word.*]—blin!

RADOST. When?

JAN. Yesterday.

RADOST. What for?

JAN. I don't know.

RADOST. There you are! He's already beginning to go mad, already, by God. Riding off, flying around at night . . . and what are you standing around for, Sir, your head dizzy? Hm! A loathing for water, eh . . . Thirst for wine?

JAN. I'm standing on guard, Sir; I have to be ready to open the window in the twinkling of an eye.

RADOST. Open it—for what?

JAN. For my master. He goes out and comes in that way.

RADOST. [*Wringing his hands.*] Crawling through windows at break of day! What better proof the fellow's mad. [*Ironically.*] And when is he returning for his wedding?

JAN. If you can believe him, he was to return at three.

RADOST. [*To himself.*] Oh, I must, I must shorten the boy's reins! There's already been much too much of this! [*A knock is heard at the window.*]

JAN. [*Going to the window.*]
Now you can scold, Sir, he's just arriving. [*Opens the window.*]

SCENE 3. Gustav dressed for riding. Jan, Radost in the rear.

GUSTAV. [*Climbing through the window.*] What an hour! Devil take it!

JAN. You speak well, Sir! Would that he had!

GUSTAV. What's that? They're still sleeping, aren't they?

JAN. It would be some sleep!

GUSTAV. I was a little late.

JAN. You're telling me.

GUSTAV. You certainly didn't get much sleep.

JAN. If only I had dozed a bit.

GUSTAV. [*Taking off his crop, cap, gloves, and wiping his face.*] Well, to tell the truth, when I was out, my teeth never chattered so before: wind, rain, cold . . . you wouldn't find a dog out.

RADOST. But you were out.

SCENE 4. Radost, Gustav.

GUSTAV. But uncle dear! [*Kisses his hand.*] How are you?

RADOST. [*Coldly.*] Welcome home!

GUSTAV. You're already up?

RADOST. You still haven't slept?

GUSTAV. There's time enough.

RADOST. The day is long.

GUSTAV. And it's just dawn.

RADOST. It's dawn, but in your head—

GUSTAV. So be it, let it dawn for the best. So long as my dear uncle loved me, I'd always be healthy, wealthy and wise. But, what's this? Scowling? Scowling? Pfaugh! The devil with scowling! Come on now! [*Looking him in the eyes.*] But . . . please . . . just a bit. The stern look will pass, your brow will be smooth, and your eyes light up with a smile. That's the way I like it, uncle dear! [*Embraces him.*]

RADOST. [*Weepingly, always admonishing.*] Gustav dear, tell me: do or do you not want a wife?

GUSTAV. I do, I do, uncle.

RADOST. For certain?

GUSTAV. I'm yearning for one.

RADOST. And this is the way you've found to go after one?

GUSTAV. Until now I haven't the slightest idea of a way.

RADOST. These excursions through windows, these nightly expeditions . . .

GUSTAV. So what of it?

RADOST. [*Losing patience.*] What of it? What about the young lady?

GUSTAV. Ah, I'm quite curious, how it can concern my young lady where, how, and when I go to sleep. If I don't—the better for her for awake I think of her and her alone, and sigh for her both day and night. But how can I sleep—is it in my power to?

RADOST. [*Weepingly.*] Gustav! I beg you, give up these flighty thoughts, and just once, for the first time, reflect a while. A few days now you're in among these worthy people and not a day goes by . . . what do I mean a day? . . . an hour, that you haven't done some mischief that'd break a person's heart. Mrs. Dobrójska looks after you herself, not like some mothers, with their noses in the air, while in their souls they beg all the saints for a son-in-law. Mindful of your parents and my friendship, she expresses her intentions toward you without fear. But everything's in vain, she troubles herself for nothing. A town dandy sees country folk in a different light, his boredom he doesn't conceal, makes no effort to be polite, and wants to make one feel the value of every moment with him. The sparrow, they say, nests only in an empty thatch, but what's in your head? Not even a sparrow.

GUSTAV. [*With sincere reflection.*] True, uncle, true, your warnings are too fair. Oh, you watch over me with a father's eyes. [*Embraces him.*] Oh, you're a treasure, a dear friend, thank you, thank you for your warnings.

RADOST. [*Embracing him affectionately.*] My good, my dear Gustav!

GUSTAV. My friend, rather my dear father! You'll see how much I'll reform, if ever I have a reason to. But just guess what amusement I have in mind for today . . .

RADOST. Oh, my God! Here's reform for you! Have pity on me! Consider, tell me, is it nice for a young suitor to sneak out through the window in order to spend the whole night God knows where?

GUSTAV. But uncle dear, I have to have fun.

RADOST. Fun!

GUSTAV. To tell the truth, in this respected home where everyone's too kind to me, where I don't abuse anything or anyone, I haven't seen any fun at all.

RADOST. Are you here for fun, for endless merriment?

GUSTAV. But not for boredom either.

RADOST. Boredom with a lovely girl around?

GUSTAV. I won't be bored when it's time to love.

RADOST. And when will that take place?

GUSTAV. When she and I get married!

RADOST. Or the other way around: when she turns you down.

GUSTAV. Oh, come on now, small chance of that.

RADOST. And how are you so certain that she won't? Is it somewhere written, inscribed in heaven, that you're the one Aniela has to marry?

GUSTAV. She'll marry me, she'll marry me, uncle dear.

RADOST. Just one thing, I can't bear that boasting of yours.

GUSTAV. Who would accuse someone of boasting who judges wisely and says that when two families wish to be united it's only natural to expect the union to take place in the end?

RADOST. It's true, if Aniela just falls a little bit in love.

GUSTAV. I beg you be at ease about it. I give you my word, everything will come out well.

RADOST. Too much confidence and confidence vanishes.

GUSTAV. Just count on me . . . but enough of these trifles. Now let dear uncle guess . . .

RADOST. Certainly, where you were last night?

GUSTAV. Where I amused myself so long.

RADOST. Speak out, speak out, or the devil choke you.

GUSTAV. We went to a masked ball in town.

RADOST. Which ball?

GUSTAV. At the *Golden Parrot.*

RADOST. In a tavern?

GUSTAV. . . . Disguised!

RADOST. Oh, God! Oh, God!

GUSTAV. No one'd blame a young fellow for that.

RADOST. [*Ironically.*] No, they'd praise him.

GUSTAV. He should be praised.

RADOST. A fine school of thought.

GUSTAV. There couldn't be a better one. In the little world, which calls itself big, where everyone cautiously threads the slippery space as though on stilts and in helmet, it's hard to tell what people are. But where a person has little value for pretense, rejects disguise and does not deceive, where will rules more than reason, take up your brush, your model's standing ready!

RADOST. There you have it! He's a new Bruyère. [*Weepingly.*] Gustav! You just now thanked me for my advice.

GUSTAV. [*Not listening.*] What an idea comes to mind!

RADOST. For example?

GUSTAV. Let's go there today.

RADOST. You and I?

GUSTAV. You and I.

RADOST. He's gone crazy.

GUSTAV. You'll be back early.

RADOST. [*Ironically.*] By the secret road.

GUSTAV. You'll go?

RADOST. Leave me alone.

GUSTAV. All right, then I'll go alone.

RADOST. Gustav! You just thanked me for my advice.

GUSTAV. [*Mournfully.*] Uncle dear! Soon I'll be married—

RADOST. [*To himself, in wonderment.*] So that's why he's up to all these pranks.

GUSTAV. [*As before, pleading.*] Now for the last time.

RADOST. I can't change him, its hopeless.

GUSTAV. I'll mount the chestnut . . .

RADOST. [*Alarmed.*] Oh! The chestnut!

GUSTAV. I'll be back before dawn.

RADOST. Then take my carriage, and let the chestnut be. [*Aside.*] The madman will break his neck yet.

GUSTAV. All right, uncle dear.

RADOST. And my coat.

GUSTAV. All right, uncle.

RADOST. Flying around in that jacket you're bound to catch a devil of a cold.

GUSTAV. All right uncle, as you wish, so be it. I always say, your advice is sacred.

RADOST. There you are, now you'll say that it's on my advice that you crawl through windows for these nightly revelries.

GUSTAV. Then you advise entering through doors?

RADOST. Talk with madmen! I advise you to go to sleep now.

GUSTAV. Sleep?

RADOST. You're so pale, it's not funny.

GUSTAV. Pale? Fine then, it hurts no one: pallor is proof of love's upset, pallor is believed sooner than words. You remember, how good it was the morning after your dinner?

RADOST. My dinner?

GUSTAV. That is, speaking honestly, it was I who gave that fine dinner, but it was uncle who paid the bills later.

RADOST. Unfortunately!

GUSTAV. I lost no skin on account of it. "Now he's in love— who can deny it—how pale, how weak—he's dying from love"—Tell me, it's true, they spoke that way and if I hadn't been too . . .

RADOST. All right, all right, all right. It's not enough he's mad, he's still ranting! Now go and sleep, that's my advice. But Gustav dear, my dear Gustav, try to get closer and please Aniela.

GUSTAV. All right, uncle.

RADOST. For mother's sake, be gracious.

GUSTAV. All right, uncle.

RADOST. And for love of God, if my friendship is still dear to you, before you say anything first, think a bit, for often words fly out as if from a sack, but their sense—Well!— There is none. But now go to sleep, you're already blinking your eyes.

GUSTAV. I'll go change. [*Kisses his hand.*]

RADOST. [*Kissing him.*] Remember, Gustav . . .

GUSTAV. You'll be amazed yourself how I'll reform this very day. [*Goes out through left side door.*]

RADOST. [*Looking after him, seriously.*] Reform! Something different every hour. Be amazed, will I? Yes! [*Suddenly overcome with feeling.*] A wonderful rascal!

SCENE 5. Radost, Albin. Albin with handkerchief in hand, assuming a tragic air.

RADOST. Albin, dear fellow, what gets you up so early?

ALBIN. Alas!

RADOST. How you sigh, how painfully you sigh.

ALBIN. Ah! Why shouldn't I sigh, when I drown in despair; when the night's minutes are counted in tears!

RADOST. And I advise you, calm yourself, don't be a Gustav— but love happily. These elegies and love plaints smite a young lady not in the least—and especially Clara, who's like a live spark, who sighs only when she yawns. Clara, who can hardly keep quiet even when she rests, is contrary and happy by nature, and afraid of despair, of which you are the perfect model.

ALBIN. Ah! Can one love and not cry at the same time? [*A short pause.*] Already two years have passed since Clara's charm excited my love beyond all bounds, beyond all measure. Not a day goes by without my pleading with tenderest glance; my every breath is already a sigh; I sprinkle her traces with tears, I sprinkle the whole road: I would have melted even a stone, but her I cannot melt!

RADOST. Even if you groaned a hundred years, it would mean nothing.

ALBIN. Oh!

RADOST. What more do you want to do?

ALBIN. What? Die from despair.

RADOST. Perhaps she loves you.

ALBIN. Loves me? I'd die from joy.

RADOST. Then order the bells rung in either case.

ALBIN. I cry, and you laugh.

RADOST. Then laugh with me.

ALBIN. Ah, hear me further, don't torment me with such an order. I thought that perseverance of the purest flames of love would change hatred into the warmest feelings, that calculated hatred for men which she nourishes in her soul, and from which she seeks glory. Ah, poor thought, alas! Deceptive hopes! Her heart grows ever colder, and mine warmer!

RADOST. [*In the same tone.*] Stay well!

ALBIN. Ah, where are you going?

RADOST. [*As before.*] Oh, just to my place.

ALBIN. You have no pity for my grief, you leave me in my hour of need.

RADOST. I would still like to go home for a while . . . [*taking out his watch*] only now it's probably . . . if I am not mistaken . . . Oho! Already too late! That's what comes from fooling with a harebrain. His idea is, leave everything for later.

ALBIN. [*Taking him by the arm.*] Wait. I must confess to you a terrible secret.

RADOST. [*Alarmed.*] For heaven's sake, what is it?

ALBIN. I'll explain the whole matter.

RADOST. Albin, I'm trembling!

ALBIN. You'll hold it sacred?

RADOST. Talk!

ALBIN. Clara and Aniela have a plan . . . Listen and weep! A plan—never to get married.

RADOST. [*Amazed and keeping himself from laughing.*] Seriously? [*At an assenting nod from Albin, Radost bursts out laughing.*]

ALBIN. What? You're laughing at it?
RADOST. I laugh, because I do not believe it.
ALBIN. I swear to you.
RADOST. And how do you know?
ALBIN. I know for certain.
RADOST. God grant it! [*Aside.*] Perhaps such a stimulus would awaken Gustav. [*To Albin.*] Thanks for the good news.
ALBIN. Good, Radost, why? If that's good, I'll die!
RADOST. You won't die, we'll both live.
ALBIN. You always laugh.
RADOST. Just you don't cry, and the fates will be kinder to you. [*Leaves through the left center door.*]
ALBIN. Oh, love, love! You cause of woe! I cannot speak ill of you, for sweet tears will flow. But Clara! When will you repay me in kind? When will you weep with me? Clara! Clara! Clara!

SCENE 6. Albin, Aniela, Clara. The girls enter before the last lines are spoken, through the right center door.

CLARA. [*Quietly standing by Albin.*] Once, twice, thrice! At summons so valiant, repeated three times, even immortal souls, like children obeying their father, forsaking their dark cells, stand ready to receive their masters' orders. Could I delay my arrival? Here I am, here I stand.
ALBIN. [*Kissing her hand.*] Ah!
CLARA. Nothing more?
ALBIN. That is so much. [*Clara laughs—then after a short pause.*] Oh, you insult love.
CLARA. [*Laughing.*] Insult? God forbid!
ALBIN. Your heart is without feeling.
CLARA. Is it a lion's, a tiger's perhaps?
ALBIN. No one can melt it.
CLARA. Not everyone, certainly.
ALBIN. I am so in love.
CLARA. And I not.
ALBIN. I cry so plaintively.
CLARA. And I laugh.
ALBIN. Cruel! You'll know what I was after you've lost me.

CLARA. Cruel! Hard! Alas! O Heavens! [*To Aniela.*] We must leave quickly, love's on guard here. Quickly, Aniela, we must not trust it. [*Sings.*] "O! Where love casts its net, don't frolic dear children, with love there's no fooling. Once it gets you, you're trapped." So granny sang to us. I'm off, while still whole.

ALBIN. Stay, cruel one, stay! I'll free your eyes from the sad object that darkens their brilliance. My torture delights you? Then enjoy it to the full: not a single blow of yours passes me, each hurts frightfully. Only one comfort remains to my soul, and that is that I did not earn the contempt which I receive today.

ANIELA. Mr. Albin! Who takes it all so seriously? Stay with us, we're only joking.

CLARA. What I said, I said sincerely.

ALBIN. And I believe everything to a word.

CLARA. He is worthy of praise who is not stubborn.

ALBIN. He is worthy of pity who falls in love with Clara, for along with pity he's lost all faith. [*Leaves through the right side door.*]

SCENE 7. *Aniela, Clara.*

ANIELA. To tease, to torture him so, that's not fair.

CLARA. Then what? Should I marry him?

ANIELA. I don't say that; but let pity sweeten the bitterness of fate, let him at least know the reason.

CLARA. Why? Let him love, weep, groan, and perish.

ANIELA. Oh, that I don't want, and you're not so hard.

CLARA. I despise love, and I cannot be moved.

ANIELA. Then find a pleasanter way; and why use words, when a sign's enough.

CLARA. Perhaps curtsying thrice before him, twirling my apron, blushing like a lobster, I'm to ask timidly that he accept without insult an answer in truth not too kind, but intended for his whole sex?

ANIELA. Oh, certainly, certainly, it would be better than continuously repeating in the poor fellow's face that his love, just like his person, neither amuses you, nor pleases you.

CLARA. Believe me, Aniela, it's all too little. You don't know how hard a man's heart is, how quickly he can pull his wounds to scars, scars which later become a source of pride. Nothing beats men's vanity, nothing makes them humble; the greater the obstacles, the more they're stubborn. Scream, despise, hate—in hatred, anger and contempt they find advantage, so that, finally, more than one of us, poor things, loses her patience, loses her head and, tired of fighting, pressed on all sides, has to fall in love in order to avoid trouble.

ANIELA. Why tell me what I know perfectly? I know men well, that race of crocodiles that lies in wait yet rests easily in order to gain our confidence and then betray us in a moment. But if they are evil, must we be the same?

CLARA. Oh, once upon a time there were good women, and what was the usual result? Happiness for the men, bitter sadness for us. Remember the book.

ANIELA. I shall never forget it: *The Philandering Life of Clorinda's Husband.*

CLARA. [*With growing excitement.*] Does one man's grief conquer your desire for vengeance—grief that he could not attain the goal he wanted? And we, must we announce to all, publicize injudiciously, our intention "never to take a husband"? Deprive all of them of hope at one time? And spare the vanity of each of them? Oh no, nothing of that, my good people! You who love to boast of your conquests, let each of your proud necks fall here at our feet. Each will personally know our contempt.

ANIELA. [*Excitedly.*] Let each one sigh!

CLARA. [*Excitedly.*] And fall in love with me.

ANIELA. Why with you?

CLARA. So that he would groan in vain.

ANIELA. My heart will not favor them more.

CLARA. Aniela! Your hand! Let's repeat our vows of eternal glory for us, and for them eternal ruin.

TOGETHER. [*Joining hands, speaking slowly and in unison.*] I swear on the unswervable constancy of woman, to hate the male race, never to be a wife.

ANIELA. To hate, yes, except for my uncle.

CLARA. And my father.

ANIELA. And my cousins.

CLARA. And Mr. Jan . . .

ANIELA. And Mr. Karol . . .

CLARA. And Józio . . .

ANIELA. Kazio, Staś . . .

CLARA. Whoa, hold on!

ANIELA. There is nothing to lose in being careful. [*A short pause.*] Then we are no longer free to love?

CLARA. One will be a lover for the other.

ANIELA. [*Reflecting.*] One for the other—oh, yes—that's exemplary, but tell me, Clara, enlighten me on this point: Do men never love sincerely?

CLARA. [*After a short pause.*] Never? Hm! Of course.

ANIELA. Why do they pretend then?

CLARA. How and why, I don't know, but what I read, I remember perfectly: "That love is worse than any adventure, that if you must love, it would be better to jump into the river."

ANIELA. Clara! For heaven's sake—into the river! That's too much!

CLARA. There's no other way! That's how it was in this book.

ANIELA. If that's how it is then it's a very strange thing that each woman loves and no one drowns because of it.

CLARA. Because each one's soul is chained to the future; she lives for heaven and loves for penance.

ANIELA. Oh, you men!

CLARA. Hell gave birth to you!

ANIELA. There isn't a land free of you!

CLARA. [*Rapid conversation.*] And our Mr. Gustav, a Warsaw dollie.

ANIELA. Oh, that one doesn't even try to pretend.

CLARA. If he speaks to you, that's already a great favor.

ANIELA. He wants to marry because he's bored sometimes. At least I spare my ears his groans.

CLARA. That certainly wouldn't comfort me at all; let each man love and find his punishment in love.

ANIELA. Ah, if one could believe in love, would there be a greater happiness on earth?

CLARA. It was that way years ago, you remember what we read?

ANIELA. Do I remember? As soon as I recall it my head spins.

SCENE 8. Mrs. Dobrójska, Aniela, Clara, Albin.
On entering, Albin rests against a wall near a small table. His arms are folded, he sighs frequently, and does not remove his eyes from Clara.

MRS. DOBRÓJSKA. [*Entering, to Albin.*] Who quarrels, loves— an old proverb.

CLARA. [*Kissing her hand.*] Did auntie ever quarrel?

MRS. DOBRÓJSKA. [*To Clara.*] You're still green.

CLARA. Oh, no!

MRS. DOBRÓJSKA. Oh, yes.

CLARA. Why?

ANIELA. Clara, mother dear, is always very wise.

CLARA. And Aniela likewise.

ANIELA. We agree in everything.

CLARA. We counsel each other mutually.

MRS. DOBRÓJSKA. When two heads advise, they do not advise in vain. So wise Clara certainly shares with wise Aniela the wise conviction that politeness, especially in one's mother's home, cannot bring the slightest harm to anyone; and on the other hand—Aniela advises Clara that indifference does not necessarily demand mockery.

CLARA. [*Bowing low to Albin.*] Mr. Albin, we thank you very much.

ANIELA. [*To Dobrójska.*] Must we try for Mr. Gustav?

MRS. DOBRÓJSKA. But don't go around scowling and pouting all the time. [*They sit down at a round table and take up their handwork, with the exception of Clara. Rapid conversation.*]

ANIELA. He doesn't see us.

CLARA. Blind and dumb.

ANIELA. Must I beg him for kinder glances?

CLARA. To speak, when he's silent; when he's bored, to amuse him?

ANIELA. [*Ironically.*] And what amusement there can be in the country!

CLARA. [*Similarly, all the faster.*] And what there is to talk about with country girls!

ANIELA. About the nice weather, or the rain.

CLARA. Perhaps he'd confuse us with his city wit.

ANIELA. Mercy, it hangs over him like a thick curtain.

CLARA. Mercy, while napping, he's trying for a wife.

MRS. DOBRÓJSKA. You've already talked me out, my pretty ladies.

ANIELA. But, mother dear! What are we to do?

CLARA. When he's stretched out on the sofa, barely mutters, half asleep already, must we sing some merry little aria? Or dance around him in garlands? [*While speaking the last few lines, Clara makes a few dance steps with a kerchief in her hand. Albin jumps up and pushes back the chair standing behind her.*]

ALBIN. For God's sake!

CLARA. What is it?

ALBIN. The chair.

CLARA. [*Angered.*] Oh, with you . . . really . . . one can't even stumble!

ALBIN. Unfortunately!

ANIELA. [*To Dobrójska.*] Very wise.

MRS. DOBRÓJSKA. [*Laughing.*] I myself am surprised. No arias, no, nor ballets either, but politeness, humility, those are your virtues.

CLARA. [*Ironically.*] Besides, there's Radost, Albin, Gustav . . . Three men! That's a court according to male rules. Three! Together! Enormous! And what do they need? What would the intelligence of woman, that weak creation of heaven, which doesn't even pretend to the right to approach theirs, what would *it* contribute to these judges of honor, these potentates of the world, these repositories of wisdom? Incapable of reaching the model—a creation always so lofty in the male soul—our feelings would always end up either trammeled or blemished.

MRS. DOBRÓJSKA. What sometimes frightens isn't always fearful. Men have their weaknesses, but so does our sex; besides, the person who chastises his own errors and is lenient to those of others is the one who carries most weight on the scale of wisdom.

SCENE 9. Mrs. Dobrójska, Aniela, Clara, Albin, Gustav. Albin stands on the right side of the stage. Near him, busy with their work, Clara, Aniela and Mrs. Dobrójska sit at a table. Gustav enters, and bowing, places a chair in the middle of the room. He sits turned to the parterre, a little toward the front of the stage. In this scene Gustav speaks absentmindedly, as though just talking for the sake of saying something, occupied at first with his clothes.

GUSTAV. Well, the rain stopped—the sky is clearer.

CLARA. Most pleasant weather, as a matter of fact. [*To Aniela.*] No one can deny now that I'm acting politely . . . And now, your turn, Aniela.

MRS. DOBRÓJSKA. [*To Clara, discontentedly.*] Clara, again? [*To Gustav.*] Albin was just saying that a new cloud threatens new rain.

ALBIN. For me it's cloudy, ah, even dark because Clara's pleasure at my despair is slowly extinguishing my hope.

CLARA. [*Impatiently.*] Oh no, not at all, I am very sad.

GUSTAV. [*Always absentmindedly, just to say something.*] The ladies are working.

CLARA. Men despise it, but this work is the quickest defense against the boredom in which a village abounds.

MRS. DOBRÓJSKA. [*To Clara, discontentedly.*] Are you bored?

CLARA. Is auntie asking me?

GUSTAV. [*Just as before.*] Who seeks a defense must be weak.

CLARA. Does one think only of oneself?

GUSTAV. [*Looking at Albin.*] Yes, and about those near you— it's nice and generous.

CLARA. [*With growing excitement.*] Near, far, either can be bored.

ANIELA. [*Aside to Clara.*] Clara, that's enough.

GUSTAV. [*Always indifferently.*] Just some general advice . . .

CLARA. There's never advice enough . . .

GUSTAV. [*Finishing his sentence.*] For spoiled children.

CLARA. I know then whom to turn to.

GUSTAV. [*Indifferently.*] The mirror.

MRS. DOBRÓJSKA. Clara cannot speak calmly. Any puff ignites that spark.

GUSTAV. [*Stretching out in the chair.*] Oh, please, this amuses me enough.

CLARA. [*Insulted, ironically.*] Is that so? Truly? I wouldn't have guessed that my words could work such a miracle. [*To Albin.*] Oh, please don't follow me with your eyes.

ALBIN. [*With a sigh.*] Even that you forbid?

CLARA. Oh, there's no end to it. [*To Aniela, aside.*] If he just winked, I could really scowl.

MRS. DOBRÓJSKA. [*After a short pause.*] Mr. Gustav could rightly be amazed that the quiet of the country, and especially at this time, can be pleasant for anyone.

GUSTAV. [*Speaks all the more slowly.*] Of course, of course . . . I'm not at all surprised . . . The country is pleasant [*trying to conceal a yawn*] really pleasant.

CLARA. [*Aside to Aniela.*] You see?

ANIELA. What?

CLARA. He's yawning.

ANIELA. Polite . . .

CLARA. [*Finishing her sentence.*] Says Auntie. [*Out loud.*] There's politeness for you . . . [*at a glance from Dobrójska changes the sense*] to praise what one doesn't like.

GUSTAV. [*Still more slowly.*] No, the country has its charms . . . I'm speaking sincerely [*trying to conceal a yawn.*] In spring, flowers . . . leaves . . . fresh grass, and in summer, in summer! . . . There are those . . . beautiful harvests; but in fall . . . [*yawning*] also . . . something happens; in winter the evenings . . . yes . . . in winter . . . evenings; there are, there are parties . . . oh, there's something every season. [*Yawns and soon begins to doze.*]

MRS. DOBRÓJSKA. Pleasure and boredom alike come from within us. If every hour is spent aimlessly and no necessary work occupies our time, if we are in a constant confusion of hum and noise, always anxious for new things, new people, then the village, like the city, in the long run bores. That's why of course the hope does not delude us that Mr. Gustav will manage to amuse himself among us.

CLARA. [*Quietly, after a short pause.*] Pst! Auntie! [*Pointing to Gustav asleep.*] He's already amusing himself.

MRS. DOBRÓJSKA. Ah! What the . . .

CLARA. Let's all of us leave.

ANIELA. Let's leave him alone.

ALBIN. Even at night I don't sleep like that.

MRS. DOBRÓJSKA. That is too much.

CLARA. Let's go.

MRS. DOBRÓJSKA. But . . .

ANIELA. [*Pulling her by the hand.*] Mother dear, please.

CLARA. [*Taking her by the other hand.*] I also offer my petition for him: as he makes his bed so let him lie in it. This is the way he's made it, let him sleep to his heart's content. [*To Albin impatiently.*] Well, come on . . . faster! Pst! Slowly now.

[*All leave. Gustav sleeps. Radost soon runs in, observes Gustav with a pained expression on his face. Folds his arms and sits in the chair in which Mrs. Dobrójska was sitting.*]

SCENE *10. Gustav, Radost.*

RADOST. [*Mournfully, almost in tears, all the louder.*] Gustav! Gustav! Cruel Gustav! [*Gustav opens his eyes and looking before him answers as if he were talking to Mrs. Dobrójska.*] Yes, Madame, I am amusing myself in the country.

RADOST. [*Bursting out in a laugh.*] And I have to laugh, when I wanted to scold.

GUSTAV. [*Bewildered, getting up after a short pause.*] I dozed a bit.

RADOST. [*Ironically.*] Is that so?

GUSTAV. [*Irritated.*] I slept, I slept. There's nothing to say.

RADOST. [*Imitating Gustav.*] "You'll be amazed, uncle, how I'll reform today"—I am amazed that you slept well and snored happily.

GUSTAV. [*Annoyed.*] All right, I slept, it's true; but on the other hand the roar of cannon hardly lulls a lover to sleep

while [*with pretended feeling*] the voice of flutes, the caressing voice of a woman does easily.

RADOST. Oh! Oh! The voice of flutes! As if someone would believe it! For heaven's sake, boy! God's plague on me! Am
I begging you and advising you for nothing? Tell me, has
your heart turned so cold that you can sleep in front of your
sweetheart as though she were already your wife?

GUSTAV. [*Annoyed with himself, pushing the chair away.*] Hm!
Devil made a chair so comfortable! Unawares . . . Somehow
. . . I got drowsy.

RADOST. And he wants to get married! There's today's courtship for you! You want to sleep, well, sleep, if you like
sleeping.

GUSTAV. But uncle, it wasn't of my own will.

RADOST. What the devil! Couldn't you have still said good-
night to everyone?

GUSTAV. All right, all right, uncle, just don't wrinkle your
brow; I'll put an end at once to all the unpleasantnesses.

RADOST. [*Taking hold of him.*] How? What? Where?

GUSTAV. I want to straighten out everything in an honorable
way.

RADOST. [*Imploring him most humbly.*] Gustav, little Gustav,
don't bring me disgrace, be wise a week, just one week
more!

GUSTAV. I will be, uncle, I will be . . . even two weeks.

RADOST. It's for your own good I'm asking.

GUSTAV. Uncle dear! I deserve your anger and rebuke. I do
appreciate and value your fatherly advice, thank you, thank
you, my dear uncle. [*They embrace.*]

RADOST. [*Moved.*] Gustav, dear! [*A short pause.*] But I'm afraid
that you thank me and again will do what you want.

GUSTAV. No, I am in love now and I'll continue to be. Albin
and I are off to the races.

RADOST. [*Holding him back.*] Ah, wait! You'll cause more woe.
They'll take the sudden change for a joke.

GUSTAV. No, I'll just sigh—once every half hour. And then I'll
look, they won't blame me for that, but how to look? I know
now. A single glance! [*Taking Radost by the hand and*

217

speaking softly.] The way uncle used to look once at a certain lady . . .

RADOST. [*Closing his lips.*] Sh, be quiet! [*Looking around.*] You're crazy, I see.

GUSTAV. But what's worse, what saddens me a bit, the young lady doesn't even give me a look.

RADOST. Ah, my Gustav, after all you are looking for a wife; would you want one who followed you with her eyes, as if to say: "who's keeping whom?" Or one who looks and sighs to herself as if whispering: "I'd marry you."

GUSTAV. No—even though I'm a scatterbrain, I want . . .

RADOST. [*With a sigh.*] Even though!

GUSTAV. . . . to have a good wife.

RADOST. And who doubts it?

GUSTAV. And if I didn't sense Aniela's qualities [*Radost in silent rapture extends his hand to him*], you wouldn't see me here this long already.

RADOST. [*Embracing him.*] Ah, what angel spoke through you?

GUSTAV. True? Can't I be wise when I have to?

RADOST. Oh, terribly, terribly, if only it'd last.

GUSTAV. Well off I go to run, sing . . .

RADOST. [*Mournfully, holding him back.*] Not that . . . [*Gustav interrupts Radost with a forceful hug.*]

GUSTAV. You'll be surprised how I'll reform today! [*Accidentally knocking the snuff box from Radost's hand, he topples over a chair running out of the room. Chasing after the snuff box, Radost looks now at it, now at Gustav, as the curtain falls.*]

RADOST. Wait! For pity's sake! Oh, God! Gustav!

ACT II

SCENE 1. Mrs. Dobrójska, Radost.

MRS. DOBRÓJSKA. Yes, yes, Mr. Radost, I share your grief, but Mr. Gustav has not pleased me at all. I find it very hard to forgive youth for self-love that denies the rights of others.

RADOST. Gustav hasn't that fault.

MRS. DOBRÓJSKA. He has only virtues and no faults? Is that true?

RADOST. Oh, he has faults, he has, unfortunately!

MRS. DOBRÓJSKA. And they are?

RADOST. Absent-mindedness, frivolousness, shallowness . . . Well, what have I to hide—he's scatterbrained!

MRS. DOBRÓJSKA. I don't see a scatterbrain in him.

RADOST. Ah, my dear lady, who can deny it now? But he has a good heart and not a bad head; those things don't pass with time like frivolousness, they're a guarantee of happiness for a wife and children.

MRS. DOBRÓJSKA. You see only good in him.

RADOST. I love him like a son. [*Mournfully.*] But only I.

MRS. DOBRÓJSKA. That is not my fault.

RADOST. But Aniela scowls.

MRS. DOBRÓJSKA. And she really has a reason to.

RADOST. Poor Gustav! Everyone's pouncing on him.

MRS. DOBRÓJSKA. And that sleeping you call scatterbrained? No —lightheadedness.

RADOST. Ah, but I woke him up!

MRS. DOBRÓJSKA. And how can I judge that when later on he flew into us as if possessed? What did he do? You were there.

RADOST. But I gave him a hint!

MRS. DOBRÓJSKA. I like young people to be gay; and real gaiety, though sometimes it goes too far, can be forgiven. Feigned gaiety, on the other hand, has no right to such consideration, and it was this kind that brought on Gustav's madness today.

RADOST. Madness! He was mad—there's no denying it, but sometimes shyness inclines us to it: you tremble, hesitate, and later wham, just like a balky horse that once started knows neither fence nor trench. And that's the way it is with Gustav—no one knows what drives him.

MRS. DOBRÓJSKA. [*Restraining a laugh.*] What? He's . . .

RADOST. [*Finishing her sentence.*] . . . shy.

MRS. DOBRÓJSKA. Gustav?

RADOST. Gustav, I give you my word.

MRS. DOBRÓJSKA. Wonderful! [*She laughs.*] Oh, poor, poor little Gustav! Can't count up to three! [*Laughs.*]

RADOST. [*Confused.*] Well . . . it is true he's too bold [*mournfully*] but what can I do?

MRS. DOBRÓJSKA. You'd best take him in hand. Speaking just between the two of us, this dear Gustav does with his uncle as he pleases.

RADOST. Oho, ho, ho!—A day doesn't go by without a paternoster flying to his ear.

MRS. DOBRÓJSKA. Oh, yes! I know that well enough: your lordship grumbles, and he pays no heed.

RADOST. Ah, how he thanks me for each warning—but if you want the truth, I can dish it out too: your ladyship is spoiling the young girls.

MRS. DOBRÓJSKA. I'm spoiling them?

RADOST. You.

MRS. DOBRÓJSKA. Mind what you're saying!

RADOST. I am. But it's so.

MRS. DOBRÓJSKA. They tremble before me.

RADOST. [*Ironically.*] Naturally!

MRS. DOBRÓJSKA. You can say it again. A pity you weren't here today when they were crying bitterly.

RADOST. Although I count for nothing, and Gustav is a lot to blame, nothing escapes me.

MRS. DOBRÓJSKA. What do those insinuations mean? Are they intended for Aniela, or Clara perhaps?

RADOST. Hm! Hm!

MRS. DOBRÓJSKA. Well?

RADOST. Some kind of vows!

MRS. DOBRÓJSKA. Childish games, about which I want to know nothing and can scarcely guess. Both spent a long time with Clara's mother; you know what kind of married life they saw there. Then a few bad books read furtively, as well as the offensive remarks of my brother-in-law, put into their young heads, not their souls, this hatred for men they're always parading. But then why bother to destroy ideas which have to change anyway?

RADOST. Change? Of course they'll change, but it's a lot of trouble for Gustav.

MRS. DOBRÓJSKA. Besides, better too little than too much feeling.

RADOST. [*Kissing her hand with feeling.*] Ah, my dear lady!

MRS. DOBRÓJSKA. The same old Radost.

RADOST. [*As before.*] The same.

MRS. DOBRÓJSKA. Go, comfort Gustav. [*Goes out.*]

RADOST. [*Threatening.*] I'll comfort him all right.

SCENE 2. Radost. (Alone.)

RADOST. What shall I do with this fellow! It's unheard of! If only I could tie him up, damn it, like a ram, drag him by force to the altar, throw him a wife, the happiness of both'd be assured. But with a scatterbrain like that—it's like trying to catch a fish in a pond, the little devil! Now you've got him, now you haven't—like sand in the eye.

SCENE 3. Gustav, Radost.

GUSTAV. Well, uncle?—A great reform, eh?

RADOST. If I didn't see it, I wouldn't have believed it.

GUSTAV. Still Anielka troubles me a bit.

RADOST. She takes right after you! You're two of a kind!

GUSTAV. She pouts at me.

RADOST. [*Aside.*] Anielka! Well I ask you!

GUSTAV. But the rarer the pleasure, the greater. Let her speak little, but love beyond measure. She's getting more of a hold on my heart.

RADOST. [*Getting angry.*] And you less and less of one.

GUSTAV. Less?

RADOST. Less.

GUSTAV. Are you joking?

RADOST. [*Ironically.*] Joking, joking.

GUSTAV. That's bad.

RADOST. [*With growing anger.*] That's good.

GUSTAV. Why is it?

RADOST. Because you deserve it.

GUSTAV. What did I do now?

RADOST. You still ask? Mercy, tell me, do you want to tear

my soul out? Did a tarantula bite your heel, that you had
to tear after everything in leaps and bolts, battering and
smashing even the poor little puppy . . . although I kept
on winking and coughing.

GUSTAV. What's so bad? I just wanted to put on an act.

RADOST. Oh, you and your acts! A master! As though he fell
from heaven—but no good where tact is needed. Who goes
from gaiety to stupidity may amuse, harming no one but
himself: but when he wants to amuse someone with idiocy,
then he insults him and is off on the wrong track.

GUSTAV. It's true, uncle, true to the last iota; what luck that
I always have you with me, that you always advise me in
such a clear way, or else I'd be ready to go on doing stupid
things.

RADOST. [*Raising his eyes toward heaven.*] You would?

GUSTAV. [*Embracing him.*] Thank you, uncle dear, for your
advice, for your sermon. From now on I'll do everything you
ask.

RADOST. [*Pleading.*] Then these conversations . . .

GUSTAV. Oh, the devil with them! This country cackling sticks
in my throat already!

RADOST. Oh . . . oh . . . angry already.

GUSTAV. It's too great an art, this amusing village ladies for
someone from the city. Mention society—"Ho, ho! Putting
on airs!" Talk about farming—"What do we care?" "Nothing else to talk about but hammer and threshing?" Talk
about literature—"My! How learned!" Joke—you're a harebrain. Don't joke—serious. Be happy—you're making fun.
Be sad—you're haughty. It's enough; in the country before people get to know you, say and do what you want—
you get blamed anyway.

RADOST. But Aniela, is she to be blamed too?

GUSTAV. What can I talk to her about? I spoke about fields,
meadows, streams, sheep and rams—what the devil else am
I to talk about?

RADOST. When you get angry and start invoking devils . . . But
what do you do in town?

GUSTAV. I don't talk with maidens.

RADOST. Maiden, no maiden, who looks so carefully!

GUSTAV. Ah, uncle dear, how you've grown old. When I can't say what's on my mind, I'll beat around the bush, and keep repeating, a hundred words to one, until slowly I reach my goal. That's because a thought is like water; the narrower the passage, the higher it rises.

RADOST. A clear argument, a beautiful comparison.

GUSTAV. With a maiden, admit it, when I groan once: "I love you," she'll answer: "I love you, too"—and the conversation ends.

RADOST. And if: "I don't love you"?

GUSTAV. That's also the end.

RADOST. But with you even the devil reaches no end. But stay, wait a moment! Hold on there! Do you know the plan of Aniela and Clara?

GUSTAV. No.

RADOST. Neither wants to and will not get married.

GUSTAV. [*With pretended alarm, leading Radost to one side.*] How is that, uncle? Ah, don't believe it! They want to ruin men, preserve their maidenly virtue? Perhaps all of them?

RADOST. [*Patting him under the chin.*] Oh, you scatterbrain you! [*Leaves.*]

GUSTAV. [*After a short pause.*] That cold glance, but loving eye, the sigh trapped deep in her chest, the clouded brow when her face smiles—on my honor, I like her, I love her, I'm going mad!

SCENE 4. Aniela, Clara, Gustav. Aniela sits down soon and begins embroidering. Gustav always directs the conversation to her. A great difference and sudden transition in his conversation. He speaks to Aniela with affection, but to Clara sarcastically or with contemptuous indifference. Clara speaks rapidly and heatedly, often for Aniela. Aniela speaks slowly, languidly.

GUSTAV. After a long war an armistice is declared.

ANIELA. I ask for peace.

GUSTAV. Who opposes it?

CLARA. [*Between them.*] Not every one deserves it.

GUSTAV. [*Not noticing Clara.*] The first condition then?

CLARA. Oh, not so fast . . .

GUSTAV. Mutual respect.

ANIELA. And my neutrality.

GUSTAV. Impossible. Let's try an offensive-defensive alliance.

CLARA. What generosity!

GUSTAV. Then I'll set the terms.

ANIELA. Jokes!

GUSTAV. I am asking.

CLARA. A lot I believe it.

GUSTAV. What?

CLARA. I advise . . .

GUSTAV. I implore.

CLARA. [Aside.] Doesn't he see me?

GUSTAV. I shall observe them faithfully.

CLARA. [Aside.] Is he making fun of me?

GUSTAV. I swear twice.

CLARA. He swears without measure who begs for faith.

GUSTAV. [Not looking at her, indifferently.] And a poor beggar, at that. Perhaps he'll find his treasure.

CLARA. He has a long way to go.

GUSTAV. [As before.] The distance of the goal doesn't lessen the hope.

CLARA. A hard prize to win.

GUSTAV. [Looking her straight in the eyes, phlegmatic.] But modesty is harder.

CLARA. [Excited.] Then war.

GUSTAV. I am armed against you.

ANIELA. I stay with Clara.

GUSTAV. I have to envy her.

CLARA. And I am with Aniela.

GUSTAV. Then there is no war.

CLARA. [With growing excitement.] And why may I ask?

GUSTAV. [Indifferently.] Because I am peaceful, not as befits a man, but rather a maiden.

CLARA. [Heatedly.] No—a man is afraid of frankness. He'd like always to cover his soul with a fog, to have two lights and stand between them.

GUSTAV. Where did you get such a bad opinion about men?

CLARA. It's quite a flattering one.

Gustav. [*Ironically.*] Profound problems! My head's in no position to solve them.

Clara. Isn't men's favorite art deceiving and betraying? Each one takes pride in it, seeks a reward for it. The more victims he can count, the more he can lie, the more noble the wreath he can crown himself with.

Gustav. Hm! I am very sorry for you.

Clara. And I am very grateful to you. But if this is pity, then what's the reason?

Gustav. [*Phlegmatic.*] That with such an innocent soul, so young, you have already experienced male treachery.

Clara. Already experienced? And who says so?

Gustav. A healthy man does not know sickness, nor a rich man poverty. The same for deceit, who has never been deceived. However, from a few books read rather hastily wisdom withholds general blame.

Aniela. But one example remains in my memory.

Gustav. [*Drawing closer to Clara.*] Oh, example! An example can be both good and bad, but the bad allures us more often. [*To Clara.*] Avenging then the wrongs of the whole female sex, lovely Clara has taken a vow never to make a single of her admirers happy.

Clara. [*Hastily.*] Who said so?

Gustav. [*Phlegmatic.*] Who? Albin.

Clara. [*As before.*] In this way Mr. Gustav will now certainly make similar vows on Aniela's part. Everyone willingly shares his own misery.

Gustav. [*Concealing the insult behind a smile.*] Hm! Miss Clara battles with the spirit of a man, and the zeal which reddens her cheeks brings the age of the Amazons before us.

Clara. [*Angrily.*] Zeal—is zeal; I know what it means . . . and I'll say it a hundred times over again: that my soul can't stand men! My mission—is to hate them—I have sworn it twice and I hold the vow sacred! [*Leaves.*]

SCENE 5. Aniela, Gustav.

Gustav. [*As though talking to Clara.*] I hold it sacred! Yes, yes, we'll see. Hatred! For all! And she swears it sacred.

[*To Aniela.*] Oh, no, don't share such thoughts, Aniela. God implanted hatred in the human heart as punishment for grievous sins; and what reason would your soul have to bear a particle of this guilt? Tell me rather that you don't believe it, that love does exist, that it can be sincere. Enough evil already awaits you in this. Ah, unbelief is like sharp thorns; experience slowly gathers them into a bouquet to hand over faithfully to old age! But pure trust, that's the blossom of youth!

ANIELA. Sooner or later the storm will ruin it.

GUSTAV. Yes, a little later a little wind will batter the flowers, and then the fruit will grow—end of the analogy. [*Moves a chair closer and sits down. Brief silence.*] I did not deserve your hatred at all, but very much your anger.

ANIELA. [*Very indifferent throughout the whole scene, occupied with her work.*] Not mine.

GUSTAV. Yours, Miss!

ANIELA. I know nothing about it.

GUSTAV. Oh, you know—but generously forgive someone who sincerely admits his own folly.

ANIELA. Why come to me with that?

GUSTAV. Ah, what a question! For whose regard could I care more? I was wrong.

ANIELA. Is that so?

GUSTAV. I am confessing.

ANIELA. [*Always indifferently.*] Then I believe you.

GUSTAV. [*Drawing near to her.*] Forgive me.

ANIELA. So be it.

GUSTAV. [*Kissing her hand.*] Sincerely?

ANIELA. Sincerely.

GUSTAV. Then I shall turn over a new leaf from now on. But in the meantime, let the goodness of Aniela grant me hope as the star of my happiness.

ANIELA. You'll get no hope from me.

GUSTAV. [*Imploring.*] The hope of hopes.

ANIELA. Not a one.

GUSTAV. [*Getting out of the chair.*] That was too sharp. [*A short pause.*] Do you know my uncle's intention?

ANIELA. I do.

GUSTAV. And that your mother is an ally?

ANIELA. I know it.

GUSTAV. And the lovely Aniela will not fulfill the dearest wishes of all?

ANIELA. No.

GUSTAV. [*Starting.*] No?

ANIELA. [*Indifferently.*] No.

GUSTAV. [*Ironically.*] Short enough an answer.

ANIELA. But honest.

GUSTAV. Too much so! [*Crossing over, he leans on the arm of the chair in which he was sitting.*] Because of your vows . . . ?

ANIELA. I know nothing about that.

GUSTAV. Don't you want to get married?

ANIELA. Not now.

GUSTAV. But later?

ANIELA. Who can guess the future?

GUSTAV. [*Pacing, excited.*] Why not guess? Oh, guess, guess, it's very easy to guess, that soon with a crash, rattle, thud, some rival will fall into the yard, and what I couldn't win today—he will tomorrow. Isn't that the way it'll be?

ANIELA. Everything is possible.

GUSTAV. [*Walking away, sits down and speaks gently.*] However, I ask one small consideration: if you don't want to— don't create hope against your convictions, but don't let your impetuosity forbid me from hoping. I ask that much . . .

ANIELA. I don't understand.

GUSTAV. [*Impatient.*] What do you mean, "I don't understand?" You don't want to understand.

ANIELA. Ah, that's possible.

GUSTAV. [*Starting up and walking around.*] "That's possible?" Ha, ha, ha! It's funny! Everything "is possible"—on my honor, it's funny! I, oh my, I don't know how to please her at all. But some neighbor, some Albin the second, a melancholic lover, gloomy aspirant, will win the prize of thousands of sighs. [*After a short pause, sitting down composed.*] I'm so distasteful to Aniela too?

ANIELA. [*Always indifferent, not looking at him.*] Distasteful? Why?

GUSTAV. [*Pushing forward with his chair.*] No?

ANIELA. No.

GUSTAV. Honestly?

ANIELA. Honestly.

GUSTAV. [*Pushing forward with his chair.*] You won't look at me?

ANIELA. [*Raising her eyes to him and then lowering them at once to her work.*] Certainly.

GUSTAV. That way?

ANIELA. How then?

GUSTAV. But so coldly.

ANIELA. And how else?

GUSTAV. [*Enthusiastically.*] Get angry with me, get angry with me at least.

ANIELA. Angry? And for what?

GUSTAV. [*Gets up and speaks to himself.*] This is unbearable. [*Walks, then stands before her.*] Does it so amuse you, is it so pleasant, that I am suffering so much?

ANIELA. Oho! Suffering already!

GUSTAV. You don't believe in my love for you?

ANIELA. I don't.

GUSTAV. [*Sitting down.*] Ask me for proof! Tell me what to do! In what way—I'll do everything.

ANIELA. Don't talk to me about it.

GUSTAV. [*Wanting to get up, but holding himself back; with dampened ardor.*] So?

ANIELA. So.

GUSTAV. I have to be silent?

ANIELA. Please.

GUSTAV. Long?

ANIELA. Forever.

GUSTAV. [*Starting, ironically.*] No, there couldn't be gentler orders, and issued in a friendlier way. [*Paces.*] Love and keep silent—fine! Excellent! Keep silent and love! For one's whole life! [*After a short pause, stands before her.*] Why this loathing? What's the reason for it? Perhaps I can lessen it, if I'm to blame, but bring it into the open so I can see it.

ANIELA. I have no loathing for anyone in the world.

GUSTAV. It's hard to love someone in just a day, but to hate him is almost impossible too. Today I'm the target of this hatred. I'm making a sad test and will set a precedent that it *is* possible to hate someone in just a day.

ANIELA. Let's forget about this unpleasant subject.

GUSTAV. Easy for you to order—beyond my power to do. [*With growing fervor.*] Listen, Aniela, listen to the voice that trustingly confides the whole future of its fate. [*Aniela rises.*] With naked soul I stand as before a divinity. In your hands is my happiness and unhappiness. Lift them on the scale, but lift them slowly . . . [*Keeps Aniela from leaving.*] Listen, I don't demand you share my feelings. Pleas won't win what is a gift of the heart, but don't despise my honorable intentions and I shall devote all my efforts, all my energies of which sincere love can be capable, to win what today I am unable to. But show me, Aniela, show me the way! . . . [*Holds her back.*] What? You leave me without a word? [*Holds her; with excitement.*] Then I take recourse to what everyone in misfortune has fair right to, though always in vain. [*Kneels.*] See, at your feet I beg your . . . mercy!

[*Aniela goes out through the right door at the rear. Gustav remains in a kneeling position. Turned to the parterre he shakes his head as if saying "I beg you." He rises at the first words spoken by Clara.*]

SCENE 6. Gustav, Clara from the left side.

CLARA. What does this mean? Prayers of thanksgiving? Or penance for too bold hopes?

GUSTAV. Your sharp guesses have led you astray this time. I got tired of constantly sitting, walking, so I knelt.

CLARA. No, no, I know what's happening. And I shall recount it accurately. Your melancholic glances were unnoticed, your sentimental sighing unheeded, your words unheard— then what remained? To your knees—love or death! But you should have had a sword in hand, a stiletto, a table knife, or at least murderers' scissors! [*She laughs.*] And now?

We stand—without feeling, without speech? And all the result of a first quarrel? Ah, so easy a victory really, it doesn't please me. I only marvel at its ease.

GUSTAV. Your quiver is already empty, so jokes aside. Oh! Miss Clara, you see me in despair!

CLARA. Oh, I'll still find a weapon for defense. But joking aside, what does this change mean? Is it perhaps the result of this morning's sleep, or a sudden crisis of wit?

GUSTAV. Too deep is the sorrow in my heart, too impartially do I judge my errors to take heed now of witty barbs. The goal of my desires, to which I was close, I now see fading from sight, and it pains the soul so terribly that I pay for my own guilt with my own happiness. And that it is too fair, I still must confess. Then whether you rebuke my lightheadedness, with which I trusted in faith beyond measure; whether you call stupidity what I did out of frivolousness, whether you regard a lack of politeness worthy of punishment—however you scold me, in whatever way, you'll always say less about me than I would myself.

CLARA. [*With feigned humility.*] The superiority of men over the judgment of women I experienced just a while ago. Now I would be too bold to dispute it. Especially when male excellence humbly places its own mistakes on the scale of wisdom, it is more fitting for me to repeat his words or remain silent. But this honest repentance and these praiseworthy regrets, from what terrible guilt do they stem?

GUSTAV. Ah, Miss Clara, I met Aniela.

CLARA. I still see no reason for despair.

GUSTAV. Having met her, I see how wrong I've been.

CLARA. [*Musing.*] Aha! Mr. Gustav truly loves her?

GUSTAV. Say idolize and you'd say too little.

CLARA. [*Reflecting.*] Hm! Isn't it only some passing fancy?

GUSTAV. The purest love heaven has given.

CLARA. But this love, will it be constant?

GUSTAV. It will last my life, and expire with it.

CLARA. And Anielka for certain didn't want to believe it?

GUSTAV. She doesn't even want to listen—that's the reason for my despair.

CLARA. [*After a short pause.*] Too bad—but perhaps she would listen to me?

GUSTAV. What love dares not, friendship may.

CLARA. If I change her mind and transform this grief . . .

GUSTAV. Ah, Miss Clara, you've guessed my thoughts.

CLARA. I'll tell her how Mr. Gustav used to be before.

GUSTAV. Use bold colors, spare me no blame.

CLARA. That he was happy, as a young man usually is . . .

GUSTAV. [*Finishing the sentence.*] A scatterbrain, lightheaded, fickle, thoughtless . . .

CLARA. [*Finishing the sentence still faster.*] Vain, malicious, proud, egotistical . . .

GUSTAV. [*Reflecting.*] That's a bit too much—much too much.

CLARA. [*More and more animated in spite of herself.*] That he saw a country bumpkin in her . . .

GUSTAV. [*As before.*] That's a bit much . . .

CLARA. That in his pride he thought that in the country politeness is something to laugh at . . .

GUSTAV. That's too much . . .

CLARA. That he lacks common sense . . .

GUSTAV. Whoa! Too much; the picture's banned!

CLARA. [*Passing suddenly from excitement to tenderness, with a smile.*] I am using bold colors, I spare no blame—but I shall also tell her on the other hand that he reformed, once he recognized his faults, that the love by which he is transported is sincere, and the slower it grows, the longer will it last; that if still it is not mutual, it should at least merit faith.

GUSTAV. Ah, yes, yes, everything, my dear Miss Clara! You read my heart, you think together with me.

CLARA. [*Bursting out in a laugh.*] Ha, ha, ha! I can't hold out any longer! Ha, ha, ha! My dear Miss Clara! Ha, ha, ha! Wonderful! I've found the way then—My weapon succeeds, his hard armor cracks. [*Seriously.*] Why does male cunning terrify us? Let our own weakness frighten us more, for the only one who won't admit [*facing Gustav*] that men are not difficult to defeat is the one who doesn't want to. Believe him genuinely and in the figure of man you'll see a slippery, poisonous snake. Resist his will, have your own opinion—he becomes a raging lion, a tiger. But play accompaniment to his little song; come out of each encounter as though defeated; always spin circles in his head—and you'll have him in a silken web. Unless I'm wrong this day's contest in no way lessens my opinion. Having expressed this fully and at length [*with a low bow*], I have the honor to remain your most obedient servant. [*Leaves by the right side door.*]

SCENE 7. *Gustav.* [*Alone.*] *From the time Clara burst out laughing, he has been standing as if nailed to the spot. A short pause.*

GUSTAV. Hm, hm, hm! So that's how it is? Because I love sincerely, act frankly, trust in frankness, I have fallen so low? Hold on, little lizard! Sharp little mind, sharp little tongue, but don't make a pair of Albin and me. You'll teach me to deceive? You want tricks? Agreed. [*He walks around thoughtfully; after a short pause.*] Aniela is good, but she's influenced—What trust rejects, let goodness get. I'll compose a romance. I'll make her my confidante—For a time I'll change the sweetheart into friend. I'll gain her pity and summon her defense. [*A short pause.*] A secret shared unites two hearts, so—I'll awaken her feelings by a picture of love, direct them to myself and stand pat all around. [*Walks around in deep thought. A dumb scene, in which it is evident that he is hatching some plan. Sits, gets up, walks about, stands. Finally, standing in one place for a while sunk in thought, gives course to words with extraordinary speed as if they were held back until then. When Albin enters he hardly sees him. Albin is surprised, and for a while stands in the doorway, only later approaching Gustav slowly.*]

SCENE 8. *Gustav, Albin.*

GUSTAV. Oh, there it is, there's the reason, the source of all the trouble here! Our Albin's shadow walks and crawls,

weeping devil knows what about! Fifty years of groaning,
sobbing; fifty years of sighing, loving. Now every girl is
bound to think that that's the way that love is spun, as if
we lived a hundred years with fifty set aside for sighing!
Pouring tears both day and night now he'll make himself a
fountain soon. And in the meantime, without aid, have I
to endure your girl friend? Don't love her so abjectly and
you'll find her loving you in turn! Don't let yourself be
ruled, be strong, she'll soon recognize your power; don't
bore with tears and with grieving and you'll conquer like
a man should. Fools alone think otherwise. Farewell! [*Leaving; in a quieter tone.*] May the devil take you . . . [*Returning.*] Where did she go?

ALBIN. Ah, who?

GUSTAV. [*Shrugging his shoulders.*] Even that he doesn't know!
[*Goes after Aniela.*]

ALBIN. [*Alone.*] Now I've hurt him—he's gone away in anger.
Where can I pour my tears, where must I lay my sighs? I
burn two years, ten years—yet I shall not change. For a moment, for the tiniest bit of a moment, let Clara look at me
and yearn a little.

SCENE 9. Albin, Clara.

ALBIN. Clara, will the weeped-for moment never come when
my heart's deep wound receives the balsam?

CLARA. Receive it can, but not from me.

ALBIN. I love.

CLARA. I know.

ALBIN. I wait.

CLARA. In vain.

ALBIN. I beg.

CLARA. Enough.

ALBIN. Cruel!

CLARA. Maybe.

ALBIN. Oh, if I could cease loving!

CLARA. [*A ball of wool falls. Albin pursues it and picks it up.*]
God grant that once the ball should fall from my hand
and your lordship not be there to get it; that once a ker-

chief should fall from the table, and your lordship not spread on the floor after it; that once I should need shears or a knife, and your lordship not search or fly after them; that once I should sneeze secretly and not hear your God bless you's! No, this is really unbearable now.

ALBIN. If I long to anticipate all your wishes, if I want to dedicate my whole life to you, attribute it to my love and your own nature. But because I have been unable to soften too hard a heart, tell me, Clara, have I thereby earned only scorn?

CLARA. No, not scorn, I don't say that.

ALBIN. But if not scorn, then what do you call it?

CLARA. Your sufferings are often painful to me. That they are sincere, I believe, but it changes nothing. Clara has no ear for any man's voice. She has sworn hatred to all, and she'll preserve it.

ALBIN. Ah, in this hatred my share is not small.

CLARA. But it's not the largest.

ALBIN. Oh, Clara, if you only cared to grasp what happens in my soul at your glance, you would certainly fulfill the hopes of my heart.

CLARA. I certainly would not fulfill them.

ALBIN. Never?

CLARA. Enough, I beg you.

ALBIN. Cruel one! That word is death . . .

CLARA. [*Laughing.*] Ah, I bring death, death!

ALBIN. The world will soon envy you this new honor.

CLARA. Until now no man ever died from love.

ALBIN. Because no one could, but more than one sincerely wanted to.

CLARA. Then desire must be taken as the cause. Honoring thus the death of Mr. Albin my grief begins from this day on.

ALBIN. Ah, I see, happy Gustav advised me well!

CLARA. [*Ironically.*] What did the Councillor of State graciously advise?

ALBIN. [*Albin speaks slowly, Clara quickly.*] "Don't love," he said "with so much feeling, and you'll be loved."

CLARA. "Don't love!"—I see, it already annoys him that some-

one is faithful and puts all his happiness in that. It so tempted him, he just had to change it.

ALBIN. "Two years you sigh, weep, and you don't know why
yourself."

CLARA. Don't know why yourself, yourself! . . . Whoever heard
anything like it?

ALBIN. "Every woman wants to impose so long a penance."

CLARA. And he prefers a day, an hour, a minute?

ALBIN. "Don't let her rule you . . ."

CLARA. Don't let her rule you!—Bravo! "Don't let her!" Well
I ask you, some right it is!

ALBIN. "And you'll rule over her . . ."

CLARA. What, what? You'll rule her? Right away, you want to
rule, to rule. How then can there be order on earth? How?
When one teaches a hundred to go wrong and the first lesson
is: "Don't let yourself be ruled!"

ALBIN. But I have no desire to heed him—I shall do what you
say.

CLARA. [*To herself.*] There's an adviser! There's a professor!

ALBIN. [*Approaching, affectionately.*] What am I to do?

CLARA. Go away. [*Bowing, Albin sighs deeply and goes out.*]

CLARA. [*Alone.*] Talk—he talks; keep quiet—he keeps quiet;
go—he goes; stay—he stays. God Almighty, let him just once
do the opposite. For that submissiveness against will and
conviction makes it impossible to hate or love him.

ACT III

SCENE 1. Aniela, Gustav.

GUSTAV. [*Entering after Aniela from the right door.*] Aniela!
Just one last word.

ANIELA. Oh, today there's no end to these last words! But to
avoid starting this all over again, I want to confess honestly now for the last time: sometime, everyone has to receive
the answer that Mr. Gustav receives from me this day. To
this undertaking then, and not you personally I ask you

to attribute all this unpleasantness. But acting in so open a
way perhaps I bring you some comfort. I would expect, however, that my confession will remain strictly a secret for all,
since I am acting against my mother's order. She understands that though the nets are visible sometimes they can
still catch you. In a word, she forbade me to announce my
intentions. I must patiently suffer confessions; I must first
know someone before I refuse him.

GUSTAV. Then I too shall follow the simple path; in spite of
Radost's order I reveal to you my heart at once: I love . . .

ANIELA. Oh, I've heard that so many times! . . .

GUSTAV. But let me go on—not you, Aniela. [*A short pause.*]
Since no opposing wishes divide us now, I place all my
hope in you. Are you surprised? I believe it—but that's the
way it is. Uncle, who took the place of my father when I
was orphaned, who almost from the cradle always graciously concerned himself with my fate, finally desired some
reward from me, but what kind, God help me! Pleas, tears,
begging, anything to incline his heart to pity. I tried everything, but everything in vain; and in the end I had to promise uncle to win your hand by all means. But when today,
with humble ardor, my trembling lips announced my love,
ah, I must confess that I was secretly afraid and trembled in
my soul. Aren't you moved?

ANIELA. Trembled? From fear?

GUSTAV. Yes, that's the way it is, alas! And your charms and
your virtues so many of which I discover daily, which only
you are not free to see, which can be as alluring as happiness, filled me, only me with anxiety. To win your smile
and friendly glance, to awaken in your heart the first sigh,
that's what I'd call heaven, not just honor or happiness.
However this caused anxiety not only to my soul.

ANIELA. Then it's love you bear another person?

GUSTAV. But how could I defend myself against you? I was
in love, when I already met you; that's why my two-faced
behavior fell under your secret censure. I felt I deserved this
and I admitted it painfully, that even though I am free
of guilt, I am however guilty. But tell me yourself, was there
another way?

ANIELA. I can only dare to say that I see only one way out of this problem: confess to your uncle . . .

GUSTAV. Ah, how many times at his feet with tears in my eyes, I begged his mercy, confessing all!

ANIELA. And what does he say to this?

GUSTAV. He repeats his orders: you have to be, alas, my wife, whom loathing more than desire gave me, whose presence does not even permit me to remember the one I love with all my heart.

ANIELA. Why?

GUSTAV. It would demand a long account, but speaking briefly, it goes back to that age-old business and the duel my uncle had with Aniela's father.

ANIELA. Aniela?

GUSTAV. Both of you have the same given name, the echo of which, beating in my heart, awakes with its charm sweet uneasiness. That is why from the first day I met you I felt an attraction to you as if to a sister.

ANIELA. Strange!

GUSTAV. Oh, if only it were I who loved, and my sufferings were only my concern! But always to feel that each pang repeats itself secretly with painful echo in another person, dearer to me than life, this goes beyond the comprehension of all suffering! It turns one's hand against oneself in order to extinguish the feeling and the mutual suffering!

ANIELA. [*Alarmed almost to tears.*] Mr. Gustav! . . . What is it . . . O God! To kill yourself, kill yourself! . . . That isn't very nice, that's a sin, a great sin; who falls into it must suffer forever in the next world.

GUSTAV. [*Talks rapidly now.*] Save me.

ANIELA. [*Also rapidly.*] I will, I will, but can I?

GUSTAV. You can.

ANIELA. [*As above.*] I'll hear no more about death?

GUSTAV. No more.

ANIELA. I'm still shaking all over.

GUSTAV. Do you want to help then?

ANIELA. But how?

GUSTAV. I'll show you the way: explain it to your mother . . .

ANIELA. All right, I'll do it.

GUSTAV. Have her forgive me.

ANIELA. Oh, I'm sure she will.

GUSTAV. Beg her!

ANIELA. I shall beg, implore, cry bitter tears, until she gives her word to help me in this matter. But don't despair, dear Mr. Gustav.

GUSTAV. In your hands, then, is my happiness, my life.

ANIELA. In mine? Oh, God!

GUSTAV. With mother persuaded . . .

ANIELA. Oh, she will be, she will be, I'm not afraid of that. But when all is said and done, what will she be able to do?

GUSTAV. Appease my uncle.

ANIELA. [*Happily.*] Right! Excellent! I am going without delay, your life is at stake here.

GUSTAV. Good God, not now! She would have reason to put too much of the blame on uncle for risking too much by wanting to entrust to me your peace, and even your whole future. That would surely wreck their friendship and I, unhappily, the object of wrath of both sides, what could I do, except jump into the grave?

ANIELA. Oh, what to do then?

GUSTAV. You do want to help me?

ANIELA. Willingly.

GUSTAV. Then let's continue as we have to this moment: I as though forever in love with you; you, looking with indifference at my love. And later on when they keep urging us I'll make an open, honest declaration. You'll refuse me in the same manner; in this way it will not shock your mother, and my uncle, though somewhat put out, will not accuse me of disobedience. Only then will I call on your defense, you'll placate your mother and then enlighten her.

ANIELA. I understand perfectly.

GUSTAV. [*Kisses her hand.*] Without hatred then?

ANIELA. I shall be happy that our plan turns out well.

GUSTAV. Acting boldly, remember always how much I trust you, how much I've confided in you. If you leave me in this sad time of need I have no one else on earth but you. You are my only protection, my only defense, without you the hope of happiness is lost. Oh, let me win my Aniela from your hand, for I do not have enough feeling, enough life, to repay you for the kindness you've shown me. Although I am not worthy of it, I shall become worthy.

[*Kisses her hand with feeling. While the last lines are being spoken, Radost enters and, unseen, shouts "bravo" and claps his hands.*]

SCENE 2. *Aniela, Gustav, Radost.*

ANIELA. He heard?

GUSTAV. What? He heard?

RADOST. Bravo, children, bravo!

GUSTAV. [*Throwing himself on his knees before Radost.*] Forgive me, uncle!

RADOST. [*Drawing back, surprised.*] Ah! What does this mean?

GUSTAV. [*Moving behind him, quietly.*] If you've already heard, then give it to me, but good.

RADOST. Gustav!

GUSTAV. [*Quietly.*] Get angry. [*Out loud.*] Have pity on my despair! [*Inclining to the rear, as though rejected.*] Don't let your hand repulse me so sternly! [*Softly.*] Get angry, uncle, will you!

RADOST. Listen here now, scatterbrain.

GUSTAV. [*Quietly.*] Better, but still too little.

RADOST. Have you gone mad?

GUSTAV. [*Quietly.*] Good. [*Out loud.*] It's already happened!

RADOST. That's too much now!

GUSTAV. [*Out loud.*] I've confessed all to her. [*Quietly.*] And now, give all you've got!

RADOST. The devil take you!

GUSTAV. [*Softly.*] That's it, that's it!

RADOST. You're making fun of me.

GUSTAV. [*Loudly, tragically.*] Uncle, uncle! You want to see me in my grave.

RADOST. [*Angered.*] Enough of these jokes, enough already, young man; do what you want, let be what has to, I don't want to find a wife for a madman. [*Leaves.*] A madman, completely mad!

SCENE 3. *Aniela, Gustav.*

ANIELA. [*Uneasily.*] What will happen now?

GUSTAV. [*To himself.*] I scraped my knees.

ANIELA. He didn't permit himself to be softened.

GUSTAV. Unheard-of thing.

ANIELA. Perhaps he didn't hear.

GUSTAV. What do you mean "perhaps"?

ANIELA. Perhaps.

GUSTAV. You said so yourself.

ANIELA. No—I was just asking.

GUSTAV. Then the whole fracas was senseless and came at the most inopportune time. I'm almost certain that he didn't hear, but what the whole business is about, it's not hard to guess.

ANIELA. Everything spoiled by his premature enthusiasm.

GUSTAV. He came in on us so suddenly and so deceptively.

ANIELA. [*Pacing uneasily.*] What can I, unhappy person, do about it?

GUSTAV. [*Aside.*] I didn't want to confide my plan.

ANIELA. [*As above.*] How in impulsive haste it's possible to ruin immediately what we undertook! How poor Aniela must be suffering!

GUSTAV. [*Taking her by the hand.*] How can one help but loving that poor Aniela?

ANIELA. One has to love her.

GUSTAV. I've sworn myself to her.

ANIELA. Oh, I believe it truly.

GUSTAV. All my desire rests on that. Then you see yourself: in you, only in you have I help, and all my hopes.

ANIELA. What can I do, and what can I change? Radost is so good, but today he's burning for vengeance.

GUSTAV. If he heard nothing I'll straighten the whole thing out.

ANIELA. Then don't waste time, go Mr. Gustav.

GUSTAV. You make sure you avoid all conversation with him, but see to it that we can meet here again for a little while, just the two of us, for further consultation about this matter. [*Takes her by the hand.*] And please always remember that my whole future lies in your hands, and even more: the happiness of Aniela from whom nothing on earth can separate me. [*Kisses her hand a few times, then goes to the door of his own room, but looking around, leaves through another door.*]

SCENE 4. *Aniela.* [*Alone.*] *Walks around meditating. Then sits down, resting her head on her hand.*

ANIELA. Strange—Strange! My ears still resound with words my soul never knew before. How he loves her! . . . And certainly he is not deceiving her: everything he says his clear glance proves. He happy with her, she happy with him, what more could they want, what more is there? Only one word more for happiness, and what happiness, what happiness—heavens! They trust each other, love each other deeply; am I happy because I don't believe in love? But this is real love, it lasts, it's proven . . . O God! I don't feel my heart in my chest any longer.

SCENE 5. *Aniela, Clara.*

CLARA. What are you thinking about? Writing something perhaps?
ANIELA. Oh, Clara, Clara, if you only knew! . . . But your friendship can't deceive us, I'll tell you everything—briefly —the whole thing: Gustav doesn't love me, but Aniela.
CLARA. Whom?
ANIELA. Aniela! But Radost forbids it; it's a big secret, don't give it away for God's sake!
CLARA. But I don't know anything about it.
ANIELA. It's already gone too far now.
CLARA. What has?
ANIELA. That stubbornness, that hatred too severe.
CLARA. [*With growing impatience.*] Whose?
ANIELA. Radost's.
CLARA. And for whom?
ANIELA. For her.
CLARA. But . . .

ANIELA. Don't torment yourself with vain fears: Gustav doesn't want to marry me at all.

CLARA. That's bad, a man should always want to, until he knows how much women despise him, especially that Gustav, who teaches people how to handle women.

ANIELA. But I'm so sorry for him!

CLARA. [*Ironically.*] Sorry?

ANIELA. He just went wrong.

CLARA. He awoke, then, I see the tenderest feelings.

ANIELA. I hate all men very much, but he places his destiny in my hands: I must defend him.

CLARA. So! And you're happy to.

ANIELA. Happy or not, I can't deceive him.

CLARA. Deceive him, deceive him, darling! Deceive the sultan.

ANIELA. Never, not ever.

CLARA. I'll help you.

ANIELA. And this Aniela who's loved so sincerely?

CLARA. Again I don't know.

ANIELA. I'll explain everything to you.

CLARA. [*Interested.*] Talk.

ANIELA. Where's mother?

CLARA. She was just calling you.

ANIELA. She's so good, I'll confide everything to her too. Just her, and no one else.

CLARA. My dear Aniela, may God protect you so that you won't carry away disgrace from men's snares; I see your hatred already weakening.

ANIELA. Oh, as I love you, I hate them.

RADOST. [*Coming up to them as they leave.*] Miss Aniela! [*Aniela takes Clara by the hand and dragging her with her, runs quickly to the right side door.*] But . . . Miss . . . please . . . [*Returning.*] Hm, hm! Scared away—Gustav had a hand in this—I'm ready to swear that it's his work. Oh, Gustav, Gustav! Sometime I'll give you a good scare! [*Gustav enters through one of the doors to the rear but catching sight of Radost goes out the other door, humming.*]

RADOST. [*Chasing after him.*] Wait now, wait! [*Runs out the door.*]

SCENE 6. Radost, Gustav.

RADOST. [*Leading Gustav.*] Come, come, I've got you birdie. [*Looking at him in the eyes, after a short pause.*] What did you mean by that: "Forgive me, uncle dear?"
GUSTAV. Just that.
RADOST. How, just that?
GUSTAV. Just that!
RADOST. What do you mean, just that?
GUSTAV. Forget it—nothing.
RADOST. Nothing.
GUSTAV. Nothing.
RADOST. It was nothing then: "Forgive me, uncle; take pity on my despair?"
GUSTAV. [*Rapidly.*] Oh, it's clear: in love it's unpleasant —who'd deny it—when sometimes there's an argument or a fight and, as though drawing strength from the power of feeling, love fights with itself or pushes itself away. Then it's really the end, the end of all the little games—Well, the matter's clear enough—understand, uncle?
[*Wants to leave.*]
RADOST. [*Restraining him.*] Wait a moment—I understand nothing.
GUSTAV. And I can't tell you any more clearly.
RADOST. Why did you kneel as if in prayer?
GUSTAV. [*With feigned ardor.*] Then uncle doesn't believe me? He doesn't believe me? [*Leaving.*] If that's the case, good— good—I know what I have to do: I'll have the carriage readied and off I go. Jan! Hey there!
RADOST. [*Going after him and patting his shoulder.*] Well now, Gustav dear, come on!
GUSTAV. [*Feigning anger.*] When I say . . . !
RADOST. [*As above.*] Enough, enough, enough, hold on, don't go.
GUSTAV. I am explaining myself well, clearly, and honestly.
RADOST. I understand now, I believe everything [*To himself.*] What a powder-keg! He's a regular spark, a flame, a fire!
GUSTAV. [*Throwing himself on Radost's neck.*] Uncle dear!

RADOST. [*Embracing him.*] Ah, Gustav, my dear Gustav [*tear-fully*], you don't listen to my advice.

GUSTAV. I listen to it and value it, and what I accomplish will be worthy of praise.

RADOST. But why does Clara . . .

GUSTAV. Oh, Clara, that Clara, she really is a divine punishment on me. She's all over the place, has a hand in everything; stubborn as a young cockerel, ki-ki-ki-ing everywhere [*demonstrating*], set up on her high horse! And you know, uncle, you know what you ought to do for everyone's sake?

RADOST. What?

GUSTAV. Marry her.

RADOST. You're crazy!

GUSTAV. Do me the favor.

RADOST. An idea worthy of your head.

GUSTAV. She upsets me very much.

RADOST. [*Shrugging his shoulders.*] Therefore an old man like me . . . She won't upset you, if you don't her. And why are you trying to get Albin stirred up against her?

GUSTAV. He's already stirred up.

RADOST. How is that?

GUSTAV. He loves Aniela like a kitten.

RADOST. Who? Albin?

GUSTAV. Albin.

RADOST. It's unbelievable.

GUSTAV. Yes, he does love her, he's almost dying from love; no disputing it, it's a known thing.

RADOST. Albin?—Our Albin?

GUSTAV. Oh, everything that glitters isn't gold; oh, he's a fickle little piece: makes vows to one, and loves another.

RADOST. But how are you getting on with Aniela?

GUSTAV. [*After a long silence, folding his arms.*] What is this magnetism business all about?

RADOST. [*Surprised.*] Ma . . . magnetism?

GUSTAV. What is it? What? Tell me!

RADOST. But why do you bring it up at such a time?

GUSTAV. [*After a short pause.*] Magnetism, they say, is that free force that conducts the spring of life from one body to another. If I have such power in me to pour my own fire into another's veins, then why couldn't I, through a strong will and burning pulses, impress the stamp of my own feeling on a fair, young soul, pure as freshly fallen snow?

RADOST. If I understand you correctly, may I be struck down!

GUSTAV. I love and I shall be loved—clear?

RADOST. Clear, quite clear, but a little too bold.

GUSTAV. Boldness before happiness, like happiness before praise!

RADOST. You shall be loved, but don't be a scatterbrain.

GUSTAV. Oh, uncle dear! You would think of that.

RADOST. Ah, don't I think and fry my brains over you?

GUSTAV. And I am always ready to thank you.

RADOST. Thank me, if you wish, but reform yourself at the same time.

GUSTAV. That has already happened at your order. And I hope everything will end well just so long as you pay no attention to what goes on; in harmony or quarrel, in tumult or quiet, let your eye sleep and your ear hear nothing.

RADOST. What will come of all this?

GUSTAV. What will come out of it? [*Embraces him.*] A wedding. [*Runs out.*]

RADOST. [*After him.*] Little sense, too much confidence.

ACT IV

SCENE *1*. *Gustav, Jan. Gustav enters sunk in thought, Jan a step behind him with a black kerchief in hand.*

GUSTAV. [*Extending his left hand without stopping.*] Tie it up! [*To himself.*] It's happened—I love her madly—But she?

JAN. [*Following him and examining his hand.*] Nothing at all . . .

GUSTAV. [*Stopping.*] What do you mean, nothing?

JAN. [*As before.*] There's nothing here.

GUSTAV. On my hand! Just tie it. [*Paces, talking to himself.*] Hm, she's agreeable, but how will it be when I change roles? How? When should I begin?

JAN. [*Unable to tie the bandage because of Gustav's gestures and his moving around.*] Please stop for just a moment. [*Gustav tears his hand away, but Jan grabs it and continues tying it while walking around.*]

GUSTAV. [*To himself.*] Stop—of course—there's a knot.

JAN. [*Letting go of the arm.*] There is a knot, Sir.

GUSTAV. [*To himself.*] But how do you untie it?

JAN. By the tip.

GUSTAV. [*Stopping in anger.*] Jan!

JAN. Yes Sir.

GUSTAV. You're stupid.

JAN. I am?

GUSTAV. [*Tearing off the bandage.*] That's not the hand. I don't write with the left one.

JAN. But which hand hurts?

GUSTAV. What does it concern you—here, take it: bind up the right one. [*Extends the left hand and continues pacing. Talks to himself.*] The first time I'm in love.

JAN. But, Sir . . .

GUSTAV. [*Continuing to pace.*] Well, get a move on! [*To himself.*] A different kind of love.

JAN. It's the same one.

GUSTAV. You're lying.

JAN. The left.

GUSTAV. [*Giving him the right hand.*] Oh, the hand—but how slow you are. [*Begins to walk pulling Jan who supports himself forcibly. Talks to himself.*] I'll make her love me . . . Ow, you'll break my hand!

JAN. Which one, Sir?

GUSTAV. Enough, damn it, let it go!

JAN. Not easy tying a bandage.

GUSTAV. And neither is shutting up.

SCENE 2. *Gustav, Albin. At a sign from Gustav, Jan leaves.*

GUSTAV. [*Aside.*] I feel moisture, a fountain is approaching! [*To Albin.*] Sad Albin! Like the morning dew the mist from your tears fills the whole house.

ALBIN. And still they haven't melted my rock!

GUSTAV. Before they become nitric acid, may I suggest another way in the meantime?

ALBIN. Advise me, advise me, but better than this morning.

GUSTAV. Did I advise you badly?

ALBIN. God will judge that!

GUSTAV. What happened?

ALBIN. I was shown the door. Advise me, advise me, but only not how to rule over women.

GUSTAV. First I'll comfort you.

ALBIN. Me? Comfort? Heavens!

GUSTAV. Clara is in love with you.

ALBIN. Your jokes are too painful.

GUSTAV. I swear it.

ALBIN. I don't believe it.

GUSTAV. One has to swear to you.

ALBIN. How do you know?

GUSTAV. [*Acting insulted.*] What is this? If you want, don't believe me—be stubborn, but don't ask me to betray a confidence.

ALBIN. [*Throwing himself on Gustav's neck.*] Oh, oh! Gustav, I'm speechless . . . my tears . . .

GUSTAV. [*Patting him.*] Sh, sh, Albin.

ALBIN. She loves me?

GUSTAV. Madly.

ALBIN. What will happen now?

GUSTAV. I'll marry Albin off.

ALBIN. Me? Me? To her? To Clara?

GUSTAV. But you'll have to play the tune as I compose it—you promise?

ALBIN. Fine, what am I to do?

GUSTAV. Break up this scheme of theirs that has become the reason for your unhappiness, and then force them to confess the truth.

ALBIN. Too much happiness!

GUSTAV. Do you need so little?

ALBIN. With her? Great heavens!

GUSTAV. You bore me—great hades!

ALBIN. What do you want?

GUSTAV. Listen to me.

ALBIN. I am listening.

GUSTAV. Make her think you love someone else.

ALBIN. God Almighty, don't finish! I'm dying!

GUSTAV. [*Persuading.*] Just for a little while!

ALBIN. Never!

GUSTAV. A day.

ALBIN. I don't want to.

GUSTAV. An hour.

ALBIN. I'll die first.

GUSTAV. [*Impatient.*] Die then.

ALBIN. I will not change my feelings.

GUSTAV. Then just pretend that they've died.

ALBIN. I simply can't.

GUSTAV. Well then—that you don't love her so much.

ALBIN. Pretend?

GUSTAV. [*Imploring.*] A little.

ALBIN. [*After a short pause.*] I don't trust my own strength.

GUSTAV. [*Aside.*] Go bust! [*To Albin.*] Then, just keep quiet.

ALBIN. How long?

GUSTAV. One day.

ALBIN. Be silent?

GUSTAV. No fainting.

ALBIN. A day?

GUSTAV. No sighing.

ALBIN. No sighing? [*A short pause.*] It's hard for me.

GUSTAV. [*With feeling.*] The second time you'll win everything;
and then for a whole day you'll be able to groan, weep,
sigh, moan, only not now, not now, damn it!

ALBIN. And when I finally do everything as you say, when
Clara sees that Albin isn't sighing . . .

GUSTAV. [*Impatient.*] Then I'll marry Albin, I'll marry
Albin . . .

ALBIN. [*After a short pause.*] Until tomorrow?

GUSTAV. But—complete silence.

ALBIN. Good.

GUSTAV. Your word.

ALBIN. But . . .

GUSTAV. You give it?

ALBIN. I give it.

GUSTAV. And now so long [*embracing him*]—wish me luck. [*Turns to the door.*] Go on.
Albin leaves.

[*Alone.*] So I'll cause some trouble for Clara. Whether she loves him or not—she's certainly curious. This change in things will interest her, and before she figures everything out, step by step I'll bring her nearer to the goal.

SCENE 3 Gustav, Aniela.

ANIELA. [*Entering cautiously.*] Did Radost hear?
GUSTAV. No, he didn't.
ANIELA. Oh, I can breathe again!
GUSTAV. I've straightened everything out.
ANIELA. I was dying of fear.
GUSTAV. [*Taking her hand.*] Such kindness so rare in this world, so many proofs of friendly interest. How much gratitude does this wake in me?
ANIELA. What have I done worthy of gratitude?
GUSTAV. You want to do good.
ANIELA. Because it's nice to.
GUSTAV. Today you have your chance.
ANIELA. Please show me how.
GUSTAV. I hurt my hand.
ANIELA. Very much?
GUSTAV. Not too badly. But I can't hold a pen at all. [*Not boldly.*] If you would care to assist me this time . . .
ANIELA. To write? What?
GUSTAV. A letter.
ANIELA. A letter! Oh, no!
GUSTAV. Two words.
ANIELA. Two—to whom?
GUSTAV. To my Aniela.
ANIELA. What? I have to write such letters?
GUSTAV. And what's bad about it?
ANIELA. You can't persuade me.
GUSTAV. [*Sorrowfully.*] I hurt my hand.
ANIELA. Then maybe someone else . . .
GUSTAV. Ah, who else on earth shares my grief? To whom

can I confide, where I can beg a favor, if I grieve before you in vain?

ANIELA. [*Walking, half in tears.*] What must I do? [*A short pause.*] Don't write at all.

GUSTAV. Aniela, you're still rich in the flower of life, you know only pleasure and no suffering; still happy, you have no idea what separation means! You don't know how when you're separated the whole vastness of the universe concentrates only on a single point, and that point is the moment of expected news. You don't know what it is to strain the eye burningly as every rustle makes you catch your breath, and what pain it is, when the hour passes—and with it your only comfort paid for ahead of time.

ANIELA. That's love! Go on fall in love, then!

GUSTAV. Yes, love, fall in love! A divine pleasure!

ANIELA. Oh no!

GUSTAV. Why?

ANIELA. I don't know, but I'm frightened.

GUSTAV. Frightened?

ANIELA. I'm afraid . . .

GUSTAV. Like a child of the doctor who nevertheless can restore his life. Ah, indifference denies nature! A soul incapable of choosing and loving another darkens every emotion with cold calculation. For such a person it's nothing to be active for others; for her, tears are nothing—people are not brothers. But when my heart beats with love, when I say: I love—only then do I live, I live happy and in pleasant confusion I draw the whole world into my embrace.

ANIELA. Yes, if love could be real . . .

GUSTAV. Love is the one . . .

ANIELA. Thousands of pretenses.

GUSTAV. Do we deny the light because darkness exists?

ANIELA. Misleading appearances force us to deny.

GUSTAV. [*With feeling, taking her by the hand.*] Ah, then don't believe that caressing look that slowly gliding rises in your eye; that trembling hand, when it is near you; don't believe that voice that forces itself into your heart. But let your own feeling be your faith: that yearning tenderness, that uncertain desire and especially that attraction fate cannot change are only an echo of similar feeling. [*At a sign of disbelief from Aniela.*] Believe me, there are souls created for each other: if destiny drives them in opposite directions, they, despite the fates, in this world or the next, will find each other, will attract each other, and will then unite just as the fragrances of two flowers different from each other, unite in the air, each one drowning in the other. [*Aniela is pensive; after a short pause Gustav continues talking.*] And what was it, tell me, that awoke in me from the first moment this trust in you? What emboldened me to make you my confidante if not the heart, which is never wrong?

ANIELA. Ah, but would anyone betray a confidence?

GUSTAV. Clara would be the first.

ANIELA. Too incorrect an opinion.

GUSTAV. The worse it is for me, the more the advantage for her.

ANIELA. Who? What? Clara?

GUSTAV. Radost is going to marry her.

ANIELA. Radost?

GUSTAV. As soon as his plan for me fails then out of vengeance he'll marry Clara, disinherit and ruin me forever.

ANIELA. That can't be.

GUSTAV. It can't be changed.

ANIELA. She won't want to.

GUSTAV. It's all arranged.

ANIELA. And her sincere loathing . . .

GUSTAV. Sincere or insincere, Radost is rich, Clara's rather greedy—there's nothing to say. As two and two makes four —if not today, then tomorrow she'll be his wife.

ANIELA. But her vows?

GUSTAV. Vows? A real dream! And you, Aniela, abandon that dark road while you still have time and I can guide you. But tell me honestly—when a flight of fancy sometimes paints for us a picture of happiness and adorns commonplace but dear objects with the purest colors of the flowers of dreams—what gathers the light, and stands in full brilliance, if not love that is constant and right, love that leads a noble pair from the bosom of their parents to the bridal altar!

Ah, all people proclaim it happiness to be loved. In my opinion it is a greater pleasure to love, to make the fate of two souls your fate, to feel and live only with the echo of dear souls, to value your life for the good of others, for them to dedicate each heart beat, to make the smallest garden a world, there to have the goal of life and the reward of life, and ending quietly one's ordained path, to carry one's hope even beyond the grave—Oh, here are the dependable virtues of happiness. And you, you want, alas, to deny them?

ANIELA. [*Transported.*] Never, absolutely never . . . [*Regaining her composure, with tenderness.*] Oh, I still don't know. [*Again enraptured.*] But I want to write; let my decision never be the cause of a single tear in the world. [*Drying her tears.*] Let me put my own happiness in that of others today.

GUSTAV. You want to write? You'll do it? O, dear angel! How much you're doing for me, how grateful I am! [*Kisses her hand.*] Oh if only you could read my heart!

ANIELA. But Gustav!

GUSTAV. But don't ask why. I would say more than I have to . . . Pen and paper . . . [*In rapture looking at her and holding her hand.*] O heavens, why this way? . . . But you'll understand me; you knew how to understand before and you'll be able to forgive me. [*Kisses her hand and suddenly goes out.*]

ANIELA. [*Alone, after a short pause.*] To hate! Yes—every woman prattles, boasts, but it's not as easy as it seems. From anger to hatred the road is very near when some treacherous deed has touched you! But when someone squeezes our hand affectionately, as I love my mother, no one could hate.

SCENE 4. *Aniela, Clara.*

CLARA. Who was here?
ANIELA. [*Avoiding the answer.*] How's that—who?
CLARA. Who was here with you?
ANIELA. Gustav came by.

252

CLARA. He unburdened his woes?

ANIELA. A bit.

CLARA. You spoke to each other so long?

ANIELA. Oh, as I love you, it wasn't that long at all.

CLARA. And what's new?

ANIELA. You won't believe it but, to make it brief, he wants to marry you.

CLARA. Me? [*Jumping and clapping her hands.*] There you are! There's my happiness! I'll torment him and torture him without measure. O, Mr. Gustav, you'll have your fill!

ANIELA. [*Angered.*] But not Gustav—Radost.

CLARA. Old Radost?

ANIELA. [*As above.*] Radost—Hm! Gustav!

CLARA. I don't want him.

ANIELA. I believe you.

CLARA. I hate him.

ANIELA. Despite your hatred, if Gustav doesn't fulfill his wishes, he'll marry you only out of vengeance.

CLARA. And who can force me into it?

ANIELA. Your father, who loves money so. Radost is a rich man —everyone knows it. There's nothing more to say—you'll be his wife.

CLARA. [*Trying to hide her growing confusion.*] That I shall not be! I'm not afraid either—my father has a will, well so do I—I'm not afraid . . . no . . . [*in tears*] what shall I do now? Once my father makes up his mind about something, everything is lost—there's no help.

ANIELA. Somehow there will be.

CLARA. [*After a long silence.*] You marry Gustav.

ANIELA. And our vows?

CLARA. Let one of us keep them at least, if we both can't.

ANIELA. But Gustav is already in love.

CLARA. Oh, what an unhappy affair! I'm going to auntie.

ANIELA. [*Looking around uncomfortably.*] Tell her, but in secret; go, don't lose time.

CLARA. She'll advise me; she won't let me die beside that old wreck.

ANIELA. [*Looking around.*] Go, go every hour is too dear to us.

CLARA. I would prefer a nunnery, or even Albin [*Goes out.*]

ANIELA. [*Calling softly.*] Listen, Clara! Clara! There you have it! She's gone. I wanted to get her opinion about this strange writing; I shouted—but since she didn't hear then what can I do? I'll have to write.

SCENE 5. *Aniela, Gustav.*

GUSTAV. [*Inkstand, pen, paper, etc., in hand.*] Here's everything, let's go to work.
ANIELA. I warned Clara.
GUSTAV. [*Aside.*] Excellent! [*Out loud.*] And what will she say?
ANIELA. To whom, and about what?
GUSTAV. My uncle.
ANIELA. I'll swear for her.
GUSTAV. How did she accept it?
ANIELA. She cried bitterly.
GUSTAV. I don't believe her tears. Anyway, whose fault is it? Albin loved her sincerely.
ANIELA. And still loves her.
GUSTAV. Oh, he doesn't love her at all.
ANIELA. I know better.
GUSTAV. He's in love, but not with Clara.
ANIELA. With whom?
GUSTAV. Hm! With whom? [*A short silence.*] I'll remain silent for the time being.
ANIELA. Someone's been making up tales, please believe me. Albin's our neighbor, he's here all the time, we know where he is and what ties he has.
GUSTAV. [*Forced.*] As long as we are speaking honestly with each other: Albin is in love—but it's you he loves.
ANIELA. Me?
GUSTAV. Yes, you. He's almost dying because of it, there's nothing more to tell—it's a fact.
ANIELA. But my God, so suddenly, just now . . .
GUSTAV. He changed slowly, because can he suffer insult in such a painful way for so many years and preserve his love at the same pitch? Perhaps spending some pleasant moments by your side, your goodness, your charms . . . in other

words, can one meet you and not fall in love with you? Will you tell me?

ANIELA. Silly question! [*A short pause.*] Then it's me he loves?

GUSTAV. [*Rapidly.*] But I advise you, don't believe him at all —his love is fickle because it's on the rebound.

ANIELA. He swears he loves Clara.

GUSTAV. He's still dreaming.

ANIELA. He sighs.

GUSTAV. Out of courtesy.

ANIELA. He weeps.

GUSTAV. Habit.

ANIELA. But . . .

GUSTAV. Really.

ANIELA. [*Taking the pen.*] Then let's write.

GUSTAV. [*With emotion.*] Dearest Aniela! [*After a short pause, when Aniela registers amazement.*] Write it, if you'll be so kind.

ANIELA. That name confuses me. [*Writes; to herself.*] Me? Is it *me* he loves?

GUSTAV. [*With envy.*] Perhaps Albin's woes, the spurned gifts, the unworthy change of affection, manage to interest, even flatter you?

ANIELA. Did I deserve such a question?

GUSTAV. Forgive me. Transported by anxiety I erred, for I know what soul yours needs; one that would love more than he could express it, although every expression becomes love.

ANIELA. Let's go on writing.

GUSTAV. We'll write—"Heaven has sent us in our unhappiness the goodness of an angel. She has taken pen in hand to bring solace to our longing . . ."

ANIELA. But it's not fitting for me to write that.

GUSTAV. But I'm the one who's really writing—and anyway, what other name could my heart give you for your goodness, your many kindnesses?

ANIELA. Then let's write.

GUSTAV. We'll write—"Don't fear any longer. The person to whom uncle wanted to marry me hates me . . ."

ANIELA. That's not so, Mr. Gustav.

GUSTAV. How else should I say it?

ANIELA. It should be changed.

GUSTAV. Correct it, if you wish.

ANIELA. Oh, I shall correct it, willingly.

GUSTAV. [*Reading over her shoulder.*] ". . . is favorable."
[*Takes her by the hand.*] Do you mean it?

ANIELA. [*Drawing her hand away slowly.*] Are words necessary?

GUSTAV. Then you know me now.

ANIELA. And how!

GUSTAV. This familiarity—could it, sometime, become friendship?

ANIELA. It is so and will remain so.

GUSTAV. [*With growing fervor.*] Always? Eternally?

ANIELA. Eternally.

GUSTAV. Enough of this already! Away all subterfuge! I love
you, Aniela, I love you more than life.

ANIELA. [*Withdrawing in amazement.*] What?

GUSTAV. [*Calming himself.*] Write it, if you please.

ANIELA. [*Bent over the paper—after a short pause, composing
herself.*] How was that? I love . . .

GUSTAV. Ah, repeat it!

ANIELA. "I love you more than life . . ." Is that the way? And
further?

GUSTAV. Further? It's pleasant to believe there's something
further.

ANIELA. Let's go on writing.

GUSTAV. Let's go on writing—but your inflection is off. The
voice should express the thought locked in the word, and
the expression "I love" declares the obligations of a person
to himself, other people, and the Creator. Should one pro-
nounce it then so coldly? You love your mother, brother,
friend, I love you, you me; just as an experiment let your
voice impart all its worth and direct it to me.

ANIELA. [*Looking at him.*] I love you.

GUSTAV. Too little feeling. [*Teaching her, with emotion.*] I
love you.

ANIELA. [*More tenderly.*] I love you.

GUSTAV. A bit too timid.

ANIELA. Oh, I love you, I love you.

GUSTAV. Getting much better, bravo! Repeat it often, you'll have it perfect.

ANIELA. Let's write.

GUSTAV. Let's write.

ANIELA. Someone's coming.

GUSTAV. No.

ANIELA. [*Getting up.*] I hear someone.

GUSTAV. [*Kissing her hand.*] Until later. [*Runs out.*]

ANIELA. [*After him.*] The letter! The letter! [*Returning.*] How well he writes!

SCENE 6. Mrs. Dobrójska, Aniela.

ANIELA. [*Hiding the letter behind her; aside.*] Someone else's secret is a holy thing!

MRS. DOBRÓJSKA. No, no, say what you will, my ladies, my way is best. I'll ask Radost; that's the shortest route, then he'll explain everything to us.

ANIELA. And Gustav? For God's sake!

MRS. DOBRÓJSKA. Gustav has been making up fairy tales. That he's in love, I believe, but that Radost knew all about it, and still knowing, brought him here, I can't believe. Certainly Gustav, like everyone, has his faults, but he is young and attractive.

ANIELA. [*Naïvely.*] I was thinking the same thing.

MRS. DOBRÓJSKA. And perhaps you can like him.

ANIELA. Perhaps, mother.

MRS. DOBRÓJSKA. And I know that his heart is better than his head.

ANIELA. Oh, better, mother dear.

MRS. DOBRÓJSKA. And would there be this trouble if you had liked Gustav even a little? [*Aniela sighs.*] No and no. For Radost such intrigues are too frivolous.

ANIELA. But I saw Gustav at his feet.

MRS. DOBRÓJSKA. That's true.

ANIELA. Their words.

MRS. DOBRÓJSKA. Their argument . . .

ANIELA. Lively enough.

MRS. DOBRÓJSKA. Who would have expected it from such a man! Well I ask you! He wants vengeance! To marry at such an age!

ANIELA. Mother dear! Don't give Clara to him.

MRS. DOBRÓJSKA. First I have to find out what father's intentions are, for I'd best counsel now the father, and not the daughter.

ANIELA. Let your advice at least comfort her now. [*During the first words of Clara with Mrs. Dobrójska, Aniela secretly gathers up the inkstand and ink and quietly goes out.*]

SCENE 7. Mrs. Dobrójska, Clara.

CLARA. Oh, what shall I do in this miserable situation?

MRS. DOBRÓJSKA. Perhaps father will not want to go against your will.

CLARA. But if he does, if he does?

MRS. DOBRÓJSKA. Then you shall have to heed him.

CLARA. That's a comfort! That's father!

MRS. DOBRÓJSKA. Don't condemn him yet; he wants your happiness.

CLARA. Beautiful happiness, I ask you—an old husband.

MRS. DOBRÓJSKA. But good.

CLARA. What do I get out of that goodness!

MRS. DOBRÓJSKA. You've forgotten that you're still under your father's authority, that not all men will allow themselves to be led around like Albin; and knowing your father, it would be easy to guess that your contempt for Albin will not be pleasant for him. Although he may free you this time from marrying, soon he may force you with a more disagreeable order.

CLARA. This Radost always seemed to be the kind that never wanted a wife! Young Albin at least knows something about love. If I have to marry a man by force, then at least I prefer Albin. [*Radost can be heard coughing from behind the door.*]

MRS. DOBRÓJSKA. And here's Radost himself.

CLARA. Already beginning to sigh.

Mrs. Dobrójska. [*Aside.*] I can't speak with him after such a favor. [*To Radost.*] I'll return in a moment. [*Goes out.*]
Radost. [*To Clara, approaching.*] I won't be bored here.

SCENE 8. *Clara, Radost.*

Radost. [*After a short pause.*] What are you thinking about, the fall of men?
Clara. I was thinking just this, which I want to explain: if I were ever forced against my will to become someone's wife, there wouldn't be a more miserable creature in the whole world than my husband!
Radost. Eh, the deuce! And what would be waiting for him?
Clara. Parties, cards, banquets and dances.
Radost. Well, that's not so bad. You'll enjoy yourself. Of course, I myself always praise merriment.
Clara. Then I don't want games.
Radost. Well, tranquility is pleasant.
Clara. I'll squander his fortune.
Radost. If your husband presents you with one.
Clara. I'll gamble and lose.
Radost. The strongest wins.
Clara. I'll dress to the hilt.
Radost. The clothes should always suit the face.
Clara. Then I don't want clothes.
Radost. Then less expense.
Clara. [*Rapidly, excitedly.*] But I'll always do everything to defy him. He'll want this, I'll that—he'll act this way, I'll that—He'll sleep, I'll talk—he'll talk, I'll yawn—When he's happy, I'll sigh, when he's sad I'll sing. I'll poke him when he writes and shout when he reads. My husband will go this way, and I'll that—a tooth for a tooth—and we're even! [*Remembering.*] And when he has gout, I'll kick him in the leg.
Radost. [*Withdrawing his leg.*] Eh, the deuce! I won't stay in the way. But who earns you for a wife for penance must be no mean sinner. As Gustav says, it could be that such happiness was predestined for me. [*Laughs.*]

CLARA. There you are!

RADOST. I'm not afraid; I don't believe your words and I know your heart. [*Tries to take her by the hand, which Clara withdraws.*]

CLARA. I don't want to, I don't want to. [*In tears.*] What shall I do?

RADOST. Don't be a child.

CLARA. Would that I still were!

RADOST. Look at me . . .

CLARA. [*Turning away.*] I know you, I know you . . .

RADOST. [*Turning all around.*] Do I look like a bridegroom? Eh? [*Capering about.*] Making merry after the wedding! [*Laughs—then serious.*] But then I'm only joking.

CLARA. I don't like joking.

RADOST. But don't cry, don't cry, nothing will come of it, nothing, and as proof, I'll send Albin to you. [*Goes away, laughing.*] An amusing affair and a strange girl!

CLARA. [*Alone.*] Yes, jokes, jokes, there are none on this point; but once he's married, then there'll be none for sure.

SCENE 9. Clara, Aniela.

ANIELA. [*Meditating.*] Clara!

CLARA. [*After a short pause.*] Aniela!

ANIELA. Do you know what?

CLARA. What?

ANIELA. I think that the other Aniela is very lucky.

CLARA. Oh, leave me alone! I have no time now, let her be as happy as she wants.

ANIELA. To be so loved!

CLARA. [*Ironically.*] As Gustav says.

ANIELA. Why should he lie?

CLARA. Why? It flatters his ego.

ANIELA. Ah, who can be grateful knows how to love!

CLARA. Don't you listen to him, that's my advice.

ANIELA. You don't know how pleasant it is when a man expresses tender feelings with worthy passion: it tickles in the ears, then something burns the eyes, it runs, runs like a shudder along the face, and from your face to your heart, and like boiling drops it rises up from your heart, up, up, up [*pointing to her breast*] and it presses here, and chokes in the throat, until in the end you're forced to sigh.

CLARA. What a child you are! To you it's something new, but not to me, dear—after all, I do have Albin.

ANIELA. Oho! It's all over with him.

CLARA. What?

ANIELA. Be happy.

CLARA. With what?

ANIELA. The change.

CLARA. His?

ANIELA. He's no longer in love.

CLARA. With me?

ANIELA. With you.

CLARA. How do you know?

ANIELA. Gustav told me.

CLARA. But just this morning he sighed.

ANIELA. Out of courtesy.

CLARA. He begged.

ANIELA. Habit.

CLARA. For sure?

ANIELA. I'll tell you something else . . .

CLARA. [*Impatiently.*] What else will you tell me?

ANIELA. That the burden has fallen on unhappy me now.

CLARA. You?

ANIELA. Me.

CLARA. He loves you?

ANIELA. So he says.

CLARA. Go believe a man! He cried as mournfully as a beaver, implored, swore, was perishing from love, and in the end furled his colors. You see how good it is that we don't love— true, Aniela?

ANIELA. Let's go to mother now.

CLARA. Isn't it true, Aniela?

ANIELA. [*Going out.*] Dinner's being served.

CLARA. [*Alone.*] He doesn't love me. [*Forces a laugh, then in anger.*] He's a snake, a snake full of poison.

ACT V

SCENE 1. Radost, Gustav.

RADOST. Gustav! For the love of God! Confess, what is this you've cooked up?

GUSTAV. Why the anxiety? I'm already in love, I won't do anything mad; I'm even amazed at my own common sense.

RADOST. Would that I could be so amazed even for half an hour! What do all these sour faces mean, beginning with Mrs. Dobrójska's? That they scowl at you, rascal, fine, but why at me? We were sitting at the table, as though there were thirteen of us, and for a little while it went devilishly bad for all of us. Aniela all trembling, now pale, now burning; the mother doesn't take her eyes from her daughter, drowns her gaze in her; Clara laughs, flutters, but always in a forced way; Albin counted all the flowers on the tablecloth over and over again. Even you aren't yourself, you only drank like yourself. Understanding nothing, surprised at everything, I was the only sensible one at the whole table, and I sat among you like Pilate in the judge's seat.

GUSTAV. [*Quieter.*] Uncle, love, love is just a riddle.

RADOST. Aniela, Clara, I fathom; but the mother, the mother?

GUSTAV. The mother can't love too?

RADOST. [*Shaking his head.*] He's gone crazy and is still mad!

GUSTAV. [*Taking him to one side.*] How do they say it uncle? About old love never getting rusty . . .

RADOST. Eh, Gustav, you cooked up something—I feel it in my skin.

GUSTAV. I'd stir up something?

RADOST. I'll disperse this cloud the easiest way by going to Mrs. Dobrójska and having a talk with her.

GUSTAV. She doesn't know.

RADOST. What doesn't she know?

GUSTAV. Not a thing.

RADOST. Once a fool, always a fool! Beg, placate, implore, beseech: nothing does any good at all. [*Going out.*] And why do I have to talk with him! It's just a waste of time. [*Leaves through the right side door.*]

GUSTAV. [*Alone.*] Dear uncle, happiness awaits you, but I still won't confide my plan to you, for he who loves never takes a wise man as a confidant. He gives advice—confesses it's the best advice, but he does as it suits him.

SCENE 2. *Gustav, Albin.*

GUSTAV. Well? Am I not a good adviser and a sincere friend?

ALBIN. Thanks to your advice, Gustav, she's already looked at me twelve times.

GUSTAV. And sighed six.

ALBIN. Oh no, only four.

GUSTAV. Well that's enough for someone who never sighs.

ALBIN. [*With a sigh.*] True, she never sighs—but who's without fault?

GUSTAV. And did you sigh?

ALBIN. Only once from afar, and that by accident, but very softly.

GUSTAV. When it hits you, go behind the door, damn it!

ALBIN. What happiness! Heavenly Providence! That I have so wise a friend who gives me such good, such sacred counsel. [*Embraces him.*]

GUSTAV. Just heed it.

ALBIN. I shall do what you order.

GUSTAV. And what you have to say to her—remember, even though she cries . . .

ALBIN. [*Painfully.*] Ah! Even though she cries!

GUSTAV. Ah? Well, if it's "ah!" the whole scheme is for nothing.

ALBIN. [*Heroically.*] Although I suffered greatly, although my brow was full of sweat, nonetheless you saw how I behaved at the table. When she looked at me—my gaze was on the ceiling; when she turned an eye away—I sneaked a glance at her.

GUSTAV. There's the way to do it.

ALBIN. She asked me for water—I said nothing. She asked for salt—I said nothing—bread, nothing.

GUSTAV. That's the idea—Then she poured wine for you—

ALBIN. [*In haste.*] But I . . . [*softer*] drank it.

GUSTAV. Because one should always drink. But I tell you, she's beginning to soften. She's now giving you a thousand proofs: she looks for you, seeks you herself. Just hold out—the whole thing depends on that, even though she comes, wants sincere agreement, even though her speech be the tenderest . . . you say: yes, or no. Not a word more!

ALBIN. Even though I should die, I'll do all you ask, for you've already convinced me your way is best. Ah, your advice is true gold for me. [*Embraces him.*]

GUSTAV. [*Imitating the tearful tone of his uncle.*] Only have pity, stop being a scatterbrain, be sensible—see, take an example from me.

ALBIN. Ah, how could I imagine comparing myself to you! [*Clara runs in, and seeing Gustav suddenly stops.*]

SCENE 3. Clara, Gustav, Aniela.

CLARA. Aniela's not here?

GUSTAV. [*Looking around.*] As a matter of fact, no. [*Aside, to Albin.*] There you are—think she's looking for Aniela? But hold on!

ALBIN. [*Aside, to Gustav.*] Bah! That's the way to do it.

GUSTAV. [*Aside, to Albin, ordering him.*] Go sit in a corner, don't move your eyes; I'll go on ahead and arrange the whole thing. [*Albin sits in the back, and so does not hear further conversation. To Clara.*] Am I to congratulate you?

CLARA. [*Ironically.*] Just in time; and for what may I ask?

GUSTAV. Your new lover.

CLARA. I know nothing about any new lover.

GUSTAV. Auntie is joking.

CLARA. Mr. Gustav!

GUSTAV. Why get angry about that?

CLARA. It's too painful a joke. [*Begins to cry.*]

GUSTAV. What's this? Tears? You mean you really don't want to become my auntie?

CLARA. I want a hundred times more to leave this world.

GUSTAV. Hm! Hm! If so, things take on a different shape.

CLARA. Different?

GUSTAV. Fate threatens us the same way; we've got to set aside all the old quarrels, advise and help each other.

CLARA. But how?

GUSTAV. How? [*After long deliberation.*] That's it, I just don't know.

CLARA. If Mr. Gustav wished to hear my advice he'd do things as his uncle wanted. We have to have a delay.

GUSTAV. Ah, I was willing, but I see Aniela herself with premature zeal has already confessed everything to her mother. The mother scowls; uncle is surprised, investigates, gets somewhere, asks around and at this moment perhaps has already discovered everything.

CLARA. What will happen now? Oh Mr. Gustav, isn't there some way of changing things? Don't think bad of me for intruding in this matter, but time is short—Radost wants to get married: tell me—do you love the other Aniela so much?

GUSTAV. Love or not, here they only despise me.

CLARA. Oh, don't believe that.

GUSTAV. Even if I obeyed uncle, Aniela doesn't want it.

CLARA. Aniela is favorable to you.

GUSTAV. Favorable! And to whom is her soul not favorable? But that inclines one only to gratitude.

CLARA. [*Impatient.*] Surmise the rest.

GUSTAV. If only I could; for it's still too fresh in my memory how Miss Clara carefully weeded out the very desires she now wants to excite.

CLARA. The circumstances explain my actions.

GUSTAV. The circumstances compel Miss Clara, but do they mean the same thing for Aniela? For what reasons can I now put faith in what secretly perhaps attracts me?

CLARA. [*More and more impulsively.*] So Aniela then . . . ?

GUSTAV. [*Finishing the sentence.*] . . . is worthy of attachment.

CLARA. And you'd sincerely want . . . ?

GUSTAV. [*As above.*] . . . to dedicate my life to her.

CLARA. Why do you hesitate, what holds you back?

GUSTAV. Uncertainty . . .

CLARA. It's gone.

GUSTAV. And willingness . . .

CLARA. It's waiting.

GUSTAV. Then Aniela . . .

CLARA. [*Finishing the sentence impulsively.*] . . . says so with my voice!

GUSTAV. [*Aside.*] Ha! That's what I was waiting for—now I can be certain; I'm at the goal, you do what you want! [*Wants to leave, but returns.*] Don't think ill of me for asking so boldly, but time is short and Radost is at work, [*with emphasis*] and someone else might still get to him! Tell me, then, without wasting too many words: [*softer, pointing to Albin with his shoulder*] are you afraid of marriage over there? You're silent—am I to guess? I wish you happiness then. But Albin . . . do you know?

CLARA. [*With growing impatience.*] I know, I know.

GUSTAV. But there is a way . . .

CLARA. I understand.

GUSTAV. Make him certain . . .

CLARA. Oh, for God's sake, I know already, I know.

GUSTAV. To go away? [*A short pause.*] With him?

CLARA. [*Restraining herself.*] Who says so?

GUSTAV. Then you'll remain?

CLARA. Tortures!

GUSTAV. Then you'll accept my advice?

CLARA. I will, I will.

GUSTAV. Honestly?

CLARA. Ah, honestly.

GUSTAV. [*Changing his tone.*] I believe that very much—To take a vow, which you call everlasting, and to change in a day's time; to hate in the morning, and to love in the evening; to hurt the innocent, and then an hour later to want to help him; if that isn't fickleness, I don't know. And who's capable of it? Certainly not a man! And so having demonstrated my point, I have the honor to remain your obedient servant. [*Bows very low and goes to his room.*]

SCENE 4. Clara, Albin.

CLARA. [*After a short pause.*] How—what is this—everything dying at once? Those jokes—his revenge!

ALBIN. [*Aside.*] Hold on, Albin!

CLARA. I believed him! I deceived Aniela!

ALBIN. [*Aside.*] Oh, she's crying.

CLARA. I'm to blame, to blame from every point of view.

ALBIN. [*Aside.*] That's the way!

CLARA. But . . . Oh, how much I'm suffering!

ALBIN. [*Aside.*] Oh, I'm afraid!

CLARA. Albin! You're already avenged.

ALBIN. [*Starts and sits down again, aside.*] That's the way!

CLARA. And how! Then I have no right even to mercy?

ALBIN. [*Starting.*] Oh, I can't hold out any longer! [*To Clara.*] You call for mercy with a vain plea?

CLARA. You can ask, knowing what it's all about.

ALBIN. What?

CLARA. Radost, Radost wants to marry me.

ALBIN. And you?

CLARA. I'd sooner die.

ALBIN. And he hopes to force you into it?

CLARA. On father's orders.

ALBIN. What? Radost and you? He won't live to see it! I'm going, I'll free you and avenge you at the same time. [*Leaves rapidly through the middle door.*]

CLARA. [*Running after him.*] Oh, Albin! Stop—[*at the door*] Stop—He'll kill him!

SCENE 5. *Mrs. Dobrójska, Aniela, Radost. Radost enters quickly, Mrs. Dobrójska after him, followed by Aniela.*

RADOST. Where is he? Where is he?

MRS. DOBRÓJSKA. Without anger, without malice.

ANIELA. [*Aside.*] Hold him, mother!

RADOST. Why didn't I know about this?

MRS. DOBRÓJSKA. I didn't believe it.

RADOST. Harboring such guests!

MRS. DOBRÓJSKA. Nothing happened.

RADOST. He stopped being a scatterbrain, and became a liar.

MRS. DOBRÓJSKA. Forgive him.

RADOST. Oh yes, certainly!

ANIELA. [*Aside.*] Hold him, mother!

RADOST. [*Wanting to go to Gustav's door.*] Now I'll straighten everything out.

MRS. DOBRÓJSKA. Wait.

RADOST. Let me go!

ANIELA. [*Aside.*] Don't let him go.

RADOST. [*To the door.*] Gustav! [*Pulls his hand away. To Mrs. Dobrójska.*] If you please! [*Goes to the door.*]

ANIELA. For God's sake!

RADOST. Well, I ask you! He's already gone somewhere. [*Peeks through the keyhole.*]

MRS. DOBRÓJSKA. Please listen to me. We first have to have an understanding.

RADOST. What is there to understand? There's clear proof here.

MRS. DOBRÓJSKA. You're getting too upset.

RADOST. I'm not upset.

ANIELA. [*Aside.*] Don't believe him, mother.

MRS. DOBRÓJSKA. Who is the other Aniela?

RADOST. Ah, beside this one I know no other on earth and never did.

MRS. DOBRÓJSKA. Who is Aniela's father?

RADOST. How should I know, if in my whole life I never knew a man who had a daughter with such a name?

MRS. DOBRÓJSKA. Someone from whom some ancient feud separates you.

RADOST. I'm not involved in any feud, and I'm not separated from anyone.

ANIELA. [*Aside, to her mother.*] He doesn't want to confess.

RADOST. It's all in her head!

MRS. DOBRÓJSKA. Can you at least recall your duel?

RADOST. My du . . . [*holding himself by the head*] God! What the rascal invents!

MRS. DOBRÓJSKA. Just be calm.

RADOST. My good woman! I could see and I felt it in my bones that he was up to something, cooked up some mischief [*woefully*] and what wounds my heart even more is that no one wants to believe that I gave it to him today but good, [*tearfully*] and what can I do? . . . But I know what I'll do: I want to give him the last warning. [*Leaves quickly.*]

ANIELA. Oh, run, mamma, hold him.

Mrs. Dobrójska. I'm running.

Aniela. Oh, faster.

Mrs. Dobrójska. [*Running.*] I can't any faster.

SCENE 6. Aniela, Gustav in the rear.

Aniela. [*Not seeing Gustav.*] Radost is impulsive, but good-hearted, he'll be moved in the end by pleas, tears, he'll forgive—Gustav will leave—and then? I'll cry, he won't grieve, he'll forget me.

Gustav. Never.

Aniela. Oh!

Gustav. No, I won't forget you: the bonds of our union are unbreakable.

Aniela. Please go.

Gustav. Go?

Aniela. Uncle threatens, curses.

Gustav. He'll ask to be forgiven.

Aniela. But he opposes everything.

Gustav. Because he's a scatterbrain.

Aniela. Scatterbrain?

Gustav. [*Shaking his head.*] Oho!

Aniela. [*Sighing.*] And I believed him!

Gustav. Certainly from fear.

Aniela. [*Naïvely.*] Not at all.

Gustav. Just think, how much trouble there'd be for you if the old state of affairs was to return. [*A short pause.*] And with it, the love so unpleasant for you. [*A short pause.*] Maybe your mother was after me too.

Aniela. Oh, she loves me so!

Gustav. What will be then?

Aniela. [*Pleading.*] What am I to say? Why the question?

Gustav. [*Taking her by the hand.*] Aniela, don't believe that caressing look which slowly gliding rises in your eye, that trembling hand when it's near you; don't believe the voice that forces itself into your soul but let your own heart enlighten you; ah, only love kindles love in return! Your heart —is silent?

Aniela. [*Looking him in the eyes.*] No.

GUSTAV. [*Taking her into his embrace.*] Aniela!
ANIELA. [*In his embrace.*] Gustav! [*Tears herself free.*] But the other Aniela?
GUSTAV. You are her, you always were her.
ANIELA. How is that, Aniela?
GUSTAV. I have no other Aniela.
ANIELA. You're not deceiving me?
GUSTAV. Oh, don't be afraid: I used a trick, but an innocent one. And would I have awakened more tender sentiments if I tried to approach you in vain; if you, forewarned, spurned me?
ANIELA. Then you weren't in love? It's not a change-about? I am the only one . . .
GUSTAV. [*Finishing the sentence.*] The only one I loved.
ANIELA. But then Clara . . .
GUSTAV. [*Finishing the sentence.*] . . . is absolved of guilt. Albin loves her, and she him.

SCENE 7. The same, Radost, Mrs. Dobrójska. Radost enters hurriedly, Dobrójska after him. Radost stands in front of Gustav, out of breath, like Mrs. Dobrójska, unable to speak. After a brief moment of silence, Gustav bursts out in a laugh.

RADOST. [*Turning to Mrs. Dobrójska behind him.*] He laughs —you see?
MRS. DOBRÓJSKA. [*Wiping her brow.*] I see.
RADOST. [*Putting his hands on his hips. To Gustav.*] My dear Sir!
GUSTAV. Oho!
RADOST. [*Exhausted.*] So: "Oho!" Do you hear Madam? "Oho," still. Tell me, then, weren't my prophecies of doom justified? What you cooked up, what you spread around! . . . But confess this: with what Aniela are you in love, and when and where?
GUSTAV. [*Taking Aniela by the hand.*] What Aniela? This one.
RADOST. Ah! [*Turning to Mrs. Dobrójska.*] Ah?
GUSTAV. [*To Aniela.*] Isn't it so?

ANIELA. Oh, yes.

RADOST. There you are! Who can understand him? But you all heard? . . . Ah! And that duel? Talk, dear fellow.

GUSTAV. [*Taking Radost to a side.*] Don't you remember, uncle dear? . . .

RADOST. [*Louder.*] What? How?

GUSTAV. [*Still louder.*] At the masquerade.

RADOST. Sh, sh!

GUSTAV. You know what happened . . .

RADOST. [*Wanting to shut his mouth.*] Shut up, you're making a fool out of me . . .

GUSTAV. [*Moving his head away.*] Probably . . .

RADOST. [*As above.*] Quiet!

GUSTAV. [*As above.*] Oh that . . .

RADOST. [*As above.*] But quiet, I say, use your head!

SCENE 8. The same; Albin runs in, Clara after him. Albin rushes to Radost from the opposite side when Radost tries to close Gustav's mouth, and shouts in his ear.

ALBIN. Before you marry Clara, you have to kill me first.

RADOST. [*Alarmed, drawing back.*] What the devil is this?

CLARA. [*Pulling him away.*] Albin!

RADOST. [*Rubbing his ear.*] I want Clara?

MRS. DOBRÓJSKA. What is going on?

RADOST. Here's the pest! Going crazy again! [*To Albin.*] Who told you?

ALBIN. You yourself.

RADOST. You believe jokes?

CLARA. You asked father.

RADOST. I? When? Who says so?

CLARA. Gustav.

RADOST. Gustav, why the latest favor?

GUSTAV. I wanted to frighten her.

RADOST. What the deuce! Am I something to frighten young girls with? [*To Albin.*] But why this burning desire for vengeance? You're in love with Aniela.

ALBIN. I? Who says so?

RADOST. Gustav.

CLARA. Yes, Gustav.

GUSTAV. Gustav, Gustav the scatterbrain, spread stories, cooked things up—but if happily [*taking Aniela by the hand, and bowing before Mrs. Dobrójska*], we'll now convince ourselves here, Aniela.

MRS. DOBRÓJSKA. [*Helping them up, to Gustav.*] I understand you.

RADOST. I am only amazed.

MRS. DOBRÓJSKA. [*Uniting them.*] And I willingly entrust my daughter's happiness to you.

GUSTAV. And now let's turn to the other pair: [*ordering*] Albin! Come close.

MRS. DOBRÓJSKA. What do you say to this, Clara?

GUSTAV. She wants it, she wants it, I give my word.

CLARA. But . . .

GUSTAV. Consider it done already.

CLARA. Oh, even if I wanted to, I couldn't be mad.

ALBIN. But you can't.

CLARA. I must love you.

GUSTAV. Then let him join you to whom you owe your thanks. [*Joining them, seriously.*] Be happy just as you love! [*To Clara, quieter.*] What about the vows? Over with! [*Similarly to Albin, aside.*] Get yourself a good pair of shoes, brother. [*Out loud.*] Now everything is fine.

RADOST. But on my soul, I don't understand a thing—tell me, Gustav dear.

GUSTAV. [*Embracing him.*] Thank you, uncle dear, for all your warnings!

END

THE VENGEANCE

A Comedy in Four Acts

*There is nothing so bad that it
cannot do some good.*

ANDRZEJ MAKSYMILIAN FREDRO

INTRODUCTION

WRITTEN in 1833 and staged for the first time in Lwów in 1834, *The Vengeance* is the richest fruit of Fredro's most productive period as a creative artist: 1831-1835. The idea for the comedy probably came to Fredro some time in 1829, not long after his marriage, when he had a chance to rummage around the fourteenth-century castle of Odrzykoń which, with other property, had come into the possession of his wife.[1] After passing from one family to the other through the centuries, the castle of Odrzykoń at the beginning of the seventeenth century was finally divided between two mutually antagonistic landowners, Jan Skotnicki and Piotr Firlej. In 1603 these two by no means untypical old Polish squires began a litigation about the minutest details of the division of the estate that dragged on for over thirty years. The litigation was no simple, peaceful affair; it developed into a full-fledged feud between the neighbors that erupted periodically into open clashes. It was finally resolved, however, in 1638 when, as in *The Vengeance*, the antagonists were reconciled through the marriage of their children.

Because of the structure of the old Polish legal system, such long-drawn-out litigation between squires squabbling over some piece of property was hardly a rare phenomenon in pre-partition Poland. Sometimes the litigation continued so long and became so much a source of embarrassment and frustration that the feuding parties took recourse to the *zajazd* or foray, whereby they attempted to settle the matter by force. Indeed, one of the classics of Polish literature, Adam Mickiewicz's verse epic, *Master Thaddeus*, deals with just such a foray, led by the Horeszkos against the Soplicas, to settle once and for all the ownership of the castle at Soplicowo which serves as the setting of the work. In one of the many notes that he wrote for *Master Thaddeus*, Mickiewicz gives us some idea of the extent to which the use of the foray was prevalent in pre-partition Poland:

---

[1] On the castle of Odrzykoń, see W. Łuszczkiewicz, "Ruiny zamku w Odrzykoniu," *Kłosy*, Vol. xv, No. 396 (Warsaw, 1873), 80.

In the time of the Polish Commonwealth the carrying out of judicial decrees was very difficult, in a country where the executive authorities had almost no police at their disposal, and where powerful citizens maintained household regiments, some of them, for example, the Princes Radziwiłł, even armies of several thousand. So the plaintiff who obtained a verdict in his favor had to apply for its execution to the knightly order, that is to the gentry, with whom rested also the executive power. Armed kinsmen, friends, and neighbors set out, verdict in hand, in company with the apparitor and gained possession, often not without bloodshed, of the goods adjudged to the plaintiff, which the apparitor legally made over or gave into his possession. Such an armed execution of a verdict was called a foray (zajazd). In ancient times, while laws were respected, even the most powerful magnates did not dare to resist judicial decrees, armed attacks rarely took place, and violence almost never went unpunished. Well known in history is the sad end of Prince Wasil Sanguszko, and of Stadnicki, called the devil. The corruption of public morals in the Commonwealth increased the number of forays, which continually disturbed the peace of Lithuania.[2]

The subject of gentry litigation and feuding, including also the use of the foray, had been treated in Polish literature before Mickiewicz's *Master Thaddeus*, notably in the play *Sarmatianism* (Sarmatyzm) by Fredro's most important predecessor in the field of comedy, Franciszek Zabłocki. In the feud between Guronos and Żegota, which is the subject of *Sarmatianism* and which like the Firlej-Skotnicki feud ends in a reconciliation through marriage, the author aimed at a satire of the manners and obscurantist outlook of the Polish gentry in the pre-Poniatowskian Saxon era, when the cultural and intellectual life of Poland suffered a serious decline.

Reading the old accounts of the Firlej-Skotnicki feud when he was going through the castle of Odrzykoń, Fredro must surely have been reminded of Zabłocki's *Sarmatianism* and

[2] Adam Mickiewicz, *Pan Tadeusz* or *The Last Foray in Lithuania*, tr. by Watson Kirkconnell (New York, 1962), p. 373.

probably then conceived the idea of doing a play along similar lines. Since Poland had been changed considerably by the partitions, the problem of the Saxon (or Sarmatian as it is often referred to in Polish) provincialism was no longer relevant in Fredro's time as it had been in the reform-conscious era of King Stanisław August Poniatowski, and there could be no thought really of the dramatist's creating a satirical comedy of manners in the style of Zabłocki. What Fredro doubtless had in mind was a comedy about two feuding squires reconciled through their children's marriage that would combine elements of both a comedy of intrigue and a comedy of character but would be free of the satire characteristic of Zabłocki's play.

Although Fredro may have had the idea for *The Vengeance* as early as 1829, he did not write the play until four years later, in 1833. Although there is little proof to go on except the texts themselves, it is possible that the stimulus for finally committing the comedy to paper was provided by the rash of Romantic works nostalgically evoking the life of the old Sarmatian-Saxon gentry that followed in the wake of the defeat of the November Insurrection and the Great Emigration. By far the most impressive of these works—Adam Mickiewicz's *Master Thaddeus* and Henryk Rzewuski's *Memoirs of Mister Soplica*—were written about the same time as *The Vengeance,* though they did not appear in print until later. Separated from the homeland, exiles they knew not for how long in foreign countries, the Polish émigrés after 1831 found refuge from the harsh reality of their circumstances in the memory of days gone by, of traditional Polish manners and customs, in general of a "Polishness" they could more easily associate with the conservative, provincial gentry of the Sarmatian-Saxon period—the seventeenth and early eighteenth centuries—than with the more progressive, more enlightened, more Europeanized gentry of the sixteenth-century Renaissance or the French-influenced reform era of King Stanisław August Poniatowski. Furthermore, the conscious evocation of a common cultural heritage, a common way of life in the past, was one method of trying to overcome the fragmentation of the émigré community into mutually antagonistic factions and cliques. That this was one of the factors motivating Mickiewicz—who took upon himself the spiritual leadership of the emigration—to write a work such as *Master Thaddeus* we cannot doubt. For Fredro, for whom the émigré world was remote and, because of the Romantic literary hegemony alien and even inimical, the nostalgic evocation of the old gentry culture—which he probably associated in part with the Romantics' adulation of the novels of Sir Walter Scott—must have seemed grossly incongruous in the light of the November Insurrection and its aftermath. With the anti-Sarmatian-Saxon satire of Zabłocki's *Sarmatianism* fresh in his mind as one of the principal sources of *The Vengeance*, Fredro may have sought to read into his comedy a parody of this Romantic "literature of nostalgia." Viewing *The Vengeance* as a comment on, rather than as another specimen of this literature, we may have a better idea of the author's intention.

Like that of *Maidens' Vows*, the success of *The Vengeance* lies largely in Fredro's characterizations and in his manipulation of a complex plot. The story is, briefly, as follows. Two Polish squires, some time in the late eighteenth century (the exact time of the action is not defined), feud over a partly ruined wall dividing their estates. One is the Cup-Bearer Raptusiewicz, and the other, the Notary Milczek. Each lays claim to the wall. We have now the makings of the familiar old Polish tale of two squires locked for years in a feud arising out of litigation over some piece of property. In the tradition of Shakespeare's *Romeo and Juliet*,[3] Zabłocki's *Sarmatianism*, and Mickiewicz's *Master Thaddeus*, the feuding squires have children (the former's niece and ward, Clara, and the latter's son, Vatslav) who secretly love each other but are afraid to declare their love because of their elders' antagonism and the feud that has been going on between them for some time now. To add to the complexity and interest of this basic plot structure, Fredro introduced an important sub-plot: the Cup-Bearer plans to marry a distant relative of Clara's, the widow

---

[3] *Romeo and Juliet* is considered one of the sources of *The Vengeance*. See Stanisław Windakiewicz, "Fredro i Szekspir," *Pamiętnik Literacki*, Vol. xxv (Lwów, 1928), 15-19.

Hanna. The woman is wealthy, owns a profitable estate, and in general seems a most attractive prospect. The Notary, however, has his own plans for her. He wants her to marry his son, Vatslav, for the same sound financial reasons that motivate the Cup-Bearer.

The Cup-Bearer's ambitious plans are aided by his factotum Papkin, a delightful character who represents the best example of the "soldier-braggart" *(miles gloriosus)* in Polish literature. Besides furthering the Cup-Bearer's scheme, Papkin has one of his own—he wants to marry Clara whom he feels the Cup-Bearer will be glad to give him out of gratitude for his service to him. As the feud between the two squires reaches the boiling point, the Cup-Bearer decides to strike the Notary's camp with a foray and entrusts Papkin with its execution. During the attack, the Notary's son, Vatslav, allows himself to be taken captive by Papkin in order to gain entry into the Cup-Bearer's home for a clandestine meeting with Clara. When the Cup-Bearer learns of the Notary's plan to thwart his own by marrying off Vatslav to the widow, he seizes on the idea of forcing Vatslav—now in his custody—to marry Clara, knowing nothing, of course, of the young people's feelings for each other. The lovers are beside themselves with joy over this unexpected turn of events and hasten to agree to the Cup-Bearer's plans for them. Eventually, however, the truth is revealed and the feuding squires are reconciled.

This bare summary of the complex but skilfully managed plot of *The Vengeance* gives little idea of the warmth, color and humor the comedy radiates. For all his genius at plot construction (of which we already have had ample evidence in *Husband and Wife* and *Maidens' Vows*) Fredro's greatest talent lay in the realm of characterization, and in *The Vengeance* he created at least three fine portraits. Apart from the conventional though well-drawn lovers, Vatslav and Clara, the romantically inclined widow, and the bumbling secretary Dyndalski, Fredro's masterful talent for character construction is best seen in the figures of the Cup-Bearer, the Notary, and Papkin. Although they represent familiar old Polish types, irrespective of any literary associations, as in the case of Papkin, Fredro succeeded in breathing so much life into them that they become three-dimensional.

The Cup-Bearer is, as his telling name Raptusiewicz (from Latin *raptus*) informs us, impetuous and bold. He is the first to inaugurate the foray that Papkin leads against the Notary's estate. The Notary, on the other hand, is of very different temperament. As befitting his profession, he prefers to rely on cleverness rather than brute strength. His legalistic approach is an expression of this. He disdains the use of force unless he has no other way out; when that happens he does not hesitate to call force into play to resolve the difficulties between himself and the Cup-Bearer. To the impetuosity of the Cup-Bearer he opposes the cunning of the lawyer, and for that reason he is known as Milczek, the "silent one" (Polish *milczeć* = to keep silent), the man of few unnecessary words. His preference for soft speech contrasts sharply with the bellowing and roaring of the Cup-Bearer, his adversary who is ready to draw his sword at a moment's notice and whose tone is always haughty and overbearing.

These basic differences between the characters are established by language no less than by gesture and manner. Since both the Cup-Bearer and the Notary are members of the gentry, their speech must reveal, initially, certain distinguishing features of the old Polish gentry idiom. Fredro has accomplished this in two ways: first, the common use by both characters of old Polish gentry terms of address and, secondly, Latinisms. The Latin language was for long a living tradition in Poland and was one of the marks of an educated gentleman; in the course of time Latinisms became a characteristic feature of the idiom of the gentry. It was something of a vestige of the Renaissance culture and while no doubt it served as a source of pride for the speaker it no longer indicated any formal training in the language or that the speaker was a gentleman in anything more than name. Here are examples of such Latinisms from the speech of both the Cup-Bearer and the Notary:

Qua opiekun i *qua* krewny,
Miałbym z Klarą *sukces* pewny. (Act I, Sc. 1)

(Qua guardian, qua relative I'd have sure
success with Clara.)

Circa quartam niech mi stanie
U trzech kopców w Czarnym Lesie. (Act II, Sc. 9)
(Let him come to me circa quartam at the three
hills in Blackwoods)

Quandoquidam już przy grobie,
Żyję tylko jeszcze w tobie. (Act III, Sc. 2)
(Quandoquidam I'm near death now. You're the
only thing I live for.)

       Podstolina
Była *quondam* ta jedyna! (*Ibid.*)
       The widow
(*Quondam* was the only one!)

Nemo sapiens, nisi patiens. (Act II, Sc. 4)

Nie jednemu *pro memoria*
Gdzieś przy uchu napisała. (Act IV, Sc. 1)

(You left etched near more than one ear *pro memoria* . . .)

Once the gentry associations of the Cup-Bearer and the Notary have been established through their speech as well as
through their dress and material surroundings, Fredro then
uses linguistic means to heighten the difference between the
characters already evident in their manners. The speech of
the Cup-Bearer is distinguished by the number of impera-
tives, curses, and imprecations which give it an aggressive,
robust flavor well suited to the specific character portrayal.
Some examples:

Cóż u djabla za szaleństwo! (Act I, Sc. 2)
(What the devil is this madness!)

Cóż u czarta! Ty spokojny
Kiedy Rejent mnie napada
I otwartej żąda wojny?
Lecz godnego ma sąsiada!
Dalej żwawo!—niech kto żyje
Biegnie, pędzi, zgania, bije! (Act I, Sc. 5)

(What the blazes! You're so peaceful while
the Notary attacks me and demands open
combat? But he has a worthy neighbor!
Lively now, men!—Let who's able run, dash,
drive, strike!)

Mur graniczny!—Trzech na murze!
Trzech wybiję, a mur zburzę!
Zburzę, zniszczę, aż do ziemi— (*Ibid.*)
The border wall!—Three men on the wall
there! I'll slay them, then smash the
wall down! I'll smash it, I'll level it
to the ground.)

Wprzódy trupem go zaścielę. (Act I, Sc. 7)
(I'll strew it first with corpses.)

Co! Jak!—Żwawo! Bij co siły! (*Ibid.*)
What? Well!—After them! Strike with all
your might! Men!)

Jak mu utnę jedno ucho,
A czej z drugiem się wyniesie! (Act II, Sc. 9)
(When I slice one of his ears off, we'll see if he
can save the second!)

Niech spróbuje!
Takąbym mu kurtę skroił! (Act II, Sc. 9)
(Let him try! I'll give him such a thumping!)

In dealing with those subservient to him, the Cup-Bearer's
language conveys his haughtiness and harshness of manner.
To Papkin, he says, for example:

I tyś milczał, ćmo przeklęta! . . . (Act IV, Sc. 2)
(And you kept quiet, damned creature!)

And:

Utarłbym cię w proch z kretesem—
Ale czasu nie chcę stracic. (*Ibid.*)
(I could grind you into powder—but I don't
want to waste the time now.)

With his secretary, Dyndalski, he is no more gentle, as in this fragment from the letter-writing scene in Act IV, Scene 5:

Milcz waść!— ...
Pisz de novo—pisz, powiadam—
Mozgu we łbie za trzy grosze!
Siadaj!—siadaj, mówię—
(Shut up! ... Write *de novo*—write I
tell you! You've a brain not worth a
farthing! Sit down!—Sit, I say.)

Z tym hebesem nie pomoże; (*Ibid.*)
(It's just no use with this dunce!)

The Notary, as we have seen, is of quite different temperament. Because of his training and experience in the law, he puts his stock in a shrewd, quiet, well-reasoned approach—devoid of the bluster and violence of the Cup-Bearer, but no less firm in its own way. This is demonstrated very well in the first scene of Act III when after the Cup-Bearer's foray against the boundary wall, he tries to squeeze every last possible drop of incriminating evidence out of his bricklayers:

Notary: Please speak boldly, master; let us note down the whole affair. In these hard times of ours such blows come like gifts of God. We'll turn every punch to profit: we all know that you were beaten.

Mason: Not so bad.

Notary: But they did beat you, my good fellow.

Mason: Only slightly.

Notary: What else happened? There was a lot of commotion over there.

Mason: Oh, a little pushing and shoving, not much else, Sir.

2nd Mason: Who'd make a case of that there?

Notary: But someone pushing and shoving isn't tickling.

Mason: Ha! Of course not.

Notary: Then he's beating?

Mason: Evidently.

The soft, gentle, even sweet firmness of the Notary is also strongly in evidence in the second scene of the same act where he refuses to permit Vatslav even the hope of some time marrying Clara, or in the fourth scene of the act where the Notary, without raising his voice or a hand, masterfully subdues Papkin whose entry is accompanied by a flourish of blustering and bravado. It is by all means one of the best scenes of the play, particularly from the point of view of Papkin's gradual shift of character from a boistering braggart to a cringing coward to the tempo of the Notary's assertion of authority. If the Cup-Bearer's speech is distinguished by shouts and threats, curses and oaths, then the Notary's is distinguished rather by a politeness and gentility that mask the toughness underneath.

Of the major characters in *The Vengeance,* Papkin is perhaps the most memorable and one of the most outstanding in Polish fiction. He is, we have seen, a Polish descendant of the Plautine soldier-braggart.[4] With Pyrgopolinices, his classical prototype, he shares a boundless braggadocio and a fondness for his sword with which he boasts he has felled innumerable opponents in wars from one end of the globe to the other, covered himself with glory and earned a vast array of medals and honors. Like Pyrgopolinices he, too, is convinced of his devastating effect on the opposite sex who find him irresistible and throw themselves at him. Like Pyrgopolinices and Terence's Thraso, and their countless progeny in European comedy, Papkin is a thorough coward with whom the demasking and humiliation all the soldier-braggarts eventually suffer catches up. In an original departure from the classical tradition, however, Fredro exposes his braggart's cowardice not only in a conventional manner (through a duel, a beating, or the public exhibition of cowardice like the behavior of Thraso —or Papkin—during a "siege") but also through the device of the "poisoned wine" Papkin believes he was given by the Notary. The discovery of this hoax completes the downfall

[4] On Papkin as soldier-braggart, see my previously mentioned article "From Albertus to Zagłoba: The Soldier-Braggart in Polish Literature," *Indiana Slavic Studies,* Vol. III (1963) , pp. 90-104. See also Tadeusz Sinko, "Genealogia kilku typów i figur A. Fredry," *Akademia Umiejętności w Krakowie, Wydział filologiczny,* Vol. LVIII, No. 2 (Cracow, 1918) , 16-17.

of Papkin; it is the point beyond which the braggart cannot hope to return.

In the development of the character of Papkin, Fredro did not stop just at the example of Plautus' Pyrgopolinices. To the basic structure of the *miles gloriosus,* he added the traditional attributes of the *parasitus* (parasite) of classical Roman comedy. Fulfilling a role analogous to that of Atrotrogus in Plautus' comedy, Papkin is a hanger-on in the Cup-Bearer's estate and lives from the Cup-Bearer's table. Fredro rounded out his braggart further by borrowing certain traits of the braggarts of Italian Renaissance comedy and the commedia dell'arte: their fondness for magnificent costume, their elegant way with the ladies, their pride in their ability to play a guitar or some other instrument with which to provide the accompaniment for the songs and verses they compose with facility and, finally, and perhaps most significantly, the Renaissance braggarts' grand manner of speaking. Papkin is never at a loss for words; even the Cup-Bearer is cognizant of his factotum's verbal skill and because of this asks him to intercede in his behalf with the widow. Papkin's "talent," his grandiloquence, resounding with compound epithets of his own invention and the bombast of image piled on image, are displayed to their best advantage—not unnaturally—in his conversation with women as on the occasion of his first meeting with the widow in Act I, scene four, or in the delightful parody of chivalric romances that characterizes his meeting with Clara in Act II, scene seven.

The success of *The Vengeance* rests not only on clever plot construction and such excellent comic creations as the Cup-Bearer, the Notary, and Papkin, but also on the form Fredro chose for his comedy. For the first time in his career as a comedy writer, he used the eight-syllable (four-foot) trochaic line consistently throughout a work. The result has been the achievement of a verve that never flags and keeps the action at a good brisk pace from start to finish. This metric pattern has a light, vivacious quality to it in Polish and is considered the most natural medium for rendering comic dialogue in Polish verse drama. By varied intonation, a skillful use of pauses, and the division of the relatively short eight-syllable line into two or three lines of dialogue spoken by more than one character, Fredro was able to make it so dynamic an idiom for comic dialogue that it is easy to agree with the opinion of Polish critics who consider it one of Fredro's finest achievements and a major contribution to the development of comedy in Poland. The same pattern was to be repeated again successfully in the play that closed Fredro's pre-"silence" career in 1835: *The Life Annuity*, a work certainly less brilliant than *The Vengeance* but enhanced to a great extent by the use of the metric formula of *The Vengeance*.

Although the trochaic tetrameter Fredro used consistently for both *The Vengeance* and *The Life Annuity* had been known and used by Polish poets ever since the Middle Ages and was the meter in which several sixteenth-century Polish dramatic dialogues were written, there is no record of its having been employed for *comedy* before Fredro. In his analysis of the metric structure of *The Life Annuity* included in *Studies in Polish Versification* (Wrocław, 1954), Karol Zawodziński assesses Fredro's contribution as entirely original. He makes the statement that

> We may consider it the result of a fortunate inspiration and the original initiative of the poet for which he had no model in the literatures, i.e. French or Italian, which he knew and which were of help to him in his own creativity.[5]

It is true that apart from the old Polish dialogues—which he doubtless knew—Fredro could have found no precedent for such metric usage in French or Italian comedy. In this respect Zawodziński's statement is correct. But what Zawodziński has failed to take into account is the possibility that Fredro could also have been following a German or Austrian example. Fredro's interest in and contact with contemporary German-language comedy were by no means slight. The German theater in Lwów (the city was known as Lemberg in German) and Fredro's visits to and brief residence in Vienna offered ample opportunity for a familiarity with the German stage of his period. His decision to use the trochaic tetrameter

---

[5] Karol Zawodziński, *Studia z polskiej wersyfikacji* (Wrocław, 1954), pp. 365-366.

for the dialogue of an entire comedy could have come about in this way. The contemporary Austrian dramatist Franz Grillparzer whose works were popular in Fredro's time and which Fredro had the chance to see in Vienna in 1831—that is before he wrote *The Vengeance* and *The Life Annuity*—had employed the same metric pattern in two works: his tragedy *Die Ahnfrau*, performed for the first time in Vienna on January 31, 1817, and his "dramatic fable" *(dramatische Märchen) Der Traum ein Leben*, presented in Vienna for the first time on October 4, 1834. In *Die Ahnfrau*, considered one of Grillparzer's best works, the trochaic tetrameter is used predominantly with occasional imperfect (i.e., cataleptic, seven-syllable) lines. The inspiration for Grillparzer's choice of meter was Calderón, whose *Devoción de la cruz* figures as one of the sources of *Die Ahnfrau*. Fredro was probably unaware of the Spanish origin of the meter of *Die Ahnfrau*, but in listening to the lively tempo of the dialogue of the play, he could have realized the potential of the meter for comedy and sought to explore it in *The Vengeance* and later in *The Life Annuity*. Thus, in addition to native sources of inspiration—the sixteenth-century Polish dialogues—the possible external influence on Fredro's choice of meter must be taken into consideration.

CHARACTERS

THE CUP-BEARER RAPTUSIEWICZ*

CLARA, *his niece*

THE NOTARY MILCZEK*

VATSLAV, *the notary's son*

HANNA,* *a widow*

PAPKIN*

DYNDALSKI,* *steward*

ŚMIGALSKI,* *servant*

PEARLIE,* *cook*

Masons, Footmen, *Hired Hands, etc.*

The scene is set in the country.

* Raptusiewicz, from the Latin *raptus,* indicating a person violent and impetuous.
* Milczek, from Polish *milczeć,* to keep silent.
* Podstolina, in the original, the wife of a *podstoli,* or Deputy Pantler, an old Polish gentry title.
* Papkin, from Polish *paplać,* to blabber.
* Dyndalski, from Polish *dyndać,* to dangle, to swing to and fro, suggesting here someone clumsy.
* Śmigalski, from Polish *śmigać,* to whip, to lash.
* Perełka, in Polish. The diminutive of *perła,* pearl. Used ironically to suggest that Perełka is anything but a "pearl" of a cook.
* Hajduki in the original Polish. This was the name given the Hungarian infantry introduced into Poland by King Stefan Batory (1576-1586), who was of Hungarian origin. The term later was used in Poland to designate manor servants dressed in the Hungarian style.

THE VENGEANCE

ACT I

A room in the Cup-Bearer's estate. Doors to the right, left, and in the middle. Tables, chairs, etc. An English guitar on the wall.

SCENE *1. The Cup-Bearer, Dyndalski. The Cup-Bearer, in a white* zhupan* *without a belt and wearing his nightcap, is seated at a table to the right. He has glasses on his nose and is reading a paper. Behind the table, a little to the rear, stands Dyndalski, his hands folded behind his back.*

CUP-BEARER. [*As if to himself.*] Capital, from every point of view. Fine forests . . . fertile soil . . . She'll most certainly make a good wife. What rents! There's a woman for you! Three farms, mind you!

DYNDALSKI. A nice widow.

CUP-BEARER. Best there is—no doubt about it. [*Puts down his papers.*] What's the matter, no soup coming? [*Dyndalski goes out.*] Must I wait with empty stomach? [*A short pause.*] No—there's no need to delay things—[*Dyndalski, meeting a servant at the door carrying a tray with a bowl, plate, bread, etc., takes it from him and returns. He ties a napkin around the Cup-Bearer's neck, then hands him the plate with the soup. There is no break in the conversation.*] Qua guardian, *qua* relative, I'd have sure success with Clara. But the girl is young and giddy. Though it's me she'd love on Monday, who'd vouch for it on Tuesday?

DYNDALSKI. No one who has any sense, Sir. It's a slippery business!

CUP-BEARER. [*Turning to him.*] That's just the rub! I'd be giving up my freedom today [*banging on the table*], so someone could . . . May lightning strike him! He'll wait a long time for that! [*A short pause, after which he takes the plate.*] Her income isn't bad either, but the widow's is far better.

* A full-length long-sleeved garment typical of the dress of the old Polish gentry.

Therefore I'll begin with her. [*A short pause.*] She's here now—staying with Clara, who's a distant relative of hers. But somehow it seems to me that . . .

DYNDALSKI. She's waiting for something more.

CUP-BEARER. [*Breaking out in laughter.*] She's waiting for . . . something . . . more . . . Oh, Dyndalski, devil take you, you and your ideas! She's waiting for something! [*He laughs.*] Ha! . . . That's really funny! She's waiting—I do believe it. [*Eating; a short pause.*] It's a fact that she's still young, but a widow—experienced—knows her place, I guarantee you. She won't make a dandy out of me, chasing after all sorts of entertainments. [*A short pause.*] Well, it's no secret I'm not young, but neither am I so old, eh?

DYNDALSKI. [*Not readily agreeing.*] Well now . . .

CUP-BEARER. [*Offended.*] Maybe you're younger?

DYNDALSKI. As for my age . . .

CUP-BEARER. [*Finishing the conversation.*] I'll give you proof. [*A moment of silence.*]

DYNDALSKI. [*Scratching himself behind the ears.*] Sir, it's only that . . .

CUP-BEARER. What is it?

DYNDALSKI. Marriage isn't always easy. And you, just between the two of us, suffer from gout.

CUP-BEARER. [*Annoyed.*] Oh, once in a while.

DYNDALSKI. Indigestion.

CUP-BEARER. After drinking.

DYNDALSKI. Sometimes rheumatism hits you.

CUP-BEARER. [*Impatient.*] What you're saying is all foolish. Such a weakness doesn't matter. Why, the Lord only knows what she's got and keeps in hiding. And I'm sure no one will ask her, just so long as once we're married we keep the score between us even.

SCENE 2. *The Cup-Bearer, Dyndalski, Papkin. Papkin is dressed in the French style, with a sword at his side, short trousers, rounded boots with folded-down tops; toupee and Haarzopf,* topped by a three-cornered hat. He carries a pair of pistols under his arm and always speaks rapidly.*

* A wig braid.

PAPKIN. God be with you, Cup-Bearer! Galloping along as ordered, I wore my nag out completely. We toppled over a hundred times, so you'll find only splinters left of what was my new carriage.

CUP-BEARER. And I'll be the first to swear that my Papkin made his way here traveling the whole road on foot, and that the gold he was given went for cards, and not for the journey.

PAPKIN. [*Showing his pistols.*] Look here, Cup-Bearer, you'll understand . . .

CUP-BEARER. I'll understand what?

PAPKIN. Shot out! Burnt out!

DYNDALSKI. [*Aside, leaving the room.*] At crows, no doubt.

PAPKIN. Where, at whom, I must keep silent, but cards are not the reason for my being delayed on the way home. Didn't even yawn, by heavens! So dies everyone by my hand!

CUP-BEARER. Everyone—no; everything—yes.

PAPKIN. Everything?

CUP-BEARER. Moths and mosquitoes.

PAPKIN. You never believe me.

CUP-BEARER. Because I'm not stupid, my good fellow.

PAPKIN. What's this I see? Breakfast here?

CUP-BEARER. Yes, breakfast.

PAPKIN. Ah, Cup-Bearer! It's been six days and six nights now since I've had anything on my tongue.

CUP-BEARER. Eat and listen.

PAPKIN. So be it. [*He sits down at the other side of the table. As though speaking to himself.*] Everyone knows how well I shoot.

CUP-BEARER. And everyone knows I've the power to have you thrown into prison, for past antics we both know of.

PAPKIN. [*Frightened.*] Prison? What for?

CUP-BEARER. For amusement.

PAPKIN. Couldn't you find some better kind?

CUP-BEARER. Sh! Not so loud! I just said it to refresh your memory, before I reveal my wishes, of what our debts are to each other.

PAPKIN. Oh, I'll carry out all your orders, I'll mount my horse in an instant . . . After all, I ride superbly—even horses not yet broken, wild as boars, fierce as lions—in my hands they're just like tame sheep. After all, I am a superb horseman.

CUP-BEARER. Oh, I wish you'd . . .

PAPKIN. Please allow me . . . I had just put my foot to stirrup when suddenly a big dispute arose that detained me on my way here. It happened like this—

CUP-BEARER. Listen here . . .

PAPKIN. Just a moment . . . I was riding, countenance bold, hair in ringlets, head held high—and what a gaze! May the treacherous sex swoon!

CUP-BEARER. Listen . . . !

PAPKIN. Just a moment . . . Along I'm riding when all of a sudden some Greek princess—an angel! a goddess! spied my figure—How these females perish for me! She glanced at me —I at her; in the end, she fell madly in love, called me over, et cetera . . . At that point the prince, a tiger, started to collect his flunkies . . .

CUP-BEARER. [*Banging on the table, which causes Papkin to jump up on his chair.*] Quiet please.

PAPKIN. How lively you are!

CUP-BEARER. And you are a godless tongue! And a chatterbox, and a liar.

PAPKIN. You're too lively, Cup-Bearer. If, like you, I also didn't keep my passions reined in tightly [*strikes the handle of his sword*], Artemis'* razor edges . . . [*Anticipating the Cup-Bearer's banging on the table.*] Please go on.

CUP-BEARER. [*A short pause.*] Clara's father bought an old castle together with the village . . .

PAPKIN. Pshaw!—My father had ten of them!

CUP-BEARER. [*Banging the table and continuing to speak.*] Here we live now, just like owls. But what's worse is that the owner of the other half of the castle is—a devil. [*Papkin registers alarm.*] Who else? The Notary Milczek—sweet and silent, face so humble, but the devil's in his soul, Sir!

PAPKIN. Nonetheless, like neighbors, calmly . . .

CUP-BEARER. If I can't get him to leave there with all my tricks, then no one can. There's not a day passes without

* Papkin has named his sword after the Greek goddess of the hunt.

fighting—but we have to have some kind of treaty. Should
I write to him? No, not to that scamp. Should I go there?
Slippery, my friend. He could secretly poison me, kill me,
and life is still dear to me. That's the reason why I chose
you: if there's need, you'll be an envoy.

PAPKIN. For this honor, I salute you! It's a great one you
do your servant. But I think I'm too ferocious—I'll cause
war instead of peace, Sir. After all, my mother bore me in
her womb for a life of knightly valor, and from infancy I
took vows never to serve as envoy.

CUP-BEARER. Papkin will be what I want him to be, for
Papkin must do as I tell him.

PAPKIN. But because he's so impetuous, if Papkin should go
choke a neighbor, if he should drill a hole in his head, if he
should chop him into *bigos** who'll then be the guilty
party? Who'll bear the punishment for it?

CUP-BEARER. I'll take all upon my conscience.

PAPKIN. Think it over.

CUP-BEARER. I've done so. Now I have one more announcement: Papkin—I am getting married.

PAPKIN. Bah!

CUP-BEARER. [*Mocking him.*] What is this, bah?

PAPKIN. I'm so happy! And I'm glad to speed the matter
along. Tell me where to sing your praises. Shall I play the
part of matchmaker? Shall I persuade the lady if she's too
timid? Shall I force her if too saucy? If she belongs to another, shall I run her tyrant's belly through?

CUP-BEARER. What the devil is this madness?

PAPKIN. Cup-Bearer, you know my courage.

CUP-BEARER. Listen, speaking just between the two of us,
without my boasting or your taking offense, I've got much
more sense than you, Papkin, a thousand times more sense.
[*Papkin wants to interrupt him, but the Cup-Bearer re-
strains him with a sign.*] But getting on with the fair sex,
you know, all that silly flirting, romantic chitter-chattering
—for the life of me, I couldn't manage it at all, Sir. So with
your eloquence you have to . . .

PAPKIN. She's already yours. I give my word. If you want a

* Polish national dish of chopped meat and cabbage.

wife—you'll have one, for I've mad luck with the ladies. I need but look and each is mine. And at each I know how to look. I'm going.

CUP-BEARER. Where to?

PAPKIN. True, I don't know.

CUP-BEARER. The widow . . .

PAPKIN. Now I get you.

CUP-BEARER. [*Restraining him.*] Wait for her here!

PAPKIN. Not a word more! In an hour she'll be ready.

CUP-BEARER. [*Going out.*] I'll find a way to thank you.

PAPKIN. One can count on the Cup-Bearer.

SCENE 3.

PAPKIN. [*Alone.*] A real volcano . . . he upsets me. If I didn't hold the reins short I don't know what would become of the world. [*A short pause.*] But I won't doze here much longer. This is how I'll handle the matter: I'll give him the widow, a somewhat antique picture; for myself I'll take fair Clara. I've had the hope a long time that her heart would open to me. We'd have been a well-matched pair now and have raised a lot of Papkins, if the Cup-Bearer hadn't always stood between us like a wall. [*A moment later.*] I must let her know I'm here. Let a song by its sweet murmur reach her dear sweet little ear—Oh, I sing as prettily as an angel! [*Sings, accompanying himself on his English guitar.*]

> Daughter mine, child of mine, what's that
> whispering in your room?
> Oh, a cat, mother dear, a kitty-cat,
> It's a cat that made the noise.
> Daughter mine, child of mine, what's that
> banging in your room?
> Mother dear, mother mine, it's the kitten
> hunting mice.
> Oh a cat, mother dear, a kitty-cat,
> It's a cat that made the noise.
> Daughter mine, child of mine, and does that
> cat have legs?

Mother dear, mother mine, and silver spurs as well.
Oh a cat, mother dear, a kitty-cat,
    It's a cat that made the noise.

SCENE 4. Papkin, then the widow who comes in from the door on the right.

HANNA. Just as I was saying—either cats or Papkin have come upon us.

PAPKIN. Always full of playful spirits, Lady Hanna! Demi-angel! Colossal image of virtue on this hemisphere of ours, blessed with love, charm, and graces! Allow me humbly to bend my brow and on the snow of your hand place the light impress of my lips. [*Kisses her hand.*] Your servant, your most humble servant.

HANNA. What is it brings you to these parts?

PAPKIN. An event pleasant to us all.

HANNA. What event?

PAPKIN. Your nuptials.

HANNA. My what?

PAPKIN. Last night it was my good fortune to have as guests for dinner Lord Pembroke, several squires, and a whole dozen chamberlains. There were not too many ladies, but what ladies!

HANNA. Whom are they matching now?

PAPKIN. There was talk that fair Hanna is getting married. Some affirmed it, others denied it, but all read the truth from my eyes, though. Then Milady, a goddess of a woman, but a little devil when jealous, pinching me constantly under the table, asked me twice, half crying: "What have you to do with Hanna?" Oh, calm yourself, I whispered charmingly into her little ear—Hanna is marrying a friend.

HANNA. But whom? Tell me whom.

PAPKIN. All agree in praise of your choice . . . But how can they fail to praise it?

HANNA. [*Aside.*] Ah, now I understand . . .

PAPKIN. A decent fellow, well off and devoted.

HANNA. [*Aside.*] He's under the Cup-Bearer's orders and in

roundabout way reaches where he's already expected. Stupid smartie.

PAPKIN. [*Aside.*] There you have it! She's glancing, she's sighing—is she wrong about the person? Is it me she loves. . . Oh, heavens! Oh, this curse, God's punishment: to young and old I'm irresistible. She's still glancing . . . is she mad? This is no joking matter. I'd eat dust from my master. And what for, why do I need this? It can't go on any longer now. [*To Hanna.*] Madame, give me your permission to congratulate the Cup-Bearer.

HANNA. I am to become his wife then?

PAPKIN. Why do you ask such a question? Was it all just a fairy tale?

HANNA. Yes, until now . . .

PAPKIN. Then it shall soon be the truth—or am I wrong?

HANNA. Why so much curiosity?

PAPKIN. If the Cup-Bearer, passion fired, overpowered by all your charms, trembling with love, and prostrate at your feet, begged for your hand?

HANNA. He'd be happy with the answer. [*She goes out through the door on the right.*]

PAPKIN. [*Alone.*] Just remember the warning—there's a devil in each woman who ignites the wanton in her. But let someone wise tell me why in the name of heaven the widow is giving her hand to the Cup-Bearer?

SCENE 5. Papkin; the Cup-Bearer enters, already dressed, from the door on the left.

CUP-BEARER. What the blazes! You're so calm while the Notary attacks me and demands open combat? But he has a worthy neighbor! Lively, men now! Let who's able run, dash, drive, strike.

PAPKIN. What's the matter?

CUP-BEARER. He's patching the wall up! The border wall, three masons are on it! He gave the order! He just dares to! The border wall! Three men on the wall there! I'll slay them, then smash the wall down! I'll smash it, I'll level it to the ground—

PAPKIN. [*Confused, repeating involuntarily.*] Smash it, level it . . .

CUP-BEARER. You with me? Gather up some men—go off with them! And if you can't use persuasion with them over there, drive them from the work by force then—You're trembling?

PAPKIN. From eagerness, Sir. But wait a moment—first listen to an exalted, beautiful ode of mine.

CUP-BEARER. What?

PAPKIN. An ode to peace, Sir—and if the desire for battle isn't silenced by the voice of the Muse . . .

CUP-BEARER. [*Threatening.*] Stay here! But . . . ! [*He goes out.*]

PAPKIN. [*Following after him with lowered head.*] Now I've had it!

SCENE 6. *Change of scene. A garden and a part of the wall. From the left side to the center the wall is intact, but from the center to the rear of the stage it is broken and half destroyed. It is on this part that the masons are working. On the left side, entirely in the rear beyond a part of the whole wall, is the bastille or tower of the Notary's castle, with a window. Somewhat to the front, on the right side, a similar tower belonging to the Cup-Bearer. A bower on the left side toward the front of the stage. Clara is passing by. Vatslav, entering through a hole in the wall, steals along the wall and appears for the second time in the bower by Clara's side.*

VATSLAV. Our homes are near each other, and our hearts nearer—yet how far apart we still are in this world.

CLARA. What new desires cloud the brightness of your brow today? Neither boundaries, nor caution—is there nothing that can restrain you, not even the love of your Clara?

VATSLAV. To see you for just one moment, then spend so many long hours without your eyes, without your voice—and I'm to praise fate's kindness?

CLARA. Just recall, recall my darling, what your words were the very first few times we met in the cloister: "Let us love each other, dearest, my tears ask for nothing more. With my love for you I'll be a god in heaven, I'll live in splendor."

VATSLAV. I didn't know what I was saying.

CLARA. Love—I said—I don't forbid you. But soon when you pressed my hands in yours with passion, you asked: "Do you love me, Clara dear?" You kept asking me that question, though my eyes gave you the answer.

VATSLAV. Who'd not want to give half his life to drink until drunk, to drink with his soul the words that come from your mouth, which still preserves a smile!

CLARA. So be it—I said finally: I love you—for I did love you, too. [*Affects his passion.*] "Oh, what happiness, joy, gladness! Praise be to the sky, the earth, the sun . . . !" Nature already spent itself fulfilling these desires. For you she had no more to give.

VATSLAV. True, I'm not afraid to admit it that nature gave me full measure. But if she increases my love, shouldn't she increase her gifts, too?

CLARA. A few days ago you said, dear: "Oh, that window, oh, that grill-work will be the cause of my ruin. See how roses twine together, how flowers bend one to the other—who prohibits us the same, dear?"

VATSLAV. When my thoughts were so confusing, what was I to do: embrace cold iron?

CLARA. I've listened to you, Vatslav. Every day we meet each other in the bower, but almost every day you wish something new of me. I owe you my happiness, and I believe— you feel the same. But why does your love keep on taking a different form each time? When the joy of being near you fills my heart to overflow you, ungrateful, at the same time keep brewing only new anxieties.

VATSLAV. Oh, I'm frightened by the present, for we still have done so little to insure our future—and our love is the future. But these constant issues, fights and quarrels between my father and your uncle foretell nothing pleasant for us. They say rather that we'll some time be separated cruelly if . . .

CLARA. Go on—show me the way. Is there anything you or I can do?

VATSLAV. Only your will can change what seems unchangeable.

CLARA. Talk, I'm listening.

VATSLAV. That you love me, that I love you more than heaven, that we want to live together, both of us know well enough. What we don't know, however, is what we have to do to destroy this awful secrecy in which we're wasting our lives now, and not be upset if happy days don't come before the sad ones.

CLARA. What must we do? Tell me.

VATSLAV. Get married.

CLARA. Oh, you're mad, what way is there?

VATSLAV. In your will.

CLARA. Say instead in my uncle's. In your father's.

VATSLAV. What hinders us will soon vanish, since there's no other way it can be.

CLARA. Oh, I understand! No, Vatslav, you'll always find me yours, wherever you want me—except in shame.

VATSLAV. Oh, but Clara, once we're married . . .

CLARA. Who, I ask, will really know that we've married once we've left here . . . What's that noise? I hear steps! Getting closer! . . . Go away fast!

VATSLAV. Just a word.

CLARA. You've had it.

VATSLAV. I'll stop living if you don't change it.

CLARA. [*With feeling, as if correcting him.*] If you want—we'll both stop living.

VATSLAV. All I ask is think it over, Clara dear . . .

CLARA. [*Almost pushing him out.*] But for heaven's sake, go on, go! [*She walks across the stage.*]

SCENE 7. Papkin, Śmigalski, several servants with sticks, later the Notary and the Cup-Bearer in their windows.

PAPKIN. Mister Mason, Sir, I ask you, decently, politely, nicely, not to do any more walling here, or you'll really suffer for it. [*A short pause.*] And you others there, good men, who are masterfully using hammers, plummets, trowels in today's unnecessary labor, all of you be off, go to the devil! [*A short pause.*] Stubborn, I see! As if deaf, this rabble doesn't hear a word I tell them. Well, Śmigalski, let's not waste time— grab them by their throats! Take their tools! Nice and decent, without tumult, let the whole affair be ended. Fear nothing—I'm beside you. [*Śmigalski surges forward against the masons with the servants. Papkin conceals himself behind a corner of the house.*]

ŚMIGALSKI. Be off! Be off!

NOTARY. [*In the window.*] Stop! What's the meaning of this?

ŚMIGALSKI. The Cup-Bearer, my master, orders that the wall be left unfinished.

CUP-BEARER. [*In the window*]. That's right, I order it, because I've the right to. Forward, forward! Lively now, men! [*Śmigalski surges forward. Papkin, who had come out, again withdraws behind a corner of the house.*]

NOTARY. What right?

CUP-BEARER. Let the border wall be just the way it was when purchased.

NOTARY. But my dear fellow, that's insanity on your part— and the wall is going to be repaired.

CUP-BEARER. I'll strew it first with corpses.

NOTARY. [*To the masons.*] Finish up your work now, friends. Just like me, ignore his empty threats.

CUP-BEARER. You want battle then?

NOTARY. Cup-Bearer, my neighbor, my good fellow, dear Sir, why don't you stop being a bandit?

CUP-BEARER. What? Well! After them! Strike with all your might, men! [*Śmigalski and his men fall on the wall. The masons withdraw in such a way that the battle remains obscured by a part of the wall that is intact.*]

NOTARY. Hola, master—I'm behind you. Don't fear anything! Let him fight if his palms are itching for it. Good! Good! Right on the head—that's it! Better! Whoever sticks his nose in! Don't fear anything! It's just what they need. Let him fight! The world's not ending! Just for this I'll put the Cup-Bearer where he won't see earth or heaven!

CUP-BEARER. [*Calling out.*] Hey! Boys! Throw me a musket, let me take a crack at his noodle—quickly! [*The Notary shuts his window.*] Ha, ha! *Fugas chrustas.** Well, Śmigalski, that's enough now. Go pass out a little money among the

---

* A humorous expression in the macaronic Latin-Polish style meaning "You're running for the bushes!"

men for their efforts, but be sure and take their weapons. That's enough, enough, for the time being. [*He shuts his window. After they all leave the stage, Papkin appears and seeing no one around any longer, addresses the wall.*] Ha! You scoundrels! Out of my way! Or I'll grind you all to a pulp—a leg won't be left among you—and I have a devilish desire today! Are there many of you there? Come on! Not one will crawl out of his hole? Oh, you rascals! Oh, you cowards! Just you wait and see, tomorrow I'll destroy the entire castle.

SCENE 8. Papkin, Vatslav.

VATSLAV. [*Coming up and standing behind him.*] Tomorrow? [*Papkin removes his hat.*] Must I go back there, to the place which will certainly be leveled to the ground by your harsh sentence? I prefer to be your captive!

PAPKIN. [*Putting his hat at a jaunty angle.*] You give yourself up?

VATSLAV. Yes, I do, Sir.

PAPKIN. Know my courage?

VATSLAV. Like a bad coin.

PAPKIN. Do you fear me?

VATSLAV. Terribly!

PAPKIN. You'll go with me?

VATSLAV. I'll go with you.

PAPKIN. Who are you?

VATSLAV. I am, Sir.

PAPKIN. But what are you?

VATSLAV. What am I? I am . . . I am . . .

PAPKIN. [*Seizing his weapon.*] Come on now, let's have it.

VATSLAV. . . . . I'm my master's deputy, Sir.

PAPKIN. What? The Notary's?

VATSLAV. No other.

PAPKIN. An unheard-of thing, I ask you! A poor country squire is barely able to crawl out from under a mess of debts— when he has to have a deputy. No wonder later when his place is up for auction: "A hundred thousand! Who bids more!" And when they shout it a third time, the squire flies out as if he were catapulted straight into the service of his former deputy as steward! But let's go now. [*Aside.*] The Cup-Bearer will be elated with my prisoner and most certainly he'll tell me when I present this booty to him: "Take Clara for your own." Come my captive.

VATSLAV. Coming now, Sir.

ACT II

The same room as at the beginning of Act One. The Cup-Bearer is sitting at a small table.

SCENE 1. *The Cup-Bearer, then Papkin, followed by Vatslav, who remains standing at the door.*

PAPKIN. [*Throwing himself into a chair.*] Ah, to hell with such labors! I can barely move, I can hardly stand. But it certainly did go briskly! To the right and left I thundered— I'm barely alive! Have some wine brought in, something old. My throat's all dried out—the sweat is pouring from my head in streams—who can fathom my deeds?

CUP-BEARER. I can, because I saw.

PAPKIN. Ha! You saw? Good, eh?

CUP-BEARER. Good—you stood in the rear.

PAPKIN. Rear or front, it makes no difference. A good knight's fearful everywhere.

CUP-BEARER. Such impertinence . . .

PAPKIN. Can't help it—such impertinence was needed to wage battle with such power.

CUP-BEARER. Telling lies again, my dear fellow . . .

PAPKIN. Listen now, it's worth your while. My first goal was the scaffolding, but I jumped with such abandon, that I landed on the wrong side. There I was—hemmed in, surrounded by masons, hired hands, soldiers, lackeys—by the hundreds—How I wound up! I grab two of them by the hair! I tear into the others with them like a mill—as though with flails I thresh all about me. Every time I turn around, more than ten of them are on the ground. So the heap kept growing bigger, and when it was level with the wall, I opened both my palms and stood again on this side. But that's not all . . .

CUP-BEARER. Pfaugh! Devil with you!

PAPKIN. Something worthy of amazement—I brought back a captive with me. Now, Sir, I'm waiting for my wreath.

CUP-BEARER. [*Seeing Vatslav.*] Who is this fellow?

PAPKIN. [*Mopping his brow.*] He's the Notary's deputy I took as captive.

CUP-BEARER. For what reason? With what purpose?

PAPKIN. I just gather what comes my way.

CUP-BEARER. [*To Vatslav.*] You be on your way, my dear sir, and inform your master please that should he give me any cause for upset whatsoever, I'll land on him so hard he won't know what it is that hit him. Now be on your way and quickly.

PAPKIN. Dedicate yourself to some good cause! Fight like Achilles, give advice like Cato, they'll just envy all your glory and pay you back in devils.

VATSLAV. [*To the Cup-Bearer.*] Pardon me, Sir, for speaking so boldly now: you're angry at your neighbor for getting in your way once in a while . . .

CUP-BEARER. Once in a while! Always!

VATSLAV. He says . . .

CUP-BEARER. Not a word about that reptile.

VATSLAV. Wouldn't there be a way, if you both gave in a little and forgot about past quarrels, to return to neighborly peace again?

CUP-BEARER. He and I in peace? My good man, sooner will the sun stop moving! Sooner will the ocean dry up, than there will be peace between us!

VATSLAV. Your mind's upset today and pronounces judgment too rashly . . .

CUP-BEARER. May God always keep us guarded from the wind, fire, and war, and moreover, from the person who bows low to everyone.

VATSLAV. Better low than not at all, Sir.

CUP-BEARER. Rot, I say!

VATSLAV. But . . .

CUP-BEARER. There are no buts!

VATSLAV. Don't forbid me to have hopes, Sir . . .

CUP-BEARER. I do, a hundred thousand times! And I want to know no more of him or of his . . . [*ironically measuring Vatslav*] preacher either, for they'll get what they're deserving. On my word as squire, they'll get it. [*Leaves through the center door.*]

SCENE 2. *Papkin, Vatslav.*

PAPKIN. Devil's stoking up the Cup-Bearer.

VATSLAV. Waste of time to try to calm them.

PAPKIN. Too much noise, too little profit.

VATSLAV. These two men—they're like fire and water.

PAPKIN. What will happen to us, young master?

VATSLAV. Ha! I'll just stay behind here captive.

PAPKIN. I've taken prisoners by the thousands whose fate depended upon my will; I battled for ten long years where bloody springs flowed so that for miles around it looked like a sea turned crimson. It was there that I earned orders, titles, and honors, but what you ask can't be granted. These models are too exalted for us. This day's scuffle's just a game, and your freedom just a trifle.

VATSLAV. I'll remain here as a prisoner.

PAPKIN. I have the right to detain you, but I've always been magnanimous, so I'll take instead a small ransom.

VATSLAV. But I must remain here captive.

PAPKIN. Know the greatness of my soul then: now you're free —go to the devil. And for freedom, give what you please.

VATSLAV. I'll remain here as a prisoner.

PAPKIN. But the Cup-Bearer won't let you.

VATSLAV. Let who captured me retain me.

PAPKIN. But it makes no sense at all, friend; don't give me a thing, just leave here.

VATSLAV. I won't take half a step from here.

PAPKIN. Go, or else I'll use my weapon.

VATSLAV. [*Always phlegmatic.*] And I, I'll just use my bare hands.

PAPKIN. [*Aside.*] What kind of a person is this, damn it! Of his own will looks for bruises. What's more, even drives me to it. [*To Vatslav.*] On your way—the devil with you.

VATSLAV. No, I won't go—I'm staying here.

PAPKIN. What a stubborn pest this is!

VATSLAV. [*Showing his purse.*] See here, brother, know what this is?

PAPKIN. Shake it up a little.

VATSLAV. Gold?

PAPKIN. Gold.

VATSLAV. It will be yours.

PAPKIN. Please sit down.

VATSLAV. But no one gives a thing for nothing.

PAPKIN. Gospel truth! But what have I to lose? Since I'm in such a miserable situation anyway: for the little due me I have to chase about as though I were courting, while in my pockets, brother dear—either empty spaces or holes.

VATSLAV. I love Clara.

PAPKIN. [*Aside.*] There you have it!

VATSLAV. And I want to stay here near her.

PAPKIN. That's bad.

VATSLAV. [*Holding on to the purse.*] Is it bad?

PAPKIN. [*Taking hold of his hand.*] That depends. But the Cup-Bearer, you realize, most certainly will act adversely.

VATSLAV. Don't let him know.

PAPKIN. If he finds out?

VATSLAV. Let him accept me.

PAPKIN. It won't be easy.

VATSLAV. [*Clinking the gold.*] Here's the start, the rest's up to you.

PAPKIN. And if the Cup-Bearer lets me have it?

VATSLAV. Doesn't mean a thing.

PAPKIN. Bah! To whom? [*Shakes his head.*] But for Clara—just some deputy.

VATSLAV. I am Vatslav.

PAPKIN. The Notary's son! Oh my heavens! And in this house! You're a danger to us both, Sir. We're both heading for a thrashing! [*Vatslav jingles the purse.*] Jingles pretty.

VATSLAV. Consider it yours, if I remain in service here.

PAPKIN. Well! I'll try . . . [*He tries to take the purse.*]

VATSLAV. [*Withdrawing it.*] A little later—but remember, from my turret shells fly quickly to the bottom. One bang from my gun and—Papkin's stretched out . . . if the desire to cheat me seizes him.

PAPKIN. In this matter's secret conduct I shall act as fitting, paying no heed to your warning. But if you have feelings for me, blow your gun out some place else today.

VATSLAV. Don't waste time.

PAPKIN. I'm going, I'm going. [*Aside.*] Devil brewed up such a triumph! I'm crawling deeper into grief; in my captive I've a rival. Either way you look it's awful—one will lock me up in prison, while the other wants to shoot me—both of them can go to hell! [*Turns back from the door.*] And the purse?

VATSLAV. It may remain here.

PAPKIN. Do you mean it?

VATSLAV. But most surely. [*Papkin leaves through the middle door.*]

SCENE 3. Vatslav, Clara.

CLARA. Oh my heavens! What's going on here? I should really be despairing, if I only had the time now.

VATSLAV. What's the matter? What's happening?

CLARA. And he laughs straight in my face yet! I know everything, because I was listening—you want to stay here.

VATSLAV. What's bad about it?

CLARA. Use your head.

VATSLAV. Where will that get me? Since we've already found out—using our heads as we had been our destinies could never be joined together now and for always. Why stay on the same old course? Onward through the by-ways, where the dawn of hope is breaking, where it's less dark before us! Let's not cast our glance sideways, for abysses are certainly around us, but raising our heads to heaven, let's go forward with a bold step. And if constancy will accompany us on our course, sometime we'll reach our goal despite strife and many barriers.

CLARA. How well you speak, let's go boldly! We gain little, you convinced me, following the simple path. You speak better than this morning when you thought we ought to flee here. But if they should recognize you? Or if Papkin should deceive you?

VATSLAV. Don't look into the abyss, dear, look instead into your own heart. Every care will vanish swiftly when your gaze sinks into love.

CLARA. Stay here in the name of God, then, you've my permission for it.

VATSLAV. Yours alone helps little, Clara, though I value it as my life.

CLARA. Maybe we can still reach uncle through the help of Hanna, the widow. You know that just this moment they've declared their mutual love—she's modest, blushed bright crimson, but promised him her hand. You won't find it hard to snare her, flattering her in every way; praise her wisdom, virtue, beauty, the bearing of her person, and what you want to be in our house you'll be before the day's out.

VATSLAV. From a deputy to actor! What would people think about it? But as always it's an honor to be in the Cup-Bearer's service.

CLARA. I'll run, I'll tell Hanna that someone's waiting for her with a request. [*Gives him her hand.*] Keep your hopes high —the bad passes. The hour of our happiness is near. [*She leaves through the door on the right.*]

SCENE 4.

VATSLAV. An hour ago she's fainting from fear; one hour later —she's a model of courage! First she sees no possibility, then she has hope enough for two people. O you pretty, gentle, fair sex! All your pleasures, all your sorrows, they're the light waves of a lake: one constantly pursues the other. One goes down, the other rises up, but always in the sun's bright glare, always pure and without end! But we, proud rulers of the earth, prisoners despite ourselves, chase like butterflies our whole lives from one moment to the other only after fleeting shadows.

SCENE 5. *Vatslav, Hanna from the door on the right.*

HANNA. Where's the supplicant? What is it he wants?

VATSLAV. [*With a low bow.*] The intruder's here.

HANNA. You, young man?

VATSLAV. [*Still bowed.*] Maybe he becomes too guilty if he raises his glance boldly . . . Well! . . .

HANNA. Can it be?

VATSLAV. [*After a short pause.*] Hanna!

HANNA. Vatslav.

VATSLAV. [*In confusion.*] Truly I don't know . . .

HANNA. This meeting . . . !

VATSLAV. Then it's you who's the widow?

HANNA. Didn't you know?

VATSLAV. [*As before.*] An hour ago . . . [*Aside.*] What can I say? What role to play?

HANNA. Didn't you know that the Steward Czepiersiński, my third husband, God have mercy on his poor soul, after marrying me in spring, went off to the grave in autumn?

VATSLAV. Yes, yes, it comes back to mind now.

HANNA. He gave up his soul on my lap.

VATSLAV. [*Absentmindedly.*] Gave up? Yes, of course he gave up.

HANNA. At first I shed bitter tears, life without a husband's painful. Even sorrow drowns in time, though.

VATSLAV. [*Absentmindedly.*] Then the Steward drowned . . .

HANNA. Who says so?

VATSLAV. It's not so? Good. But I must go.

HANNA. [*Restraining him.*] What's he thinking? What's he saying? Oh my soul, you're going crazy!

VATSLAV. That may be.

HANNA. [*Tenderly.*] I'll tie you up, I'll imprison you, my dear prince.

VATSLAV. Oh, please don't repeat that word! Look how I'm burning all over with shame for my youthful peccadillos. Vatslav no longer possesses either name or princely title, for they were—

HANNA. What?

VATSLAV. Just pretended.

HANNA. Everything?

VATSLAV. To the last detail.

HANNA. You're no prince . . . ?

VATSLAV. Not in the slightest.

HANNA. Why the pretense?

VATSLAV. No good reason—youthful madness . . . Silly urges . . . In a word—just something senseless, like most of our stupid actions.

HANNA. And what of your love for me?

VATSLAV. [*Aside.*] Now she's got me in her trap!

HANNA. This blush—coloring your forehead, what does it mean? I waited, then looked for you all over Lithuania, but about a Prince Rodoslav, no one knew, or really could know.

VATSLAV. I was . . . young . . .

HANNA. [*Repeating ironically.*] "I was young!" you say. But quite talented at your art?

VATSLAV. That I don't know.

HANNA. But there are proofs.

VATSLAV. Proofs? What kind of proofs?

HANNA. Your treachery.

VATSLAV. It's possible I've changed since; it's not easy to love constantly! But if I deserve to be chastised should a different Hanna do it? Your search didn't take you too far, your wait didn't last a long time—no sooner does the lid close on your husband when the Cup-Bearer comes calling, and should he yawn his last today, there'd be someone new to-morrow. I'm not making accusations—on the contrary, my blessings. But the rights that you're permitted should be given every person. If I've changed my feelings toward you, I just followed your example. Either we've deceived each other, or there's no deceit at all here.

HANNA. Vatslav dear, I'm now a widow.

VATSLAV. And I almost a married man.

HANNA. Well-known friend, who are you really?

VATSLAV. Vatslav Milczek.

HANNA. The Notary's son? Here, in this house . . .

VATSLAV. [*Finishing the sentence.*] I just stumbled.

HANNA. My whole being's filled with terror . . . Everything's grown dark . . . My heart beats faster . . . When the Cup-Bearer finds you here! . . . When he sees a rival in you!

VATSLAV. Oh, he'll find no rival in me.

HANNA. Don't make any vain denials. After all you did beseech me to come to you, is that not true? What do you
want?

VATSLAV. May I perish if I know myself. Keep well!

HANNA. [*Restraining him.*] Just the way you used to be! Stay,
don't go away!

VATSLAV. [*Aside.*] Ah, Papkin, some captivity you gave me!

HANNA. You're the only one I've loved—I prefer you to a hundred princes! Come on to my room in secret, you'll be out
of danger there, dear. I'll protect you with my life if need
be and at least seek praise in that way.

SCENE 6. Hanna, Vatslav, Clara from the door on the right.

VATSLAV. [*Seeing Clara, painfully.*] Oh!

CLARA. [*Happily.*] What is it?

HANNA. That is . . .

VATSLAV. Nothing . . .

CLARA. [*To the widow.*] What does he want?

HANNA. [*Aside.*] What can I tell her?

CLARA. [*Aside.*] Things look good—she's siding with him.
[*Aloud.*] Perhaps I should know?

VATSLAV. Oh, what for?

HANNA. It's a rather serious matter and needs some deliberation. For that reason, please say nothing that you know about
his presence—I'll explain the whole thing later.

VATSLAV. [*Quietly, to the widow.*] I'll leave here.

HANNA. [*Also quietly.*] I won't permit you. [*Out loud.*] Would
you please come with me now, Sir? His is such a complicated matter—I've some papers to look over. [*To Clara, kissing her on the forehead.*] And remember please, Clara dear,
not to say a word to anyone.

CLARA. No one in this house will find out . . .

HANNA. It would cause us all some trouble; I'll tell you later
what it's about. [*She goes out casting a glance at Vatslav,
who leaves with her through the door on the right, his head
lowered.*]

CLARA. [*Alone.*] What on earth could be funnier than to watch
the deceived deceiving! Oh, how Vatslav with humility

seemed to call her to defend him! I could hardly keep from laughing. But hold on there, whoa young lady! You've no right yet to a triumph; though you've had a good beginning, the game has hardly been won yet.

SCENE 7. *Clara, Papkin.*

PAPKIN. Just as in Arabian deserts the gold-strewing gaze of Phoebus bears death to lilies in its heat till their white heads bow low, and a fertile dew-drop, gathered in the azure sky, brings new life to the withered flowers and transports them to the heavens—in this way your gracious presence, honey-flowing Clara [*with a bow*], was for me, your humble servant, just as potent and effective. I myself was close to fading when your gaze changed everything. Would that sometime the gods let me bear you a sweet recompense, and e'er time briskly wields its scythe, be your glowing fire, your dew. [*Bows deeply.*]

CLARA. [*Ironic throughout the entire scene, returning his bow.*] Every woman dreams of finding husbands as renowned for rhyme as military valor. But since these days all the young men like to plait the wedding wreath with loving and respectful phrases, it's always hard to trust them.

PAPKIN. Can you not believe, great heavens, that fair Clara's truly loved? Must one take an oath to it?

CLARA. That I'm loved—there's no need swearing, but that it will always be so even swearing can't assure me.

PAPKIN. Ah, let your tiny grain deign to fall on the fertile bed of my heart, and that small seed that comes from you will strike an eternal root.

CLARA. In days of yore a true knight either won a wreath of glory or engaged in bloody battles before making a declaration of love. For the honor of his loved one he entered tournaments. In these he scored bravely with his lance, unseated almost a dozen men and only then, when he bent down to take his prize from a beloved hand, did he beg her open her heart and permit him to love her—and be free, fighting under her colors, to break lances, to cross swords, and to love or die just for her!

PAPKIN. From this costume and this armor you see a foster-child of Mars who as knight errant has raced from one pole to the other. Would that my trusty Artemis, fearful to the world that blade, swollen with blood like a wet sponge, were able to speak just this once to you of faith, and to me of glory. [*With still greater passion.*] Where there was a fortress on a cliff, where there was a wall besieged with cannon, where there were sharp waves of bayonets, where there were vaults of pikes and sabers—there was Papkin—lion undaunted! Devilish swordsman! Divine shot! Groan, moan, shout, roar, death was all around—here an unarmed man asks pardon, here a maiden pleads for mercy, a mother cries, a child whimpers, but my trusty blade-arm falls: those who lived, no longer live. [*Clara bursts out in a laugh.*] Please forgive the zealous thunder of my knightly exaltation, but you see: I have enough fame. All I lack is the permission to take my place with the fortunate of whom Clara will be the goal.

CLARA. I'll permit you.

PAPKIN. [*Kneeling.*] Take my vows then . . .

CLARA. Hold on! There come years of test now in which you must offer proof of obedience, endurance, and courage.

PAPKIN. O Queen of All-Beauty! Ornament of all Mankind! Say: "Jump in the fire, Papkin"—and in the fire your Papkin perishes. [*He rises.*]

CLARA. My demands aren't so severe; the jewel of the knightly caste will not be sacrificed to fire. But I repeat to your lordship: I demand proof of your obedience, endurance, and courage.

PAPKIN. In each I'll find cause for glory.

CLARA. To reveal the measure of your obedience, for six months you must say nothing.

PAPKIN. Not to say a thing?

CLARA. Yes—nothing more. I'll believe in your endurance if you live on bread and water . . .

PAPKIN. Please, I beg you, not for too long.

CLARA. One year and six days.

PAPKIN. [*Painfully.*] I'm in the grave . . . [*With a bow.*] But your servant now and always.

CLARA. As for your courage—you'll give proof of it in the manner I tell you. In a land far distant from here there is famed a monstrous creature who strikes terror in the heart even of the bravest and is called a—crocodile. You go capture it and bring it for my amusement, for I'm frightfully curious to see this monster in the flesh. That is my unchallengeable will—who succeeds in what I've ordered will lead me to the altar. Only such a man would I consent to marry. [*After bowing, she goes out by the door on the right.*]

SCENE 8.

PAPKIN. [*After a long silence.*] Crrrrocodile! [*Ironically.*] A mere nothing! What a madness, devil take it! Young girls have crocodiles in their heads now because they're all seeking excitement. What's fashionable, charming, and pretty these days is what's deadly, what's hideous! Once upon a time a young girl said pleasantly to her lover: "Get me, dear, a small canary." But instead each one today says: "If you don't wish my destruction, then fetch me a crocodile, dear!" [*A short pause.*] Fast, silence—they're just trifles—she won't station a guard around me. But this monster's no plaything. Let the devil go, not Papkin. [*He goes toward the door on the right and meets Vatslav who comes running out of it.*] Well!

VATSLAV. What?

PAPKIN. Nothing.

VATSLAV. [*Throwing him the little purse.*] There you are—but keep your mouth shut—or else!

PAPKIN. [*Seizing the purse.*] I know. [*Vatslav goes out. A short pause.*] I know? I know nothing! If he stays here, if he goes, why he gives me gifts, I don't know. I know it's gold, though; I know that he did well giving, but I don't know if the Cup-Bearer won't make me pay dearly for it. I know if I cheat this wooer he's all set to blow my head off. But I don't know, I just don't know if when all these maneuvers are over I'll still have my head in one piece. I know—yet I don't—how maddening: here a bullet, there a saber—well, as Mister Benet* said once: [*tossing up the purse*] *Beatus qui tenet.*†

SCENE 9. *Papkin, the Cup-Bearer from the center door.*

CUP-BEARER. Wish me well on my success, Sir! We've exchanged vows today. Finally, and no postponing, the widow gave her promise.

PAPKIN. I know how smoothly it all went—after all, it's all my doing.

CUP-BEARER. Oh! Your doing! Just look at him! You ask me about it now, Sir! [*Glances around.*] I came there at a good moment. She received me nicely, sweetly, gave me glances, flirtatious ogling—right off I began to woo her. What a mighty fuss she made then—not this, not that, this way, that way, while I kept on coming closer. 'Midst the giggles, 'midst the chatter, closer . . . closer . . . smack! And finally— [*Benevolently.*] Ah! Some shame I caused the woman; like a beet she blushed all over—then confusion took hold of me. So much so I thought of leaving, running fast from there like lightning. Just then guess what happened next, Sir. She called to me: "Hold on, Mathew—let it be as your will wishes—I accept it in humility—take this ring—God give His blessings!

PAPKIN. Devil take it! Great performance!

CUP-BEARER. [*In anger.*] Say it reverently, damn it! Or . . . [*He points to the door.*]

PAPKIN. You're always in a bad mood. My, what quarrels there'd be here if my blood was any warmer—but there are more important things we have to talk about.

CUP-BEARER. Fine with me.

PAPKIN. That young flunky of the Notary, who'll remember me a long time, asks if he can possibly stay behind here in your service. He'll be nimble, fit and faithful, but what of it? [*Secretly.*] There's a rumor that he likes the bottle.

CUP-BEARER. Whether he likes it, or doesn't like it—there's no

---

* The titular character of Fredro's comedy *Pan Benet*, about a typical old Polish squire.
† Happy is he who has.

place he'll warm in my house. I won't pick up from the ground what falls from Milczek's nose . . . If he puts up a fight, however, and really insists on staying, I'd then accept him out of spite. You'll soon find out, for I'm taking a different tactic now. On account of my prank today, and because the wall's still got a hole in it, Squire Milczek wants to sue me. I prefer the sword to end it. You shall go and summon him, Sir; let him come to me *circa quartam* at the three hills in Blackwoods. [*To himself.*] When I slice one of his ears off, we'll see if he can save the second!

PAPKIN. Better to write him.

CUP-BEARER. God forbid it! Explanations and persuasions—you need a tough head for such matters.

PAPKIN. I have something to confess, Sir: my last weakness left me stupid!

CUP-BEARER. That may be.

PAPKIN. Then . . .

CUP-BEARER. There's no way out.

PAPKIN. Keep God in your soul, man, don't send a wretch like me to him. Before you slice both his ears off in the forest, something shameful will befall me—you yourself said this morning: "My life is still precious to me; he could secretly poison me, kill me."

CUP-BEARER. Secretly? On God's earth he won't!

PAPKIN. [*Disturbed.*] Eh, I'm not sure what he'll do there!

CUP-BEARER. He won't knock your head off right under my nose.

PAPKIN. The devil never sleeps!

CUP-BEARER. Humbug!

PAPKIN. But if he should . . . [*Indicates hanging.*]

CUP-BEARER. [*Threatening.*] Let him try to! I'll give him such a thumping!

PAPKIN. Lot of good that's going to do me, dangling somewhere at rope's end.

CUP-BEARER. [*Soothing him.*] Know what, Papkin—handle this well and your pocket will be heavier. [*He kisses him on the forehead and leaves through the door on the left. Papkin, with a wry expression on his face and shaking his head, leaves through the middle door.*]

315

ACT III

SCENE 1. Notary, Masons. The Notary is seated at a table and writing. Two masons are standing at the door.

NOTARY. Please speak boldly, master; let us note down the entire affair. In these hard times of ours such blows come like gifts of God. We shall turn every punch to profit. We all know that you were hit.

MASON. Not so bad.

NOTARY. But they did hit you, my good fellow.

MASON. Only slightly.

NOTARY. What else happened? There was a lot of commotion over there.

MASON. Oh, a little pushing and shoving, not much else, Sir.

2ND MASON. Who'd make a case of that?

NOTARY. But someone pushing and shoving isn't tickling.

MASON. Ha! Of course not.

NOTARY. Then he's hitting?

MASON. Evidently.

NOTARY. When sticks count up all the bones in a person's back, then the person's hit—don't you know it? And who's been hit, has been beaten. Well?

MASON. Aha! What you say is right, Sir, he's been beaten.

NOTARY. Then you have been beaten in fact, a clear matter, my friend.

MASON. Somehow getting all the clearer.

NOTARY. [*Writing down.*] Were you injured?

MASON. Oh, God forbid!

NOTARY. No, my dear, not even somewhat?

MASON. Oh, no.

NOTARY. Is there any sign of something, a small scratch perhaps?

MASON. [*After talking with the second mason.*] Perhaps we'll yet find something.

NOTARY. And a scratch, I'm sure you realize, is a small wound, nothing else.

MASON. So it seems.

NOTARY. Big, tiny, every single wound, in short, comes from what?

MASON. I guess . . . it comes from . . .

NOTARY. From an injury.

MASON. No doubting.

NOTARY. Having a wound means the same as having a body that's injured. Since the scratch is really a wound, we can then assure the whole world that indeed you have been injured and deprived therefore of your livelihood.

MASON. Oh! About that . . .

NOTARY. Deprived, brother, and for the reason that you won't get a crumb from me—[*He writes.*] since in fact you have been injured, deprived therefore of your livelihood, with a mother . . . wife . . . four children.

MASON. I've no children.

2ND MASON. I've no wife.

NOTARY. What? You haven't? No harm done then—you can have them—you're so young yet.

MASON. Ha!

2ND MASON. It's true.

NOTARY. [*After writing.*] The deed is finished. Now you'll also testify that the old Cup-Bearer, seized by a fit of madness, made an attempt on my life by shooting at me.

MASON. I didn't see it.

NOTARY. He yelled for a gun.

2ND MASON. I heard nothing.

MASON. True he called: "Toss me a musket!" But he wanted to shoot some noodle.

NOTARY. Some noodle . . . Some noodle . . . Well, that's enough of this now—witnesses I'll find all over—no lack of witnesses in this world. Now come here—Closer! Closer! Sign with the sign of a cross here: Michael Kafar a bit lower—that's it— Mathew Miętus—lovely! For this small cross you'll be paid well, and the Cup-Bearer will burst from anger.

MASON. Now most humbly I implore you for what's long already due us.

NOTARY. The Cup-Bearer will pay for all.

MASON. Somehow, Sir, that's not nice . . .

NOTARY. Just so long as you lose nothing.

MASON. I've been working here . . .

NOTARY. [*Pushing him toward the door.*] Go with God, or you'll soon be on the doorstep.

MASON. Everyone would say, the wages here . . .

NOTARY. [*Shoving him in the direction of the door.*] Go on, darling, or you'll get it.

MASON. [*At the door.*] But . . .

NOTARY. [*Shutting the door.*] Good-bye for now, good people! [*Returns.*] I may have to become bankrupt, but I'll smoke the Cup-Bearer out of here if it's the last thing I do. Later on he'll have plenty to tell the courts about. But if all my secret reports tally fully with the truth, I'll hit him hardest with what now comforts his heart.

SCENE 2. Notary, Vatslav.

NOTARY. You've come just at the right time, son. Let's sit down and have a little talk. [*He sits down and gives a sign for Vatslav to be seated also.*] From many of your actions I've taken fullest confidence that in following your father's footsteps you're traveling on the road of virtue. And that evil thoughts and bad counsel never can take you from it brings pleasure to my heart! *Quandoquidem* I'm near death now, you're the only thing I live for. [*Wipes his tears away.*] All these torments—bitter toils—I humbly place for your sake in the fickle wheel of fortune at the feet of God Almighty. In this world the only thing I still aspire to is your happiness, my child.

VATSLAV. Though my father's favors are rare, they're still very dear to me.

NOTARY. You're the only hope that's left me, but my enemies envy me it. They wish to split son from father, then take pleasure at my suffering. Everywhere lurk evil spirits with nets set to capture your youth.

VATSLAV. I don't understand.

NOTARY. You don't, eh? This girl Clara . . .

VATSLAV. She's a fine girl . . . Adoring her . . .

NOTARY. You do in secret.

VATSLAV. If I did keep it secret, it was just because I first wanted to make peace between neighbors.

NOTARY. Between me and the Cup-Bearer? Oh my God! Who could desire it more than I, a righteous man?

VATSLAV. Then permit Clara and me to . . .

NOTARY. That is simply out of the question; the Cup-Bearer looks for trouble, while all my desires are peaceful.

VATSLAV. But what blame is it of Clara's that her uncle's sometimes crazy?

NOTARY. Whether guilty or not guilty, you've need of a different wife, son, and a different one it will be.

VATSLAV. It's too harsh a sentence, father . . .

NOTARY. And will not be changed, my dear son.

VATSLAV. But you said your one goal in life was just to see your son happy.

NOTARY. That's for God to see and judge me.

VATSLAV. I love her.

NOTARY. [*With a laugh.*] It seems so.

VATSLAV. I can't bear a separation.

NOTARY. You can't frighten me on that score.

VATSLAV. I swear it.

NOTARY. [*Sternly.*] Will you be quiet! [*Sweetly.*] What fate decrees, you must accept: Let heaven's will be done. But, my dear, if you're so constant what about your older ardors? Silent, eh? [*Ironically.*] It's unbelievable how the old man knows about everything!

VATSLAV. My youth . . . perhaps . . .

NOTARY. The widow *quondam* was the only one! The chosen one! The loved one! Now she's staying at the Cup-Bearer's.

VATSLAV. [*Hastily.*] She's engaged to the Cup-Bearer.

NOTARY. Thats' something I won't believe until I hear it from her own lips.

VATSLAV. From her lips? From the widow's?

NOTARY. I asked her about the matter, and if God grants it, she'll accept the hand of my son.

VATSLAV. But your son will not accept hers.

NOTARY. An obedient son, thank heaven. I have drawn up a marriage contract where it is expressly stated that the first party to break the contract pays the other one hundred thousand złotys.

VATSLAV. My happiness is worth much more.

NOTARY. Such a wife will bring you happiness.

VATSLAV. I'll be six feet under first . . . But if the Cup-Bearer's still living he'll stop us before we get very far.

NOTARY. [*Phlegmatic as usual.*] Ha! He'll be hanging long before that. Let heaven's will be done; one must always accept it.

VATSLAV. Father!

NOTARY. Son!

VATSLAV. It's a sharp knife you're plunging into your son's heart.

NOTARY. There's no bad without some good.

VATSLAV. Change your order.

NOTARY. Quite unlikely.

VATSLAV. [*Throwing himself at his feet.*] Pity, please!

NOTARY. You've had your share, son! See: I'm crying!

VATSLAV. [*Getting up.*] Can I have hope?

NOTARY. No, my dear, that cannot be now.

VATSLAV. I'll go mad from grief.

NOTARY. See, I'm crying . . . not a word more! Virtue, son is a structure, it's a seed which sows . . . [*Vatslav goes out. A short pause.*] Still terribly young.

SCENE 3.

NOTARY. What inclined our Hanna, a well-off, comely widow, to fall for a reptile like that is still a puzzle. There's no reason to doubt, though, that she'll be happy to change her mind. [*Straightens himself.*] Even though old age is hearty, youth has its privileges. But the Cup-Bearer, once he discovers how he has been made a fool of, maybe . . . maybe . . . I'm afraid, he'll be seized with apoplexy . . . Well, let heaven's will be done, one must always accept it.

SCENE 4. Notary, Papkin.

PAPKIN. [*Entering cautiously.*] May I enter?

NOTARY. Please, I beg you.

PAPKIN. [*With a very low bow, and humbly.*] If I am correct does a great and unexpected honor fall to me this very moment to see in your worthy person the master here and Notary?

NOTARY. [*Humbly.*] So it is—your humble servant. May I please ask in return, Sir, whom I'm honored now to greet here?

PAPKIN. [*Aside.*] Hm! An humble little squire. Every word he's diving lower—all my worries were unfounded. [*Bolder.*] I am Papkin. [*The Notary, bowing, indicates a chair standing in the middle of the room. Papkin carefully looks over the Notary who, as always, stands motionless with his arms folded over his chest. Papkin says further in an aside.*] As I figured, I don't need help with this matter. [*Out loud—stretching himself in the chair.*] I am Papkin—lion of the North, chevalier and famous warrior—[*With a gesture indicates his ribbons.*] known, as you see, the world over. Wise in counsel, fierce in battle, the spirit of war, the foe of peace. The Swedes, Mohammedans, Saxons, Italians and Spaniards know how sharp Artemis is and the skillful arm that wields her. In a word, speaking briefly, the whole globe knows Papkin. Now, brother, have some wine brought in.

NOTARY. [*After a moment's vacillation, aside.*] Nemo sapiens, nisi patiens. [*He takes a bottle from under a table covered over with a small cloth. Holds it up to the light and examines it, then pours out a small measure and hands it to Papkin.*]

PAPKIN. [*Aside.*] Oh! My brother squire's a coward through and through . . . After taking care of the Cup-Bearer's commission, I may pick up a little something extra for myself. [*Covers his head; drinks.*] Weak stuff! [*Drinks.*] Hog-wash! [*Drinks.*]

NOTARY. [*Aside.*] A bit too bold.

PAPKIN. Real swill, brother. Nothing better 'round the house, eh?

NOTARY. Forgive me, there's nothing else, Sir.

PAPKIN. There's our Polish gentry for you! [*With contempt.*] Sits in the country—plows, sows, grumbles—idles, growls, barks—but to serve good wine—that it can't do. [*Goes to the little table, pours out some wine for himself. The Notary, not moving, follows him with his eyes.*] Should a bottle come along though, the sight of it's enough to scare you. Then he'll beg you: "If you please, Sir"—country lout, don't beg, don't idle, just serve something better, damn it!

NOTARY. Oh, but come now, my good fellow . . .

PAPKIN. [*Drinking.*] Dull drink, sour beyond belief—perfect swill, my dear Notary!

NOTARY. [*Aside.*] This requires much patience; let heaven's will be done.

PAPKIN. Visit all my wine cellars—you'll find drinks from half the world there; a hundred casks stand in a single row! If you find your kind of stuff there, I'll give you a horse and bridle.

NOTARY. [*With a bow.*] Permit me to ask, my dear Sir, since I do not know the reason, what has brought the son of Mars here to this miserable threshold of mine.

PAPKIN. [*Spreading out further in the chair near the little table.*] What? You want to know?

NOTARY. I'm asking.

PAPKIN. Then know that I'm here, you scoundrel, on behalf of his excellency, the Cup-Bearer Raptusiewicz whom a foul horde of your servants, indeed worthy of their master, dared attack in his castle this morning.

NOTARY. Would your lordship speak a bit more softly, his servant hears quite well enough.

PAPKIN. I speak always as I wish to.

NOTARY. But my head is aching.

PAPKIN. [*Still louder.*] Because someone's ears are twinging, because someone's head is ailing, Stentor's voice is never changed to a nightingale's singing.

NOTARY. [*Sweetly.*] But I have some men around here; I'll order you thrown out a window. [*At the Notary's words Papkin slowly rises, taking off his hat.*] And it's a good way to the bottom.

PAPKIN. Oh, there's no need.

NOTARY. Is someone there! Hey!

PAPKIN. Please don't go to any bother.

NOTARY. You'll fly out of here just like a feather! [*To his servants.*] Four of you wait behind the doors there!

PAPKIN. What's the point of all this, neighbor, of such a parade between us?

NOTARY. Now I hear your lordship clearly. [*Seating him virtually by force.*] Please be seated—please be seated—[*Sits near Papkin and opposite him.*] On what business have you come here? [*Does not remove his eyes from Papkin.*]

PAPKIN. You're a little bit too lively. I had no idea, as God's my witness, that you had such tender hearing—please forgive me, if by accident—I utter some small word too loudly.

NOTARY. May I learn why you've come here?

PAPKIN. [*Very quietly.*] Right away—The Cup-Bearer requests that . . .

NOTARY. Eh?

PAPKIN. Still louder? [*At a sign of assent from the Notary, he continues.*] The Cup-Bearer requests that . . . that is . . . rather the Cup-Bearer informs you that in order to end immediately the unpleasantness that . . . happened . . . [*Unable to avoid the Notary's gaze, he becomes more and more confused.*] Yes, I'm speaking right . . . that happened . . . the unpleasantness . . . as is known . . . that since . . . that is . . . that . . . he ag . . . rees . . . [*Turns around, aside.*] That's an evil eye he's got there, my tongue's getting all twisted.

NOTARY. I'm not able to follow you, you're complicating matters so.

PAPKIN. [*Rising.*] On account of . . . these . . . Forgive me, Sir, your wine proved a bit too potent, and I've no talent for speeches . . . [*Quieter.*] Are those four men still on guard there?

NOTARY. In just one word, my esteemed Sir, what is it my good neighbor wishes?

PAPKIN. But the envoy's somewhat . . .

NOTARY. [*Finishing.*] . . . frightened. Please be unafraid, my dear Sir.

PAPKIN. Well, the Cup-Bearer requests that *circa quartam* you be present at the three hills in Blackwoods—with a sword to end the dispute.

NOTARY. [*Ironically.*] Old Cup-Bearer's still got spirit!

PAPKIN. [*Getting bolder.*] Bah! Everyone certainly knows that his blows always hit their mark—after all, he's creased the noses of all the squires in this whole district. And still . . .

NOTARY. Softer, please.

PAPKIN. [*Glancing in the direction of the door.*] Softer, certainly. Softly then, I bring his polite request here and to it add one of my own for a short, lucid answer.

NOTARY. That I'll give to him in writing. But how can we make arrangements, since tomorrow is his wedding?

PAPKIN. [*More boldly.*] One thing won't interfere with the other: in the morning a ring—mid-day a saber—evening a tankard—at night . . .

NOTARY. [*Sweetly.*] Please, softly.

PAPKIN. Softly, yes. [*Aside.*] Nasty business, no doubt about it. How the devil did I ever land in such a mess?

NOTARY. [*Ironically.*] Does his future wife adore him?

PAPKIN. You should see! She faints three times a day just from love—The Cup-Bearer, likewise inflamed, burns for her just like a candle. They'll be a perfect couple. That she'll be true in every respect I'll wager both my hands and feet.

SCENE 5. Notary, Papkin, Hanna.

HANNA. Well here I am at your summons, in your home, my dear Notary. I trust this will prove to you that my former plans have been changed. I didn't lose much time in unnecessary thinking—for I do not think too often, though I'm hardly slow in acting—and without saying to the Cup-Bearer: 'Bye for now, stay well, old fellow, I prefer your neighbors to you—I shall sign all your agreements and be settled here shortly. [*Hands him a folded paper.*] I am giving you one copy; the other will remain with me. Since we have our guarantees now and have exchanged our mutual pledges, may I greet you as your son's wife.

NOTARY. This is a great honor for me, kind and gracious lady. Fortune in a golden vessel unfurled her sails for me when you willingly and kindly took unto your splendid heart all my humblest proposals. So it is, my gracious lady, a great honor for me truly—and one still greater can descend on all my future heirs, for you wish by your great kindness to share

my son's bed. I ask that I be allowed now on this poor patch
of my earth here to fall before your tiny feet as your servant,
your humble servant, offering you assurance of springs of
everlasting favor and whatever services you may require of
me. [*Kisses her hand.*]

PAPKIN. [*Aside.*] What do I hear? What the devil! Snapped the
Cup-Bearer's wife from him, and he's matching her with
his son! But when the Cup-Bearer finds out, he'll rip him
open like a trout.

HANNA. Please don't think however, my dear Notary, that I've
undertaken this new course just because I've a taste for
change. Your son, Vatslav, was known to me, very well
known—in a word, there's no reason to conceal it: I loved
him, and he loved me sincerely.

PAPKIN. [*Clapping his hands.*] That's the way it was!

HANNA. What's this? Papkin here?

PAPKIN. Yes, Papkin's waiting until Hanna deigns to view him.

HANNA. [*To the Notary.*] Sir, you tolerate that person? [*To
Papkin.*] Out of my sight!

PAPKIN. [*Hastily.*] Off I go.

NOTARY. Wait!

PAPKIN. Waiting.

NOTARY. Don't forget the letter.

HANNA. It was he who with his lying eloquence wrung from
me, just a weak woman, promises I've since regretted.

PAPKIN. I?

HANNA. And were it not for this change, I, poor woman, would
have gone right into a tyrant's power.

PAPKIN. [*To himself.*] A day of woe!

NOTARY. [*To Hanna.*] The will of heaven—one must always
accept it. But now this is my judgment: Since the Cup-
Bearer still knows nothing of this change to our advantage,
though my note makes mention of it, it would be good if
on his part Papkin would take a confirmation and repeat
what's in this letter.

PAPKIN. [*Aside.*] Wants to ruin me, obviously!

NOTARY. Now, my dear, give him your message and I'll add a
few words to it. [*He goes out.*]

SCENE 6. Hanna, Papkin.

PAPKIN. [*Following him out with his eyes.*] Hanna! Is all this true? What does this mean? Where is your conscience?

NOTARY. [*Showing his head in the door.*] Please be quieter.

PAPKIN. Right, quiet. [*Aside.*] Even hears through walls, this devil. [*Quietly to Hanna.*] Oh, what are you doing, woman? On account of you we'll all perish—don't you know the Cup-Bearer? He won't tolerate this insult. Armed with torches and steel flashing, he'll come hurling death at your walls and leave this house smashed to smithereens. Fear the Lord, let's leave together. [*Looks around, then draws her farther aside.*] Ah, you don't know where you've come to . . . you're in such fearful depth here . . . Sh! . . . if Artemis' awful strength wasn't in the palm of this hand . . . we'd already . . . Sh! . . . May God preserve us! . . . Out the door and down the staircase.

HANNA. [*Tearing herself away.*] The way is clear now.

PAPKIN. Not entirely. He's got four men on guard.

HANNA. But first take this farewell message to the Cup-Bearer. Greet him very courteously; tell him, if you will, how my soul is painfully consumed with sorrow that I have to leave him this way—let him not pursue me rashly . . .

PAPKIN. It's all stuff and nonsense, Madam, he won't hear such things from my lips.

SCENE 7. Hanna, Papkin, the Notary.

NOTARY. Quieter, if you please.

PAPKIN. Yes, quieter.

NOTARY. Here's the letter for my neighbor.

PAPKIN. Devilishly slippery mission!

NOTARY. Good-bye, Sir.

PAPKIN. [*Bowing.*] Papkin salutes you and thanks you for receiving him. [*Bowing and ceremony until the end of the scene.*]

NOTARY. Think nothing of it.

PAPKIN. Oh, on the contrary.

NOTARY. [*Leading him out.*] Your humble, humble servant.

PAPKIN. Please go back.

NOTARY. That's hardly proper.

PAPKIN. I implore you.

NOTARY. You don't have to.

PAPKIN. I won't let you.

NOTARY. Someone there? [*The doors open and four of the Notary's men are seen waiting on the outside.*]

PAPKIN. Oh, no need for ceremony.

NOTARY. [*To his men.*] Show this gentleman the way out.

PAPKIN. I salute you—I can manage.

NOTARY. Take him under the arms—but gently—the stairs are dark—you have to grope your way—

PAPKIN. I salute you—you're too kind—[*From a bow he finds himself behind the doors in one bolt. The doors shut. A thud is heard as if someone hurtled down the stairs. The widow goes over to the Notary.*]

NOTARY. [*Returning.*] Let heaven's will be done, one must always accept it.

ACT IV

A room in the Cup-Bearer's house. Apart from the side doors, larger ones to the rear, to the right of a chapel. Tables along both sides. On the table to the right an inkstand and writing materials; a bottle and a few glasses. In the rear, floral decorations are being put up.

SCENE *1. Cup-Bearer, Dyndalski. After the curtain rises, Dyndalski stands behind the Cup-Bearer, who is seated at the table. He is holding two sabers; the Cup-Bearer is examining a third while the first lines are being spoken. In the background, Śmigalski and Pearlie.*

CUP-BEARER. [*Holding the saber.*] Well, Śmigalski! Time is rushing, get on with you, on your horse now. Bear my invitation like lightning and fulfill all my orders smoothly. Repeat to everyone three times if need be that tomorrow I, the bridegroom, invite them to my wedding feast. Understand?

Well, on your way then. [*Śmigalski leaves. A short pause.*]
Hey, Pearlie! See to it that you don't spoil a thing tomorrow,
or I'll have you boiled in oil! Tomorrow show the world
your stuff. My good man, see you're not sparing of cinnamon
and nutmeg and all kinds of aromatics, so everything be as it
should. For the fish you've got fresh parsley, and more than
enough desserts—let it be good, little brother.

PEARLIE. What initials should be put, Sir, in the middle of the
table?

CUP-BEARER. M. H.—M. H.—Mathew, Hanna. Hearts on top,
below *Vivat*—make sure everything is in good taste.

PEARLIE. All your wishes will be seen to. [*At a sign from the
Cup-Bearer, he goes out.*]

CUP-BEARER. [*After a brief pause, looking over the saber.*]
Papkin's been gone for some time now. The Notary sits like
a holed-up fox; smoking him out of there won't be easy. But
my arm will pull him out, if he wants such ceremonies.

DYNDALSKI. Bah! Who gets in your way, Sir, soon enough
finds his nose tickling.

CUP-BEARER. [*Giving back one saber and taking another.*] But
these gentlemen of the bar are all devils in slippery skin.
There's no keeping up with them, even though they fall out
of step sometimes.

DYNDALSKI. Bah!

CUP-BEARER. [*Drawing out his sword.*] He, he, he, Lady
Barska!* How well you served me at Słonim, Podhajce,
Berdyczów, Łomza. That was quite a different thing then!
Youth, so active, fierce in battle, has made way for elders'
councils, just as God has us all numbered. But now it's come
to pass the eggs are wiser than the hens. [*A short pause.*]
Sturdy handle this, I tell you, but the damascene's my preference. [*Changes swords.*] Eh, you whirler! Once you let
loose, you struck out from candidacy more than just a
single envoy. You left etched near more than one ear *pro
memoria:* [*brandishing the sword*] "When it's raised, it
barely flashes—when it whines, go greet your Maker!"

* So named because it was acquired during the Bar Confederacy (1768-
1772), a patriotic rising of Polish gentry aimed against Russian interference in Polish internal affairs. Its defeat led to the first partition of
Poland in 1772. Słonim, Podhajce, Berdyczów, and Łomza were places of
battle during the Confederacy.

SCENE 2. The Cup-Bearer, Papkin. Dyndalski, after help-ing the Cup-Bearer tie on his sword, leaves through the door on the left.

CUP-BEARER. Here at last . . .

PAPKIN. [*Hat at a jaunty angle, but hair and coat a bit di-sheveled.*] My throat's parched badly—give a drink here! What a business! [*Pours himself out a glass and drinks.*] First I stuffed his nose with pepper till it grew three times its own size.

CUP-BEARER. Now we're really going to hear it!

PAPKIN. But that Notary's a lively little piece, and besides a real devil. I came awfully close to drawing Artemis from her scabbard, but I feared to, speaking frankly. Once that devil sniffed my blade-arm, he'd find a way to stop it.

CUP-BEARER. How this *nequam* can weave stories! What about the Notary though? Will I ever find out?

PAPKIN. Oh, he graciously received me—asked me have a seat —brought wine out—

CUP-BEARER. [*As if to himself.*] Doubtless poisoned . . .

PAPKIN. What's that? What's that?

CUP-BEARER. Nothing, nothing . . .

PAPKIN. But . . .

CUP-BEARER. And what else?

PAPKIN. Poisoned, you say?

CUP-BEARER. There's no joking with that scoundrel, my dear Sir.

PAPKIN. I've enough without that . . . something's burning me.

CUP-BEARER. How did he receive my summons? Well? [*Silence.*] What went on there? Are you deaf and dumb? [*Papkin, aghast, hands him the letter without looking at him.*] Ah! We'll find out from the letter. [*He reads.*] What, what, what, what? [*Quickly.*] What, what, what, what? [*In violent anger advances to Papkin with each step shouting "what" as if unable to find the proper words. Papkin retreats until he is behind the little table standing on the left side of the room.*] What, what, what, what?

PAPKIN. Yes, that, that, that!

CUP-BEARER. The widow . . .

PAPKIN. [*Tearfully finishing the sentence for him.*] . . . has deceived us.

CUP-BEARER. To the Notary . . .

PAPKIN. [*As above.*] . . . she made off.

CUP-BEARER. To the Notary . . . the Notary? And she wants . . . to marry . . .

PAPKIN. [*Terrified.*] . . . Vatslav.

CUP-BEARER. And you kept quiet, damned creature! . . . But the whole affair won't last long . . . O treacherous sex! Unworthy of respect! Would that you were in my hands now like this letter. [*Crumpling the letter.*] Like this letter . . .

PAPKIN. [*Regaining his speech, aside.*] She'll certainly hear about this!

CUP-BEARER. I'd grind you into powder—but I don't want to waste the time now. I've got to hire a fiddler for their wedding sarabande—let him play until their ears burst! Until the Notary's twisted in knots! Once the festival is over, he'll know not to mix in my broth! Hey, boys! Hey there, fellows! [*Goes out through the center doors.*] After me, Papkin!

SCENE 3. Papkin, later Dyndalski.

PAPKIN. [*After a long silence, contorting his face, then feeling about his abdomen.*] Something hurts here. Oh! Ah! It's burning—Oh, that wine! Such awful poison! O you traitor! O you damned one! Such a lovely rose you're destroying! [*Dyndalski enters from the door on the left.*] Oh, Dyndalski, worthy fellow! Oh, tell me, if it's possible?

DYNDALSKI. Is what possible?

PAPKIN. That that snake, that devil in the form of the Notary, is killing me today with poison?

DYNDALSKI. Eh, come now!

PAPKIN. You don't believe it?

DYNDALSKI. Now who over there would covet your lordship's petty existence?

PAPKIN. Nothing bad will happen to me?

DYNDALSKI. Eh, no.

PAPKIN. But the Cup-Bearer just said . . .

DYNDALSKI. Well that's something else again now—Our master knows everything on earth like a person knows his own home. Poisoned you! I ask you! What mischief!

PAPKIN. Tell me, what's your advice now? What must I do, what must be done?

DYNDALSKI. Ha! [*Takes snuff.*] You've got to call a priest in. [*Leaves through the center door.*] What a scoundrel, I ask you!

SCENE *4.*

PAPKIN. [*Throwing himself into a chair.*] Dying! Dying! Oh, great heavens! [*A short pause.*] But where was my head? I bellowed at him, abused him, so he fixed up a treat for me. And the great speed with which he took out the bottle, with which he poured in a whole glass—and it still wasn't enough for me! So I swallowed, and I'm poisoned. Since this is one I won't squeeze out of, I'll make out my last will and testament now. [*With exaggerated weeping.*] After that I'll pay for my funeral—then—*requiescat in pace.* [*Frequently wiping tears from his eyes, Papkin writes for some time.*]

SCENE 5. *Papkin, the Cup-Bearer, Dyndalski.*

CUP-BEARER. Hold on, I won't do it that way—all that's nothing but soap-bubbles—I'll think up a better vengeance. But I've got to use new tactics. If only I had his son trapped, I've a good cage ready for him. I'm not worried by his papa, time enough for that—[*To Papkin.*] Move over.

PAPKIN. [*Not looking up.*] I'm making out my testament.

CUP-BEARER. I don't want a word about it, or I'll send you to a madhouse.

PAPKIN. [*Rising.*] You mean it? [*To himself.*] Now I'll seal it. [*Papkin takes himself to the small table on the left side of the room.*]

CUP-BEARER. [*To Dyndalski.*] Sit down over here—wet your pen, and write what I'm going to dictate now.

DYNDALSKI. I don't wield a pen too surely.

CUP-BEARER. Good, we need a woman's hand here. Life for ransom, hook the suitor—It'll work out well.

DYNDALSKI. [*Sitting down opposite the Cup-Bearer and with his side to the audience. Puts on his glasses.*] Thanks be to God!

CUP-BEARER. Now you've got to write exactly as Clara would to Vatslav.

DYNDALSKI. Oh! Oh!

CUP-BEARER. Well, what? Why the "oh! oh!"?

DYNDALSKI. [*Getting up.*] But, Sir, that would be offensive to her.

CUP-BEARER. It's not your place to ask about that! Dip your pen—write and that's it! [*Dyndalski sits upright on the edge of his chair and dips his pen in the ink. During this scene Papkin is also writing. At times he rises, walks back to the rear of the stage, dips his pen in the inkstand on the small table at which the Cup-Bearer is sitting and again sits down. He weeps constantly, but without exaggeration.*]

CUP-BEARER. [*After a short pause.*] Just keep in mind, Sir, that pretending takes much talent. All the usual nonsense, rubbish, all that silly lovers' babbling . . . [*Thinks.*] How shall we begin, Sir?

DYNDALSKI. [*Getting up.*] My truly beloved . . .

CUP-BEARER. Oh . . . oh . . . oh! . . . Like a wife writing—you need half a word here, or a quarter of a word, not just any old way, but as though she's trying to say: "I'd like to, but I'm afraid to." There now—you know! Well! That's the way . . . but you have no training for it. Write: [*hums*] A moment—[*Hums. Dictating.*] Be so kind as . . . [*Points to the paper.*] What's that?

DYNDALSKI. [*Getting up. He does this whenever he speaks to the Cup-Bearer.*] B.

CUP-BEARER. That?

DYNDALSKI. Capital B—*a capite*, Sir.

CUP-BEARER. [*Looking across the table.*] B?—That's a dash—where are the loops?

DYNDALSKI. One below, another on top.

CUP-BEARER. [*Fetching his eyeglasses.*] What the devil. [*Takes the paper.*] You're right—it is—[*At this point Papkin leans across the Cup-Bearer in an effort to dip his pen in the ink-*

*stand. The Cup-Bearer knocks him away, saying what fol-
lows, then later pursues him with his eyes until he returns
to his seat.*] Go to . . . [*Pushed away, Papkin leaves, but moving from the rear to the small table he steps on Dyndalski's foot.*]

DYNDALSKI. You! . . .

CUP-BEARER. [*Looking the letter over.*] B, capital B. If you
think about it, you'll guess it. Well, well—write—but accurately. [*Dictates.*] Be so kind as . . . my esteemed Sir . . . my
esteemed Sir . . . to consider . . . my esteemed Sir . . . this
petition . . . my esteemed Sir, to consider, as proof of trust
in a person . . . my esteemed Sir, or Your Lordship, who although known little to you . . . who although known little
to you . . . [*Indicating with his finger.*] What's this?

DYNDALSKI. [*Getting up.*] It's just a blot, Sir, but I'll make it
over into a letter.

CUP-BEARER. If you spill any more drops you'll get such a solid
rapping you'll think you were back in grade-school. Read it
—[*Dyndalski wipes the perspiration down to his neck.*] Well!
What have we got there?

DYNDALSKI. [*Reads.*] Be so kind as, my esteemed Sir, my esteemed Sir, to consider, my esteemed Sir, this petition, my
esteemed Sir . . .

CUP-BEARER. [*Grabbing the paper and tearing it up.*] Devil take
you with that empty head of yours! "My esteemed Sir"—
the blockhead writes!

DYNDALSKI. But those are your very own words.

CUP-BEARER. Shut up! Rewrite it *de novo*; omit "esteemed
Sir" everywhere.

DYNDALSKI. [*Wanting to gather up the pieces.*] Won't be easy
from these pieces.

CUP-BEARER. Write *de novo*—write, I tell you! You've a brain
not worth a farthing! Sit down! Sit, I say.

DYNDALSKI. I'm sitting.

CUP-BEARER. And repeat now [*dictates*]: Be so kind as, my
es . . . [*Covers his mouth.*]

DYNDALSKI. [*Repeating what he has written.*] My es . . .

CUP-BEARER. [*Starting.*] My es . . . ? Meaning? It's just no use
with this dunce. It's got to be done differently. Maybe it'd
still be better if I send a fellow from here with an oral re-

333

quest. Yes, that's just what I'll do. Listen. Go . . . Hold on a moment! There's no one here who knows what the Notary's son looks like.

PAPKIN. [*Indifferently.*] Everyone here can recognize him, since he was here this very morning.

CUP-BEARER. What? That young fellow? The one who called himself—the Notary's deputy?

PAPKIN. That's the one.

CUP-BEARER. Steals into my rooms, just in order to upset me, and this one keeps quiet, says nothing!

PAPKIN. [*Indifferently.*] He gave me gold to keep my mouth shut.

CUP-BEARER. [*Holding himself by the head.*] Oh my God! You scoundrel!

PAPKIN. Who's got one foot in the grave already isn't afraid of your anger any longer. [*Throws the small purse on the floor.*] What good is money to me at such a time?

CUP-BEARER. Oh, keep quiet!

PAPKIN. Who values it? What use can I make of it now? [*When Dyndalski wants to pick up the purse, Papkin forestalls him, at the same time finishing what he was saying.*] Except to keep the pockets full.

CUP-BEARER. Quiet, quiet, without tumult, please. There's no time now for such matters. But upon my word as squire, you'll account to me for your action—[*To Dyndalski.*] Now go—and send old Rosie, have the old witch sneak into Milczek's and be sure to tell young Vatslav, the young master—well, you know—say that Miss Clara asks him to come kindly for a moment and say not a word about it to anyone, and that he should not be frightened since the Cup-Bearer's not at home now. Well, understood?

DYNDALSKI. To the letter.

CUP-BEARER. In the meantime you get yourself busy. Put some fellows in the bushes near the break in the wall there. And as soon as the young fellow sets one foot across the boundary, *lapes capes**—have them grab him. And if he doesn't want to come, have them tie him up.

---

* The Polish expression "łapu-capu" meaning "hurry-scurry" with the -es ending borrowed from Yiddish.

DYNDALSKI. It's a shame, Sir, to treat him like he was some ruffian.

CUP-BEARER. You were and still are a bumpkin. Let it be as I've ordered. [*He wants to go out.*]

PAPKIN. [*Intercepting him.*] Cup-Bearer.

CUP-BEARER. What?

PAPKIN. [*Handing him a pen.*] As a witness.

CUP-BEARER. Go to hell! [*He goes out with Dyndalski through the center door.*]

PAPKIN. [*Alone, repeating.*] Go to hell! There's the gratitude of people, the greatness of this world—Everyone thinks just of himself and sees others just as tools. As long everything's all right—it's gold and baubles; when it's bad—it's "Go to hell!"

SCENE 6. Papkin, Clara from the door on the right.

PAPKIN. Oh, goddess of my thoughts! O, you alone merciful! Poison tears the thread of life now but my heart, as though in a coffer, always keeps its love for you.

CLARA. What's happened?

PAPKIN. I live no longer. I'd have fetched that crocodile, I'd have won your hand in marriage. But my final earthly hour's come; today I end my knightly suffering.

CLARA. [*Aside.*] Utterly lost all his senses.

PAPKIN. I entrust this testament to you: Please, bear with me like a mother, and weep for me when I'm buried. [*He reads, frequently wiping away the tears.*]

I, Joseph Papkin, the son of my father, Jan Papkin . . . [*Tenderly.*] Jan, Jan—Jan was his name. [*Reads.*] Being completely of sound mind and body, but unable to know when I am to die . . . Naturally, because I have been poisoned by a glass of the Notary Milczek's wine . . . A glass of wine. I am writing this testament or last disposition of my movable and immovable property. The immovable I cannot dispose of because I have none . . . I cannot—The movable I am distributing as follows: To her whom I have always loved, honored and deified, Clara Raptusiewiczówna, daughter of the *starosta* of Zakroczym, I leave my English guitar

and a rare collection of butterflies, presently in pawn. My
Artemis . . . I wanted to give it to the Cup-Bearer before, but
now I have changed my mind. The Artemis shall go to the
most valiant knight in Europe, on the condition that he erect
a monument on my grave. As for the rest of my movable estate, I wish to be buried with it [*dries his tears*]. His excellency the Cup-Bearer, and the starosta's daughter, as execu-
tors of this will and testament, I beseech not to pay all my
remaining debts in so far as I desire to leave them as me-
mentoes to my brothers of different rank and faith.

Joseph Papkin

Joseph Papkin incognito—there's no room for my titles—
take it then—and what's inscribed here, let your memory
preserve forever.

SCENE 7. Papkin, Clara, Vatslav from the door on the left.

VATSLAV. Clara, Clara, what's happening? Fate pursues us too
severely—all our fondest hopes may be shattered in a
moment.
CLARA. Speak carefully.
VATSLAV. [*Catching sight of Papkin.*] He was paid off. The widow's in our house now—for my father's plan won't be
changed. He's forcing me to marry her.
CLARA. God forbid!
VATSLAV. And that vile soul, without pity or embarrassment,
paying no heed to my pleading, bends her ear just to his
will.
CLARA. Oh, Vatslav, I haven't the strength to speak, to tell you
what to do in this emergency, for I'm afraid for you here.
Ah, you don't know my uncle! There are no bounds to his
rashness.
VATSLAV. There's no need for you to fear. He doesn't know me
as Vatslav.
PAPKIN. [*Indifferently.*] Oh, that story's worth nothing now.
VATSLAV. So you betrayed me?
PAPKIN. I told him.

VATSLAV. Ah, you scoundrel!

CLARA. [*Restraining him.*] Oh, my darling don't give me more cause for worry.

VATSLAV. At least let me punish him.

CLARA. You'll cause your Clara's death yet.

PAPKIN. Who's got one foot in the grave now, threats can't frighten any longer.

VATSLAV. What's he saying?

CLARA. Same old nonsense. Go away, go on, don't lose a moment.

PAPKIN. Oh, and I advise the same thing, for the Cup-Bearer is planning to trap you here right in his claws—he's dispersed several of his men to seize and tie you up, if need be.

CLARA. Is that still too little for you?

VATSLAV. What will happen . . . ?

CLARA. [*Anxiously.*] I'll write later.

VATSLAV. Tonight . . .

CLARA. I hear noise, get going . . .

VATSLAV. What I meant was . . .

CLARA. [*Pleading.*] Later, later.

VATSLAV. [*Going to the door.*] I'll go now, but when I get back . . .

SCENE 8. Clara, Papkin, Vatslav, the Cup-Bearer, Dyndalski, footmen from different sides.

CUP-BEARER. [*Blocking his way at the door on the left.*] Hold on there, hold on, my good fellow! I've got you trapped like a bear.

VATSLAV. And what's going to happen to me? I see many adversaries, but don't think I'm afraid. [*To the Cup-Bearer.*] If you're a brigand—you've got me, I'm yours. If you're a man of honor, let me have some sword or other—I have faith in God I won't die.

CUP-BEARER. Boy, I'm glad you've shown some spirit—but we've other things to talk of. Just pay heed to what I'll tell you: the Notary stole my fiancée so you could become her husband—in this way he'd have his triumph. But I'm able to take measures—either you'll go to my prison below,

where you won't be found so easy, or—you'll give your hand
to Clara. But if she doesn't want to travel with you to the
altar, we have here her second cousin whom I'll order you to
marry. For you, a nymph-like bridie, for the widow, old
maids' day dreams, for the Notary a thumping, and for me
the perfect vengeance—that's how we'll end the whole affair. [*Silence.*]

VATSLAV. But . . .

CUP-BEARER. No buts here.

VATSLAV. Just a moment . . .

CUP-BEARER. Now or never!

VATSLAV. [*To Clara.*] Can it be true?

CLARA. Ha, let's believe it—[*To the Cup-Bearer.*] Will the wedding be today?

CUP-BEARER. Today. [*Clara turns around to Vatslav as though
expecting an answer from him.*]

VATSLAV. Well, in that case, we'll get married.

CUP-BEARER. Then give the girl your hand—seems she doesn't
have objections. Priest's already in the chapel—come on now.
[*Aside.*] The Notary's finished. [*They all go out to the
chapel.*]

PAPKIN. [*Testament in hand.*] Oh you little tigress—Fortune!
First the poison, then a wedding—That's just too much!
That's just too much! [*Goes out to the chapel.*]

SCENE 9

DYNDALSKI. [*Collecting fragments of his letter.*] Once he gets
something in his head, you can't get it out with a crowbar.
That I could write, as they call it, as I've lived this long
with God now, I never said at all; such a presumption
would be sinful. But I'd like to know, however, why this day
I descended to the level of a schoolboy? What fault could
he find, I ask you, with the way I made that B? Is the letter
missing something? Is it lacking in form, is it lacking
in measure? That's my cross and I must bear it. [*Sits down
and arranges the pieces.*]

SCENE 10. Dyndalski, Notary. The Notary enters looking around on all sides.

NOTARY. [*Placing his hand on the shoulder of Dyndalski, who has not seen him.*] A good evening to you, brother. What's the matter, has the plague struck? Not a living soul around here who'll tell me if the master's at home.

DYNDALSKI. I'm here, Sir, at your service.

NOTARY. This is quite a curious business. The Cup-Bearer summoned me to a duel, though it's not my kind of amusement. Nonetheless I said: heaven's will, one must always accept it. So I went, I waited for him, but my waiting was for nothing. Maybe he predicted too smugly that the Notary'd be absent? But the Notary was ready; it's the upstart who's still absent.

DYNDALSKI. Eh, listen, my good Notary, don't dare call him to a duel. When he twirls his sword about, he'll cut you to shreds, I swear it. [*Voices from the chapel.*] Hooray! Hooray! Long live the bride and groom!

NOTARY. Who is it being married here?

DYNDALSKI. The Notary's son.

NOTARY. [*As if scalded.*] That's impossible!

CUP-BEARER. [*Off stage.*] Hey, Dyndalski! Devil take you! Go and saddle up my horse! [*Going out.*] Damn, it's already past four now.

SCENE 11. Notary, Cup-Bearer. After coming to the front of the stage, the Cup-Bearer sees the Notary. He stands as if nailed to the spot. The Notary bows low. A moment of silence, as they look each other straight in the eye. The Cup-Bearer reaches for his sword, the Notary does the same. A short period of hesitation. The Cup-Bearer appears to be struggling with himself. Dyndalski runs to the chapel.

CUP-BEARER. [*Aside.*] Don't lead me into temptation, Great God of my forefathers! Since he's stepped across my threshold a hair mustn't fall from his head. [*Takes off his sword and throws it onto a table. The Notary hangs his hat on the handle of his sword.*] What do you want?

NOTARY. My son.

CUP-BEARER. Ha! Ha! A pleasure it will be! You shall have your satisfaction—but with or without his new wife?

NOTARY. [*Restraining himself.*] That . . . is too much . . .

CUP-BEARER. What is too much? That you stole my widow from me to make her your daughter-in-law? I detained your son in turn here to arrange a wedding for him—There you've got it: tit for tat.

SCENE *12. The same, Clara, Vatslav, Papkin, Dyndalski, courtiers, women—all enter from the chapel carrying bouquets of flowers.*

VATSLAV. Oh, father!

CLARA. Oh, uncle! Let all this unpleasantness end!

VATSLAV. [*Kneeling.*] Forgive me, father, and please give your blessings to our mutual love!

NOTARY. Get up, son, and come with me.

SCENE *13. The same, Hanna.*

HANNA. Can I believe what's happened, Vatslav and Clara.

NOTARY. [*Aside.*] I'm going crazy!

HANNA. Yes, I believe it, it's already happened! I've something then to tell you—and no little. I wanted to get married as soon as possible so as not to be left entirely in want—the fortune that was left me was mine only for a short time, and as true and permanent gift falls today to lucky Clara.

NOTARY. [*Aside.*] Two estates—a tidy morsel—uncle doubtless grieves this windfall.

CUP-BEARER. [*Aside.*] Uncle's gone and made a change, For an axe he's got a cane.*

HANNA. But despite it I lose nothing. The Notary owes me a hundred thousand . . .

CLARA. No—I'll pay it from my own money. [*Hanna passes to the right side of the stage.*]

* In Polish: "Zamieniał stryjek/Za siekierkę kijek. A proverbial saying meaning to exchange something valuable for something of little value. The Cup-Bearer evidently has the widow's losses in mind.

CLARA. [*To the Notary.*] Don't resist it any longer; extinguish what's left of your anger. Give your blessings to your children. [*She kneels together with Vatslav, to whom she gives her right hand.*]

NOTARY. Let heaven's will be done, one must always accept it. [*He makes the sign of the cross over them and then has Vatslav and Clara rise.*]

PAPKIN. [*To Vatslav.*] Can I count on your word really? Will you swear my health's not been damaged? [*At a sign of assent —to the Cup-Bearer.*] Now I call upon your lordship! Have them bring us in some goblets, let the house resound with fanfare, you and I shall drink the first pair! [*Passes to the left side of the stage and tears up his testament.*]

CUP-BEARER. Today let there be a wedding in our hearts as was in deed. [*Extending his hand to the Notary.*] Sir, let there be peace between us. [*The Notary accepts his hand with a low bow.*]

ALL. Peace! Peace!

VATSLAV. [*Stepping to the middle of the stage so that Clara on his right side gives her hand to the Cup-Bearer, while he [Vatslav] gives his hand to his father on his left side, and then advancing to the front of the stage.*]

So be it, peace, and God will then extend his hand.

E N D

THE LIFE ANNUITY

A Comedy in Three Acts

The miserly and greedy carry their souls in their purses.

ANDRZEJ MAKSYMILIAN FREDRO

INTRODUCTION

ALTHOUGH not performed as often as his other major plays, *The Life Annuity* is generally regarded now as one of Fredro's better comedies, along with *Husband and Wife, Maidens' Vows,* and *The Vengeance.* The idea for the comedy may have been conceived as early as 1829; its final version was ready, however, only in late 1834 or early 1835. This means that chronologically *The Life Annuity* comes at the end of the most productive period of Fredro's long career. It was thus the last major comedy the dramatist wrote before the "time of silence." Its premiere was celebrated on June 12, 1835, in the Lwów Theater, and in 1838 it was included in the fifth volume of Fredro's collected works.

The Life Annuity has not had a consistently good reception in Poland. While it has been recognized for its many fine comic scenes and its lively brisk pace, the comedy has been at times dismissed as little more than an adaptation, a Polonization of Molière's *L'Avare,* a work with which it is usually compared because the central characters of both plays, Harpagon in the French, and Patch in the Polish, are avaricious money-lenders. Even the astute critic Boy-Żeleński viewed the comedy in this light and in his introduction to a Polish version of *L'Avare* treats *The Life Annuity* as something of a clever Polish version of Molière's original, reminiscent in a way of the successful Polish adaptations of French comedy by Bohomolec and Zabłocki in the second half of the eighteenth century.[1] The Polish literary historian, Stanisław Windakiewicz, wrote about *The Life Annuity* that it was written as a kind of relaxation by Fredro after his work on the great comedies of the "pre-silence period."[2] With *Maidens' Vows* and *The Vengeance* behind him, Fredro sought—and found—diversion once again in reading Molière, and *The Life Annuity* grew out of this reading.

[1] Molière, *Skąpiec,* tr. and ed. by Tadeusz Boy-Żeleński, *Biblioteka narodowa,* Series II, No. 6 (Wrocław, 1950), p. xxviii. Boy-Żeleński does agree, however, that Patch is one of Fredro's finest character studies.

[2] Quoted in Aleksander Fredro, *Dożywocie,* ed. by Karol Zawodziński, *Biblioteka narodowa,* Series I, No. 93 (2nd edn.; Wrocław, 1949), p. xi.

Similarities between *L'Avare* and *The Life Annuity* undeniably exist. The central characters, we have seen, are miserly, greedy money-lenders; they both plan to marry much younger women whom they eventually give up in the face of possible financial loss. In the case of Harpagon, the woman he insists on marrying is Marianne, with whom his son, Cléante, is secretly in love. Patch has no son, but in the protective guardian's role he comes to assume in his relationship with Leon Birbancki there is a somewhat analogous situation with *L'Avare*. Leon loves Orgon's daughter Rose, but faces the prospect of losing her to the wealthy Patch. Given the near father-son relationship of Patch and Leon, the triangular love intrigue of *The Life Annuity* does recall that of Molière's comedy. In both comedies the elder suitors retreat from a position of intransigence and eventually surrender the reluctant bride-to-be to her younger suitor when the maintenance of their positions threatens a loss of money. Harpagon relinquishes Marianne (to Cléante) in order to retrieve the 10,000 crowns Cléante and the servant La Fleche have pilfered from him precisely in order to force this move; Patch surrenders Rose to Leon rather than endure the loss of income he draws from Leon's life annuity that would result from Leon's threatened suicide (again planned to force Patch's hand).

Apart from the above similarities, there are also a few lesser points of contact between *The Life Annuity* and *L'Avare*. Harpagon's anger over his son's and daughter's "extravagant clothes" reminds one of Orgon's lamentable attempt to attire himself as a fashionable gentleman, and Patch's remarks about the fine outfit he equipped Philip with when the latter was in his service. Finally, the "sons" of both comedies—Cléante and Leon—are passionate card players.

The differences between *L'Avare* and *The Life Annuity* are far greater, however, than any similarities. The French play is essentially a comedy of character in which the author exposes to ridicule a single human failing: greed. Fredro, on the other hand, was not writing a comedy of character in *The Life Annuity* but a comedy of intrigue. For *The Life Annuity* the avarice of Patch is of secondary importance. What matters far more is the richly ironic and absurdly comic situation in which Patch comes to find himself in his relationship with Leon. To understand this relationship fully, we must first consider the significance of the title of the play.

In old Poland, a life annuity, *dożywocie* in the original Polish, was a fixed monetary pension a person received throughout his life from the income of an estate, property, or other possessions. It was, in a certain sense, an inheritance in the form of regular installments payed out for the lifetime of the person to whom the annuity or *dożywocie* was bequeathed. Now this income could be transferred or sold to another party, usually for a lump sum of money, when ready cash was needed in some financial crisis. This means that the income in whole or in part, depending on the terms worked out between the contracting parties, would go to the new purchaser of the annuity for the rest of the life of the *original* possessor. It is on this axis that the Fredro comedy revolves—and what makes it so different a work from *L'Avare*. In *The Life Annuity*, Leon Birbancki, a young gadabout, has lost his life annuity to Patch, presumably in order to get the cash he needs to pay for his heavy gambling and high living. At first, this would appear to be a potentially profitable arrangement for Patch. Leon is a young man and seems a good risk; for the rest of his [*Leon's*] life Patch stands to draw an income from his annuity. (When the original possessor of the annuity died, of course, all contractual obligations ended and the purchaser of the pension ceased to draw an income from it.) To Patch's profound dismay and chagrin, however, he discovers that Leon is anything but a good risk. On the contrary: he is a high liver, fond of drinking, gambling, partying and late hours who seems hell-bent on his own destruction. In order to safeguard his investment, Patch must now protect Leon from himself! The greedy money-lender is forced by circumstance to assume the completely unexpected role of Leon's mysterious "guardian angel," even to the point of abandoning his own intention of marrying Rose in order to prevent Leon from taking his own life. Patch thus appears in the paradoxical position of having to safeguard his own interests by acting *against* his own interests. The irony of this paradox stemming from Patch's dual role, as it were, is the foundation on which the comedy of

The Life Annuity rests. As we can see, it is a play far removed from Molière's *L'Avare* and one which indeed surpasses *L'Avare* in its cleverness and humor.

Once the basic premise of the *dożywocie* is grasped in its various implications for both Patch and Leon, the logical development of the plot is easy to trace. Although some Polish critics have insisted that the financial agreements in *The Life Annuity* are not clear, that the appearance of the Lagena brothers is superfluous, and that Patch's position strains credulity, these appear relatively minor problems in a consideration of the overall structure of the work. We can appreciate this better by comparing it to the Molière comedy. It is quite true that in *L'Avare* and *The Life Annuity* the basis of the plot is the familiar situation of young lovers temporarily prevented from marrying because of the selfishness of a parent or guardian. In *L'Avare* it is Cléante's father, Harpagon, who comes between Cléante and Marianne, and in the sub-plot between his daughter and Valère. In *The Life Annuity*, the young lovers are Leon and Rose who are prevented from marrying each other by the intention of Orgon, Rose's father, to marry her instead to Patch. This traditional formula was of greater importance to Molière than to Fredro. In *L'Avare* the action revolves mainly about the father-son love rivalry and secondarily Harpagon's refusal to permit his daughter to marry Valère. The solution comes in a conventional and mechanical way. Harpagon learns that Marianne and Valère are sister and brother and of noble birth; this makes it possible for him to permit his daughter to marry Valère. Harpagon's lust for money, and the pressure of Marianne's father, Anselme, force him to abandon his own claim on the girl in favor of his son. In *The Life Annuity*, the relations between Leon and Rose, and Orgon's plan to give his daughter to Patch, are less significant in the structure of the comedy than the transition of Patch from a greedy usurer to a guardian angel who like an anxious mother protecting her young makes every effort to keep Leon from harm.

Apart from its originality of conception, *The Life Annuity* abounds in excellent characterizations which owe nothing to Molière: Patch himself, one of Fredro's most interesting and original characters, and far more rounded than Harpagon; Hardcoin, whose unrelenting avarice makes him more similar to Molière's Harpagon than Patch is; Leon, the impetuous but not witless young hellion who recalls Gustav in *Maidens' Vows*; Orgon, the frustrated, bitter and impoverished squire who attempts to improve his financial position by forcing his daughter into a marriage of convenience with Patch; and even Doctor Hugo, who warns his patient (Leon) against further drinking and high living and then joins him in washing down oysters with a few glasses of champagne.

With all the rich humor of *The Life Annuity*, the comedy also has an undercurrent of almost bitter social comment that has not gone unnoticed. The Polish Naturalist dramatist Gabriela Zapolska, who worked for a time as an actress in Antoine's Théâtre Libre in Paris, found the comedy gloomy because of it. In 1900 she wrote in a review:

> I don't know what impressions other viewers carry away, but I cannot laugh during a performance of *The Life Annuity*. I have, on the contrary, a negative impression. These revelries of Birbancki, these pursuits after a penny, this phrase-mongering squire [Orgon] bartering with his own daughter, this band of usurers playing with a human life, with pistols, with doctors' prescriptions all represent a human menagerie for me. I look at it from behind the grating and see these instances of human malice and stupidity in the light in which Fredro's talent shows them to us. It is some kind of a miserable chase after a handful of money, and Birbancki, a romantic decadent, pale from dissipation and drunkenness, seems a wretched impostor to me in his love for Rose. . . . In my opinion the play is a much deeper satire than seems evident from appearance.[3]

The case may be easily overstated, as I feel Zapolska has overstated it. Leon is a partly negative character in his aimless pursuit of pleasure and in his questionable morality; in his nerve-racking lust for money and his view of a wife as nothing

[3] The article appeared in *Słowo polskie*, No. 476, Dec. 12, 1900. It was reprinted in Gabriela Zapolska, *Dzieła wybrane*, Vol. XVI (Cracow, 1958), 118.

more than a watchdog for his moneybags, Patch does become grotesque and ludicrous; Orgon's understandable bitterness about his position in life loses power to evoke sympathy in the face of the "sale" of his daughter to improve his social and financial standing; in his dedication to self-gain and in his uncompromising toughness Hardcoin may easily emerge as the most thoroughly unappealing character in the play. *The Life Annuity* is certainly not free of social commentary, but it is hard to see the author's purpose as didactic. Although Fredro makes a statement about his time in the comedy, his emphasis falls less on chastisement through public exposure of the sin of avarice than on the comic exploitation of this human failing. That is why the paradoxical Patch-Leon relationship is central in the plot. For Fredro the absurdity into which the lust for money can lead was of greater importance than any reaffirmation of the sinfulness of this lust. The rapid pace of the plot and the concentration on comic situation (the series of "crises" through which Patch passes in his career as Leon's "guardian angel") never permit the social commentary to gain the ascendancy or remain too long prominent, and the impression the play finally creates is one of clever situations, successful characterization, brisk dialogue, and good humor—in short, the chief ingredients of a first-class comedy. *The Life Annuity*, the last of Fredro's major comedies, is this above all.

As in *The Vengeance*, a good part of the appeal of *The Life Annuity* in the original lies in Fredro's use of the trochaic tetrameter throughout the work and the varied rhyming patterns ranging from the simple aabb, abab to the more complex abaccb, etc. On the matter of Fredro's verse, Boy-Żeleński once summed up his own feelings—and those of many of his countrymen—in the following words:

> To know his verse by heart and to be able to enjoy it in the living word, to seize from the mouth of a good actor every phrase, tasting and swallowing its pronouncement, that's the only real approach to Fredro. Until you know this pleasure, dear readers, don't speak to me of your literary culture, you're ignoramuses, pshaw![4]

[4] Boy-Żeleński, "Obrachunki fredrowskie," p. 248.

CHARACTERS

Leon Birbancki*

Doctor Hugo

Orgon

Rose, *Orgon's daughter*

Patch*

Hardcoin*

Raphael Lagena

Michael Lagena

Philip

MUSICIANS, JEWS, ETC.

The scene is set in an inn in the city.

* Birbancki, from Polish *birbant*, someone who leads a wild life.
* Łatka, in the original Polish.
* Twardosz, in the original Polish.

THE LIFE ANNUITY

ACT I

A room in an inn. A number on the door. On the right, beneath a window, a small table with smoking candles, wine glasses, cards, etc. Same things along with a few bottles on the floor. On the left, Raphael and Michael asleep on a sofa. In the rear, with instruments in their hands, musicians asleep on chairs. On the music stands in front of them—bottles and candles going out. Overturned chairs and disorder throughout the entire room.

SCENE 1. Patch, Philip cleaning up.

PATCH. [*Peeking in.*] Psst! Philip!
PHILIP. [*Blowing out the candles without turning around.*] Come on in, come on!
[*Patch enters and looks around, shaking his head.*]
PATCH. Fiddlers here, drunkards there. Oh, Philip, my dear, it looks bad.
PHILIP. [*Yawning.*] Why, what's happened?
PATCH. [*Kicking a bottle with his foot.*] Judging by this wreck, the party . . .
PHILIP. Wasn't bad, not bad at all.
PATCH. This staying up almost night after night, all the revelry, this kind of living certainly doesn't add a thing to one's health and Master Leon doesn't have too much to spare. Oh my, these youths are nothing but a lot of trouble. They live as though they were immortal. Tell them: "You'll die!" They won't believe you, till priests come to fumigate them, till the time comes to plant them six feet under. Then . . .
PHILIP. [*Interrupting him.*] They believe you.
PATCH. Right you are there! But by that time they've lost everyone who . . .
PHILIP. [*As above.*] Loves them with all their heart and soul . . .
PATCH. Right you are! And also those who lay out thousands in cash to acquire life annuities they could lose a day later.

And not one of them is mindful of the fact that his health was bought by someone—and he wastes it as though it was still his own!

PHILIP. [*Ironically.*] Wastes it, wastes it, then kicks the bucket; and the life annuity—poof! Gone to hell.

PATCH. Poof! Philip dear, that's the way it is, yes, poof! What losses! It's as though I was standing now on hot coals . . . Oh, what troubles! What went on here at this party?

PHILIP. What?

PATCH. What?

PHILIP. They drank.

PATCH. I guessed it, I guessed it. Bad, unhealthy . . . Did they drink modestly or a lot?

PHILIP. A round each.

PATCH. That's some wise answer! A round each! Say—just a swallow, but a hundred thousand swallows. And our Leon?

PHILIP. He had the most.

PATCH. He drank, he drank?

PHILIP. Like a fish.

PATCH. Like a fish? God! He's his very own worst enemy. His chest is like a sparrow's. He chokes from coughing. He's plunging a dagger in himself, a dagger! What else did they do?

PHILIP. They gambled.

PATCH. Gambled, eh? Good—that pastime always brings some kind of profit, for what someone can't lose he'll pawn with us for a song.

PHILIP. I can't squawk about the playing—it brought me in ten gold pieces.

PATCH. Ten gold pieces! Ah, Philip, you were born a lucky fellow, I see. So you've taken up a trade now?

PHILIP. I hope it doesn't show on me! After all I finished your school: never risking things uncertain, always taking what comes easy.

PATCH. How'd you get that ten-spot, Philip?

PHILIP. For card tipping—it's an old custom.

PATCH. Ten from tipping—a nice take-in! Not a bad income on the side, eh?—Come on, show me those ducats.

PHILIP. Nothing special. Here you are.

PATCH. No gold rubbed off?

PHILIP. No, they're perfect.

PATCH. Now what happens?

PHILIP. I don't get you.

PATCH. After all . . . That ten-spot . . . Eh? . . . Well? . . . People everywhere . . . in this world. One hand . . . washes . . . Oh, you know it . . .

PHILIP. [*Wanting to leave.*] I've no time now.

PATCH. [*Holding him back.*] Want me bankrupt?

PHILIP. What? The wealthy Mister Patch wants to share, to take a half of what his poor servant gets his hands on cracking his skull day and night? Oh, that's a real disgrace!

PATCH. Oh, Philip, there's nothing disgraceful about it. People like to hold on to their money, others like to grab it from them. But listen, Philip dear. If the two of us split even, that's the reward I get for all my efforts. When I bought Leon Birbancki's life annuity I wanted someone clever who'd stay by him all the time, someone who'd keep watch over his esteemed health, over his life, which is so expensive for me, who'd care for him like he would for his own eyes. I chose you out of respect for the services you did me, for the zealous way you cared for all my interests in the pawnshop. And in spite of all the troubles it took, at great cost, and with great effort, I fixed you up with a job here, my friend, where they pay you pretty well now.

PHILIP. But you take five percent of what I make.

PATCH. While it's ten you ought to be paying. After all, I'm the one who gave you the income you've got now. And besides, I first outfitted you like a little master.

PHILIP. Outfitted me? That's a joke!

PATCH. Didn't I give you a hat with a tassel, a pretty hat?

PHILIP. Some worn-out junk. Good for frightening sparrows maybe.

PATCH. But the tassel!

PHILIP. A lovely hat.

PATCH. But the tassel!

PHILIP. [*Ironically.*] . . . Fine! Dandy! And what did I get out of the gift?

PATCH. But the tassel, brother, the tassel . . .

PHILIP. What the devil's with this tassel?

PATCH. And the lining wasn't bad, either. I also gave you some length of nice livery.

PHILIP. Left-overs!

PATCH. A fine umbrella.

PHILIP. Some great profit!

PATCH. Handsome shoes, too.

PHILIP. There was just one.

PATCH. One? Perhaps—but it's from Paris. I gave you a robe with pretty flowers on it.

PHILIP. After six years in your service I come out rich as hell— in just one shoe and a robe.

PATCH. But that's not what I came to talk about. When I bought the life annuity . . .

PHILIP. Bought it? Bought it? Snatched, you mean, Sir.

PATCH. Ah, my dear Philip! You've got to watch that sharp tongue of yours. "Snatched it! Snatched it!" That's just the trouble—I think I paid too much for it.

PHILIP. I'm also afraid you did. But why'd you put another name on the contract, not your own?

PATCH. Why is that my servant's business?

PHILIP. And why are you very careful to conceal it from Birbancki? Whose annuity is it now? Who's the real benefactor? Trying to avoid some trouble, are you?

PATCH. Growing devil's horns, I see.

PHILIP. Let them grow for all I care. But to make sure they don't prick you I'm through with this job and the low gain —now let someone else look out for Birbancki when he's sick.

PATCH. What? He's sick?—Or ill? I'll go get a doctor right away.

PHILIP. Doctors won't be of much help to him.

PATCH. What's the matter with him? What's the matter with him? I'm going to faint!

PHILIP. [*Indifferently.*] What? Consumption, for sure.

PATCH. Great heavens!

PHILIP. He'll bust a vein in his lungs.

PATCH. Bust? A vein? In his lungs?

PHILIP. He'll moan, he'll groan—and then it's all over.

PATCH. Then it's all over!

PHILIP. You've got to handle him like an egg.

PATCH. I'll run fetch a doctor quickly. What times these are! What times!

PHILIP. [*Alone.*] Miser! Niggard! Scoundrel! Devil! I should watch out for your interests and not connive a little when I'm able? I'd have to be without a conscience for that. But it's time I was on my way now, too; the wind's shifting, I'm afraid. I've got my bags and my belongings. But Birbancki, the poor fellow, squeezed all out like a lemon, soon'll be among the beggars.

SCENE 2. Leon, Philip, Michael, Raphael, and musicians asleep.

LEON. [*Judging by his suit, it is obvious that Leon did not change at night. Coughs frequently while he talks.*] Philip!

PHILIP. Yes, sir.

LEON. [*Sitting down, supporting his head with his hands, and talking to himself.*] Quite a party! Excellent in all respects! Pockets empty, my head bursting. Philip!

PHILIP. Yes, Sir.

LEON. Any borsht around?

PHILIP. Coming.

LEON. Sour?

PHILIP. Ha! Our cook knows how to make the best borsht . . .

LEON. [*Calling after him.*] A glass of water! Hear! With sugar.

PHILIP. [*Coming back.*] I'll put sugar in. And perhaps a little lemon? Eh?

LEON. Ha! Fine. [*Calls after him.*] Wait, never mind it . . . My head's bursting, chest hurts awfully. I'm so weak I feel like fainting, and you're pouring lemonade now—Go to hell with such a treatment!

PHILIP. Maybe then . . .

LEON. What is it this time?

PHILIP. A few drops . . .

LEON. Of what now?

PHILIP. Of some rum? Eh?

LEON. Hm!—Pour me out a little. [*Calls after him.*] Or . . .
know what—don't add water. Who the hell wants that re-
freshment! I don't want to hurt myself any more! I'd have to
be crazy for that! If I'm going to drink some rum then I'll
take it without water. Bring me in a little bottle. Know what
kind? The Rose brand. [*Philip goes out. A short pause.*]
Rum always helps me. [*After a short pause, approaches the
sleepers.*] Michael dear!—My old friend Raphael! Brothers
both of equal strength. Raphael's got a bump?—The devil!
The card Jan hit him on the head with was kind of hard, I
see. Just so long as he believes us when we tell him that he
just dreamt the whole thing. [*A short pause.*] Well, so far
life's been pleasant—parties, gambling, cards and dances.
But what's ahead, I just don't know—not even a roof
above my head. Completely bare and empty—and as for
credit—oh, my God! It's already reached its last breath, it
can hardly shake a finger any more. [*A short pause.*] What
will I do with myself then? Ha! What's there to think
about? I'll just settle in a monastery somewhere and I'll
write on all my letters: the year eighteen hundred thirty-
five—and the first of my destitution.
[*Awakened, the bass player draws his bow a few times.*] Anyone there?

PHILIP. [*Off stage.*] Coming, coming. [*Entering.*] Here I am, Sir,
with your order. [*Brings the rum.*]

LEON. Now get rid of all these fiddlers. Pick up the cards,
collect the bottles.

PHILIP. This amusement doesn't last long. By the way, Sir,
there's a great friend of ours waiting a long time to see you.

LEON. Which one? Who?

PHILIP. The one with the little red beard.

LEON. Red?—Even if it were blue it won't make my money jin-
gle . . . you know why.

PHILIP. He's got some summons, and wants . . . [*indicates
money*].

LEON. Give him a good boot, we'll be even.

PHILIP. And what if he wants to pay us interest on your prom-
issory note?

LEON. Take it. And today you can let all our Jewish brothers know that from now on I've got a completely new financial system: after taking a strict accounting of what I've still got and what I can get, I don't plan to give them a penny! But since the talk's about finances, I wanted to know, and ordered you to investigate, in what hole, pit, or puddle the filthy robber has hidden who grabbed my life annuity. I've got to find him, because I'd like to either politely incline him to some agreement, or bring suit for all my losses, or beat the daylights out of him.

PHILIP. One's better than the other. Hard to choose from those three weapons. But nothing will come of it—since the shyster's in Berlin now. When the installments are due he just collects your life annuity through some banker there, as if he had been left it. But that fellow is still waiting, Sir.

LEON. Tell him I'm in a bad mood—let him beat it.

PHILIP. He won't listen.

LEON. Blast it in his ears!

PHILIP. He says he won't give up his station.

LEON. [*Banging the table with his fist.*] Then waltz the upstart down the stairs!

VIOLINIST. [*Waking up.*] Waltz?—Coming up—[*To the musicians.*] A waltz! A waltz!

[*They begin to play one after the other, but falsetto.*]

PHILIP. [*Trying vainly to tear the bows away.*] Quiet! That's enough! Sh! Quiet!

VIOLINIST. Sometimes a person dozes off against his will.

PHILIP. [*Pushing them out the door.*] Go on! Go on! March, march!

VIOLINIST. [*At the door.*] A march, Sir? Right away. A march! [*They begin to play a march.*]

PHILIP. [*Closing the door.*] Oh, shut up! Just as though the devil tuned them!—Now they play, last night they guzzled— [*One can hear the sounds of music fading away in the distance. When Philip returns a clarinetist so far unnoticed lying in a far corner of the room begins to play a falsetto accompaniment.*]

PHILIP. [*Walking toward him.*] What the hell's going on now?

CLARINETIST. Clarinet's got somewhat dried.

PHILIP. Seems to me it got soaked.

CLARINETIST. It should . . .

PHILIP. [*Conducting him to the door.*] Go on . . . Go on—Sleep well! [*Shuts the doors.*] Thank heavens! [*Gathers up the candles and leaves.*]

SCENE 3. Leon, Raphael, Michael.

RAPHAEL. [*Awakened, he begins to sing while still lying down.*]
When we think the time is fitting,
And the time is here,
Our host's health we all drink toasts to,
He's our comrade dear!

MICHAEL. [*Jumping up and sitting straight.*] Whose hand is it? Health? Whose health? [*The two of them, still sitting, look around on all sides. Brief silence.*]

LEON. Ah, good morning.

RAPHAEL. My dear Leon. Quite a banquet, as they call it. They'll be talking about it everywhere. But . . . [*Begins to look for a shoe.*]

MICHAEL. [*Sighing.*] BUT—a big but. I know . . . Brother dear, it's going to be bitter.

RAPHAEL. [*Still looking for the shoe.*] I'm sure I left a shoe here. [*Finds it and puts it on.*]

MICHAEL. Oh, what troubles I've got into!

LEON. What's the matter?

MICHAEL. How can I face my wife today?

RAPHAEL. Looks bad, Michael!

MICHAEL. Looks bad, Raphael.

LEON. What the devil! To be so afraid of one's wife. She'll nag and growl a little, but she won't smoke you in a chimney, she won't take your scalp for punishment—and the matter's hardly worth talking about.

RAPHAEL. Easy to say: won't take my scalp . . . But why's my head so itchy? Did something give me a good bite? [*To Leon.*] Is it red? Eh?

LEON. Just a speck there.

RAPHAEL. A mosquito probably . . .

LEON. Or an earwig . . .

MICHAEL. All in all, last night's amusement in such company . . .

RAPHAEL. The whole night . . .

MICHAEL. Wasn't worth a damn, the whole thing. And it was your doing, brother.

RAPHAEL. Just don't put the blame on me, hear! I went over to my lawyer's with a neighbor. I was supposed to be back home in half an hour, they were expecting me for dinner . . . But what went on there! Oh my heavens!

MICHAEL. I went out to buy tickets for some *Norma** they were playing yesterday—I'm still carrying them around with me. Then I had the luck to meet you: "Come with us, come on!" —I make excuses. That won't do though: "Come on! Come on!"—"Where to?"—"Just for a little herring." Liking herring, off I went . . . Pretty herring I got into, eh?

RAPHAEL. It seems just like I dreamt I played cards yesterday . . . Don't you remember, brother? [*Raphael recovers his wallet.*]

MICHAEL. No, I don't.

RAPHAEL. [*Turning first his wallet, then his pockets inside out.*] Well, here's the answer!

LEON. Are you missing anything there?

RAPHAEL. Missing anything, are you joking? Sister sent three hundred guilders just so I could do some errands for her . . . devil with these small-town errands! A real plague descended on us!

LEON. You might conquer stubborn fate yet and tomorrow win . . .

RAPHAEL. I swear it, I'm all through with cards—forever. Three hundred, brother, three hundred.

MICHAEL. [*Snapping out of his reverie.*] If I could only remember what I've done here all these hours—maybe you remember, brother?

RAPHAEL. I don't remember.

LEON. [*Laughing.*] Lovely!

RAPHAEL. But there's nothing here to laugh at—rotten joke it would be, damn it; after all, we're both married.

---

* The opera *Norma* by Vincenzo Bellini (1801-1835), which first appeared in 1831, was popular in Poland as elsewhere in Europe.

LEON. I give you my word, there'll be no fuss.

MICHAEL. Some poor time I picked to go out.

LEON. I'll take all the blame on myself—I'll straighten you out with your wives.

RAPHAEL. Very well, then, come home with us.

LEON. I'll come later.

MICHAEL. Hell with later!

RAPHAEL. Know what, Leon, I've a favor to ask: you know how to smooth out even the maddest quarrel with pretty phrases—write my wife a little letter.

MICHAEL. And mine also.

RAPHAEL. Just a few words.

MICHAEL. She regards you very highly.

RAPHAEL. And mine trusts you very much, too.

LEON. I could do it—and I even predict my two notes will straighten everything out. I'm afraid that on my desk, though, you'll find a bottle faster than a pen. Wait—I have a pencil I use for notes. I'll go right now and scribble out a few words. [*Goes out.*]

SCENE 4. Raphael, Michael. Silence

MICHAEL. What do you say?

RAPHAEL. What?

MICHAEL. What?

RAPHAEL. And you?

MICHAEL. I—nothing.

RAPHAEL. Nothing?—Me too.

MICHAEL. Only that it's bad, damn it, my first quarrel with my lady.

RAPHAEL. Mine won't say a thing. She won't even raise an eyebrow. But she'll go to church to offer a sacrifice for all her sufferings. Once she's home again, though, she'll start bringing it up slowly. And the next day she'll repeat it, and the day after, then two more, for a week, and then another, always softly, nice and friendly—and just like water from a dripping faucet always falling on the same spot, till it almost bores a hole in your head. She'll start yapping, yapping, yapping. She could yap till doomsday, if I didn't get so bored finally that for her sake as well as mine I promise not to cook up anything else like this. I'd promise anything just so as not to give her something new to nag about.

SCENE 5. *Raphael, Michael, Leon.*

LEON. Here are your testimonials: loyal, diligent, and sober. Sober—eh? And furthermore, I beg their forgiveness for the time you lost with me.

RAPHAEL. God repay you for your troubles.

MICHAEL. You'll go to heaven for this service.

LEON. I'm hoping their anger won't last long, but just see to it that they don't learn that they both have the same letters.

RAPHAEL. [*Kissing him on both cheeks.*] Splendid! Splendid! Many thanks, friend, for helping us in this mess.

MICHAEL. [*Kissing him on both cheeks.*] I'll reciprocate this favor if ever [*sighing*] God gives you a wife.

LEON. Now have faith in my protection, you've got nothing more to think of. What's happened—happened! [*Taking Michael under the arm, Raphael puts on his hat in a nonchalant manner.*]

RAPHAEL. Certainly! Let's go like men now! [*The hat, too large, falls down all the way to his chin. Freeing his head.*] This hat . . .

MICHAEL. [*Trying it on.*] Isn't yours, brother—nor mine either.

RAPHAEL. It's too big.

MICHAEL. [*Looking.*] But where's mine?

RAPHAEL. [*Looking.*] Isn't that nice! Just a week ago I had it blocked and cleaned!

MICHAEL. But I did have one—or did I just dream it?

LEON. [*Pointing with his foot under the table.*] Something's lying here.

MICHAEL. Mine was new.

LEON. Take what's there.

MICHAEL. [*Putting on the hat, which stays on the top of his head.*] This one's a bit tight.

LEON. Nonsense, it's just like your own.

RAPHAEL. Being hatless is like being headless!

LEON. Oh, forget it, don't waste time now—just so long as you've got something on your dome! And if someone asks, say it's the style.

RAPHAEL. Right you are! And I do like it—wine is wine— and water, water . . . Let's go, brother! Just be fearless. What's happened—happened! [*They go away arm in arm, one in a hat too big, the other in one too small.*]

LEON. [*Alone.*] Nothing but a social menace these husbands, these pendulums swinging from the marital virtues to "Let's live it up a little"! Teach each one the ABC's of some innocent amusement from drinking to gaming—oh, what torture and what torment! Should you happen to succeed though— which don't count among the wonders—you'll see how fast they take to it! The husbands soon outdo the bachelors!

SCENE 6. Leon, Philip.

PHILIP. [*With a package in his hand.*] Very early in the morning someone left a package for you. No one knows from where or whom, since, as usual, it came secretly.

LEON. A package, you say? A package for me? Heavy? Light? Eh?

PHILIP. Why it's very—

LEON. Heavy?

PHILIP. Light.

LEON. [*Taking it.*] Makes no difference, even if it were lighter than a feather. Just so long as it's been sent here by your hand, my guardian angel, you who always watch out for me and with loving wings protect me! No, you are not just some fancy of mine. Each day I have new proof from you! You may be a Sylph sent down to me, which is why I call you Sylphid. Your protection brings my heart joy, your gaze never takes leave of me. Or perhaps you are some earthling whom my mind clothes with the beauty of a goddess. My breast waits for you enamored to embrace your soul forever!

PHILIP. Please be kind to take a look at what this Sylphid sent you. A little money'd do nicely today. After all, you even owe me something.

LEON. Right you are, especially since today's the day my fortune's perished. [*Tenderly.*] She's eager to bring me help and for a start sends me something to support me. Or perhaps at just this moment I've an unknown cousin who's given his ghost up maybe in Calcutta, and my Sylphid sends her gnomes here with his will made in my favor—all the millions I'll inherit! [*Holds the package high in the air.*] Oh, you! Earthling or spirit, open up your secrets to me! Let me count your many treasures—for I need them rather badly! [*Opens up the package, and with astonishment.*] Oh!

PHILIP. [*As Leon takes out the contents.*] A jacket . . . pair of stockings . . . and a nightcap—old, however . . .

LEON. [*Picking up everything and throwing it in Philip's face.*] Go to the devil!

PHILIP. What did I do? Let your Sylphid go instead.

LEON. Out of my sight, out you scoundrel! Or I'll also play you such a joke now you'll wind up with your neck in two.

PHILIP. You act like this joke was my fault. [*Picks up the items on the floor.*] Everything is made of flannel . . . It's really no calamity—warm and good for the health.

LEON. Shut up!

PHILIP. Aha!

LEON. [*Impetuously.*] What?

PHILIP. There's a letter. Maybe this nightcap's something magic? When you stick it on your head, Sir, the mystery'll clear up.

LEON. [*Reading the letter.*] "Value health the way you should, for when you die, you lose your life."

PHILIP. Ah, you see, Sir, you see?

LEON. [*Looking around.*] No, I don't see any stick around here —I could really use one now.

PHILIP. [*Retreating.*] I'll go see if I can find one in the hallway.

LEON. Hold on, hold on.

PHILIP. Right away, Sir. [*Goes out.*]

LEON. [*Alone.*] Mocking me again, the rascal! [*A short pause.*] But this time there's a reason. My donor's dumb or just insulting—pair of stockings for a person who's lost every cent he once had! [*A short pause.*] Or perhaps—I could believe it—it was meant as a friendly warning; even though it was done strangely, there's no reason to be angry. Once again it proves, however, that my welfare still concerns her, that she's a tireless genie, who keeps me guarded every way she can.

PHILIP. [*Announcing.*] Doctor Hugo. [*Goes out.*]

SCENE 7. Leon, Doctor.

DOCTOR. What the devil! Leon's weak—Leon's ailing, the Doctor races, hardly breathing, and Leon's healthier than the doctors, the lot of them together!

LEON. Who? Me? Sick?

DOCTOR. Otherwise I wouldn't be here.

LEON. What does it mean? More things I don't seem to fathom.

DOCTOR. What?—I've been sent to see you.

LEON. Although I'm always happy when you come to pay a visit, please forgive me if just for that I don't rush to get sick. So explain the whole thing clearly to me, because I sense there's something strange going on.

DOCTOR. I had just stepped out of my house, when a person unknown to me, almost breathless, pale from fear, rushes headlong into my path, and embracing me by the knees, asks me, begs me, implores me, to rush to you since you need help. I came straight here as fast as I could . . .

LEON. Ah, my Sylphid, my Sylphid, how couldn't I recognize you in that person! Please describe her to me, doctor. Say she's lovely, fair, a goddess! Youthful, dewy-fresh, charming! Tell me, tell me, my dear doctor!

DOCTOR. [*Laughing.*] I gave my word I'd say nothing, but upon my soul I never would have guessed that the person's name was Sylphid.

LEON. I'm the one who gave her that name, since she's my guardian spirit. Although she always soars above me and keeps me sheltered with her wings, she's never been close enough for me to see her so I'd know if she's an earthling, or some creature sent from heaven.

DOCTOR. Earthling? From heaven? Now I see there's a reason why I was sent here—you have to have your blood let.

LEON. Listen, then I'll do whatever you want. For more than a

year now some strange power that's always with me, guarding every step I take, helps me out of every trouble. When
at public masquerades sometimes nasty brawls break out
around me, I'm instantly surrounded by Harlequins and
Doctors. If I'm somewhere and it's pouring, though I've said
a word to no one, somehow a coach comes to fetch me. If
I lose or damage something or get lost somewhere while traveling, someone comes from out of nowhere, eager just to be
of service. Even when I come home late at night sometimes not so steady on my feet, someone's hung a lantern
for me, or an arm comes out to help me. [*Sighs.*] Although
she's more generous with good advice than with presents,
I'm no less grateful to her. Who's without fault on this
earth, eh?

DOCTOR. That it's strange, no one will argue . . .

LEON. Since she sent you here to see me, maybe I am weak,
after all. I do cough some—my head's burning.

DOCTOR. [*Taking his pulse.*] As concerns your head, brother,
only a surgeon can help you now. He'll take off the old one
and put a new one in its place.

LEON. [*Pulling his head away.*] Go to hell!

DOCTOR. Healed already? And your Sylphid? [*Leon gives back
his hand.*] Coughing?

LEON. Coughing.

DOCTOR. Eating much now?

LEON. Hardly any.

DOCTOR. Do you sleep about twelve hours?

LEON. For the last two nights I haven't slept a wink.

DOCTOR. Coughing kept you up?

LEON. No—playing cards.

DOCTOR. There's a drug for such a weakness. Commonly it's
called—jail. But joking aside, my dear Leon, please try to
think about your health some, for, I swear, you're in for
trouble. She in whose defense and protection you've placed
so much faith tries through my voice to remind you to
consider, even for a moment, that every hour there's that less
life left.

LEON. [*Interrupting him.*] And every doctor, too—that's not
new.

DOCTOR. Better if the doctor finishes you, than having to moan and groan a long time.

LEON. My do-gooder Doctor Hugo.

DOCTOR. I'm talking as a friend now. If you want to—go ahead, ruin your health. Once you lose it, the grave awaits you. But you won't succeed this way, you won't break the thread of this endless misery so easily. After losing your inheritance, you'll be left without a penny to your name. You've been used to wealth and comfort, and you think, I'm sure quite nobly, that if it happened, after all, you'd not be scared by the picture! What a life—through your own errors a burden to yourself and the whole world, living from one hour to the next groveling like a common beggar!

LEON. And my Sylphid?

DOCTOR. Stay well!

LEON. Hold on! My prescription?

DOCTOR. I'll give it to the one who's for sure doing penance watching out for you.

LEON. But why do that?

DOCTOR. For this reason: [*Philip enters.*] I'll keep an eye on the apothecaries so that they make accurately what you'll doubtless throw out later.

LEON. [*Reading a note brought in by Philip.*] Hooray for trade! Hooray for the ocean! Fresh oysters have arrived today!

DOCTOR. [*Happily.*] What's this? Oysters?

LEON. Come on, doctor, this isn't anything to put off. Let me open the first with you!

PHILIP. But you've got to think of your health!

DOCTOR. Oysters won't do any harm though . . .

PHILIP. But the champagne that goes with them . . .

DOCTOR. Well, just one glass!

LEON. Then a second.

DOCTOR. Yes, a couple . . .

LEON. [*Taking his hat.*] Just a couple . . .

DOCTOR. It can never ever harm you.

LEON. Let's have some.

DOCTOR. In moderation.

LEON. Since I'm your patient, doctor—you start first and then I'll follow. [*Takes him under the arm and goes to the door with him.*] Tell me, doctor, what's the best thing I could take now for my illness?

DOCTOR. I'll give you some pills and tonic . . .

LEON. Oh, how well he knows my nature!

[*They go out.*]

ACT II

Desks and sofa removed. On the left, a small table and chair.

SCENE *1. Orgon, Rose, Servant. Orgon dressed in traveling clothes, cap on his head, long moustaches, watch on a wide fob, etc. Behind him, Jews and servants from the inn.*

SERVANT. [*Pointing to the door on the left.*] Number five. There are two rooms there.

ORGON. And how much for them for a day?

SERVANT. We'll settle the accounting later.

ORGON. It's this "later" I'm afraid of. Can you let me know the price now?

SERVANT. Just a florin.

ORGON. Silver?

SERVANT. Silver, Sir.

ORGON. Silver florin, awfully expensive.

SERVANT. But they can't be any cheaper.

ORGON. But everywhere else it's cheaper—let it go for half a florin.

ROSE. Father, please, I beg you, don't bargain.

ORGON. My what pride she's got! Just see here! He has no shame when he bargains for a penny and makes us say "it's expensive" just to embarrass us, when he's simply over-charging. [*To the servant.*] Well then, take two paper flor-ins or I'll leave—Eh? . . .

SERVANT. Just for you, Sir, I'll let it go for that price, so you'll get to know us better.

ORGON. [*To Rose.*] You see there's no ounce of shame here, and you still have something left in your pocket.

SERVANT. I'll have your things brought in.

ORGON. Wait, wait—tell me, friend, if you're so kind, do you know the residence of a Mister Patch?

SERVANT. Patch? The one they call the "friend of youth"?

ORGON. Who's just called Prosper Patch, short and sweet. I don't know of any surnames.

SERVANT. His house isn't far from here.

ORGON. Please be so good, go and tell him Mister Orgon asks him to come here—and have Mathew bring our things in. [*Enters the room on the left.*]

ROSE. Even if he's bad, ugly and old, I'd still go to the altar with him willingly since such a sacrifice is needed for my father and our family. But to have to marry a money-lender, a man without faith and honor—it just tears my soul to pieces, it's driving me crazy. Yet I must, I must, I must.

ORGON. [*Coming in.*] Every turn you take there's cheating— two rooms he said! There's just one here divided by a curtain.

JEW. I'm a broker.

ORGON. I don't need one!

SECOND JEW. Money-lender?

ORGON. I don't need one!

SECOND SERVANT. Can I serve you?

ORGON. I don't need you! I'll repeat it: I don't need you! Oh, damn! My God, what a punishment!
[*They leave.*] No sooner do you set foot in town, screeching crowds gather around you, just like jackdaws chasing owls. [*A porter comes in and hands him an announcement. Orgon looks him straight in the eye for a while. The porter bows to him.*]
Here's a tip—but the next time, my dear Sir, please spare us another favor! [*The porter leaves. Orgon to himself.*] If you let them, they'll all serve you, and you'll end up a pauper. [*Reads the announcement.*]

"A trip into space—which H. Carlo Bombalini will have the honor to undertake in a huge balloon, the likes of which have not been seen in Europe until now. He is offering without charge a seat next to him and invites anyone who has the desire to appear in the above designated place from which at four sharp, to the echo of Janissary music, the released balloon will rise to an unseeable altitude."

[*Throws the announcement on the table to the right.*] Let the Lord show him the way there together with that free seat of his. Let whoever wants to take his place there, and the two of them go traveling. God forbid I'll ever do it!

[*Together with the janitor, Mathew brings in a big bundle. Orgon pushes the janitor away.*]

What's he doing meddling in here? Every minute a new face! [*To Mathew.*] Couldn't Kaśka mind the horses while Mykita brought it all in?

JANITOR. I am . . .

ORGON. You're polite—I see it—God save us from such politeness! But I despise politeness and repay it with ingratitude. [*To himself.*] Or sometimes with this cane of mine. [*To Mathew, taking the bundle with him.*] Well, step lively! Hurry up, dunce! [*They carry out the bundle.*]

ORGON. [*Out of breath.*] In and out they like to carry. No one asks them, yet they do it . . . [*With a gesture.*] They get something for it, yet still have the nerve to ask for a tip. A real swarm of locusts!

SCENE 2. *Orgon, Rose, Patch.*

PATCH. Your humble servant.

ORGON. How are things with you, my dear Sir?

PATCH. Please permit me to embrace you, guest we've been waiting for so long! [*They kiss each other. To Rose.*] To my beautiful Miss Rose a hundred little kisses on her little hands. [*Kisses her hand.*] Whether at home or traveling, she's always pretty! A real heart-stealer! Looks exactly like her name—[*Aside to Orgon.*] Ah, my friend, what ever possessed you to throw yourself into this place? They'll pluck you like a chicken here; when it comes to that they're devils. Ah, you've somewhat lost your senses!

ORGON. I know what it smells of here, but I had to. There's no other place in the whole town.

PATCH. I'll get you something else tomorrow.

ORGON. I won't warm this place too long.

PATCH. Why is Miss Rose looking sternly?

ORGON. My poor child!

PATCH. It's my hope that she won't be poor at all, Sir, once she becomes my wife.

ORGON. [*With sadness.*] Yes! Of course! But there are sorrows —for her home, for her family. I give my word they'll pass soon, however. Rose is a good, level-headed child. Well, so as not to lose much time, I'll go look around the stores now. You stay here and rest yourself, Rose. Let me think about your trousseau.

PATCH. Why observe the customs so strictly and make a big fuss about a trousseau, just so the Jews can take your money? [*Takes him aside.*] After all, everything you need you'll find at my place: from diamonds to distaffs, from booties to bedding. And I'll let you have everything wholesale, because the pawn terms expired long ago.

ORGON. I don't want someone else's shoes.

PATCH. Are you mad, what are you saying! "I don't want someone else's shoes." Ah, it's just your pride talking, pride, ambition, stuck-up nose! But I'm just proposing something, you're free to make your own choice. [*Aside.*] Let him buy what he wants to—just as soon as I'm married, I'll sell some things and exchange the others.

ORGON. I've some matter to take care of.

PATCH. Saving money? All my blessings.

ORGON. I'll tell you briefly what it's about. A year ago, during the fair season, I did something stupid. Trying to catch the city style, I ordered a tailor brought in to me. What a sight! You should have seen him—with a compass, an eyepiece, a ruler like a saber. He lays out his measuring table, and while I stood there all astonished, he measures me from every side. Then between two parallels from my shoulders he drops a straight line down from my nose, divides my stomach into triangles, draws four lines slanted fashion, makes two levels at the very bottom, and up above a circle and half-circles. Then he writes, makes drawings, counts, then demands some more material. Once he's gotten what he wanted, out comes not a coat—but a jacket! Not at all the thing I ordered. When I sued him on account of this, he takes a shoemaker for a counsel, because the fellow really knows the law. So the case has been dragging on for a whole year now. But if, God forbid, I don't end the affair before this day's out, mark my words, I'll pound this tailor-geometrician to a pulp, Sir. For the time being now, farewell—Adies!

PATCH. Adiu!

SCENE 3. *Rose, Patch.*

PATCH. The time has come, never too soon for the heart, when the lover is permitted to put an engagement ring on his beloved's little hand.

ROSE. [*Withdrawing her hand from him.*] It's enough I'm getting one ring!

PATCH. Pearls, precious stones, all gold . . .

ROSE. Gold, silver—what do I care!

PATCH. Heavens, Rose dear, gold is gold. Let's not blaspheme, my child, if you want happiness on earth. Take it, my little turtle-dove, my little pigeon, my little cuckoo, my little squirrel, my little darling. [*Wants to put the ring on her finger.*] Take it, put it on this little thin one, on this one, this teeny-weeny little finger.

ROSE. [*Tearing her hand away.*] No, no, and no.

PATCH. Oh, how strange, upon my soul—while I give, I still have to beg. That has never happened to me before! Let me have your little hand here, come on, if you love me.

ROSE. Just hold on now! Where did you get the idea that I love you? Surely I never said so.

PATCH. Oh, my dear Rose, you must be joking—after all, what will soon take place between us is your very own wish. [*Rubs his hands together.*] Soon, quite soon, fine and dandy, a little capital will fall my way—[*indicating children*] the little percentages will grow, who can guess how many of them.

ROSE. Yes, of course, my very own wish . . . Anyway, it's clear my father would have had to lose his village to pay off the debt he owes you. So—the debtor gives his daughter. But it doesn't mean, however, that I'm obliged to love you, or that I would ever love you! I'll be your wife, but no more.
[*Goes out.*]

PATCH. [*Alone, after a short pause.*] From her father's debt I deducted six thousand for this marriage. No great sum, it's certainly true; nonetheless, I've given plenty. "I'll be your wife, but no more." That's all I ever wanted, too—whether Violet or Rosie, whether frigid glance or tender, just so long as I had a guard at home, just so long as my purse was cared for—that's all I wanted, and that's what I'm going to have. But the annuity matter's worse! If I don't dispose of it soon, I could land in serious trouble. This Birbancki's something awful. Looks like death's about to take him. Coughs and coughs—like from the graveyard. Skin's all yellow . . . No—he's awful . . . I'll ask three percent not six now. Just let Hardcoin hand it over . . . Here he's coming. Thank God!

SCENE 4. Patch, Hardcoin.

HARDCOIN. [*Talks slowly, his eyes always lowered, and without the slightest emotion on his face. Aside.*]
Hm! Doesn't see me . . . looking down . . . saying prayers . . . the old miser! [*Comes closer.*] Oh! Forgive me . . .
[*Wants to withdraw.*]
PATCH. [*Pretending surprise.*] Jan, dear fellow!
HARDCOIN. I just lost my way . . .
PATCH. Wait, hold on!
HARDCOIN. Number four they told me.
PATCH. But Jan, please don't run away now! [*Takes him by the shoulders and looks tenderly into his eyes.*] Well, would you ever believe it! You're so handsome—like a daisy— every hour you're getting younger. [*They embrace a few times.*] Jan, my dearest friend, my dear Jan—come sit down —let's talk a while, eh? [*Takes his hat. Both of them sit down.*] That's right—That's right . . . [*Puts his hand on his knee.*] My dear fellow! [*A short pause.*] What's the good word for today, Jan?
[*Hardcoin sits very straight, his legs crossed and hidden under the chair. Eyes lowered all the time, he looks at Patch's fingers moving over his knee. Sits as though made of stone.*]
HARDCOIN. Nothing.
PATCH. [*After a short pause.*] Windy . . . looks bad out . . .

HARDCOIN. [*After a short pause.*] Bad.

PATCH. Why?

HARDCOIN. Because it's windy.

PATCH. [*Aside.*] He's in no mood to talk business . . . caught me by the neck—caught me and holds me! [*Out loud.*] Ah, my friend, it's truly sinful that you never come to see me. You'd have a bite once in a while, modest of course, but always in pleasant company. [*A short pause. Aside.*] Damned crook! Nothing doing with him!

[*In the following speech, Patch anticipates an answer after every sentence. Hardcoin, however, moves his head each time as if saying: "Ha! What do I care."*]

You didn't close your deal this morning . . . An hour later you'd have gotten more . . . But I still haven't sold yet . . . And I put it off a while . . . If it means hurting my friends, I don't want even the greatest profit.

HARDCOIN. [*After a short pause.*] You won't get so much from me now.

PATCH. [*Jumping up, then sitting down.*] "You won't get so much! You won't get so much!" Oh, my dear friend, please don't say that. Why it's just like you were shoving a heated iron into my hands! "You won't get so much! You won't get so much!" Am I not a true believer? Am I a mason, am I a libertine, am I a bankrupt? Please don't say that, Jan, I beg you, please don't say that, or my soul will burst from sorrow!

HARDCOIN. I'm not saying . . .

PATCH. Why this talk then?

HARDCOIN. Because Birbancki isn't healthy, he'll surely croak . . .

PATCH. [*As if hurled into the chair.*] Let the Lord's hand protect his dear head! [*Laughs forcefully.*] Have you lost your senses, Jan? "He's not healthy! He'll surely croak!" . . . He's as fit as Hercules, Sir—he'll be a new Methuselah. What a build he has! What a chest, what a head! What bones he has—like a giant! You won't find another like him anywhere on earth! All your senses must have left you, if this is the way you talk, Jan! [*Jumps up.*] But know what? I'll tell you something . . . One word . . . just one little word . . . no more. [*Takes Hardcoin by the head with both hands.*] Come let's bargain—[*Kisses him on the forehead.*] A hundred thousand . . . [*Jumps away—looks around—Hardcoin shakes his head indicating that he does not agree. Patch advances, and slapping him on the shoulder, says.*] Make it ninety . . . [*Acts as before.*] Then give eighty—[*As before.*] Oh, you dearest friend of mine Jan! What's the matter! God Almighty! You want to ruin me forever, you'll squeeze the blood right out of me! [*Pulls him by his coat and shakes him.*] Heavens, man, why after all have some pity in your heart, have a conscience. In this world business is easy but remember your salvation! Make it seventy! [*As above.*] Since you wish to murder me—to murder me terribly—better do it with a razor! [*Sticks out his throat.*] Cut it, cut it! . . . Go on, cut it! Cut it here where it's smoothest, since I have so much to lose now. Or knock my head off with a club. Just don't let me suffer too long. [*Hardcoin wants to get up. Patch pulls him in such a way that he sits down forcefully and assumes the same position as before.*] Give me sixty! [*As above.*] Listen, Jan—let paralysis [*pointing to his throat*] strike me here! Let me break my legs in four! Let my bones fall to nothing! If I can go down a penny, or even a half a penny—from the fifty . . . [*When Hardcoin wants to get up, Patch pulls him back to his seat and talks rapidly.*] Make it forty. [*Pulls him by his coat.*] What? Not even that?—Not even forty? . . . On the Mother of Seven Sorrows have some pity, heartless person! [*More and more emotionally, almost in tears.*] I'm unfortunate, impoverished, I can barely make ends meet, I'll soon be naked, without any shelter over me, and you want to finish me off . . . I'm burdened with a family: an old father, a blind mother—I must support them to the end . . . Soon I'll have a wife and children. Have some mercy on my infants, on the innocent little children . . . Jan, I beg you, for God's sake, don't drive me out among the beggars! [*Hardcoin gets up and takes out his purse. Silence.*]

HARDCOIN. I'll say just a word, just one little word . . . [*Silence. A servant enters with some medicine bottles.*] No delay . . . I'll give you cash now . . . On the table . . .

SERVANT. [*Standing behind Patch.*] Please . . .

PATCH. [*Impatiently.*] What is it?

SERVANT. Sir, are these medicines here for Mister Birbancki?

PATCH. [*Holding the hand of Hardcoin who is hiding his purse, and trying to conceal the servant with his body.*]

PATCH. [*To Hardcoin.*] How much? How much?

SERVANT. Here?

PATCH. [*Right in the servant's ear.*] Go to hell! [*To Hardcoin.*] How much?

[*The servant puts down the bottles and goes out.*]

HARDCOIN. [*Taking his hat.*] Let the ailing man be healed first!

PATCH. "Ailing! Ailing!" How's that—ailing! What on earth's come into your head! The doctors want to weaken his excess of health with these drinks here. These are really friends of ours, Jan! [*Takes a bottle and talks while drinking from it.*] See! Look here!—Lemonade! Take a sip . . . See how I drink it! And you know I'm certainly healthy . . . Good . . . First rate . . . See how I'm drinking—

HARDCOIN. Bye bye! [*Leaves.*]

PATCH. Oh, you gypsy! Jew! Turk! Renegade! Even Satan in his lair wouldn't get a penny from you! [*Shakes himself and spits.*] Break your neck, I'll send a candle—or at least the promise of one. [*Spits.*]

SCENE 5. *Patch, Leon. Leon in high spirits, but not drunk, comes into his room whistling a tune. Finding it locked, he turns around and calls.*

LEON. [*Coughing frequently.*] Philip! Philip!

PATCH. [*Aside.*] Ay, how he shouts! He'll start coughing . . .

LEON. I'll shoot him! Philip! Philip!

[*With every shout, Patch shakes as though struck.*]

PATCH. [*Aside.*] Now that's too much! His lungs could burst with that shouting. [*To Leon.*] What is it you'd like to have, Sir?

LEON. And what business . . . [*Coughs.*]

PATCH. [*Finishing the sentence Leon started.*] . . . is it of yours? None of mine, not in the least bit . . . Don't you talk . . . I can figure it out, and we'll understand each other by gestures . . . Just don't shout that way, I beg you.

LEON. But I want to shout.

PATCH. Oh, my God! I'll just say . . .

LEON. [*More and more loudly.*] Who'll prevent me?

PATCH. Lord Almighty!

LEON. [*Coming closer to Patch's ear.*] And if someone . . .

PATCH. [*In an undertone.*] But your lungs, your lungs!

LEON. My good sir . . .

PATCH. Oh, your lungs!

LEON. My ears are ringing . . . [*Coughs.*]

PATCH. Saint John, I beg you, help me!

LEON. Why don't you clear out of here now!—I'll keep shouting . . .

PATCH. Saint John, help me!

LEON. Just so long as I have breath to—Ha! Hu! Ha! Hu! [*Coughs.*]

PATCH. God Almighty! Holy Joseph! Oh, your poor lungs! Please permit me to explain, Sir, that my plans for you were different . . .

LEON. I'll shout if I want to!

PATCH. [*To himself.*] Useless! [*Runs out.*] Saint John, help me! What will happen to his lungs! Help me!

LEON. Go to hell! [*Sits down.*] Why who the devil . . . brought him here . . . I must be silent . . . I must . . . I must . . . or I'll give my soul up coughing. [*Rests his head in his hands.*]

PATCH. [*Bringing water.*] Here's water, with a little sugar. Drink some, it should help you. It'll give your lungs some moisture and ease the chafing phlegm . . . All I wanted was to serve you.

LEON. Serve! [*Drinks a little.*]

PATCH. [*As if drinking himself.*] That's the way, yes . . . it soothes . . . it softens . . . You have to guard your body just like your soul! God commanded us to protect ourselves from illness, for He gave our bodies as gifts. Just so long as we're healthy then there's joy and happiness.

LEON. [*Pointing to a poster with his head.*] What's that?

PATCH. [*Trying to guess.*] What?

LEON. [*Louder.*] That.

PATCH. [*As if someone struck him.*] Talking loud again . . .

LEON. Give me!

PATCH. I'll read it—rest your chest.

LEON. Give me!

PATCH. [*Giving it to him.*] Here, it's about some madman bent on breaking his neck today, flying a balloon way up high. May the Lord God bring him the light!

LEON. [*Getting up.*] Madman? Oh, no, but one would have to be himself mad to call him one. Shouldn't we instead envy those who fly beneath starry heavens? [*As if talking to himself, not paying attention to Patch.*] What bliss! Even for a moment just to fly high amidst the clouds and cast a sage's quiet eye on so much stupidity and misery. As you fly on higher, higher, this mud-drop, the heart of our world, this whole ant hill of ours— how small and petty it seems! And those splendid ants below, full of desire, wisdom, pride —how they seem like some wretched, laughable creature! Thrown out by the spark of life onto the broad expanse of the earth it soon flees it as if it had become inflamed with an eternal blaze of lightning. Trampling everything it climbs up, unaware of what it crushes, be it a heart, be it a life, so long as it keeps going higher, so long as it reaches the top sometime! [*Ironically.*] Where are those great earthly works by which nature must be surpassed? Where, in the grief of tears and blood, is the clamor of triumphant murders? Where is fame's resounding echo? Where are all those voices of praise which must strike the very heavens?—There, on high, one can hear nothing . . . only silence . . . blissful silence . . . There it's possible to breathe freely—far from people, closer to God! [*Falls into reverie.*]

PATCH. [*Aside.*] Now he's raving feverishly; getting worse and worse—my God! A little vein in his lungs can burst, just like a thread on a distaff. When it busts, then it's all over! First you yawn, and then the head shakes, and to hell with life annuities! [*Leon, his mind elsewhere, comes closer to Patch, and holding the poster in his right hand leans his left elbow on Patch's right shoulder. Under this weight, and with each movement, Patch moves his right foot now back, now forward. Leon looks straight ahead, and so does Patch. After a long pause, Patch speaks in an undertone, then finally as though he were reciting prayers, mournfully.*] God

Almighty! How he's tottering! How his elbows and legs are trembling—something frightful's happening to him . . . What a burden! God Almighty! He's dug his whole elbow into my shoulder . . . God, oh God! He'll surely crush me —I can't stand it any longer; Holy fathers, help me, help me—he'll crush me, he'll break me—and I can't move an inch away, or he'll fall flat on the floor . . . God Almighty! He'll crack his skull . . . Holy Saints John and Anthony, please come to my rescue! Oh, my God, I'm almost dying! [*Before Patch's last sentence, Leon raises the poster and reads.*]

LEON. Ha!

PATCH. [*Turning toward him.*] Colic? Eh . . . ? [*Grabs him as Leon is about to fall on him because Patch moved his shoulder.*] He'll fall, he'll die!

LEON. He invites us to go flying; very well, I'll go.

PATCH. Help! I'm dying!

LEON. [*Looking at his watch.*] After three now. In one hour I'll split the heavens with my head! Well, believers, fond farewell now! Philip! Hey! My new tuxedo! Two packs of cards . . .

PATCH. [*Throwing himself on him and trying to hold him back.*] I won't let you. I won't let you, dreadful person! I'd prefer to die at your feet!

LEON. Something new come to his mind now?

PATCH. Not a step!

LEON. Out of my way! [*Pushes him away from the table with such force that Patch lands at the other end of the stage where, after coming to a halt, he speaks with his face beaming and happy. Leon goes out.*]

PATCH. There's strength for you! There's health for you! There's a life worth half a million! But what of it?—Devil's done it . . . Once you fall from a balloon, sick or well— you'll die no matter. [*Searches for a plan.*] Bust the balloon?—I'll pay for it; who wants that . . . phew! Keep him guarded? . . . Either way's worth nothing.

LEON. [*Coming back.*] Ah, that Philip! Aha, that rascal! [*Makes a threatening gesture.*] If I had him here, he'd get it!

PATCH. [*Coming closer to him in a mysterious way.*] If you please, Sir. [*Points to door on the left.*]

LEON. What?

PATCH. Over there, Sir . . .

LEON. What?

PATCH. He's hiding.

LEON. For what reason?

PATCH. He's afraid.

LEON. [*Entering Orgon's room.*] Oh, you idiot, now I'll show you how to be bold!

PATCH. [*Closing the door behind him and locking it.*] Doors of oak, bars on the window—for a madman you need at least that much! [*Puts a small chair before the door and sits down.*] Wait here now for your four o'clock . . . [*Jumps up.*] But Rose? . . . [*Runs toward the door then stops.*] And the life annuity! My love—and thousands—behind one door! [*Goes to the door.*] However . . . [*Listens and then steps back.*] Ah, what nonsense! [*Goes out.*] One must after all trust virtue and modesty. Yes, modesty . . . for he'll break my neck, that's certain, the moment I open the doors. On the other hand . . . in anger, or perhaps, sometimes, in fever he could . . . Holy fathers, please protect us!

SCENE 6. *Patch, Philip.*

PHILIP. [*Aside.*] Peddling something, the old miser—[*Out loud.*] Trying out a new key, are you?

PATCH. Ah, it's you, Philip, my dear friend, it's a wonder I'm not dead yet. Well, Satan must have brought this Italian here with his balloons; and this Leon, devil incarnate—Lord have mercy on us all!—wants to fly with him to the stars.

PHILIP. [*Ironically.*] Your humaneness then forbids it?

PATCH. That's right, Philip, it forbids it, since my capital could be injured.

PHILIP. For it doesn't wish for such a journey.

[*Patch runs to the door, listens, and then comes back.*]

PATCH. Help us then, save me and Leon . . . Go on, fast as you can, beat him to it, take his place there in the balloon!

PHILIP. [*Smiling, after a short pause during which he appears amazed.*] But he'll order me down as soon as he sees me.

PATCH. Then play deaf.

PHILIP. He'll wave.

PATCH. Close your eyes.

PHILIP. So he'll pull me.

PATCH. Makes no difference, you'll be up above him.

PHILIP. He'll shoot.

PATCH. He'll surely miss.

PHILIP. No, no, Sir; this is something I don't want any part of.

PATCH. Ah, dear Philip, if you just knew how nice and pretty it is up high. You'll be sitting on some cloud there just like old Jupiter used to.

PHILIP. Praise it all you want, urge me all you want—you're just wasting your time. I haven't reached the point where you could make a complete fool of me.

PATCH. You won't?

PHILIP. I won't.

PATCH. Pretty stubborn.

PHILIP. True.

PATCH. Well then, the matter's finished. Make believe I was joking. But don't spare your legs now, Phil dear, go on, run fast to the balloon. When it climbs and gets up higher come back quickly to report it. But be fast, for love of heaven! Every moment is precious now! Philip, Phil, for love of heaven, make it fast, fly like a bird, please! Here's a tip. [*Hides it.*] I'll give it to you later. [*Philip goes out.*] But what eats my heart out is that he doesn't try to force the door down. [*Listens.*] Not a murmur. Like the grave. [*Looks through the keyhole.*] There's a screen hiding him from me!

SCENE 7. *Orgon, Patch. Orgon comes in followed by two Jews with packages who are scrapping with each other and pushing each other away from the door. Orgon comes back and locks the door.*]

ORGON. What the devil's going on here? This crowd's looking for a beating!

PATCH. [*In despair.*] Orgon!

ORGON. Out! Out! [*Comes closer.*] Ah, my dear Sir, whatever you ask, everything's high now. Only cheap thing is our grain. They just skin us best they can, Sir. [*Takes out different samples from his pocket.*] I took along various samples, maybe Rose will find one she likes. But they all have odd names that stick in your throat: there's a *satan*,* one's called *shvali*,† another's *grugru* . . .** But all first-rate! Or rare! Or . . . oh, what rubbish, just so's they can milk the gentry.

PATCH. [*Aside.*] I'm scared to keep quiet and scared to open my mouth.

ORGON. And for dresses—what a racket! Has the fashion gone insane now? Folds everywhere—on top, at the bottom, in back and in the front! I'll tell you frankly, it's terrible to get married this way. A person can't be sure exactly what it is he's really getting . . . [*Shows the samples.*] Give me your advice: they're all right for blankets, aren't they? Why, what is it makes you so pale?

PATCH. Me? . . . Me? . . . No . . . Where? [*Aside.*] I'll drop dead now!

ORGON. You're shaking.

PATCH. No, just laughing. [*Laughs.*]

ORGON. That's a sign of . . .

PATCH. [*With concern.*] Of what, tell me?

ORGON. That your stomach must be aching. I'll give you some drops I've with me—made from vodka mixed with sweet-flag.

PATCH. [*Blocking his way.*] Go back to the city, Orgon!

ORGON. For what reason?

PATCH. I'm afraid you went shopping in the wrong places . . . Maybe the stuff's old, maybe new . . . You've got to . . . [*Aside.*] I'm losing my senses.

ORGON. Just a moment. Rose!

PATCH. [*Closing his mouth.*] Sh! Softly! Don't yell "Rose!" She can't hear you. Don't shout, don't shout.

---

* A corruption of the French *satin*, satin.
† A corruption of the French *chevelu*, a hairy material.
** A corruption of the French *à gros-grains*, coarse-grained.

ORGON. Leave me alone.

PATCH. [*Pleading.*] Go back to the city, Orgon! [*Gently pushes him away.*]

ORGON. Stop holding me up for nothing. Rose!

ROSE. [*From her room.*] I hear you.

ORGON. Come!

ROSE. I can't.

PATCH. Go on Orgon, time is wasting . . .

ORGON. [*Closer to the door pulled shut by Patch.*] Why?

ROSE. Because they've locked me in here.

LEON. And I have to stay with Rose now like some Capuchin in his cell.

ORGON. What? Who? How? With whom? [*Takes his thick cane.*] We'll see now! I'll put an end to all this soon enough. Open! Open, or I'll smash the door down!

PATCH. [*Pulling him back.*] Go back to the city, Orgon . . .

ROSE. But, papa, there's no key here.

LEON. Some Patch's got hold of it.

ORGON. [*To Patch.*] Hand it over, or I'll choke you!

PATCH. Go back to the city, Orgon.

ORGON. The key, I say!

PATCH. I don't have it.

ORGON. What the devil's going on here! Just one answer— smash the door down.

PATCH. [*Standing in front of the door as if crucified.*] Only over my dead body!

ORGON. [*Addressing the middle door.*] Hey! Anyone there? Come who can! What's going on here? What's going on here?

[*A servant and Mathew enter.*]

PATCH. [*Aside.*] He'll destroy him with the first blow. As it is he's barely alive.

ORGON. [*To the servant.*] Break the doors down!

SERVANT. As you say, Sir.

PATCH. [*In the shape of a cross, stamping his feet and shouting at the top of his lungs.*] Help! Oh, help! What are you doing? It's my own life you're taking! Help me! Help me!

ORGON. He's gone crazy!

[*Leon, who all the time has been shaking the doors, and*

consequently Patch as well, now opens them after striking them solidly. Knocked over together with the doors, Patch falls into Orgon's embrace.]

PATCH. Hold him! Hold him! Or he'll hit me! . . . Hold him back, for love of heaven! People! Whoever believes in God, please don't let him loose, I beg you!

SCENE 8. Orgon, Leon, Patch, Rose.

ORGON. Leon!

LEON. [*To the servants.*] Go away!—Well, Orgon, [*Slapping him on the shoulder*] well, old man, it's quite surprising that we should all come together here today. But my heart is full of sorrow, that your daughter, my beloved, my darling little Rose, who's loved me from the cradle and was brought up by my mother, has to marry this man Patch, marry this man, with his crooked nose, just because of his miserable money. Have a look at him and tell me, if this sallow-looking owl's head, these cat-like eyes, this hawk-beaked nose, if they're fitting for my fair Rose?

ORGON. Oh, dear Leon, what can I say?

LEON. Ah, dear Orgon, it's not easy! I know pretty well how things stand, but approve them—that I can't do.

ORGON. All your words are just in vain now!

LEON. You who governed my estate once, you know full well what I had—but what you have no idea of is that today I've been left with nothing.

ORGON. But your life annuity?

LEON. Vanished! Having made this introduction as a pledge of my sincerity, I'm now asking for Rose's hand.

ORGON. But Leon . . .

LEON. I'll also add—that I'm worth more than three Patches.

ORGON. But this is a mad idea—since you can't count on my gifts.

LEON. I have nothing, neither does she—that's what they call —a perfect couple. [*As if to himself.*] And isn't Sylphid worth a million?

PATCH. Maybe that estate's for sale?

LEON. Half a life wouldn't be enough reward for such a treasure.

PATCH. [*Aside.*] Which in half a year he's bound to lose anyway.

ORGON. For you I'd put my hand in fire, but, Leon dear, it just can't be. It would only mean more trouble. [*Rose withdraws with lowered head. With emotion.*] Your head was always . . . God have pity on me!—but you had a good heart. It's to your heart I'm talking now. Please don't trifle with my daughter. She's my one salvation. Think of her as well as me . . .

LEON. But to marry such a person! Such a person!

ORGON. Everything will work out somehow.

LEON. [*Turning around.*] The balloon . . .

PHILIP. [*Entering.*] Above the Cloisters.

ORGON. [*Beside himself.*] My poor children!

PATCH. [*In the same manner.*] Luck is with us! [*They all stand submerged in thought.*]

ACT III

SCENE 1. Patch, Hardcoin. They sit by a table to the right. Hardcoin near the wall counting his money—a few bags of it in front of him.

PATCH. Oh, my God, what I'm losing!

HARDCOIN. Oh, my God, what I'm paying!

PATCH. [*Giving him the pen.*] Sign it, sign it, Jan dear.

HARDCOIN. [*Turning over the papers.*] Two and three makes five . . .

PATCH. Please sign it.

HARDCOIN. Five more ten, and five, fifteen . . .

PATCH. Pen's drying . . .

HARDCOIN. Makes no difference . . . Five makes fifteen, and then nineteen . . .

PATCH. Now let's do it properly. First we'll sign it, then I'll take everything, without any accounting; that way trust

won't grow into deceit between us. Thousands exchange
hands with us like this—and no fuss made.

HARDCOIN. Two thousand, three thousand, four thousand . . .

PATCH. But, Jan, have a look at this please—this bill here's
badly torn.

HARDCOIN. It'll pass, it'll pass!

PATCH. There's no crest on it.

HARDCOIN. Then it won't prick you.

PATCH. Ah, it won't prick. Pranks are fine, jokes are fine. But
when a big loss looms up it's nothing to joke about. And
this fiver looks like a rag . . . Jan, I ask you, have a
conscience!

HARDCOIN. I don't make them, I can't change them.

PATCH. Hell with it!—But afterward, Jan, we'll sit down and
talk about it. Now just sign it, Jan good fellow, sign it, sign
it, damn it, let the business be ended once and for all!

HARDCOIN. Ah, signing it's no trifle . . .

PATCH. Oh, for goodness' sake, Jan dearest, for the love of
God Almighty, please don't bore me so mercilessly. Till you
get around to something, you can so tire a person, so torment him, so torture him, bore him so silly, it's enough to
turn his blood to gall.

HARDCOIN. [*Taking the pen, phlegmatically.*] That's the way
I've been since I was born. [*Takes the pen, looks it over and
begins to fix it, when the Lagenas and Philip enter the
room. Listening to them carefully, he hides packet after
packet of money in his pockets, not taking his eyes from
them while they talk.*]

SCENE 2. *Patch, Hardcoin, Raphael, Michael, and Philip.*

RAPHAEL. Hey! Birbancki!

PHILIP. [*Impatiently.*] But he's not here. I'll say it once again:
he's not here!

RAPHAEL. Quiet, peasant!

PHILIP. [*Arrogantly.*] Who's a peasant?

RAPHAEL. The one who'll get it with this stick here, if he
won't keep his tongue guarded. My, how arrogant he is now!
What a braggart, what a show-off, all because he's in the

service of a knave and scoundrel who throws a big party
once in a while, and then not at his own expense, because
he's got creditors swarming all around.

PHILIP. It's not proper for a servant to reply to such a matter.
But my master will soon be here and himself will answer
all the charges.

RAPHAEL. He'll answer what he'll answer!

PATCH. Psst, Philip, not a word more.

RAPHAEL. Today they're going to level to the ground this
house of sin and shame.

MICHAEL. [*As though to himself.*] Where nobody doubts his
honor.

RAPHAEL. Today they'll close this place of scandal and corruption, where the pocket always trembles anxiously—full
in the evening, empty by morning.

MICHAEL. [*Aside.*] Three hundred guilders down the drain!

RAPHAEL. Today's a day of judgment. Out of this hell today
the furniture'll go for debts, the stick for servants, and the
owner himself—to the spirits!
[*Hardcoin gets up. Patch flabbergasted. Philip leaves, making a gesture with his hand.*]

MICHAEL. I'm also stirred by vengeance; after all, I was humiliated, too.

RAPHAEL. I'll be first, and then you second.

MICHAEL. Why, of course, and I'll come second. But looking
at it another way, you talk a little too much, my brother,
because what can come of these quarrels?

RAPHAEL. [*Drawing out pistols.*] What? Here's what—I'll
drill him in the head and then bury him! [*Puts the pistols
on the table on the left.*]

MICHAEL. God grant it. Yet, however, I must tell you, that
though nobody can deny he wronged us both quite badly,
he'll still be free to have one shot when we come to settling cases.

RAPHAEL. [*Giving him his hand.*] Let him shoot, and let him
kill me. After all, you'll still be alive to take him—you gave
your word.

MICHAEL. And will keep it. But . . .

RAPHAEL. There's no chance here for agreement.

MICHAEL. None, of course, but nevertheless . . .

RAPHAEL. There'll be one less person alive today. [*Sits at the table on the left.*]

PATCH. Well, now if this isn't something—how could I not recognize you! Masters Lagena—in person. Peter Radost, at your service. I had the honor to know your father. Yes, indeed, a real honor. I remember both of you, too. Yes indeed, how well I knew you. You were only just this high then, and already such rare humor. Your father's brains, your mother's looks! People came from all around just to look at such wonders the likes of which they never saw before in the whole city. Well, now if this isn't something! How could I not recognize you!

MICHAEL. I'm so very pleased, you must allow me to embrace an unknown friend now. [*Embraces him.*]

PATCH. Your servant, Sir. But what were those words of yours that suddenly disturbed my hearing? How could anyone as pleasant as Birbancki cause you insult? Tell me about it, for I'm so frightened I can hardly breathe.

RAPHAEL. What's there to say!

MICHAEL. A nasty business!

PATCH. Oh, gentlemen, a nasty business, eh? But killing's worse though—it's a frightful business. What could this young fellow have done? Of what great crime is he guilty? Why my dear friends, he's an angel in human form!

RAPHAEL. He can praise him who's not married, but he's a devil, Sir, a devil incarnate. He's a scoundrel without morals or faith, and he won't escape our vengeance.

PATCH. Well, well—it's true, all too often his head's filled with silly nonsense, but his heart—is pure! Pure, I tell you, gentlemen. His word's as good as cash, like a contract signed and sealed. [*Casts a glance at Hardcoin.*] Business with him's crowned with gold. Let him be as mean as he likes; if you stick through what you've started with him, you'll gain an easy hundred percent, gentlemen, a hundred percent, and yet you're still burning with anger at him!

MICHAEL. Not a word about percentage.

PATCH. Then about the capital.

MICHAEL. Sure, he's already given our capital a good shake up—but I'll tell you the whole story, so you'll know the kind of person he is. In my brother's company last night, somehow, not really wanting to, just for a little while I thought, I landed at a celebration here. When morning came—it was bad. My brother also got his feet wet. Leon has a good laugh at the expense of the two of us, but offers his assistance, lest our wives . . . you must know, after all, Sir, that with people in our position things are a bit different. Sometimes it's simple, sometimes it's not simple. For our sakes he writes letters, but somehow the letters are different from what he promised. Instead of calming our wives down, they tore our peaceful households apart as if lightning struck from heaven. Quarrels, envy, brawling, shouting—gone all shame and rights together! And when the curtain fell, it came out in the course of things that Mister Leon for a whole year now . . . [*Whispers into Patch's ear.*]

PATCH. You're not the first, Sir, or the last.

MICHAEL. And my brother, too, that's clear now.

PATCH. And just for that you want to spill blood, just because your pride's been somewhat . . .

MICHAEL. Pride nothing, it's my wife I'm thinking of.

PATCH. Worldly vanity, my dear man.

RAPHAEL. You're an imbecile! Hell with you!

PATCH. Oh, come now, what kind of a joke is that: "Hell with you! Hell with you!" [*Embraces him.*] You're quite a fellow! All your jokes aside now, gentlemen, think it over. Human life isn't a coin. Once you break it, you can never put it back together again. Oh, what a dreadful thing to think of. Blood will flow, your foe will perish, and then what, what will be after?

MICHAEL. My dear Sir, it will be frightful.

PATCH. Ludmir, who's well known around here, once summoned a friend to a duel and killed him. From that time on he's had no pleasure, no peace, no sleep at night. And when he falls from exhaustion, all at once some bloody corpses start in making merry with him. First they choke him, then they tickle him, then they shove their bones in his throat.

[*Raphael sits sunk in thought, Michael standing behind him.*]

MICHAEL. It's a frightful business, brother.

PATCH. If you want I'll fall on my knees and embrace your legs. [*Kneels.*] There I've done it, now you've got me. I beg you, give up your awful plan. For blood that's spilled is— dreadful!

RAPHAEL. And what business is it of yours?

PATCH. [*With growing affection, which Michael shares.*] Oh, my king! My precious master! I raised this little Leon, fondled him, rocked him—I love him just like a son. He's my one and only pleasure; he's all I have left in my life. If it's blood you're thirsting after for some silly pranks he's pulled, then shoot me—and let the bullet graze me a little somewhere—in the thigh, say.

RAPHAEL. [*Taking the pistols and getting up.*] So be it. [*Patch jumps and hides behind Michael.*]
Come on, Michael. I'm touched by his devotion. Let's just drop the whole affair.

PATCH. [*Coming to again.*] Splendid, splendid, simply splendid!

RAPHAEL. [*Putting his hand on Patch's chest.*] There's a man for you! There's someone I can respect! O, let any foe of mankind look into this man's heart here and let him still tell me afterward that friendship has gone out of this world of ours. [*Embraces him and leaves.*]

MICHAEL. [*Kissing him.*] May God keep you well!

PATCH. [*Seeing them out.*] Be assured of my gratitude, any time you say I'll prove it. Your humble, humble servant. [*Returns.*] Cowards! Cowards! Just plain cowards! Fast enough at making threats. But hold your ground, be bold— right away they'll back down. Well, let's finish what we were doing.

HARDCOIN. They won't be back?

PATCH. Bah! They've clouds of dust behind them! [*Hardcoin takes out his money.*] Sign it, sign it, then you'll count it.

HARDCOIN. [*To himself.*] "First I'll drill him, then I'll bury him."

PATCH. Half in paper, half in gold.

HARDCOIN. Once your thoughts oppose each other, it's not easy to get back to yourself again.

SCENE 3. *Patch, Hardcoin, Doctor.*

DOCTOR. Well! It's our mysterious guardian! [*Laughs.*] No—
it's Sylphid! Multitude of charms! Youth, beauty, angel,
deity! What is it you wish again here? How's our favorite
patient doing? What new troubles has he caused? Oh, don't
throw away the disguise by which you keep hidden from
him, if you want to keep your head on, if you want your
wits in ready. But I must congratulate you for the sharp
thorns in your vigil. No matter how grave the sins you've
gotten yourself into this time, they'll nonetheless save a
soul. They'll be a source of everlasting joy to you. But
joking aside now, I must tell you as a doctor . . .

PATCH. Later, later.

DOCTOR. That you must think soon about Birbancki's health.
It's devilishly bad now!

PATCH. Lord have mercy!

DOCTOR. Ha! It's painful, eh? I know it all too well—I feel the
same way.

PATCH. Oh, have mercy!

DOCTOR. Evil should be kept on short rein right from the
start otherwise, you see, it spreads fast. On your request today, Sir . . .

PATCH. But . . .

DOCTOR. I was there and found him in not at all the best
condition . . .

PATCH. Oh, doctor, you're ruining me!

DOCTOR. I wrote him out a prescription . . .

PATCH. Don't finish, don't finish!

DOCTOR. Not at all, Sir! Since he's someone who concerns
you, it's my physician's duty to inform you, while there's
still time . . .

PATCH. Oh! . . .

DOCTOR. Don't let his face deceive you; he's ill, he's really ill
now.

PATCH. You're ruining me!

DOCTOR. And if he keeps living like he is, goes on drinking
like he's drinking, spending his nights like he spends

them, even doctors won't be of any help, and he won't remain long with us.

PATCH. Oh, doctor!

DOCTOR. I share the sadness with which I wound your heart,
but he's bound to get consumption. And when that occurs,
my dear friend, it will progress rapidly and go into the last
stage at a gallop.

PATCH. Help!

DOCTOR. And before he can cry out, he'll go quietly like a
chicken.

PATCH. Oh, doctor! Doctor! Would that you were struck by
lightning!
[*As in the previous scene, Hardcoin conceals his money to
the tempo of the bad news he hears, then sneaks out unseen.*]

DOCTOR. Calm your feelings of despair, it can't be any other
way now. Either he'll live differently, or soon find himself in the grave. [*Goes out.*]

PATCH. [*Turns around expecting to talk to Hardcoin.*] Don't
believe all this . . . [*Dumbstruck.*] Oh, the devil must have
ordained my destruction today! In what accursed puddle did
I set foot today? For the last three hours I look at gold, and
I can't reach it. I'll get out of here, I'll pull some deal yet
to make up for this day's losses. But what? Where? From
whom? Makes no difference, just so's it's gold! Just so's it's
gold! [*Meets Orgon with Rose in the door. Grabbing Orgon
by the shoulders, he says.*] You'll give me? Give!—It's you!
[*Runs out.*]

SCENE 4. *Orgon, Rose.*

ORGON. [*With a few packages under his arm.*] What the devil's
going on here? Did a wasp fly up his nostril, that he's spinning like a top today? Or has the whim again seized him to
take someone half insane, twist him dizzy, break his bones
up—and then out of pity for him lock him up with some
young girl? [*Ironically.*] 'Pon my soul, if I have not seen
for the first time in my whole life a way that's fast and certain to drive someone really crazy! Ha! A person's always

learning, learning till they close his eyelids. Well, go on, Rose, get your things now! [*Indicates the packages lying on the table.*] Crying again?

ROSE. I'm not crying. After all this Mister Patch is quite rich.

ORGON. Ah, when I see tears in your eyes, it's as though a snake crawled into my heart. [*With sorrow.*] Leon pulled a fast one on you.

ROSE. Oh, no, father—but he grieved me, for he even more convinced me how the whole world loathes this Patch. But I'll take him for my husband, and just as I share his name, so will I also share his shame. [*With feeling.*] Maybe in time my once-proud heart will finally fall to slumbering.

ORGON. What? You think the whole world will despise you? Oh, believe an older person—just be wealthy, darling, and the world will bow before you! I and my neighbor Krętarski are the best examples of this. Because I wear long moustaches and a none too stylish headgear; because I'm thrifty, for I've little; because I don't *perle franse*, though I am, if I may say so, a man honest and without fault—hardly do I show myself in town, when what do I hear on all sides: "No good title! Just poor gentry! A real nothing!" . . . and etcetera. And though I make nothing of these young parrots' stupid babble, its nothing flies in just with the wind. I hear and feel the world's barbs. But Krętarski, the old scoundrel, just because he jingles his purse, since he robs one day and squanders the next; just because he jokes and flatters, hurls out lies as though from a sling-shot, just because he's always *à la mode* there; and says *bon jour* day and night; just because he plays cards heavily, he's called *comme il faut* and enjoys respect, honor, and freedom!

ROSE. I'll become Patch's wife, since it has been so decided. But there are those who also wed thinking perhaps only of money, but who still have some respect for the person.

ORGON. [*With forced laughter.*] "Who still have some respect for the person!" God forbid it!—God forbid it! Nowhere on earth is it like that, you're just dreaming, my child. With our marital arrangements, a young man doesn't come to a girl with the usual words of courtship, but with statements of finances making his pitch at the dowry. Here the person matters little; what you are, nobody asks you—what you have—that's the question. Who has plenty catches plenty, who has little stays in the corner. So thousands go with thousands, and millions go with millions. That's the way the parents match them. Whether love ever blossoms, whether heaven or hell's ahead of the young people, that's for later—as God wishes.

ROSE. I'll be Mister Patch's wife then, but there's no happiness in wealth.

ORGON. [*With growing bitterness.*] Ask, if you ever meet one, some sweet dollie prettied up nice, with her angel eyes turned townward, to tell you what happiness is all about ... But it doesn't help to question, she'll just answer: "Love and virtue"—and herself be thinking: "Gold, gold." That's what each one wants, and the one who doesn't have it had best be ashamed or run away; to the world he's not a person any longer.

ROSE. Oh, father, must I hear such words coming from your lips?

ORGON. Because I'm losing my poor head. I've the usual road before me, and can't find a way to leave it—straight ahead or back—it's bad either way. Reason says I shouldn't care much if my child likes it or doesn't, yet I've no strength to look at tears and not wish instead for a smile ... All around it's a devilish matter, just woe and trouble everywhere you look.

ROSE. [*Kissing his hand ingratiatingly, not boldly.*] I'm still curious to find out what papa thinks about Leon ...

ORGON. Empty, penniless, and crazy.

ROSE. If he blunders, then it's from goodness.

ORGON. Devil cares—how he hits me, if from goodness or from folly. There's no difference—all blows hurt!

ROSE. Yet I have the feeling, papa, that he would certainly change, certainly ... if he got married, if he'd find the proper person, someone who's thrifty and mature ...

ORGON. Yes, small, with an up-turned little nose.

ROSE. [*Lowering her eyes, confused; a short pause.*] Papa doesn't want ...

ORGON. [*Finishing her sentence.*] To scold you, so do me a favor, therefore: don't discuss what in a day's time will have already left his mind!

ROSE. But he calls it his happiness.

ORGON. One week's joy, a year of peace, followed by a life of misery and anguish.

ROSE. But with sincere desire, sound advice . . .

ORGON. Not a penny to his name—that's too little for things at home to be all right. Then keep silent—sound advice. Get going now.

ROSE. But . . .

ORGON. [*Kissing her on the forehead and turning away.*] Not a word more! [*Rose goes out.*]

SCENE 5.

ORGON. [*Alone; after a short pause, striking with his cane.*] World, you old trickster you! World, world without honor, without faith! Would that you could now appear before me in human form. I'd let you have such a beating, you'd start to bite your heels! Then I'd say: "Now talk straight: what do you respect the most? Money or conscience?" I'm honest—My reward then? . . . I always seem to be sinking into deeper water. Any dandy looks at me from above and makes fun of a poor little squire—Ha, let him go on with his scoffing. God doesn't miss a thing, though! When there's any trouble, fops and dandies splash the water and slip away fast like eels—while the squire, sincere and willing, isn't sparing of himself and takes on even a greater burden than he can carry. [*With bitterness.*] Until finally, with bloody sweat . . . Ah, better shut up about it! [*Waves his hand, and goes off to his room.*]

SCENE 6. Leon, Philip.

LEON. Come, Milord, a little closer . . . Closer, closer— a bit closer . . . Let's the two of us have a little chat, for I've a desire to talk now—but if you lie even an iota, I'll give you such a fondling, your hair will stand on end!

PHILIP. Sir, you're upset, since this morning . . .

LEON. Tell me—who's this fellow Patch who's always hanging around me? Something funny going on here, the whole thing's kind of puzzling. His meeting with me earlier, his behavior like a madman's—all will be explained by you, Sir.

PHILIP. What the devil have I to do with it?

LEON. But I'm asking you . . .

PHILIP. I must go now . . .

LEON. Do it for me . . .

PHILIP. No, I won't, Sir. I'm off . . .

LEON. [*Grabbing him by the collar.*] I'll make your trip shorter, you thief, for I'll toss you out of this window in a second if you come out with just one lie! What were you and he discussing the moment I caught the two of you in the hallway? When you saw me, why'd you scurry, just as though the two of you had been scalded? The truth! Or else . . .

PHILIP. So be it. There's no point in hiding further. This here Patch—is your Sylphid.

LEON. Thief!

PHILIP. He's with you everywhere, Sir; his vigil and guarding hand keep you from every kind of trouble. Since he's got your life annuity, he's in great fear of your dying.
[*Silence.*]

LEON. Well it's clear, I see it plainly. He's the one, the thief, who managed to trap me in his nets so shrewdly so I'd understood what happened only when I'd already lost the rest of my estate! [*A short pause.*] Well! I'd like to pay him back now! Philip! Listen!

PHILIP. At your service.

LEON. What would you prefer best: three ducats or a couple of good, solid wallops?

PHILIP. Ah, the ducats!—Without thinking!

LEON. [*Sitting down to write.*] Go and get my pistols for me. What are you waiting for?

PHILIP. I'm just thinking . . . Is it good that I'm so scared now?

LEON. Go on—there won't be any shooting here.
[*Philip goes out. Leon reads aloud what he wrote.*] "Af-

ter losing you, dear Rose, nothing's left for me but death. One shot will quiet the heart which has always been yours. My pistol is already loaded. Farewell—be happy!—Leon." [*Folds the letter and gives it to Philip who has returned with the pistols.*] You've deceived me so many times, deceive me now, but do it smoothly. This is a letter for Miss Rose, who is soon to become Mrs. Patch. By your wit you'll infer that it's a love-letter. Then betraying all my orders you'll give it to Patch.

PHILIP. That's all? You have no more orders for me?

LEON. No—now go, and come back later for the ducats I promised you.

PHILIP. For them—I'll come like I had wings on. [*Goes out.*]

SCENE 7.

LEON. [*Alone.*] Now I have to let Rose in on my intentions. [*Goes to the door then returns.*] But if that old fox suddenly happens to fall in and finds me here—he may get wind, he may guess what's going on and ruin my plans. No . . . [*Sits down.*] I'll write her what's happening. [*Writes fast.*] Yes, my dearest, keep your hopes up . . . [*Enters Rose's room, then comes out a moment later.*] If I had to pawn myself, or give up the last of my strength, I must save you, I must, from this Patch's foul clutches! [*Sits next to the small table on the right and puts the pistols in front of him.*] Now—with wild despair on my face, my eyes mad, my hair unruly, I'll wait here for my opponent . . . Here he comes rushing like a madman!

SCENE 8. *Leon, Patch, later Orgon and Rose. Patch runs in and throws himself on the table, covering the pistols with his body.*

PATCH. Help me! Help me! Call police in!

LEON. What's the matter?

PATCH. Police! Police!

LEON. Just be quiet!

PATCH. I have to shout—Oh, oh, help me!

LEON. What the devil, people . . .

PATCH. Help!

LEON. [*Grabbing him by the throat while sitting down.*] Shut up, or I'll choke you.

PATCH. [*Stifled.*] Help me . . . help me! [*Released, quietly, losing his strength.*] Help me, help me! [*Begins to weep and howl, to the point where he begins to tremble, all the while lying on top of the pistols.*]

LEON. Has this man lost all his senses?

PATCH. [*Blubbering.*] No . . . no . . . but . . . I've . . . p . . . p . . . payed . . . Lo . . . lo . . . lots . . . of . . . lots of money . . . And I have your—life annuity!

LEON. Makes no difference.

PATCH. Oh, a big one—shooting yourself—in the head . . . you're quite clearly . . . shooting at me. [*Jumps up and grabbing the pistols passes the left hand of Birbancki who is turned with his back to the door of Orgon's room.*] But no . . . no . . . I know what I'll do—I'll take you to court . . . I bought your life and it's mine now. No one's got any right to it, and whoever makes threats at it, is a killer, a traitor, a swindler. He's a robber, he's a—murderer! Help me! Help me!—He's a murderer! Yes!—I'll fall before the judges, I'll tell them about your foul thoughts, I'll tell them about your intention, and the kind court, the considerate court will hand down a ten-year sentence—not counting all the expenses of the trial.

LEON. As you wish, go on and sue me—but once you've won the case against me, put your sentence on my gravestone.

PATCH. [*After a short pause.*] Then I won't sue—but I'll achieve the same goal by a shorter route—Philip's gone—to get the police.

LEON. Hm! That's no joke!

PATCH. Ah, no joke at all! Some will come who'll be able to subdue you. Once I tell them how I'll charge you, once I properly convince them that you made threats on my life—I've the gun now, and I'll show it.

LEON. And so what?

PATCH. Then off to prison they'll take you and lock you up there!

LEON. But I won't deny your charges. Let them try me and hang me, that's the way they'll make me happiest!

PATCH. [*Beaten down in turn, in an undertone.*] How I wish you'd break a leg! [*Points to the window, after a short pause.*] But, for heaven's sake, my good man, why such terrible despair? See how the whole world is happy . . . Look at the clouds there, those mountains, the streets, the churches, those coaches there, those stands, these beauties of nature! Where'd you get this urge for death? Why do you delight in torturing a miserable poor wretch like me? [*Orgon and Rose appear in the background.*] Why's it my fault, why I ask you, that you turned with godless anger on a poor old wretch like me, why?

LEON. [*As if to himself.*] Rose is lost to me forever.

PATCH. Take her, damn it! Go on have her! Either a bullet or a wife—it all comes out to the same thing. The life annuity always perishes.

LEON. I no longer want a wife now, for my plan hasn't been altered.

PATCH. Oh, dear Leon, my good fellow, don't wish my eternal ruin—Oh, Leon! My dear treasure! I prostrate myself before you, trample me, kick me, my lord, my master! But fulfill my last desire! If you have to shoot yourself—then shoot already, for love of heaven . . . but act decently before death, I'll get you a cross if you do—just postpone your death awhile, take yourself in hand, take treatment, try the doctors, take the waters—maybe you'll regain enough strength so I won't lose so much on you . . . Once your cheeks take on more color, maybe someone there'll be tempted. I won't stand on ceremonies. Then—when your shot strikes like thunder, I won't be left out in the cold. Oh, Leon! My treasure! Save my life annuity! That's no great favor, is it? You've got all eternity ahead of you, half a year more on this earth here won't spoil it for you in the least.

LEON. The end must come this very day.

PATCH. Then you yourself redeem it. I'll make it cheap, cheap —Give me back . . . How much? Give me half— [*Weeps.*] No more than half back. Then I'll be glad to fire the shot myself.

LEON. I don't even have a penny.

PATCH. In an hour?

LEON. Not in ten—

PATCH. In a year, perhaps? If you've got some kind of mortgage . . .

LEON. I've got none.

PATCH. On your Sylphid? Eh?

LEON. Are you joking?

PATCH. Oh, God forbid it, who'd be joking in such grief? Give me your word then. [*Orgon gives a sign to Leon to give his word.*]

LEON. You have it.

PATCH. That a half . . .

LEON. I'll pay in a year.

PATCH. That you'll respect our arrangements—there won't be any bang?

LEON. You've my word now. But what guarantee do I have?

PATCH. [*Giving him papers.*] Here—the papers are my pledges . . . but there won't be any bang bang?

LEON. Life would be more pleasant if I had a wife like Rose here. Will you let me have her, Orgon?

ORGON. After all, he said: "You take her!"

LEON. And you, Rose?

ROSE. Oh, Leon! I owe you my life.

LEON. [*Pointing to Patch.*] It's to him, to him we owe thanks for tearing the gun out of my hand. True enough—it wasn't loaded, but he didn't know about it. What he took, he gave back richly, decked our brows with myrtle wreaths, gave a wife to look out for me, and to Patch—brought back honor. Long live my annuity!

[*Patch who withdraws as far as the chair during Leon's speech, falls dumb, and after the last line slumps into the chair.*]

END

BIBLIOGRAPHY

Editions of Fredro's Works

The following editions of Fredro's works have appeared in Poland:

1. 1826, Vols. i, ii, Vienna (Pichler).
   1830, Vol. iii, Lwów (Kuhn and Milikowski).
   1834, Vol. iv, Lwów (Ossoliński).
   1838, Vol. v, Lwów (Wild).
2. 1839, 2 Vols., 2nd revised edn., Lwów (Wild).
3. 1853, 5 Vols., Warsaw (Orgelbrand).
4. 1871, 5 Vols., Warsaw (Gebethner and Wolff).
5. 1880, 13 Vols., Warsaw (Gebethner and Wolff).
6. 1897, 5 Vols., Lwów (Księgarnia polska; ed. by Henryk Biegeliesen).
7. 1898, 3 Vols., Warsaw (S. Lewenthal).
8. 1926, 6 Vols., Lwów-Warsaw-Cracow (Ossoliński; ed. by Eugeniusz Kucharski).
9. 1930, 2 Vols., Lwów-Warsaw (Księgarnia Polska; ed. by Henryk Cepnik).
10. 1955—, 12 Vols. (to 1962), Warsaw (Państwowy Instytut Naukowy; ed. by Stanisław Pigón).

The most recent edition of Fredro's collected works, which the State Scientific Institute (P.I.N.) began publishing in 1955, is by far the best. The translations in this book are based on it.

The Polish National Library (*Biblioteka Narodowa*), an excellent series of Polish and foreign classics known for its copious notes and detailed, comprehensive introductions, has published five comedies of Fredro to date:

1. *Maidens' Vows* (Śluby panieńskie), Series i, No. 22, 3rd edn., ed. by Eugeniusz Kucharski.
2. *The Vengeance* (Zemsta), Series i, No. 32, 3rd edn., ed. by Eugeniusz Kucharski.
3. *Mr. Joviality* (Pan Jowialski), Series i, No. 93, 2nd edn., ed. by Karol Zawodziński.
4. *The Foreign Way* (Cudzoziemczyzna), Series i, No. 97, ed. by Stanisław Windakiewicz.

Works about Fredro

Although there is a mass of periodical literature on Fredro in Polish, only two major studies have appeared to date: Ignacy Chrzanowski's *O komediach Aleksandra Fredry* (Cracow, 1917), and Tadeusz Boy-Żeleński's *Obrachunki fredrowskie* (Warsaw, 1934). The first is a valuable book, arranged topically, by now antiquated in many respects. The second is provocative, polemical, more engaging than Chrzanowski's, devoted for the most part to the "revision" of what Boy-Żeleński views as erroneous traditional attitudes toward Fredro and his plays. Three other Polish books on Fredro represent collections of public lectures or articles that appeared separately: Stanisław Tarnowski, *Komedie Aleks. hr. Fredry* (Warsaw, 1876); Wacław Borowy, *Ze studiów nad Fredrą* (Cracow, 1921); Stanisław Pigoń, *W pracowni Aleksandra Fredry* (Warsaw, 1956). Important materials are in Juliusz Kleiner's *O Krasickim i o Fredrze* (Wrocław, 1956); Stanisław Pigoń's *Z ogniu życia i literatury* (Wrocław, 1961); and Tadeusz Sivert's *Aleksander Fredro* (Warsaw, 1962). A special study devoted to *Maidens' Vows*, by Wanda Achremowiczowa, *Śluby panieńskie Aleksandra Fredry*, was published in Warsaw in 1964, in the series *Biblioteka analiz literackich* (The Library of Literary Analyses). The introductions by Kazimierz Wyka to Vols. I and VII of the newest edition (P.I.N.) of Fredro's works may be considered collectively one of the most valuable new studies on Fredro. The closest anyone has come to a full-length biography of Fredro is Stefan Majchrowski's fictionalized biography *Pan Fredro* (Warsaw, 1965). Outside of Poland, only one study of Fredro has appeared to date: the very slight *Pessimismo ed ottimismo Fredriano*, by Antonio Stefanini (Rome, 1930).

Translations of Fredro

The Soviet edition of six of Fredro's comedies translated into Russian by various hands and published by Iskusstvo (Moscow, 1956), represents the first foreign collection of his plays. The comedies contained in the Soviet edition are: *Mister Moneybags, Husband and Wife, Ladies and Hussars, Mister Jo-*

viality, *The Vengeance*, and *A Great Man for Small Matters.*
They are preceded by a short introduction by K. Derzhavin.

The following translations of Fredro into English have appeared:

1. *Ladies and Hussars*, tr. by Florence Noyes and George
   Rapall Noyes, publ. by Samuel French, New York and
   London, 1925. The translation is incomplete in places:
   part of the dialogue has been omitted from Act I, Scene
   15, and from Act II, Scenes 7 and 17. There is a one-
   paragraph note on Fredro.

2. *Maidens' Vows or The Magnetism of the Heart*, tr. by
   Arthur Prudden Coleman and Marion Moore Coleman,
   publ. by Electric City Press, Schenectady, N. Y., 1940.
   The translation is in prose, with a four-page introduction.
   Although there are a few mistranslations, the work on
   the whole is accurate.

3. *The Vengeance*, tr. into prose by May Bamforth Hum-
   bert, ed. and with introduction by Marion Moore Coleman, publ. by Alliance College, Cambridge Springs, Pa.,
   as Vol. VII of *The Alliance Journal* (1957). The translation is very bad with numerous errors and omissions.